I Tatti Research Series

2

SEACHANGES

Music in the Mediterranean and Atlantic Worlds, 1550–1880

edited by
Kate van Orden

I TATTI

I TATTI

I Tatti – The Harvard University Center
for Italian Renaissance Studies
Via di Vincigliata, 26
50135 Florence – Italy
itatti.harvard.edu

Project coordinator: Thomas Gruber

Published and distributed in Italy by

OFFICINA LIBRARIA

Officina Libraria
Via dei Villini, 10
00161 Rome – Italy
officinalibraria.net

Project coordinator and Publisher: Marco Jellinek
Art director: Paola Gallerani
Layout: Ivano Bettin
Color separation: Premani, Pantigliate (Milan)
Printed and bound by Esperia, Lavis (Trento)
Copyediting: Sandra Creaser
Index: Gabriele De Melis

Publication of this volume has been made possible by

The Myron and Sheila Gilmore Publication Fund at I Tatti
The Robert Lehman Endowment Fund
The Jean-François Malle Scholarly Programs and Publications Fund
The Andrew W. Mellon Foundation Fund for Scholarly Programs and Publications
The Barbara and Craig Smyth Fund for Scholarly Programs and Publications
The Lila Wallace-Reader's Digest Endowment Fund
The Malcolm Wiener Fund for Scholarly Programs and Publications

Worldwide distribution by Harvard University Press
Italian distribution by Officina Libraria

ISBN 978-06-74278-40-0 (Harvard University Press)
ISBN 978-88-3367-150-5 (Officina Libraria)

CONTENTS

ACKNOWLEDGEMENTS

Seachanges began with a conference on Music in the Mediterranean Diaspora at I Tatti in 2017. For that precious opportunity to think together about cross-cultural musical entanglements in the past, we are indebted to Alina Payne, director of I Tatti, and to the staff, whose hosting of the conference and concert by Jordi Savall and Hespèrion XXI made the whole experience a joy. Thomas Gruber helped assemble these essays, and Marco Jellinek and his design team at Officina Libraria assured that they look as striking as they are thoughtful. Harvard University supported both the conference and this publication most generously, for which we are all extremely grateful. Further acknowledgements have been integrated into the Introduction; readers will find them beginning on page 26.

K.v.O.

INTRODUCTION
Music and Mobility

Kate van Orden

The evidence is in: it is no longer tenable to conceive of early modern cultures as bounded, fixed, and primordial. In the last decade, histories of traveling musics and musicians have multiplied with force, shattering the coherence of static accounts rooted in national, religious, and ethnic identity into a glittering array of new subjects privileging hybridity, cosmopolitanism, and the global. International research projects have produced border-crossing histories of early modern music in Slavic lands of the Mediterranean like Croatia and Dalmatia[1] and comprehensive archival studies of "foreign" musicians in Rome, Venice, and Naples.[2] Two recent collections exploring music's mobilization via diplomatic networks begin with early modern embassies as models of soft power in international relations.[3] A new volume on Euro-American interchanges edited by Javier Marín López argues that "all studies of colonial musical culture in one way or another reflect the dynamics of interchange (whether by assimilation or rejection in various degrees)" and presses for flexible approaches to Hispanic-American musics.[4] Reinhard Strohm's paradigm-shifting Global History of Music project, funded by the Balzan Foundation from 2013 to 2016, has produced two volumes juxtaposing local histories from across the globe with narratives of musical reciprocity and "cross-examinations" (*regards croisés*) reflecting encounters among the musics of Europe, Asia, and Latin America, many from the early modern period.[5] Finally, a volume on acoustemologies in contact in early modernity appeared while this book was in production.[6] And this is only to cite some of the most recent, collective endeavors.

The tide of historiography has turned, and this seachange brings us to a disciplinary turning point: when we accept that music has always moved, what happens to our intellectual frameworks for understanding it? Now that we have exposed the extent to which cultural "purity" is a myth of colonialism and the nation-state, what do we make of it? How can we avoid merely adding minority repertories and marginalized musical communities to historical canons that otherwise remain unchanged?[7] Most urgently, as we grapple with the expansive geography and cultural plurality tied to the very mobility of music itself, what questions will guide our research and choice of historiographic models? Old histories of Western European polyphony featuring the cyclic masses of Giovanni Pierluigi da Palestrina and symphonies of Ludwig van Beethoven were already "global" in the sense that their authors had successfully generalized from the particulars of score study and biography to the universality of a canonic repertoire that is, in fact, broadly dispersed and remains remarkably enduring throughout the world. Simply sighting these musics on the move is risky: new global histories of music require framings designed to expose cultural imperialism and move beyond it.

Microhistory

The essays in *Seachanges* are incisive: each unfolds with the immediacy of musical time, at the scale of human lives. Many are works of microhistory. No matter how peripatetic the musicians and how extensive the circulation of instruments, practices, and repertoires in the past, we believe that the micro-realities of musicking require local, individual, connected explanations. While the geographical reach of this volume extends from Constantinople to Cuzco, and its chronological span encompasses several centuries, from around 1550 to 1800 CE, these are not "big" histories of the sort that seek to discover global unities or musical universals.

Our object is not to add unknown or "quirky" micronarratives to music history, but to contest conventional, composer-centric histories of Renaissance and Baroque music from below.[8] Following the lead of Carlo Ginzburg, a number of our authors concentrate on biographies that have been neglected in prior histories: Emily Wilbourne studies a Black singer who starred in Venetian operas, Philippe Canguilhem identifies two Indigenous musicians who were trained by Dominican missionaries in Mexico and then traveled to the Guatemalan Highlands, and Pedro Memelsdorff considers—among others—a flautist of color from Saint-Domingue named Atys, who made a career in Paris and Vienna. Inasmuch as possible, these scholars take the lived experiences of individual musicians as openings that allow them to address the massive cultural upheavals caused by the enslavement of sub-Saharan Africans, Spanish missionization, and French colonization in the Caribbean.

These examples illustrate the *jeux d'échelles* at work throughout this volume, and the ways that our authors play with scales of analysis. Many chapters move from deep readings of a single biography or primary source to the geopolitical configurations it reveals. Others drill down to the human dimension of large-scale histories in musically contextualized studies of diplomatic relations, war, or imperial expansion. These moves between micro and macro align our methods with what historians are calling "global microhistory," a form of microhistory that aims to populate models and theories of global historical structures with real people.[9] Here culture comes strongly into play, and musicology stands to make significant interventions, for our histories illustrate the benefits of countering hard forms of world history destined to discover the global unities created by economic, colonial, and—eventually—industrial processes with soft forms of global history that take into account cultural variabilities and the crossing of peoples, religions, musics, and languages.[10] The cultural responses to globalization must be part of these expanded histories. Francesca Trivellato argued as much in her landmark essay on microhistory and global history when she cautioned: "no matter how much global historians set out to challenge earlier Eurocentric and teleological narratives, they sometimes reproduce generalizations closely indebted to those very narratives, especially when their accounts unfold on the macro-scale."[11] As musicology finds its footing in the broader field of global history, our studies suggest the importance of microhistory as a model for music historians and the methods by which our discipline's traditional strengths in textual criticism, source study, and archival work might be leveraged to new ends in studies which begin by identifying subjects that defy assignment to a single place, language, or ethnicity.[12]

Many chapters in this volume highlight their own incompleteness, a quality intrinsic to the microhistorical approach. As Ginzburg put it so eloquently when describing his experience working with Inquisition records, the obstacles interfering with the research are constituent elements of the documentation and must be part of the account. As a result, microhistories actively investigate voids and lacunae:

> The same for the hesitations and silences of the protagonist in the face of his persecutors' questions—or mine. Thus, the hypotheses, the doubts, the uncertainties became part of the narration; the search for truth became part of the exposition of the (necessarily incomplete) truth attained.[13]

We find that reckoning with ephemeral figures and marginalized repertoires requires a narrative style that refuses to fill in documentary gaps to obtain the polished surfaces of traditional histories. Indeed, these often elusive subjects are the very stuff of a fully cultural history of music, and elite and mainstream musical cultures cannot be understood without them.

Orality

Historical musicology is always a business of interpreting partial evidence, for writing can never convey the sound of a song or cantillation or a castrato voice. Even exactingly notated choirbooks of polyphonic masses or early opera scores require reading with an ear for pacing, timbre, instrumentation, diction, tuning, and affect. As we are reminded by modern experiments in historical performance practice, notation is not a finished product, only an invitation to do something, to sing or play, just a script. "Listening in" has emerged as a core value across these chapters as we test new means for hearing beyond the printed and manuscript sources that are the stock-in-trade of historians.

Listening for background information becomes essential when investigating migratory musics, for they often traveled in blended patterns mixing oral and written transmission. Several of our contributors examine unwritten musics that moved into foreign terrain where they were subsequently written down. Such is the case with the Spanish strumming techniques studied by Cory Gavito, who explains that Italians—lacking direct experience of them—found it necessary to produce textual supports for guitarists aspiring to learn the style and chord changes of this unfamiliar repertory. The *chansons turcquesques* featured in my own contribution appear to have been composed in Algiers and transcribed by ear by a Francophone musician. By contrast, the Jewish synagogue music studied by Francesco Spagnolo was an entirely oral practice: it sedimented in Corfu in distinct layers over centuries as displaced Jews arrived on the island from Spain, Apulia, Livorno, Venice, and Thessalonica, where it continued to coexist with written compositions that were added to the repertory in the nineteenth century. Recognizing the cultural systems of religious and musical training that sustained repertoires without notation and examining transitions from one system to another can help break down false segregations between written and unwritten musical traditions and illuminate the vast middle-ground of face-to-face training that included everything from biblical cantillation in Hebrew to the rigorous partimento drills of Neapolitan conservatories and the *meşk* system of the Ottoman court.

Many of the sonic readings essayed here attend to lyrics for what they suggest of interconnections across the early modern world. Passages of slave jargon in a Florentine opera libretto from 1657, a song in Latin, Czech, German, and Italian celebrating the Battle of White Mountain (1620), a book of Roman Catholic devotional songs from the island of Tinos in *Frangochiotika* (a transliteration of spoken Greek using the Latin alphabet)—again and again musical sources seem to capture the rawness of languages in practice, the extreme displacements of musics and musicians, and the cross-cultural traffic sustained by singing. Yet making cultural sense of these linguistic migrants remains problematic. Often few in number, pieces representing "minority" speech are frequently marginalized. Nonsense syllables in songs may script vocal patter or—conversely—only *seem* like nonsense when they actually record the sounds of dialects and "foreign" speech. Deciphering such texts requires extraordinary linguistic competence and imagination, and even so the results are oftentimes only partial translations. But in their refusal to speak in the idealized and literary forms of languages codified by academies such as the Accademia della Crusca (est. 1583) and the Académie française (est. 1635), in their moves across scriptural traditions (Hebrew, Arabic, Greek, or Latin), they spark new analyses that are sociolinguistic in approach and can better address the sounds of speech in places where people, languages, and cultures were in constant contact.[14]

Working to understand past oralities is enhancing our discipline's critical toolkit, encouraging collaborations that bring complementary and alternative forms of knowledge to bear in our histories, and expanding our range of source materials. Early music practitioners, specialists in Ottoman modal systems, and literary historians have all had hands in this research. Spagnolo's disentangling of the various strains of Jewish ritual on Corfu employed an archive of mid twentieth-century field recordings made by ethnomusicologists, a strong reminder that written records, too, can be studied as "sound recordings" from the past. Jordi Savall's research has been entirely collaborative and practice-based as he learned from musicians expert in performing traditions adjoining his own.

We hope that these studies will encourage methodological eclecticism and more tacking among practices as research unfolds. Moving forward, listening closely to texts that require extra decryption, identifying the codes governing perplexing marginalia, and attending to the convergences of oral and written traditions can broaden the scope of music history to better account for diasporic musicking and the people and musics we encounter in our studies. In our experience, keeping musicians at the center of history allows us to write from the vantage of a philosophical "elsewhere" that validates all forms of musical knowledge.

The Western Sea

Seachanges adopts a geographic configuration that allows us to map new connections in the early modern world and remap present-day intellectual cartographies. This work began in 2017 with a conference on "Music in the Mediterranean Diaspora" organized and hosted by I Tatti, the Harvard Center for Italian Renaissance Studies just outside Florence. Conversations there ran from Livorno to Ethiopia and the Bosphorus to Brazil, and they included scholars, composers, and musicians. We debated the nature of evidence, compared research strategies, and came away transformed. *Seachanges* provides a snapshot of the trajectories charted at I Tatti, and we see parallels all around as early modernists and musicians specializing in historically informed performance move beyond "Europe," pursuing diasporic studies, collaborating with musicians versed in Armenian, Greek, and Arabic performance traditions, and elaborating new scholarly networks like the Global History of Music study group of the International Musicological Society, which launched in 2019, and the Mediterranean Music Studies study group, which works closely with the International Council for Traditional Music.

The Mediterranean features in *Seachanges* as a place—one place—from which to unsettle Eurocentric histories of music. From the time of Fernand Braudel's *The Mediterranean and the Mediterranean World in the Age of Philip II* (1949), Mediterranean histories have challenged separatist, Eurocentric views of the world.[15] Whether or not one agrees with Braudel's insistence on the unity of the Mediterranean and the "shared destiny" of the Muslim and Christian worlds bounding it, turning to the sea does stage perspectival shifts that bring new cultural cartographies into view. Indeed, Mediterranean Studies have generated what historians are calling The New Thalassology: "sea studies" designed to counter smaller terrestrial histories from the expanded scale of seas and oceans.[16] Gone are the old boundaries segregating history into national narratives or aggregating them into familiar geopolitical regions: for global historians, these models of a maritime world replace terra firma with ocean as the unifying feature of new histories that promise to destabilize the hegemony of continents like Europe, Asia, and South America by turning perspectives inside-out; for scholars who espouse "connected" accounts like Sanjay Subrahmanyam's study of the Indian Ocean, seas allow us to reconfigure histories of human relations.[17] And where "terraqueous" histories might nonetheless run aground, imaginative scholars are spying "virtual seas" typified by in-betweenness and liminality: "spaces of danger and variable communications—mountain ranges, forests, or arid wildernesses such as the Sahara."[18]

The intellectual benefits of casting out to sea are nicely illustrated by considering the first known map of the world (see figure 1). In this map, made in Palermo in 1154 by the Arab cartographer Muḥammad al-Idrīsī, South is up, islands are overblown—Sicily, Crete, Cyprus—and the Italian coastline bulges with out-of-proportion inlets and harbors. Cities are evident, and it

Fig. 1. Konrad Miller, modern copy (1929) of the 1154 world map of Muḥammad al-Idrīsī, *Nuzhat al-mushtāq fī ikhtirāq al-āfāq* (The Excursion of One Who is Eager to Traverse the Regions of the World), also known as the *Tabula Rogeriana*, with the names transliterated into Latin characters. Note the mirrored configuration of the Indian Ocean (the "Eastern Sea") and the Mediterranean (the "Western Sea")

is possible to spot Rome (ruma), Genoa (ǵanua), and Florence (fluranaia), but the representation is largely topographic: mostly rivers, seas, and mountains, with ports so evenly spaced along well-traveled coastlines that they look like strings of dark pearls (see figure 2). Based on the accounts of travelers to Palermo, which al-Idrīsī assembled over a period of fifteen years, the map provides a littoral sense of the routes taken by nomads, pilgrims, exiles, and crusaders, the prevalence of travel, trade, and cultural encounter, and the importance of mobility as a critical lens. Waterways are clearly delineated, from the vast Nile Delta to the Bosphorus (disproportionately large). Recapturing the social and cultural dimensions of these thalassic imaginaries requires following the southern compass point implied in al-Idrīsī's "down is up" cartography and embracing island-centered histories that include coastal cities as virtual islands, local yet linked like archipelagos by small boats and short-distance exchange.[19]

The ancient Romans called the Mediterranean Mare nostrum, "Our Sea," yet one of the most fascinating aspects of the early modern Mediterranean is that it did not belong to the West. Whereas the overarching narrative of the early modern world is Europe as colonizer and the "rest of the world" as colonized, the Mediterranean was *not* colonized, something witnessed by the ongoing

Fig. 2. Detail of the *Tabula Rogeriana* showing the Italian Peninsula

embroilments of West and East that resurfaced again and again after the fall of the Roman Empire. The loss of Constantinople in 1453 proved definitive: notwithstanding the triumph of the Knights Hospitaller at the Siege of Malta (1565) and the victory of the Holy League at the Battle of Lepanto (1571), which aimed to regain Catholic control of the Eastern Mediterranean, ultimately every major island came under Ottoman rule: Rhodes (1522), Cyprus (1573), and fertile Crete (1669). Renaissance poets and historians papered over these centuries of failure with accounts of philosophical progress from East to West, creating paradigms that sighted culture on a naturally occurring westering trajectory from ancient Greece to Rome, France, and England, but we should recall that these myths of cultural reincarnation were necessitated by defeat.[20] In *Cultural Mobility: A Manifesto* (2010), Stephen Greenblatt reminds us that the triumphal symbolism of *translatio imperii*—by which power and authority were transferred successively from Persia to Greece, Rome, and the capitals of early modern Europe—masked political failures left behind: "the symbols, regalia, and other literal trappings of Roman imperial power were physically carried, when the empire was no longer able to defend itself, from the ancient capital of the world to a succession of new sites of global ambition."[21] As we reckon with the devastating impact of colonization on the Indigenous peoples of the Americas, the cultural complexity evident in Mediterranean musics stands as a reminder that colonial projects and Catholic missionization also failed. Western European powers did not dominate everywhere. On the contrary: Mediterranean histories of music blur the boundaries of a "Europe" that was only coming into being.[22]

Nonetheless, claims of Western exceptionalism prove quite persistent, and even as scholars challenge continental hegemonies from the Mediterranean, the sea's prestige as the "cradle of Western civilization" remains deeply inscribed, surfacing with a vengeance when discussion turns to cultural production. It is not by chance that when Braudel sought to affirm the "greatness" of the Mediterranean world, he summoned forth cultural icons from Italy and Spain in support of his claim:

> The greatness of the Mediterranean … lasted well after the age of Columbus and Vasco da Gama, until the dawn of the seventeenth century or even later. This "waning" of the Mediterranean, to borrow the word Huizinga used of the Middle Ages, had its autumnal fruits: Titian and Tintoretto at Venice; Caravaggio and the Carracci at Rome and Bologna; Galileo at Padua and Florence; in Spain, Madrid and the Golden Century; and the rise everywhere of the theater and music we still love today.[23]

By attributing timelessness and universality to Caravaggio and "the music we still love today," (What music? Who are "we"? Whose "today"?), Braudel casts a very specific set of artistic values across the entire Mediterranean world in a cultural *longue durée* that matches the slow march of environmental and social time.[24] We witness Braudel falling victim to Enlightenment presumptions of Western cultural superiority, and—alarmingly—it is but a small step from his assertion of "Mediterranean" cultural greatness to global projections of Western Art Music as an art form transcending time, space, and cultural difference. Braudel himself staked out just such an intellectual trajectory in *Out of Italy*, a late work describing the "exceptional destiny" of Italian culture: "Between 1450 and 1650, for two extraordinarily eventful centuries, one country—dazzling, multicolored Italy—beamed a radiance out beyond its own frontiers, a light that spread to every corner of the world."[25] Not only do these critical moves reveal how quickly Mediterranean Studies can collapse into merely rebranded forms of European history, they illustrate how deftly music can be enlisted in totalizing histories that ultimately reinforce narratives of Western cultural imperialism.[26] These tensions are dramatized in *Mare Nostrum* (1975), a piece of *Musiktheater* composed by Mauricio Kagel, an Argentinian-born composer living in Germany. Clearly conscious of his status as an outsider, Kagel created an inverted history of colonization in a piece that recounts the "Discovery, Pacification, and Conversion of the Mediterranean by a Tribe from Amazonia" and explicitly references the Roman Empire in its Latin title.

In short, setting out to sea does not in itself release history from Eurocentrism. But seas and oceans—the Mediterranean, the Atlantic, the Indian Ocean—*are* places from which to turn back toward "Europe" to question the power relations and exclusions written into histories of Renaissance and Baroque music. At this stage, our subjects are decidedly opportunistic: we begin with microhistories of musical migrants, contacts, repertoires, liturgies, and practices in motion. We look for fissures, weak patches, chinks, and gaps in nationalistic and European narratives of cultural wholeness. They are openings, apertures that can let the dazzling, multicolored, musical radiance of the early modern world ring brightly in our histories.

Seachanges offers pathways toward the new horizons opened up by mobility studies with essays designed to stake out new methodological points of orientation for scholars eager for leads. Models complement and contrast with one another even as all address basic features of musical mobility, such as hybridity, translation (verbal, practical, instrumental, notational), and polyglotism. Some chapters identify patterns of cultural encounter precipitated by economic migration, colonization, war, enslavement, or exile; some investigate cultural crossings on a single island or within a multiethnic empire (Ottoman, Venetian, Spanish); and some analyze the internal evidence of iconographic, literary, liturgical, theatrical, or musical sources. Constructions of racial, religious, and ethnic identities are analyzed at every turn and from multiple vantages that themselves crisscross and look back at each other. Small but fierce, our approaches to cultural mobility are perhaps even "guerrilla," in the sense that they employ unconventional tactics drawn from ethnomusicology, historical performance practice, sociolinguistics, and anthropology. Readers are encouraged to consult the index to this volume, as it is an essential resource for navigating these constellations of subject matter and method.

Chapters that intersect along geopolitical themes are grouped together according to regional designations—the Mediterranean, Italy, the Spanish and French empires—and these are introduced below. But as one should anticipate in a book of mobility studies, these essays do not stay put, and many defy the regions to which they have been assigned, crossing political borders at every turn. National designations such as France, Italy, and Spain are employed as conventions and not intended to invoke the nineteenth-century ideologies of nation-states.

Orient-Occident: The Mediterranean

Seachanges opens with a set of Mediterranean essays that examine the western and eastern parts of the Great Sea. To a large extent, Mediterranean historiography has been dominated by accounts of the civilizational clashes of the Western Mediterranean, which have been projected across the entire sea: the ultra-Catholicism of Spanish monarchs and their systematic persecution of Jews and Moors created blunt dichotomies between Christian and infidel that did not pertain elsewhere, wringing ambiguity out of the Mediterranean world and intensifying the identification of meridional cultures in France and Spain as different from those of the north.

In France, these polarities largely effaced the country's Mediterranean past. As Megan C. Armstrong and Gillian Weiss explain, French historians, including Braudel, have long assumed "that the Mediterranean—whether as a body of water or a social construct—had little to do with the economic, political, or cultural formation of metropolitan, if not colonial, France."[27] My chapter joins a series of new studies elaborating France's connections to the sea with a microhistory of two isolated *chansons turcquesques* ("Turkish songs") that were printed in Paris in 1604. Previous scholars presumed that the *chansons turcquesques* were fakes—nonsense parodies of Turkish song composed by French musicians for court festivities—but I piece together an alternative history of their oral transmission from Algeria to France by working collaboratively with Turkish, Iranian, and Greek musicians and scholars of Ottoman lyric. Underpinned by new information from the Archives diplomatiques, in my account the songs emerge as a sonic record of Franco-Ottoman relations in the Western Mediterranean and a caution against projecting Saidian Orientalism back in time. This new reading emphasizes the political and musical significance of France's Mediterranean history and urges sustained investigation of cultural entanglements across the sea that predate French colonial rule.

Distinctions between Christian and Muslim worlds break down entirely in the Eastern Mediterranean. Molly Greene has shown that this part of the sea had "a dynamic all its own, one that is not adequately conveyed by the struggle—or absence of one—between Christianity and Islam."[28] Her study of Crete, *A Shared World* (2000), stresses the Mediterranean history of Eastern Orthodoxy, adding intricacy to binaries opposing Latin Christianity and Islam. Cretan history, in particular, also destabilizes characterizations of religious identity as fixed and religious communities as segregated. In Crete, religious identities were fluid, and shifting alliances based on shared commercial interests could foster cooperation among traditional stake-holders in the region as the Venetians and Ottomans faced common threats from "northern intruders" like France, England, and Holland. Greene explains that the "overemphasis on the Christian-Muslim divide obscures the fact that, in the early modern Eastern Mediterranean, the real battle would prove to be between this *ancien régime* and the 'northern intruders' ... They upset the balance in the Mediterranean not because they were Christian but because they were new."[29]

The cultural effects of successive regimes are identifiable in local liturgical traditions, which evince an array of continuities, ruptures, and hybridizations. In her study, **Théodora Psychoyou** describes the Greek Archipelago as strongly multi-confessional: highly Christian, mainly Orthodox but also Catholic in some areas, and the whole situated within a broader sphere of Ottoman hegemony. Enter the Jesuits, who established enduring missions on several Greek islands (Naxos, Syros, Tinos, Chios) and enrolled hundreds of students in their schools by the end of the sixteenth century.[30] In this first glimpse of a larger study, Psychoyou charts the hybrid ritual forms that emerged at this extraordinary encounter of eastern and western Christians. For instance, Jesuits printed catechisms in *Frangochiotika*, and French and Sicilian priests worked out their own rough scripts for baptisms and marriages by translating Latin liturgies into Greek and writing out the results phonetically. Sacred music is equally tangled, with Byzantine and Roman Catholic elements mixed together in contrafacts of pre-existing chant and song.

In his chapter, **Francesco Spagnolo**'s meticulous interpretation of liturgical music reveals the composite identities created by Jewish migration to Corfu, an island in the Ionian Sea that—exceptionally—remained under Venetian rule until 1797. Across the centuries, displaced communities of Greek, Italian, Sephardic, and Ashkenazi Jews took refuge on the island, bringing their own liturgical traditions with them and creating what Spagnolo calls a liturgical *koiné* particular to Corfuan Jews. In a virtuosic unraveling of these interlaced liturgies, Spagnolo draws upon written accounts and liturgical texts as well as a remarkable set of archival field recordings made by Leo Levi in the second half of the twentieth century. The Jewish diaspora, confronting millennia of displacement, here reveals its potency as a paradigm for understanding other cases of communal mobility: music and ritual sustained uprooted peoples, who counted on the expression of shared beliefs to maintain a sense of togetherness. Yet liturgies responded to time and place as well, and diasporic studies inevitably confront conditions prompting the sorts of métissage, translation, and polyglotism seen across this volume as a whole. Next steps for the field would include more sustained consideration of relationships with homeland and hostland and—following Spagnolo's leads—interrelationships among communities of the diaspora.[31]

The title of this section, Orient-Occident, honors the pathbreaking series of recordings made by Hespèrion XXI and **Jordi Savall**, the Catalan conductor and viola da gambist whose artistic vision of pan-Mediterranean musicking has created an entirely new register of convergence across the sea. Tellingly, the project originated with a gift: during his first concert tour to Istanbul in 2000, friends there gave Savall a new edition of Dimitrie Cantemir's *Science of Music*, a seventeenth-century collection of instrumental music from the Ottoman court. Struck by the beauty of Cantemir's *maḳāms*, Savall "set about studying both the music and the composer in order to learn about a culture which, despite its proximity, seems remote to us as a result of sheer ignorance." These revelations ultimately launched a decade-long project in which Savall and Hespèrion XXI partnered with musicians from Turkey, Armenia, Israel, Morocco, and Greece to perform programs of music from Constantinople, Persia, Iberia, Italy, and beyond. In 2008, Savall was designated a UNESCO Artist for Peace in recognition of his dedication to intercultural dialogue and his commitment to preserving the intangible cultural heritage of the Mediterranean. His Orpheus XXI ensemble, made up of around twenty refugee and migrant musicians, performs Mediterranean repertoire in Europe, preserves musics that are under threat, and teaches young refugee and migrant children about the music of their homelands.

Into Italy, Out of Italy

Italy holds a central place in the early modern Mediterranean, and its history is tied to the sea. The great republics of Genoa and Venice faced outward, culturally, onto maritime empires that were their lifeblood (each year, the doges of Venice tossed a gold ring into the Adriatic, affirming the marriage of Venice to the sea), while the Kingdom of Naples was itself part of a "Spanish" thalassocracy, the Crown of Aragon. In addition to the mobility generated by Venetian and Genoan maritime trade in spices, textiles, and other goods, Rome was a destination for pilgrims, diplomats, and clerics from across Christendom, and

Venice was the launching point for pilgrim ships to the Holy Land. Islands and ports cities like Corsica, Livorno, and Naples thrived on the subjugation of Mediterranean captives and enslaved sub-Saharan Africans trafficked via trans-Saharan routes and by sea from Mauritania, Upper Guinea, and the Gulf of Guinea via Lisbon, Lagos, and Seville, beginning in the fifteenth century.[32] The chapters gathered here stress the extent to which people and musics were constantly on the move, both into and out of the Italian peninsula.

No broad history of cultural mobility can ignore the ramifications of enslavement, but as Olivia Bloechl observed in "Race, Empire, and Early Music" (2015)—a manifesto calling for race critical and postcolonial studies of early modern European music—early musicology has hardly grappled with race and racism.[33] **Emily Wilbourne**'s study rises to the challenge with a Black history of the seventeenth-century Italian opera stage that brings to light the career of Gio: Buonaccorsi, "il Moro" (the Moor), an enslaved member of the Medici household. By crossing the evidence of baptismal records, pay records, a painting, letters of engagement, libretti, and scores that identify Buonaccorsi and his roles, Wilbourne not only elucidates how normalized racial and religious slavery was in early modern Italy, she troubles the presumed whiteness of European music-making. Black singers on the operatic stage, she concludes, "were not an imagined, fantasized representation symbolizing something allegorical, but a reflection of the mundane, day-to-day co-existence of white and Black Europeans."

Cory M. Gavito's study exemplifies the impact of Spanish imperialism in Naples and Rome, and it demonstrates that colonization moved in all directions. By 1600, one third of Rome's inhabitants were Spanish, with communities representing the entire social spectrum from stratospherically wealthy cardinals to workers, provisioners, and the poor.[34] One musical vestige of Spanish Rome and Naples is a distinctive style of guitar playing that Gavito recovers from Italian accounts and musical sources. Whereas these Ibero-Arabic dances and strumming patterns were the stock-in-trade of Spanish guitarists and quite familiar in the Iberian peninsula, where they required no written instructions to perform, Italian musicians textualized them in a new form of tablature, *alfabeto*, beginning in the Spanish orbit of Naples and Rome. Gavito's deft analysis of Italian cultivation of guitar playing *alla vera Spagnola* exemplifies both the advantages of oral traditions and desires to convey unfamiliar musics in writing, in this way contributing to broader histories of memory and haptic knowledge that spanned the Mediterranean.[35] Moreover, by critiquing the cultural and social meanings of *alla Spagnola* in early seventeenth-century

Naples, Rome, and Florence, his study provides new reference points for how to theorize perceptions of musical difference that ran along ethnic lines.

Dinko Fabris, in his chapter, also considers the mobility of a musical practice: the Neapolitan style of musical training and composition. By 1700, Naples' four selective conservatories had launched approximately 4,000 students on professional careers after eight-to-ten years of intensive training in what Fabris describes as an "almost industrial level of production." Singers including Neapolitan castrati dominated opera stages and filled choirs across the peninsula and in European capitals, instrumentalists were in equally high demand, and musicians moved far and wide through intricate professional networks established over generations of student-teacher relationships and institutional genealogies. Whereas Braudel's oblique reference to "the theater and music we still love today" suggests that the success of "Italian" music was self-evident—preordained by the destiny of Mediterranean culture—Fabris illustrates the benefits of a truly Braudelian analysis that aggregates data on the careers of musicians and employs diasporic models of migration.

There is no question that Italian was a musical and courtly language of prestige north of the Alps, though we have much to learn about its traction in the time before Italian opera was cultivated abroad. **Scott Lee Edwards** turns his attention to the early seventeenth century and the printing of Italian *laude* in Bohemia, working outward from aristocratic circles to argue for Italian as a spoken *lingua franca* in very real terms emerging from waves of Italian immigration to Bohemia in the late sixteenth century and reinforced by the incursion of Habsburg armies from Italian and Spanish territories in the seventeenth century. In Edwards's reading, the *laude* printed in Bohemia witness "a linguistic culture sustained by various diasporas from the Italian peninsula, but by no means limited to those who spoke fluently." The drastic circumstances of the Thirty Years War, which brought far-flung civic, military, and religious communities into jarring contact, made multilingual communication especially urgent, and the singing of *laude* became a means for Bohemians to navigate a new and intensely heteroglot environment.

The Spanish and French Empires

Scholars concerned with questions of cultural mixing in early modern empires regularly focus on Spain, which engaged in projects of colonization in the Mediterranean, across the Atlantic, and beyond. Spain's global expansion was financed by silver and gold from Mexico and Peru, which significantly shifted the balance of power in European Christendom. American gold paid for the construction of roughly a hundred ships that by the late sixteenth century allowed the Spanish navy to defend the Papal State against the Ottoman Empire and secure Spanish claims to Rome itself as Philip II lived up to his title as Most Catholic King.[36] Spain's ultra-Catholicism has magnified accounts of the Mediterranean as the site of irresolvable conflicts between Christians and Muslims (more true in the Western Mediterranean than the East), but more interesting, from a comparative standpoint, is how the extreme religious intolerance evident in the Spanish Inquisition and the militarism of the Jesuit Order (est. 1540) defined imperial forms that did not pertain in the great multiethnic Eastern Mediterranean empires of the Venetians and Ottomans.

Spain's imperial expansion in colonial Latin America was justified as a quest for souls, and musicians became frontrunners in missions to convert and "civilize" Indigenous peoples. **Geoffrey Baker**'s wide-ranging essay begins by considering the professional careers of Indigenous church musicians and the ways they might secure positions within the new social orders that came with colonization.[37] In this respect he resists blunt oppositions between oppressed peoples and oppressor imperialists, but he also moves on to question celebratory histories of religious syncretism and the flourishing of a "mestizo" musical culture as Indigenous song, dance, and instruments were introduced into Catholic ceremonies. Mapping the evidence shows that "mixture was more likely to take place at the margins and in backwaters," whereas repertoire performed in major centers like Cuzco Cathedral projected the social codes of "elite *criollo* institutions dedicated to the reproduction of European cultural values."

Baker argues that because church music was a domain that promoted the performance of sameness, it can be challenging to spot cultural hybridity in written sources. In this light, **Philippe Canguilhem**'s precious discovery of traces of mestizo musicking in the margins of a manuscript from the Highlands of Western Guatemala makes complete sense, originating as this source did far from Mexico City, Merida, or any major city and cropping up as these traces do at the edges of a polyphonic manuscript. Canguilhem's reading of this neglected musical fragment shows how the unusual notation and onomatopoetic syllables are both unlike the conventional white-note polyphonic notation being taught to local singers and similar to "marginal" notational forms associated with early organum and the mnemonic techniques of instrumentalists. Analytically, it exemplifies the "lateral" moves of connected history called for by Sanjay Subrahmanyam and a critical perspective that is less a zooming out than a stepping aside, getting off the paths worn by presumptions of sameness and difference to allow previously unseen connections to come into view.[38]

Olivia Bloechl shifts from the real-world geographies of colonial expansion to the fictional cartographies of the operatic stage. In a sustained analysis of Jean-Baptiste Lully's *Proserpine* (1680), she shows how the descent of mythological characters from earthly settings to the underworld and back again spectacularizes monarchic power in spatial terms. Drawing on a formulation of Edward Said, Bloechl argues that the make-believe orders comprised by opera's celestial, terrestrial, and infernal realms establish an "imaginative geography" that performs the important cultural work of demarcating "a familiar space which is 'ours' and an unfamiliar space beyond ours which is 'theirs'."[39] In this way, cartographic divisions of the known world (as, for instance, into "East" and "West") map onto the political cosmography of the French stage in ways that can reveal the latent Orientalism of hellish *enfers* and other marvelous settings far more prevalent than the geographically distant "elsewheres" represented by the Sicilian myth of Proserpina, Eastern Mediterranean locations, and the otherness of characters such as Dido, the Afro-Phoenician Queen of Carthage.[40]

Pedro Memelsdorff draws our attention to the French colony of Saint-Domingue (Haiti), the most exploitative settlement in the Caribbean. At its apex, Saint-Domingue produced 40 percent of the sugar and 60 percent of the coffee imported into Europe. Its theatrical life has recently emerged as a locus of scholarship on early modern music and race thanks to the wealth of information that survives pertaining to performances at its multiple play-houses.[41] Memelsdorff opens his chapter on opera in pre-revolutionary Haiti with the biography of the superstar coloratura soprano, Minette, the first known French opera singer of color to be cast in a title role. While the broad outlines of Minette's career have been known, surprisingly little consideration has been given to her artistic persona or the significance of her most famous performances. Memelsdorff discloses Minette's complex bonds with the mixed-race audiences of Port-au-Prince through an intricate reading of one of Minette's hits of 1786, *L'amant statue*. In the second half of his essay, he considers the possible identities of the enslaved flautists whose playing from the orchestra pit "animated" the flute-playing statue opposite Minette on stage. Drawing together the Enlightenment fascination with musical automata, the prevalence of actual statues of Black flautists in France and America, and the career of Louis, an enslaved flautist at the theater of Port-au-Prince, Memelsdorff argues that for contemporaries, *L'amant statue* raised questions over "animation" itself as it pertained to the souls of the enslaved and their status as human beings.

International collaborations and cross-cultural conversations have been integral to the genesis of this volume. Our work would not have been possible without all the musicians, cultural informants, academic colleagues, translators, and archivists who broke a code, corroborated an intuition, suggested a new lead, corrected a misunderstanding, and rallied to support this research. We have done our best to respect the epistemological sovereignty of the past peoples and musics we study and disclose the motives behind our studies, but we offer up this volume with the recognition that the potential to misread remains. Expanding beyond traditional areas of expertise brings with it various degrees of uncertainty and individual discomfort, but the payoff comes in the form of new intellectual connections and networks. The in-betweenness of seas and oceans can provoke worry that "this is not my field," but we stand encouraged by the great Italian ethnomusicologist Tullia Magrini, instigator of the Mediterranean Music Studies group of the International Council for Traditional Music, who reputedly told hesitant scholars that their anxieties were "not a matter of concern, the journey will be transformative."[42] We are immensely grateful to all the collaborators whose on-the-ground knowledge anchors so much of this volume and has begun to transform our field.

Our deepest thanks owe to Alina Payne, the visionary director of I Tatti, who encouraged this disciplinary plunge into the Mediterranean and Atlantic worlds, and her superb staff, especially Thomas Gruber. We also thank all those who participated in the conference that gave rise to this volume, which also included Guido Guerzoni, David Irving, Cemal Kafadar, Kay Kaufman Shelemay, and session chairs Martin Alan Brody, Bonnie Gordon, Stefano Lorenzetti, and Michael Wyatt, who added so much to the discussion. Finally, we acknowledge the invaluable advice of the anonymous reviewers for the press.

To be honest, the gathering at I Tatti in May 2017 was organized in the spirit of a workshop to test ideas and define approaches to mobility studies; publication of conference proceedings was not part of the plan. But a sense of urgency coalesced at the meeting, for then—as now—the world was seized by crisis. To introduce this book without mentioning the almost two million migrants, refugees, and asylum seekers who have crossed the Mediterranean Sea since 2014 would be irresponsible. Italy alone had received 624,747 individuals by the end of 2017, most of them via the hazardous Central Mediterranean route from North Africa. NGOs, Italian coast guards, and merchant vessels rescue thousands from rubber rafts and dinghies, but as of this writing, the International Organization for Migration estimates that 17,862 migrants have died en route from Libya to Malta and Italy.[43]

Nothing exposed the failure of international coalitions to establish safe paths of migration more pointedly than the photos that had been published in September 2015 of a young Syrian boy, Alan Kurdi, lying drowned on a Turkish beach. His death symbolized the obstacles faced by refugees and the tragedies resulting from systematic resistance to immigrants. Instead of making diasporic communities a lived reality, democratic societies across the world have reacted to refugees with varying degrees of fear. In the United States, voters in the 2016 presidential election endorsed the explicitly anti-Muslim, anti-immigration campaign of Donald Trump in a rising tide of nationalism. Responses in Europe have ranged from Sweden's embrace of asylum seekers to the controversial detention deal between the European Union and Turkey, which shut down migration via the Greek Islands.

As we work to understand the circulation of music and musicians in the past, these pictures, statistics, and isolationist policies have stayed with us, casting shadows across our research. Our studies will not bring relief to refugees, but they can refute claims of nationalism; histories of migration and cultural complexity are more pressing than ever. At a time when colonial philosophies continue to justify economic, military, and cultural imperialism, the euphemistically named Age of Discovery emerges as twinned with the present, in dyad with this now. Indeed, the Mediterranean, the Americas, and their roles in Europe's past have yet to be fully discovered.

Notes

1. For publications, see Gurrieri and Zara, eds., *Renaissance Music in the Slavic World,* research undertaken within the framework of the European program "EACEA—Culture Programme 2007–2013 Aux confins de l'Humanisme musical: monde slave et culture méditerranéenne," developed between 2010 and 2012 by the Centre d'Études Supérieures de la Renaissance in Tours, France, the Matica Hrvatska—Ogranak Dubrovnik (Mediterranean Study Centre of Dubrovnik), the Univerzita Karlova v Praze, and the Università degli Studi di Palermo. From the HERA-funded program managed by Vjera Katalinić, "Music Migrations in Early Modern Europe," www.musmig.eu (accessed November 22, 2019) see zur Nieden and Over, eds., *Musicians' Mobilities and Music Migrations in Early Modern Europe*, and Katalinić, ed., *Music Migrations in the Early Modern Age.*

2. Goulet and zur Nieden, eds., *Europäische Musiker in Venedig, Rom und Neapel. Les musiciens européens à Venise, Rome et Naples*, research undertaken by the program MUSICI, www.musici.eu (accessed November 22, 2019), an ANR-DFG research program at the École française de Rome, in collaboration with the German Historical Institute.

3. Ahrendt, Ferraguto, and Mahiet, eds., *Music and Diplomacy*, and Ramel and Prévost-Thomas, eds., *International Relations, Music and Diplomacy.*

4. Márin López, "Introduction. Musical Interchanges in the Atlantic World: A Paradigm under Construction," 24.

5. Strohm, ed., *The Music Road*, and idem, ed., *Studies on a Global History of Music.*

6. Wilbourne and Cusick, eds., *Acoustemologies in Contact.*

7. Madrid, "Diversity, Tokenism, Non-Canonical Musics, and the Crisis of the Humanities in U.S. Academia."

8. On musicology's turn from new historicism to an obsession with objets trouvés and quirky micronarratives, see Mathew and Smart, "Elephants in the Music Room: The Future of Quirk Historicism."

9. Andrade, "A Chinese Farmer, Two African Boys, and a Warlord," 574, cited in Ghobrial, "Introduction: Seeing the World like a Microhistorian," 14. Ghobrial's invaluable introduction fronts an issue of *Past & Present* devoted to the subject of global history and microhistory.

10. On hard versus soft models of history, see Green, "Maritime Worlds and Global History," 514–15. Green argues that global histories often fail to work through cultural responses to larger processes and the "uneven trajectories and diametric strategies forged by individuals and communities in the face of globalization" (514).

11. Trivellato, "Is There a Future for Italian Microhistory in the Age of Global History?" I.

12. For an overview of the working methods of microhistory and macrohistory that can illuminate the degree to which musicological studies of the early modern period align with the former (even if few musicologists explicitly identify as microhistorians), see ibid., III.

13. Ginzburg, "Microhistory: Two or Three Things That I Know about It," 23–24.

14. See Pennycook, *Language and Mobility: Unexpected Places*, a forceful analysis of nationalistic ideologies of language, global Englishes, and linguistic imperialism.

15. Following the lead suggested by Braudel, two of the most notable recent studies of the Mediterranean vastly expand Braudel's *longue durée*: see Horden and Purcell, *The Corrupting Sea*, which takes an ecological and partly synchronic approach to history across two millennia, and Abulafia, *The Great Sea*, which charts humankind's relationship with the sea from around 22,000 BCE to 2010.

16. See Horden and Purcell, "The Mediterranean and 'the New Thalassology'," and Miller, *The Sea: Thalassography and Historiography.*

17. Subrahmanyam, *Explorations in Connected History: Mughals and Franks.*

18. Horden and Purcell, "The Mediterranean and 'the New Thalassology'," 723; on virtual seas, see Abulafia, "Mediterraneans," and for a new model of maritime history, see Bashford, "Terraqueous Histories."

19. On island-centered histories, see Molly Greene's studies of Crete (*A Shared World*) and Malta (*Catholic Pirates and Greek Merchants*).

20. On Renaissance philosophies of the westward movement of culture, see Ferguson, "The Exile's Defense," 280–82.

21. Greenblatt, "Cultural Mobility: An Introduction," 7–12. Greenblatt presents two "powerful traditional models for understanding cultural mobility": *translatio imperii* and "the account that theologians developed for describing the ways that Christianity 'fulfilled' the Hebrew Scriptures and hence transformed the Torah into the Old Testament" (7). Both are inherently Mediterranean.

22. On the construction of Europe at this time, see Piechocki, *Cartographic Humanism*, especially her discussion of al-Idrīsī and the designation "Western Sea" at 199.

23. Braudel, *The Mediterranean and the Mediterranean World* 1:14.

24. Tomlinson, "*Il faut méditerraniser la musique*: After Braudel," is an almost unique example of a music history embracing Braudel's *longue durée*.

25. Braudel, *Out of Italy*, foreword. My warmest thanks to Cemal Kafadar for recommending *Out of Italy* (*Le modèle italien*, Paris, 1989) and several precious conversations concerning Mediterranean Studies.

26. On the tenaciousness of these ideologies, see Irving, "Rethinking Early Modern 'Western Art Music'."

27. Armstrong and Weiss, "Introduction: France and the Early Modern Mediterranean," 2.

28. Greene, *A Shared World*, 4.

29. Ibid., 5. Also see Greene, "Beyond the Northern Invasion."

30. Shore, "The Jesuits in the Orthodox World," 321–23.

31. See Butler, "Defining Diaspora," for ways "to look beyond the *labels* of diaspora currently in use to the fundamental differences between *types* of diaspora" (197).

32. See the data compiled at www.slavevoyages.org, accessed November 25, 2019.

33. Bloechl, "Race, Empire, and Early Music," 77–78.

34. Dandelet, *Spanish Rome*, 9.

35. See, for instance, Bouza, *Communication, Knowledge, and Memory in Early Modern Spain.*

36. Dandelet, *Spanish Rome*, 7–10.

37. Also see Baker, *Imposing Harmony: Music and Society in Colonial Cuzco.*

38. See Subrahmanyam, "Connected Histories: Notes towards a Reconfiguration of Early Modern Eurasia." Subrahmanyam defines connected history in opposition to the comparative methods of area studies still prevalent at the time of his writing, which depended on segregated histories: "Nationalism has blinded us to the possibility of connection, and historical ethnography, whether in one of its western variants of high Orientalism, or whether practiced in the East, has aided and abetted this unfortunate process" (761).

39. Said, *Orientalism*, 54.

40. On Purcell's *Dido and Aeneas* and its place in "turning the Mediterranean-centered consciousness of European memory into an Atlantic-centered one," see Roach, *Cities of the Dead*, 42–48, this quote at 45.

41. For resources see the database curated by Julia Prest, "Theatre in Saint-Domingue, 1764–1791."

42. Cited by Philip Bohlman in *Antropologia della musica nelle culture mediterranee*, 12.

43. "Missing Migrants Project," https://missingmigrants.iom.int, accessed December 24, 2019.

Bibliography

Abulafia, David. "Mediterraneans." In *Rethinking the Mediterranean*, ed. William V. Harris. Pp. 64–93. Oxford: Oxford University Press, 2005.

Abulafia, David. *The Great Sea: A Human History of the Mediterranean.* London and New York: Allen Lane, 2011.

Ahrendt, Rebekah, Mark Ferraguto, and Damien Mahiet, eds. *Music and Diplomacy from the Early Modern Era to the Present.* New York: Palgrave Macmillan, 2014.

Andrade, Tonio. "A Chinese Farmer, Two African Boys, and a Warlord: Toward a Global Microhistory." *Journal of World History* 21 (2010): 573–91.

Armstrong, Megan C., and Gillian Weiss. "Introduction: France and the Early Modern Mediterranean." *French History* 29 (2015): 1–5.

Baker, Geoffrey. *Imposing Harmony: Music and Society in Colonial Cuzco.* Durham: Duke University Press, 2008.

Bashford, Alison. "Terraqueous Histories." *The Historical Journal* 60 (2017): 253–72.

Bloechl, Olivia. "Race, Empire, and Early Music." In *Rethinking Difference in Music Scholarship*, ed. Olivia Bloechl, Melanie Lowe, and Jeffrey Kallberg. Pp. 77–107. Cambridge: Cambridge University Press, 2015.

Bohlman, Philip V., Marcello Sorce Keller, and Loris Azzaroni, eds. *Antropologia della musica nelle culture mediterranee: interpretazione, performance, identità: alla memoria di Tullia Magrini = Musical Anthropology in Mediterranean Cultures: Interpretation, Performance, Identity, in Memory of Tullia Magrini.* Bologna: Edizioni Clueb—Cooperativa Libraria Universitaria Editrice, 2009.

Bouza Alvarez, Fernando J. *Communication, Knowledge, and Memory in Early Modern Spain.* Philadelphia: University of Pennsylvania Press, 2004.

Braudel, Fernand. *The Mediterranean and the Mediterranean World in the Age of Philip II*, trans. Siân Reynolds. 2 vols. New York: Harper & Row, 1972.

Braudel, Fernand. *Out of Italy: Two Centuries of World Domination and Demise*, trans. Siân Reynolds. New York: Europa Editions, 2019.

Butler, Kim D. "Defining Diaspora, Refining a Discourse." *Diaspora* 10 (2001): 189–219.

Dandelet, Thomas James. *Spanish Rome, 1500–1700.* New Haven: Yale University Press, 2001.

Ferguson, Margaret W. "The Exile's Defense: DuBellay's *La Deffence et illustration de la langue françoyse.*" *PMLA* 93 (1978): 275–89.

Ghobrial, John-Paul A. "Introduction: Seeing the World like a Microhistorian." *Past & Present* 242, Supplement 14 (2019): 1–22.

Ginzburg, Carlo. "Microhistory: Two or Three Things That I Know about It," trans. Anne C. Tedeschi and John Tedeschi. *Critical Inquiry* 20 (1993): 10–35.

Goulet, Anne-Madeleine, and Gesa zur Nieden, eds. *Europäische Musiker in Venedig, Rom und Neapel. Les musiciens européens à Venise, Rome et Naples.* Special issue of *Analecta musicologica* 52 (2015).

Green, Nile. "Maritime Worlds and Global History: Comparing the Mediterranean and Indian Ocean through Barcelona and Bombay." *History Compass* 11 (2013): 513–23.

Greenblatt, Stephen. "Cultural Mobility: An Introduction." In *Cultural Mobility: A Manifesto*, ed. Stephen Greenblatt et al. Cambridge, UK and New York: Cambridge University Press, 2010.

Greene, Molly. *A Shared World: Christians and Muslims in the Early Modern Mediterranean*. Princeton: Princeton University Press, 2000.

Greene, Molly. "Beyond the Northern Invasion: The Mediterranean in the Seventeenth Century." *Past & Present* 174 (2002): 42–71.

Greene, Molly. *Catholic Pirates and Greek Merchants: A Maritime History of the Mediterranean*. Princeton Modern Greek Studies. Princeton: Princeton University Press, 2010.

Gurrieri, Marco, and Vasco Zara, eds. *Renaissance Music in the Slavic World*. Collection "Épitome musical" 92. Turnhout: Brepols, 2019.

Horden, Peregrine, and Nicholas Purcell. *The Corrupting Sea: A Study of Mediterranean History*. Oxford: Blackwell, 2000.

Horden, Peregrine, and Nicholas Purcell. "The Mediterranean and 'the New Thalassology'." *The American Historical Review* 111 (2006): 722–40.

Irving, David R. M. "Rethinking Early Modern 'Western Art Music': A Global History Manifesto." *IMS Musicological Brainfood* 3 (2019): 6–10.

Katalinić, Vjera, ed. *Music Migrations in the Early Modern Age: People, Markets, Patterns and Styles*. Zagreb: Croatian Musicological Society, 2016.

Madrid, Alejandro L. "Diversity, Tokenism, Non-Canonical Musics, and the Crisis of the Humanities in U.S. Academia." *Journal of Music History Pedagogy* 7 (2017): 124–30.

Marín López, Javier. "Introduction. Musical Interchanges in the Atlantic World: A Paradigm under Construction." In *Músicas coloniales a debate: procesos de intercambio euroamericanos*. Colección Música Hispana. Textos. Estudios 22. Madrid: Instituto Complutense de Ciencias Musicales, 2018.

Mathew, Nicholas, and Mary Ann Smart. "Elephants in the Music Room: The Future of Quirk Historicism." *Representations* 132 (2015): 61–78.

Miller, Peter N. *The Sea: Thalassography and Historiography*. Ann Arbor: University of Michigan Press, 2013.

"Missing Migrants Project." https://missingmigrants.iom.int/, accessed December 24, 2019.

Nieden, Gesa zur, and Berthold Over, eds. *Musicians' Mobilities and Music Migrations in Early Modern Europe*. Bielefeld: Transcript Verlag, 2016.

Pennycook, Alastair. *Language and Mobility: Unexpected Places*. Critical Language and Literacy Studies 15. United Kingdom: Multilingual Matters, 2012.

Piechocki, Katharina N. *Cartographic Humanism: The Making of Early Modern Europe*. Chicago: University of Chicago Press, 2019.

Ramel, Frédéric, and Cécile Prévost-Thomas. *International Relations, Music and Diplomacy: Sounds and Voices on the International Stage*. Cham, Switzerland: Palgrave Macmillan, 2018.

Roach, Joseph R. *Cities of the Dead: Circum-Atlantic Performance*. New York: Columbia University Press, 1996.

Said, Edward. *Orientalism*. New York: Vintage Books, 1979.

Shore, Paul. "The Jesuits in the Orthodox World." In *The Oxford Handbook of the Jesuits*, ed. Ines G. Županov. Pp. 318–48. New York: Oxford University Press, 2017.

"Slave Voyages." www.slavevoyages.org, accessed November 25, 2019.

Strohm, Reinhard, ed. *Studies on a Global History of Music: A Balzan Musicology Project*. Abingdon, Oxon, and New York: Routledge, 2018.

Strohm, Reinhard, ed. *The Music Road: Coherence and Diversity in Music from the Mediterranean to India*. Oxford: Oxford University Press, 2019.

Subrahmanyam, Sanjay. "Connected Histories: Notes towards a Reconfiguration of Early Modern Eurasia." *Modern Asian Studies* 31 (1997): 735–62.

Subrahmanyam, Sanjay. *Explorations in Connected History: Mughals and Franks*. Oxford India Paperbacks. New Delhi: Oxford University Press, 2011.

"Theatre in Saint-Domingue, 1764–1791, Plays, Ballets, and Operas." https://www.theatreinsaintdomingue.org, accessed June 30, 2019.

Tomlinson, Gary. "*Il faut méditerraniser la musique*: After Braudel." In *Music and Historical Critique: Selected Essays*. Pp. 327–45. Aldershot, UK and Burlington, VT: Ashgate, 2007.

Trivellato, Francesca. "Is There a Future for Italian Microhistory in the Age of Global History?" *California Italian Studies* 2 (2011), https://escholarship.org/uc/item/0z94n9hq

Wilbourne, Emily, and Suzanne G. Cusick, eds. *Acoustemologies in Contact: Sounding Subjects and Modes of Listening in Early Modernity*. Open Book Publishers, 2021.

PART I

Orient-Occident: The Mediterranean

Hearing Franco-Ottoman Relations circa 1600: The *chansons turcquesques* of Charles Tessier (1604)*

Kate van Orden

In April of 1589, a French gentleman named Jacques de Villamont boarded the *Nana Fera*, a Venetian merchant vessel destined for Tripoli on the Syrian coast.[1] Thirty-six barques pulled the great craft out to sea from the Lido, whence it set sail on a journey planned to last through summer. The passengers came from near and far: France, Florence, Lombardy, Armenia, Cyprus, Greece, and more. The Venetian merchants traveled in high style, bringing along "spinets, lutes, citterns & other instruments" to pass the time, much to Villamont's delight.[2] This was not the only music on board. Each evening, the captain made sure the *Ave Maria* was sung, and on Saturdays the litanies of the Virgin and a *Salve Regina*; the cabin boys sang their prayers at reveille.[3] Although the *patron* in this way imposed Roman Catholic devotions on board the *Nana Fera*, the passengers were of diverse faiths. Some were Christians such as Maronites, Armenians, Georgians, Cretans, and Greeks, while others were heading home to the Islamic world, "Mores, Perses & Turcs," as Villamont calls them, including a Persian cleric.

Villamont took his meals in the great hall at the rear of the ship, which accommodated thirty-nine, and we have to imagine that table talk mixed multiple vernaculars. In its farrago of peoples, the *Nana Fera* aptly represents the blends of polities, languages, and religions that coursed throughout the Mediterranean basin: groups pooled together for part of a journey, only to drain and be replenished in new concoctions as ships docked en route for fresh provisions.

I begin my essay here, with these travelers embarking on still further travels to unsettle presumptions about where people and things belong in histories of music. Villamont and six other pilgrims on the *Nana Fera* were on their way to the Holy Land, one for the third time. Villamont's wildly popular *Les voyages du seigneur de Villamont* (1595) provided prices for the journey between Marseille and Tripoli and tips on what to pack, and its twenty-three reprintings witness a burst of trans-Mediterranean travel.[4] The end of Turkish-Venetian wars in 1573 facilitated decades of tourism, with "pilgrim ships" setting sail each spring and longer routes establishing a "Grand Tour" including Cairo and Constantinople.[5] Travelogues like Francisco Guerrero's *El viaje de Hierusalem* (1590), Villamont's *Voyages*, and Jean Palerne's *Peregrinations* (1606) set the stage for maritime histories of cultural mobility that defy segregated framing according to language, nation, or faith.

This essay contributes to a growing body of scholarship designed to situate early modern France in the broader field of Mediterranean studies. Histories of France that venture beyond "the hexagon" generally sight the kingdom's destiny to the West, finding in the Atlantic its "trajectory to modernity as a nation and as a colonial power," as Megan C. Armstrong and Gillian Weiss explain.[6] Even Fernand Braudel's magisterial *La Méditerranée*, begun in French Algiers in the 1930s, barely mentions France or its southern coast.[7] Such exclusions have had follow-on effects in musicology, tacitly validating perspectives biased toward Paris and the French royal court in the north, even though—as I show here—music history can provide new data points for studies of cultural exchange in the Western Mediterranean.

One reason France has remained so easily cordoned off from Mediterranean history relates to ideologies of the French language and written representations of speech in the early modern age. Here, too, Villamont is instructive: throughout his journey, Villamont relied on Italian as a bridge language and knew enough "moresque" to catch fragments of conversation and respond.[8] Clearly polyglot, he used languages resourcefully, mobilizing some sort of *lingua franca* as he traveled.[9] And yet, Villamont recounts his *Voyages* in French. Monoglossia—increasingly typical of French literary production—silences direct speech, suppressing what Mikhail Bakhtin described as the "intense interanimation of languages that took place during the Renaissance."[10] Villamont spoke in the tongues of bazaars filled with civet and musk, and the bartering lingo of places like Cairo, filled with people from "the Indies, all of Asia, Africa, and Europe."[11] His mother tongue was probably Breton. But he wrote in French.

France was itself a place of heteroglot borderlands, and port cities like Marseille were full of resident foreigners. One place to listen for the polyglotism that bathed French shores is in songs. Uncensored by the monotonicism of high literary genres, the linguistic errancy of song repertoires enables Bakhtinian critical moves that can turn scholarship toward polyglossia and the interanimation of languages and cultures, calling into question the purity of essentialized ethnicities keyed to "national" languages like French.

Villamont's *Voyages* provides tantalizing details about music on the move in the Eastern Mediterranean, and it can be charming to imagine spinets on their way to the Levant and Venetian gentlemen whiling away empty hours singing *ottave rime* stanzas from Ariosto's *Orlando furioso*. And yet, the charm of such a history, which would reinforce narratives of Venetian supremacy, lies entwined with myths of Western exceptionalism that must be corrected here at the outset. Ottoman maritime technology easily rivaled that of the Venetian and Habsburg empires, and the sultans wielded extraordinary political power. Goods and people moved in all directions across the sea, and with them ideas, mental constructs, ornamental styles, furnishings, fabrics, and song. Rather than adding to the cultural history of European expansionism charted, for instance, in repeating accounts of keyboard instruments being gifted to Ottoman sultans, I hear music as a cultural frontrunner, which traveled as readily as one could sing at sea.[12]

Segregated histories

The centerpiece of my essay is the *Airs et villanelles Fran. Ital. Espa. Suice. et Turcq.* of Charles Tessier (Paris, 1604), a polyglot anthology pitched to a niche market for songs in foreign tongues. Tessier claims in his dedication that after "tasting the sweet nectar of the Muses and being admitted to their most delightful fields in France, Italy, Spain, Germany, and Arabia," he gathered together this bouquet.[13] As is true for so many musicians, biographical information about Tessier is scant, and there is no way to verify his claims to have collected songs abroad. He was almost certainly the son of the Breton composer Guillaume Tessier, and he definitely visited England, possibly as early as 1582: his *Premier livre de chansons et airs de cour tant en français qu'en italien et gascon* (London, 1597) is signed "di Londra," and three letters written in England likewise attest to his presence there.[14] Tessier traveled to Marburg to present the 1604 *Airs et villanelles* to the Landgrave of Hesse-Kassel, but his 1610 dedication to the King of Hungary was signed in Paris, as "Musissien dela chambre Du Roy."[15] We have no hard evidence that Tessier traveled to Italy, Spain, or the Arabian Peninsula, though given the fact that even his employment at the court of Henry IV has proven impossible to firmly corroborate, the flowery language of his dedications may well convey some truths of his peregrinations.[16] In content, Tessier's *Airs et villanelles* certainly resembles a musical travelogue, and it reflects the song-collecting of French travelers like Jean Palerne (d. 1592), who kept a manuscript full of his own poetry and song lyrics in Occitan, Tuscan, Bergamasque, Neapolitan, Spanish, and Turkish, and a diary of his youthful adventure to the Holy Land and Constantinople, places he described as "quite frequented these days by our French" ("aujourd'huy assez frequentee par noz Françoys").[17]

Tessier closed his 1604 *Airs et villanelles* with two "chansons turcquesques" that might well have been picked up on a Mediterranean voyage or from a traveler, sailor, or captive, and these are what drew my attention to the collection in the first place, for they seemed to represent what Sanjay Subrahmanyam has called "the at times fragile threads that connected the globe."[18] Yet scholarship on them has remained resolutely hexagonal, with disbelief and misreadings cutting short investigation into the context of their publication. By far the most striking omission in the secondary literature is the failure to relate the *chansons turcquesques* to the political event that almost certainly defined their reception: the signing of a landmark set of Franco-Ottoman trade capitulations in May 1604.[19]

The capitulations, which endured until 1923, culminated decades of negotiation by the French, who badly needed Ottoman support to strengthen their geopolitical position. Already in 1535, François Ier had joined with Süleyman the Magnificent in opposition to Charles V, after which the French became the first Europeans to establish a permanent diplomatic embassy in Galata, in 1536.[20] Not only did this benefit French trade, Süleyman's galleys, commanded by Hayreddin Barbarossa, subsequently captured Nice in the name of France (1543–1545), defended French interests against Spain, and even wintered in the port city of Toulon, where the Cathédral de Saint-Marie was turned into a mosque for the sailors.[21] French soldiers fought alongside the Ottomans against the Habsburgs in Eastern Europe, and in 1572, the Poles elected Henry de Valois as their king in an effort to please the Sultan.[22] After he became king of France, ultra-Catholic detractors called Henry "le roi Turc" for his "unholy" alliance with Murad III. By 1599, the Franco-Ottoman coalition proved so powerful that the Persians attempted to forge a counter-alliance with the Habsburgs against their Ottoman enemies. Nonetheless, studies of the *chansons turcquesques* fail to mention the 1604 trade capitulations and their protection of Levantine commerce.

Rather, most assessments of the songs relegate them to the fictionalized realms of court festivity, attributing them to Oriental fantasies. Frank Dobbins, editor of Tessier's *Œuvres complètes* and the composer's most energetic biographer, described the songs as "exotic," "parodic," and "probably related to masques or other revels presented at the French or English courts."[23] Alex Robinson followed Dobbins's lead, noting that "exotic themes were rather common in ballets at this time" ("les thèmes exotiques étaient assez communs dans les ballets à cette époque"), and citing a "Ballet pour une troupe de Turcs Armez" of 1596 as one example.[24] Indeed, numerous contemporary ballets featured Saracens, Ottoman princes, and "Turcs": even a cursory search of Margaret McGowan's

L'art du ballet de cour turns up a "ballet des étrangers" including Turks, Persians, and East Indians (1598), a "ballet des Turcs" (1600), a "ballet: le Roy des Maures Nègres" (1600), and a "ballet des Janissaires" (1604), all dating from the years just before Tessier's *Airs et villanelles*.[25]

What distinguishes Tessier's *chansons turcquesques* from Turkish-themed *ballets de cour* is their language: *airs* from contemporary court ballets are almost invariably in French, no matter what character is being portrayed.[26] To take one notable example, René Bordier provided French lyrics for the Grand Turk, the African Chief, and Atabalipa, the King of Cuzco, in his famous *Grand bal de la douairière de Billebahaut* (1626).[27] Such adherence to French makes sense given that these roles were regularly played by French courtiers and the declarations of these characters might be quite recitative-like.[28] Antoine Boësset wrote a magnificent bass *air* for the Grand Turk, full of octave leaps and in G with affective flats that project the power of the persona (see figure 1). Described as "comically serious" in the livret, when the Grand Turk descended from his (real) horse, he took large steps to exaggerate his rigid comportment (see figure 2). This burlesque scene turns on a heightened masculinity projected through the low voice, athletic vocal leaps, large moustache, and the oversized turban, and the role was taken by le sieur Marais, a lead much appreciated for his comic talents.[29] Each stanza ends with a ponderous alexandrine line, and the poetry is beyond regal, designed to parody the ostentation of the French court through hyperbolic language that is funny precisely because it is so familiar.

Occasionally ballets employed a foreign tongue, but the instances are extremely rare. One such moment occurs in the African scene of the *Grand bal de la douairière de Billebahaut*. Just before the African Chief sings his *air* from atop an elephant, he addresses his entourage in their own language: "he held forth in his song, & his subjects answered him in such excellent jargon that one could understand neither him nor the others" ("il cause en son ramage, & ses sujets luy répondent en si excellent jargon, que l'on n'entend ny les uns ny les autres").[30] This break from convention owed entirely to the casting, for the African Chief was played by "le sieur Delfin," a Corsican courtier who seems to have worked up the scene in jargon himself.[31] Though the audience could not understand what Delfin said, they praised his delivery as "excellent"—this was obviously a convincing performance by a fluent speaker, an off-script interpolation keyed to his abilities. The same ballet includes a Spanish song and a troupe of guitar-playing "Musiciens de Grenade," and here, too, we should probably assume that Spanish-speakers took a role in producing the performance, perhaps musicians in the entourage of Anne of Austria, the queen consort.[32]

SECOND RECIT
E regne à la ſource du jour, Où le So-
leil me faict la Cour Dans vn Empire plein de char- mes:
La Fortune ſuit mon ardeur, Et le dieu Mars ne prend les

Fig. 1. Antoine Boësset, Air for the Grand Turk

Fig. 2. [Atelier de Daniel Rabel], Seconde entrée du grand Seigneur, *Grand bal de la douairière de Billebahaut*. Paris, Bibliothèque nationale de France

The working relationships that can be discerned from the situations I have just described suggest that Tessier collaborated with a speaker of Turkish in producing the *chansons turcquesques*, and yet scholars have not pursued this avenue of research. One possibility is Francesco Andreini, whose *commedia dell'arte* troupe played at court in 1603–1604.[33] Their repertory included Turkish-themed plays like *La fortuna di Lelio*, in which Isabella Andreini, the leading lady, sang songs disguised as a "little Turk" ("Turchetto"); not only did Isabella and Francesco both employ Turkish on stage, Francesco had been captured while fighting the Turks in 1568 and spent eight years in Ottoman captivity.[34] Though the plots of these plays were fictitious—this is not ethnography, after all—the players did put actual life experiences to use on stage in performances that spun together authentic vocabulary, delivery, and song in carefully crafted sonic identities.[35]

This is to say, even if Tessier's songs were employed in *ballets de cour*, we need not necessarily dismiss them as fake. Nonetheless, Dobbins uses the term "*turquerie*"—analogous to *chinoiserie*—to describe one song, implying that it is a Western product styled *à la turque*.[36] Georgie Durosoir, in her study *L'air de cour en France*, twice cuts short any discussion of the Turkish songs with an exclamation point, simply mentioning "deux airs turcs!" with no further remark, as though their mere existence is stupefying.[37] Finally, Damien Vaisse doubles down on the Orientalist interpretation in the liner notes for a 2006 recording made by the ensemble Le Poème Harmonique:

> As for the "chansons turcquesques," ... they are purely whimsical pieces, corresponding to the wave of interest in the East aroused by François I's privileged relations with the Sublime Porte. ... Tessier was apparently the first to publish songs in a pseudo-Turkish gobbledegook ["un sabir pseudo-Turc"], and his example was followed by others and culminated in the *turquerie* of *Le Bourgeois gentilhomme* by Molière and Lully (1670).[38]

That Damien Vaisse's translator renders "un sabir pseudo-Turc" as "pseudo-Turkish gobbledegook" fully exposes how swiftly songs, poems, and tongues that seem to be out of place can be dismissed as parodic nonsense.[39] Unsurprisingly, reviews of the recording pick up the Orientalist tone, describing the songs as a "spicy sonic journey" and "tasty" morsels, as though listening to them is equivalent to dining out on meze and kebab.[40]

Chansons turcquesques / türkīs

Certainly one obstacle to interpreting the *chansons turcquesques* has been the difficulty posed by their lyrics. Dobbins seems not to have attempted a translation, and Jean-Louis Bacqué-Grammont was unable to identify the language, which seemed to be neither Turkish nor Sabir, the *lingua franca* of the Western Mediterranean.[41] But the *chansons turcquesques* cannot be read like literary texts written in normative orthography. Songs that travel from one speech community to another are often transcribed using local phonetic systems, and reading them can be laɪk ˈridɪŋ aɪ-pi-ɛɪ wɪˈθaʊt ˈnoʊɪŋ ðə koʊd (like reading IPA [the International Phonetic Alphabet] without knowing the code). Unfamiliar phonemes may be rendered with more habitual sounds, breaks between words may fall in different places, and words can dissolve into a staccato sequence of disconnected syllables.

Giving *He vel a queur* and *Tal lissi man* a fair hearing thus began in the voice. In 2016 during a music seminar at the Fondazione Cini in Venice, I worked with a Turkish early music singer, Ozan Karagöz. As a specialist in historical performance practice, he knew sixteenth-century French pronunciation and could sound out enough of the lyrics to translate some individual words. Next, two generous colleagues at Harvard pitched in: first Himmet Taskomur, from the

Tessier, *Airs et villanelles*	Turkish (modern)	English Translation
He vel a queur si hu geau ne my Guierler molac kara guiu selly Ba ha durly durly gie far *Guie lere mi ci guie lere mi ci* *Cara guiu selly*	Evvela gör şu gönnümü Görürler m'ola kara gözlüyü Bana dürlü dürlü cefa *Görürler mi ki, görürler mi ki,* *kara gözlüyü*	Look at this heart of mine first I wonder if they could see that black-eyed one [s/he inflicted?] All sorts of pain upon me *Will they ever see, will they ever see* *that black-eyed one.*
Occu la dam ha te la ha hyn Es cherine catte la ha hyn Cula la hin sa tu la ha hyn *Guie lere mi ci guie lere mi ci* *Cara guiu selly*	Oku? aldım? atılayım Eskerine katılayım Kul olayım satılayım *Görürler mi ki, görürler mi ki,* *kara gözlüyü*	I seized the arrow, let me jump (rush) Let me join his/her soldiers Let me be [his/her] slave and be sold *Will they ever see, will they ever see* *the black-eyed one.*
Tal lissi man he ra his he hi der Va ra lon bo hi hon da ul duc Iol lo na co hor ba ho la lon *Al dic ca hic ol da celar* *Ka ter galarey*	Dalışman'a reis Haydar Varalım boyunda öldük? Yoluna kurban olayın *Aldı kayık yoldaşlar* *kadırgalara*	Haydar is captain to Dalışman [or, Dalışman's captain is Haydar] Let us go, join his "tribe" (forces?) Let me sacrifice myself in his path *Comrades embarked* *on [took] boats to(ward) the galleys*
Hi gri mi alti ol dacch belle hy Ho chi ha hin helin de naldy Tal lissi man ia ra lin moldy *Al dic ca hic ol da celar* *Ka ter galarey*	Yigirmi altı yoldaş ile hey O cihanı elinden aldı(?) Dalışman yaralı m'oldu *Aldı kayık yoldaşlar* *kadırgalara*	With twenty-six mates, hey He took the world from his [some rival captain's?king's?] hand Was Dalışman wounded? *Comrades took boats to(ward) the galleys*

Table 1. Song texts and translations

Department for Near Eastern Languages and Civilizations, and finally Cemal Kafadar, Harvard's Professor of Turkish Studies.

Producing the translations in table 1 required reading the lyrics against the spoken forms of Ottoman Turkish, and yet despite the expertise of my collaborators, portions of *Tal lissi man* remained impossible to render until Kafadar identified the author as Dalışman, a poet active in sixteenth-century Algeria who "signed" the song in the opening line ("Tallissiman" = "Dalışman").[42] This was the final key. Tessier's chansonnier is the only known source of *Tal lissi man he ra his he hi der/ Dalışman'a reis Haydar*, but other poems by Dalışman survive in manuscript, and one includes the line "Dalışman der Reis Paşa biz n'olduk" and the words "yoldaşlar kadırgalara" in the refrain, as in this chanson, confirming the attribution.[43]

Little about their transmission can be determined directly from the texts. Tessier's transcriptions employ (mostly) French orthography, inasmuch as francophone biases of pronunciation and spelling can be discerned from such a small amount of text (and given the fact that French is far from phonetic).[44]

The songs appear to have been transcribed by a French speaker who worked by ear with little comprehension of Turkish or recognition of Dalışman's name.

With their repetitive rhymes, brief stanzas, and catchy heterometric refrains, these lyrics resemble the strophic poetry of Turkish-language songs known as *türkī*s, which often state the pen name of the poet in the last stanza.[45] Their prosaic handling of rhyme and meter, in which assonance or a final consonant can stand in for full rhymes and line-lengths vary, accords with the songs created by singer-poets known as *ʿāşıḳ*s, who entertained patrons of taverns, coffeehouses, gardens, and other pleasure spots for music, wine, and love.[46]

*Türkī*s were also heard at the Sultan's court, and much of what we know about them owes to a Polish-born musician, santûr-player, and interpreter at the Ottoman court, ʿAlī Ufuḳī (ca. 1610–1675, also known as Wojciech Bobowski and Albert Bobovius), who compiled several collections of music that include instrumental repertory from the court, *türkī*s, and urban art music.[47] ʿAlī Ufuḳī also produced an insider's description of life at Topkapı Palace, *Serai Enderum*, with precious details about the education of palace musicians, rooms where musicians rehearsed, and the musical genres in their repertoire.[48] Although these sources post-date *He vel a queur / Evvela gör* and *Tal lissi man / Dalışman* by several decades, they remain indespensible to music historians for the very reason that they are the earliest known notated collections of that musical repertory. Yet they are extremely difficult to decipher. My work has benefitted enormously from the recent publication of Judith Haug's magisterial study *Ottoman and European Music in ʿAlī Ufuḳī's Compendium, MS Turc 292: Analysis, Interpretation, Cultural Context* (2019, 2020) and Haug's analysis of the *türkī*s recorded by ʿAlī Ufuḳī.

Mobility is a defining characteristic of the *türkī*: the *ʿāşıḳ*s who devised *türkī*s were poet-singers who traveled the countryside performing at fairs, dervish gatherings, and Bektaşi lodges; moreover, the number of *ʿāşıḳ*s known to have been Janissaries, and the longstanding association of the *çöğür* (a fretted instrument with metal strings) with both the *türkī* and Janissary regiments and marines marks out the military as a source of musical circulation to destinations far beyond Topkapı Palace and Constantinople.[49] ʿAlī Ufuḳī describes the *türkī* as a popular style of song telling of local warriors, their victories, loves, longing, and suffering, which neatly captures the substance of the *chansons turcquesques*.[50] Indeed, the *ra'is* (Muslim corsair captain) mentioned in Dalışman's song may be Haydar Ra'is (ca. 1492–1572), a poet, painter, and captain in charge of the Ottoman Imperial Naval yards known for his portraits of Barbarossa and François Ier.[51]

The nautical themes of *Tal lissi man / Dalışman* bring us to the Western Mediterranean, where Dalışman worked, aptly evoking the significance of Algiers as a military stronghold and the reliance of the regional economy on maritime warfare, ransom, and plunder.[52] The poet hastens to serve his captain, Haydar, setting off with twenty-six mates toward galleys and full of admiration for his commander. The swirl of activity turns on the poet's desire, expressed as the lust for martial contest and yearning of a subservient to die for love. Such amorous hierarchies are equally evident in *He vel a queur / Evvela gör*, in which the poet is a slave to love, suffering at the hands of his beloved and rushing toward desperate ends. Enslavement was a fact of life in the Mediterranean, and the trope of the captive lover was a lyric commonplace at the time, particularly in Ottoman lyric, where it referenced not just enslaved servants or oarsmen on galleys, but the elite Janissaries and *kul*s, who were taken as prisoners of war or forcibly recruited through the *devşirme* (child levy).[53] The ambiguous gender of the beloved in *He vel a queur / Evvela gör*—common in Ottoman lyric—allows for double reading, though the masculine dynamics energizing both poems registers the barely masked violence of male society with its scripted aggression.[54]

European singers able to understand these lyrics may well have found their poetics familiar. The symbolism of dark eyes and arrows were ubiquitous in lyric traditions throughout the Mediterranean, while the melancholy longing and subordination of the lover in *He vel a queur / Evvela gör* shares much with Petrarchan lyric, making it instantly legible across cultures as a poem of courtly love.[55] Such foundational parallels between Ottoman and European love lyrics have led Walter G. Andrews and Mehmet Kalpaklı to see the Renaissance as a pan-Mediterranean whole, an "age of beloveds" in which the desire for a corporeal union that can never be achieved inevitably results in poems of separation and longing: "If there is a point at which Ottoman and European, Hafezan and Petrarchan love intersect completely, it is in the taste for melancholy as the dominant theme."[56] Whether or not Tessier fully appreciated the "Arabian muses," these songs make a nice bouquet with the more sorrowful French court *airs* in his volume.

The *chansons turcquesques* seem to be genuine examples of *türkīs*, yet how Tessier came by them remains unclear. *ʿĀşıḳ*s did produce written collections of their verse, but the phonetic spellings suggest living, breathing transmission, encounters that involved a singer of Turkish and a writer of French. The orthography also eliminates bilinguals with dual literacy from consideration, since someone like the French ambassador François Savary de Brèves, who could read and write Turkish, Arabic, and Persian, would have provided more accurate transliterations of the lyrics, with syllables grouped together in words.[57]

Tessier's lyrics evince—at most—only spoken command of Turkish, multiplying the possible agents of transmission exponentially and likening the songs to the "lullabies, dance melodies, and sea shanties" that Owen Wright posited might travel between cultures across the Mediterranean.[58] Did they come to France on the lips of an Ottoman merchant? An enslaved Muslim, ransomed Christian, or Christian convert? Entirely possible at a time when three thousand French captives were being held in Algiers and—following the expulsion of the *moriscos* from Spain—Marseille was so full of foreigners that some considered it "more Moorish than French."[59] Could they have come via Constantinople? If so, they would be further evidence of the small-scale verbal exchanges charted so exquisitely by John-Paul Ghobrial in *The Whispers of Cities*, a musical instance of the way "personal encounters between Europeans and Ottomans in Istanbul produced conversations, news, and stories, which consistently, albeit unpredictably, experienced a second life in scribal and print media in Europe."[60] It is still too soon to provide full answers, since studies of minority languages and polyglotism in France and the cultural effects of trans-Mediterranean mobility are still coming online. My focus, in the research that follows, has been to concentrate on the French court and flesh out the categories of potential "carriers" that can be adduced from the archives.[61] Given their date, Tessier's *Airs* certainly seem related to the diplomatic efforts of Henry IV in 1604, but this stock-taking has a larger goal, for sifting through the archives for records of "foreign" tongues, the ceremonial performances of emissaries and foreign courtiers, and echoes of Mediterranean song models musicology's ability to amplify historical connections that might otherwise remain quite faint.

Emissaries, dragomans, and captives at the royal court

The political and legal history of Mediterranean relations makes it difficult to locate speakers of Turkish, Andalusian Arabic, and Berber languages on French soil. At the top level of diplomatic interchange, Ottoman embassies to Europe were rare, and most French negotiations with the sultans took place at the Sublime Porte. At the bottom end of the social scale, the legal maxim that "no one is a slave in France" has made enslaved "Turks" and "Moors" particularly difficult to trace and relegated accounts of them to port cities like Marseille and Bordeaux.[62] Notwithstanding, archival records for the French royal court do witness Ottoman diplomatic missions to France, ownership of the enslaved by courtiers, and the presence of official interpreters (dragomans) capable of translating spoken Turkish. Each of these categories represents a specific form of early modern mobility.

Table 2

Ottoman Embassies to the French Court, 1550–1610

Bold= embassies that followed the granting of trade capitulations

1552	Ottoman ambassador from the king of Argos[a]
1559	Mahmud Bey[b]
1562	Assun Aga, envoy from the king of Algiers[c]
1565	Hajji Murad, a *bey* (gentleman)[d]
1567	Hajji Murad, a *bey*[e]
1569	**Ibrahim Bey, a dragoman and *müteferriḳa* (five times)**[f]
1571	Hajji Murad, a *bey*, spring[g]
1571	Ottoman envoy named Mahumet (imprisoned in Verona, turned back), spring[h]
1581	**Gabriel de Bourgoigne, dragoman, with letter from the Sultan, September 19**[i]
	Hasan Aga, a *çeşnigīr* (official taster), November–December[j]
	Ali Aga, a dragoman and *müteferriḳa*, scribe to the Sultan, November–December[k]
1598	Muteferrika Mutahher (recalled)[l]
1599	Ali *çavuş*[m]
1601	Barthélemy de Coeur (physician of Mehmed III), mid-June[n]
1602	A *çavuş* arrived in September with letter from the Sultan[o]
1602	A *çavuş*, Mustafa, arrived with a letter from the Sultan dated December 16[p]

a. The entourage numbered at least seven or eight. See Coulas, *Henri II*, 357; McGowan, *Dance in the Renaissance*, 149.

b. Unat, *Osmanlı Sefirleri ve Sefaretnameleri*, date: 1559.

c. Presumably Hassan the Eunuch, a Sardinian renegade and Barbarossa's lieutenant in Algiers and effectively its ruler until 1545. Setton, *Papacy and the Levant*, 837.

d. Setton, *Papacy and the Levant*, 836–41. Işıksel, "Haci Murâd," 252–53; Skilliter, "Catherine de' Medici's Turkish Ladies-in-Waiting," 198–99; Isom-Verhaaren, *Allies with the Infidel*, 176.

e. Işıksel, "Haci Murâd," 253–55.

f. Unat, *Osmanlı Sefirleri ve Sefaretnameleri*, date: 1569; Ibrahim had also been sent to Venice in 1567. See Pedani Fabris, *In nome del Gran Signore*, appendix 1.

g. Işıksel, "Haci Murâd," 256–57.

h. Charrière, *Négotiations*, 3:175–84.

i. Traveling with Hasan Aga, Gabriel ran letters from the Sultan and Venice to Paris and back again while Hasan Aga's party waited to proceed. Gabriel was a dragoman for the French embassy in the Sublime Porte. Charrière, *Négotiations*, 4:72–74. Skilliter, "The Sultan's Messenger," 54.

j. Jensen, "The Ottoman Turks," 466–67; Charrière, *Négotiations*, 4:114–17; "Relation des ambassadeurs envoyez par le Grand-Seigneur, Empereur des Turcs"; L'Estoile, *Journal*, 1:222; Skilliter, "The Sultan's Messenger," 54–55.

k. Ibid (that is, all the above citations relate to this embassy as well). For a copy of the French translation of the Sultan's letter, made and delivered by Ali Aga, see AAE MD Turquie, vol. 2, fol. 62r; Skilliter, "Catherine de' Medici's Turkish Ladies-in-Waiting," 188–91 provides the original text as preserved in the official register of the Ottoman Chancery with English translation.

l. Hammer-Purgstall, *Geschichte des Osmanischen Reiches*, 2:635; Baudier, *Inventaire de l'histoire générale des Turcz*, 441–42. Baudier gives the name and title as Muttafer Aga.

m. Unat, *Osmanlı Sefirleri ve Sefaretnameleri*, date: 1599.

n. Yirmisekiz Mehmet Çelebi, *Le paradis des infidèles*, 23; L'Estoile, *Journal*, 3:310; Barthélemy de Coeur was also in Venice in April, 1601. See Pedani Fabris, *In nome del Gran Signore*, appendix 1.

o. Chalcondyle et al., *Histoire générale des Turcs*, 869–70, with reproduction of the letter.

p. AAE CP Turquie, vol. 3, fols. 16r–23r.

1607	**A *çavuş* delivers a letter from the Sultan May 22[q]** **Mustafa Aga received at Fontainebleau June 27[r]**

q. L'Estoile, *Journal*, 4:58. May 22, at Fontainebleau. "Traitement fait en France au chiaoux que l'empereur des Turcs envoya au roi Henri IV en 1607," AAE MD Turquie, vol. 10, pièce 2, fols. 37r–38v.

r. Héroard, *Journal*, June 27, 1607, at Fontainebleau. Given his high status, it seems unlikely that Mustafa Aga was the "chiaoux" received at court in May. Rather, the messenger likely announced Mustafa Aga's embassy. Savary de Brèves was present at both royal audiences. The intensity of contact in 1607 is attested by multiple missives from the Sublime Porte. See the letters sent "par ordinaire" from the Sultan, Grand Vizier, and Mustafa Bassa (=Pasha) copied in AAE MD Turquie, vol. 5, fols. 74r–87v.

Table 2. Ottoman embassies to the French court, 1550–1610

Between 1550 and 1610, the French royal court welcomed a series of envoys from the Sultan, some of very high rank, who traveled with entourages and stayed for months (see table 2).[63] Two well-documented embassies occurred in 1581 and 1607, though even for these, surviving diplomatic correspondence, diaries, and court payment records are incomplete. Moreover, some missions attested in Ottoman archives cannot be confirmed from the French side, and we know of others that had to be abandoned, as happened in 1571 when an envoy named Mahumet was forcibly detained by the Venetians at the height of the *Lega Santa*.[64] Decades later, in 1598, Muteferrika Mutahher was sent to France with a gem-encrusted sword and orders to bring thirty-six richly harnessed Arabian horses as gifts for Henry IV, but he was recalled before he reached France.[65]

The embassies of 1581 and 1607 were both diplomatic missions of the highest order, led by powerful ambassadors with entourages that spent months in France. In 1581, worried by English initiatives to establish the Levant trading company, the French ambassador in Constantinople worked behind the scenes to have the English trade agreement revoked and strengthen the French capitulations already in place.[66] As a result, Sultan Murad III granted to France the most definitive privileges to date: diplomatic precedence over other Christian nations, exemption from personal taxation, and mandates that the English trade under the French flag. Two Ottoman delegations then traveled to France, one led by Hasan Aga, a *çeşnīgīr* or official taster to the Sultan, who extended an invitation for Henry III to attend the circumcision ceremony of the Sultan's son; Hasan Aga apparently traveled with his own son and at least two retainers.[67] The second party was led by Ali Aga, a dragoman in French royal employ and *müteferriḳa* to the Sultan, who carried the new capitulations.[68]

Both parties stalled at Venice, where they awaited an invitation to proceed to Paris as Henry III deliberated over whether to receive them. The conciliatory politics of the Valois toward the Huguenot "heretics" in their own country continually threw into question the Catholicity of the French crown, and receiving the "infidel" ambassadors had political ramifications for the king. Indeed, propaganda campaigns begun by Charles V and continued by Philip II regularly cited French alliances with the Turks as evidence of French heresy, to such an extent that Christine Isom-Verhaaren sees in these Habsburgian polemics the origins of "Europe" as a cultural and religious entity defined in stark opposition to the Ottoman Empire.[69] But France needed her Ottoman allies, and eventually Henry III welcomed the Sultan's ambassadors to France, sending mounted dignitaries to escort them to Paris and housing the dozens in their parties in lavishly furnished *hôtels* in the faubourg Saint-Germain where they were attended to by his own servants and had multiple audiences with the king, queen, and queen mother; Pierre de L'Estoile, the Parisian diarist, says they stayed for a month, from November 8 to December 10.[70] It was this embassy that occasioned Catholic extremists to dub Henry III "le roi Turc."[71]

Royal audiences were highly public, and Henry III recounts that he was attended by the whole court and infinite numbers of other people. Hasan Aga kissed his hand and those of the queens, read the Sultan's letter aloud (with the dragoman Gabriel de Bourgoigne there to translate), and at the end of his mission, the *āġā* was given a silver cup richly lined with gold for the Sultan, bolts of scarlet fabric for the Sultanas, and a magnificent clock for the Sultan's son, all items that were highly prized in the Levant.[72]

In similar fashion, in 1607, Ahmed I sent his closest advisor to France, El-Hajj Mustafa Aga, Chief Eunuch and one of his favorites.[73] Mustafa Aga arrived in high style at Fontainebleau accompanied by "a Janissary, two other Turks, and two slaves"; after his royal audience, he was entrusted to the care of François Savary de Brèves, France's long-time ambassador to the Porte, who had negotiated the 1604 agreement and liberated seventy-two French captives from Tunis on his way home from Constantinople in 1605–1606.[74] Mustafa Aga had accompanied Savary de Brèves on that eighteen-month journey and represented the Sultan's desire to protect French interests in Tunis and Algiers; given the mutual perils they survived on the way, the two must have been quite close.[75] While at court, Mustafa also visited the young dauphin, Louis, bringing him green damask and a Turkish tunic decorated with flowers. Jean Héroard, Louis's physician, recounts that the five-year-old dauphin received the *āġā* in his own apartments in a dignified fashion, with whipped-together accoutrements of a rug and little throne, the whole time maintaining a steely, confident gaze.[76] These encounters find their artistic parallel in the "ballet des nations" discussed earlier, in which rulers from distant parts of the globe pay their respects to the French king.

Ceremonial performances weighed heavily in court society throughout the Mediterranean, where only face-to-face proclamations could ratify agreements, and the size of embassies, the status of ambassadors, and displays of wealth materialized the *éclat* of kings, emperors, and sultans. The diplomatic archives are but written records of verbal accords that required the presence of high-ranking courtiers to guarantee their validity: ambassadors represented their rulers in the most literal sense of reproducing the authority of their very being in a distant place, for which reason accounts concentrate on physical signs of deference such as kneeling and kissing the hand or mantle of the king; reports from French ambassadors to the Sublime Porte are equally attentive to etiquette at Topkapı and the rites of passage through the palace complex, which evince shared understandings of comportment.[77] A negative example is offered by the 1601 embassy of Barthélemy de Coeur, personal physician of Mehmed III (see table 2). He came to ask that the king recall the duc de Mercoeur from Hungary, where he was fighting the Ottomans on behalf of emperor Rudolf II, and to sweeten the Sultan's request, de Coeur brought extravagant gifts as tokens of esteem (a scimitar and a dagger, both with golden handles and ruby-studded scabbards, and a plume of heron feathers in a gold and turquoise setting).[78] But Pierre de l'Estoile, for one, remarked that de Coeur had "ni la suite ni le titre d'ambassadeur" (neither the entourage nor the title of ambassador), and in fact, Henry IV refused to intercede on behalf of his Ottoman allies.[79]

Barthélemy de Coeur brings into earshot a host of transnational go-betweens that facilitated diplomatic exchanges at consulates and courts. De Coeur was a native of Marseille who converted to Islam and held a sufficiently high position as the Sultan's doctor that he was sent on a European mission taking him to the French royal court, the court of Elizabeth I, and to Venice.[80] The circum-Mediterranean trajectory of his life from Marseille to Constantinople and round again was not extraordinary, for the Ottoman polity was largely governed by renegade elites like de Coeur, who were brought to the Porte through the *devşirme* or as captives.[81] Most came from the Balkans, but renegades from the Western Mediterranean were not uncommon. These individuals often became dragomans and, like de Coeur, presented natural choices as emissaries.[82] Ali Aga may have been a French native as well, since he personally translated the 1581 trade capitulations into French.[83]

The French embassy to the Porte employed its own dragomans, renegades like Domenico Olivieri, Gabriel de Bourgoigne, and Martin de Bourgoigne, and they, too, exemplify the cultural entanglements of life in the Mediterranean.[84] Gabriel was the son of a French consul to Alexandria. As a youth he was captured in Venetian waters by Dalmatian brigands and sold as a slave into Turkey, where he converted to Islam and took the name Maḥmūd ʿAbdullāh Frenk; in Constantinople he worked as an importer of luxury goods for the Imperial Household, during which time he became an agent of the Grand Vizier and parlayed his connections into employment at the French embassy as a dragoman. By 1581, he knew Italian, Turkish, vulgar Greek, and some Latin, and had already engaged in espionage in England, Holland, and Venice on trips purportedly made to procure "clocks and mechanical instruments" for the seraglio.[85] The ultimate middle-man, he epitomizes the go-betweens that Emrah Safa Gürkan sees as typical of Constantinople's unique plurality, the small-scale ransom agents, merchants, and information-traders that "used their in-betweenness and liminality to weave dense networks of patronage ... in quite an entrepreneurial fashion."[86]

In France as well, dragomans (*truchements*) were retained by the court, but little is known of them. Under Henry IV (if not earlier), when messengers arrived with letters from the Sultan, the *çavuş* was brought before the king where the contents were read aloud in Turkish by the messenger and then translated by the king's *truchement*, who responded in Turkish to the envoy.[87] Eventually Jean-Baptist Colbert would institute official training of *truchements* with the *jeunes de langues*.[88] The linguistic reach of the royal court audibly expressed power—the power to dominate, the power to govern—and like the exotic animals kept imprisoned by kings and dukes, foreign tongues could inspire wonder by symbolizing the geographical compass of a monarch's authority, to say nothing of the brutality securing it.[89] That said, multilinguals could imperil themselves by freely exercising their linguistic abilities: in 1558 someone penned a letter in Turkish to the desperate mother of two captive girls who had been made ladies-in-waiting to Catherine de' Medici, causing a diplomatic uproar. The French ambassador at the Porte counseled the king to seek out and expel the perpetrator from the kingdom, which suggests that numerous persons could have been suspect.[90]

The scandal of the Turkish girls exposes yet another stratum of polyglots at court: enslaved Muslims.[91] The girls had been captured along with their brother while on pilgrimage to Mecca in 1557 by François de Lorraine, who gifted them to Catherine de' Medici and Marguerite de France; their brother may have ended up on a Maltese galley. Thanks to their mother's persistent pleas in Constantinople and the intervention of the Sultanas, the Ottomans pressed for the girls' return for decades, making their liberation a point of negotiation during the embassies of both 1565 and 1581. Nonetheless, "Catherine" and "Marguerite" (named for their owners), "La Turque et La More," remained in France, and must stand as reminders of the other enslaved individuals who disappear in court records behind Christian names when baptized, and who, having accepted the Catholic faith, were not relinquished to infidels.[92] At the very least, we know that Diane de Poitiers also owned a number of enslaved Muslims, and that at her marriage in 1533, Catherine's retinue included a young "Moorish" girl and two "Turkish" girls.[93] Perhaps they assisted in the 1552 "Mascarade à la mauresque" honoring an embassy from the King of Argos, which featured ladies dressed in Turkish fashion who twisted their bodies as they danced.[94]

The unremarkable tone in which enslaved domestics are mentioned underscores just how ordinary they must have been. Nathalie Rothman's research locates numerous enslaved "Moors" in Venetian households throughout the seventeenth century.[95] Emily Wilbourne's contribution to this volume attests to intergenerational families of enslaved sub-Saharan Africans at the Medici court, including a talented singer.[96] Further south, we know that in 1581 Luigi d'Este, Cardinal Protector of France, purchased ninety-seven "Turkish" captives, which he paraded in chains through the streets of Rome before taking them back to Tivoli.[97] These sinister histories ran deep: in the fifteenth century Philip the Good outfitted an entire troupe of "Moorish" dancers in animal collars and costumes with Arabic letters.[98]

At the French court, an aside made by Jean Héroard attests to a singing Turkish boy there, probably enslaved: in 1606, Héroard mentioned a song the dauphin had been singing that day, "Houja Criaqué Chinchin, Criaqué, pista, christa, Criaqué," which he had learned the year before from "le petit Turc de M. de Vendosme."[99] The "little Turk" would have belonged to one of the dauphin's older half-brothers, César (b. 1594) or Alexandre (b. 1598), and was probably a boy himself. Not only did the *devşirme* systematically target children between the ages of ten and eighteen, even younger children were forced into servitude on both sides of the Mediterranean.[100] This boy was probably a Greek captive, since the lyrics sound more Greek than Turkish—something like *Houda Kyriaki, chinchin* (?) *Kyriaki, pistá christá Kyriaki* (Houda Κυριακή, chinchin Κυριακή, πιστά, χρηστά, Κυριακή), reminiscent of a devotional song: "Lord on Sunday, [chinchin] on Sunday, faithfully, kindly, on Sunday."[101]

Tessier's songs need not have come from Vendôme's "petit Turc." Rather, both "Houja Criaqué" and the *chansons turcquesques* witness the face-to-face contacts that we should acknowledge as commonplace throughout the Mediterranean basin. As they traveled on when sung by the dauphin, in bourgeois homes, perhaps in theaters, the very sound of *Houja Criaqué*, *He vel a queur*, and *Tal lissi man* continued to build up cultural memories based on hearing and oral communication. Along with plays, storytelling, news, and reading aloud, songs echoed Mediterranean encounters long after voyages and lives had ended, their rough phonetic transcriptions allowing singers to inhabit sonic representations of pashas, diplomats, and captives that were equally present in dictionaries, phrase books, travelogues, *commedia dell'arte* plays, and the first wave of picaresque novels coming from Spain. Overfull of *k*s (as in "al dic ca hic") and foreign consonants like the aspirated *h*s of "he ra his he hi der" and studded with comprehensible code words like "galarey" (*galère* or galley)—the only three-syllable word in either song—the very sound of *He vel a queur* and *Tal lissi man* established affective meanings through which singers could imagine the songs of *ʿāşıḳ*s or mariners and speech patterns of the seraglio and *eschelles*.[102] Singing probably resulted in creative mishearings as well—"cara" as the Italian *cara* ("dear" instead of "black"), or "queur" as *coeur* ("heart" instead of "see")—leading some to adduce that *He vel a queur* was a love song. Some singers may well have taken them to be French parodies of *türkī*s and adopted a burlesque style, but others could have correlated them into horizons of expectation established by amorous tales like *Les estranges avantures* (1580), in which a heart-broken chevalier from Seville ends up enslaved as a "serf du jardin" for six years in an Algerian palace, where he learns to converse "en langue Moresque, de fort bonne grace," charms a local lady by singing to the lute with "gracieuses parolles," and eventually sings his way to manumission.[103] In sum, although we cannot account for details of their reception, it would be a mistake to suppose that these transcriptions stood alone, silent, meaningless, and disconnected from surrounding sonic frames of reference. Finally, printing them was not neutral: it presumed an audience for *türkī*s, construed them as *chansons*, and marketed them as flowers from Parnassian "elsewheres" located in a mythological realm unmarked by Orientalism's imaginative geographies of barbarian lands.[104]

Musical translation

The Turkish lyrics of *He vel a queur / Evvela gör* and *Tal lissi man / Dalışman* encourage closer consideration of their melodies, even as we remain mindful that musical analysis cannot recover the sound of these *türkī*s: for the songs have not simply been transcribed, they have been *translated* into a polyphonic musical system governed by diatonic harmony and the simple rhythmic proportions of mensural notation. The analyses that follow do test Tessier's Westernized melodies using the theoretical toolkit of Ottoman court music—the melodic system of *maḳām*s and the rhythmic system of *uṣūl*s—but not with the goal of "authenticating" them, which would be highly problematic for several reasons. In the first place, the melodies of *türkī*s did not necessarily adhere to the *maḳām*s and *uṣūl*s that governed the performance practices of Ottoman art music; rather, the tunes of *türkī*s were more akin to ways of singing a song that were reused across the repertoire of the *ʿāşıḳ*s.[105] Secondly, performance practices have evolved across the centuries, making it difficult for modern *ʿāşıḳ*s to judge seventeenth-century songs.[106] Thus even for Ottoman repertoires that have not traveled, disentangling originals from the twists and turns of transmission across time remains a fraught enterprise. What we *can* do is allow the songs to retain their in-betweenness, rather like Sabir, and to concentrate on the "chansonization" process itself. Listening for *maḳām*s and *uṣūl*s in the *chansons turcquesques* puts pressure on Tessier's texts, opening up gaps for a critical operation that asks what would have been required to bridge between European and Ottoman theoretical systems.

I began my musical investigations in consultation with the ethnomusicologist Payam Yousefi, a specialist in Persian classical music, who quickly steered our conversation toward meter. Yousefi heard the sixteen-beat *uṣūl* Nīm ḫafīf operating in *He vel a queur / Evvela gör*, particularly at the opening of the chanson, where the *uṣūl*'s signature "short short long" pattern is quite evident: "düm tek tek, düm tek tek, düm tek düm düm, tek teke" (see examples 1 and 2).[107] The *uṣūl* would have been tapped out on a frame drum or the knees, a practice described by ʿAlī Ufuḳī in the *Serai Enderum*.[108]

The *uṣūl* Nīm ḫafīf neatly matches the four-square phrasing of Tessier's *He vel a queur / Evvela gör*, with its sixteen-beat units, but it is possible to hear the shorter four-beat *uṣūl* Ṣōfyān in this piece as well, something suggested by another of my informants, Mehmet Sanlıkol, musicologist and director of the ensemble Dünya, who pointed to the dactylic rhythms of the refrain and their reversal of the opening anapests in double time.[109] If identifying a 16/4 or 4/4 *uṣūl* in *He vel a queur / Evvela gör* seems inconclusive (given how common

1604 ff. 42

6. Oc-cu la dam ha te la ha hyn
Es che-ri-ne cat-te la ha hyn,
Cu-la la hin sa tu la ha hyn
Guie-le-re mi ci, gui-e-le-re mi ci
Ca-ra gi-u se-ly.

Example 1. Tessier, *He vel a queur / Evvela gör*, ed. Dobbins in Tessier, *Œuvres complètes*

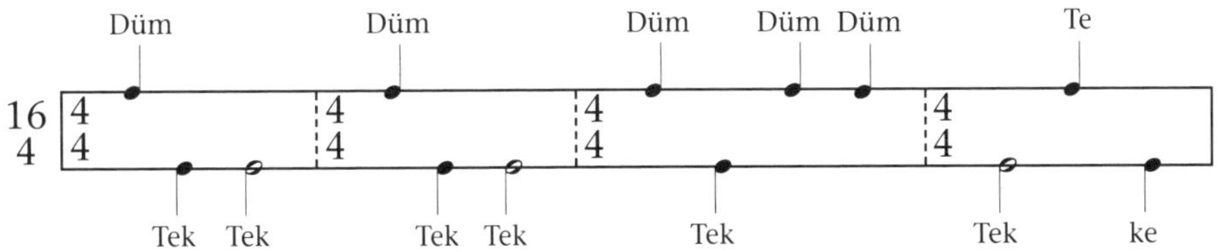

Example 2. *Uṣūl* Nīm ḫafīf

four-bar phrases in 4/4 meter are in other repertories), we might note that none of Tessier's other pieces fall into regular meters. Frank Dobbins correctly cites the "square repetitive rhythm" as "quite unlike the French or Italian airs" in the volume.[110] Indeed, in order to accommodate Tessier's barrings, throughout his edition Dobbins refrains from adding bar lines and often resorts to multiple meter signs. Such metric irregularity is evident in *Tal lissi man / Dalışman*, for instance: as Yousefi began to play through it on his *kemençe*, he remarked that "the rhythm makes no sense" and quickly abandoned the notated rhythms (see example 3). Sanlıkol, who agreed that *Tal lissi man / Dalışman* was not based on an *uṣūl*, guessed that even though the lyrics are in the form of a *türkī*, the piece might be a *gazel*, a genre of poetry sung in a rhythmically free improvisation over a drone.

Tal lissi man / Dalışman quickly turned the attention of both Yousefi and Sanlıkol toward *maḳāms*, with Yousefi hearing the *maḳām* Beyātī in the *dessus* (transposed up a fourth) and Sanlıkol hearing the *maḳām* Nihāvend or—if imagined with a microtonal quality—the *maḳām* Ḥüseynī, which predominates in the seventeenth-century repertoire of *türkīs* and *türkī*-like folk music (example 4).[111] At stake in these differing assessments is whether the fourth or fifth scale degree operates as a structural pitch (*c* or *d*).[112] Yousefi acknowledged that the opening leap up to *d″* is not typical modal behavior in the *maḳām* Beyātī, at least in the present day, though the initial resting place on *c″* is typical, as is the *seyir* or overall sweep down to $\hat{2}$ and $\hat{1}$ as the phrases progress, which struck Yousefi as "quite modal" (see example 3). In his performance, shown in example 5, Yousefi extrapolated significantly from Tessier's diatonic notation, adding in a half-flat second scale degree (*a*𝄳*′*) and affective ornaments, which—coupled with the flattened sixth scale degree (*e*♭*″*), elongations of *c″* (around 8 seconds in), and rhythmic freedom—significantly transformed the melody.

Present-day difficulties hearing *maḳāms* in these melodies when working from harmonized sources in staff notation and at the distance of half a millennium should not be underplayed. For instance, Yousefi found it impossible

1604 ff. 42v

Example 3. Tessier, *Tal lissi man / Dalışman*, ed. Dobbins in Tessier, *Œuvres complètes*

Example 4. *Maḳām* Beyātī (transposed) and *maḳām* Nihāvend

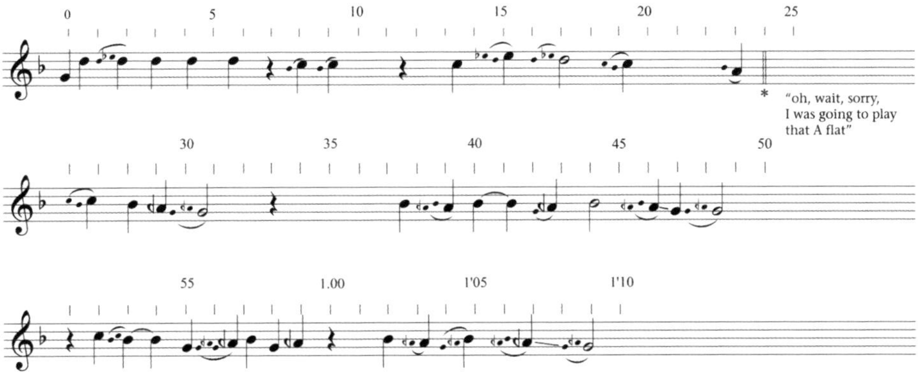

Example 5. Transcription of Yousefi performance of *Tal lissi man / Dalışman*

to hear a known *maḳām* in the *dessus* of *He vel a queur / Evvela gör* (example 1), whereas Sanlıkol felt that the melody's *seyir* strongly resembled the *maḳām* Segāh or ʿIrāḳ, despite the atypical leaps between *a*′ and *c*″. A seventeenth-century Ottoman musician might have had a completely different *maḳām* in mind, and we will never be able to reconstruct this. Nevertheless, the appraisals of today's musicians establish valuable points of orientation from which to reconsider the "hexagonal" perspectives that often frame the analysis of chansons.

In his critical edition, Frank Dobbins remarks that *He vel a queur / Evvela gör* has a "limited melody with strange mode and cadences."[113] He never specifies what he finds "strange" about the mode, and his reading of cadences is rather garbled, since he identifies every arrival on a semi-breve as a cadence, despite the fact that chansons often have phrases that end without cadences; he also mislabels the "cadences" in the first phrase as g-F and g-D (instead of G-F and G-D). These slips in the critical commentary are particularly surprising because they produce the chord changes D-g-F-B♭-F-g-D: read in G minor, the progression is V-i-VII-III-VII-i-V. Far from "strange," this is a folia bass pattern, replete with the vamp's signature B♭ in the bass at the move to III and the obligatory *f*♯s in D chords that create the dominant of G minor (see example 1). A favorite of improvisers and amply evident in the late sixteenth-century chanson repertoire, folia-based songs were stock-in-trade of French musicians, who used the bass pattern in homophonic settings such as those in Nicolas de La Grotte's extremely popular *Chansons de P. de Ronsard, Ph. Desportes, et autres* (Paris, 1569).[114] One song, *Quand le gril chant*, opens with the same harmonization found in *He vel a queur / Evvela gör*, with the top two voices moving in parallel motion over the folia bass line, beginning with *f*♯s in the alto. Moreover, because the entire polyphonic fabric of folia songs is generated from the bass, with root-position chords, the melody in the *dessus* results "bottom up" from the chord progression. If Tessier was working with a Turkish song, he apparently retained the rhythms and devised a chordal setting beginning with the folia bass in G minor and shifting to D minor in the second part of the song.

One could excuse Dobbins's oversight by noting that *He vel a queur / Evvela gör* ends on a D major chord (is it I of a folia in D minor? V of a folia in G minor?); this is indeed a special moment. Some contemporary folia chansons that begin with the stock G minor folia pattern do end elsewhere tonally, in F, for instance, and many have a raised third in the final sonority, but its placement here in the *dessus* is extraordinary.[115] Could the *f*♯′ have come forward with the *türkī*? Sanlıkol observed that it is not at all unusual for a number of *maḳāms* to end in this way, citing ʿIrāḳ as an example. Again, we cannot resolve these questions, but raising them models the kinds of eclectic analysis and cross-repertorial investigation that may payoff more decisively another time.

Unfortunately, what this brief analysis does expose is how quickly Dobbins dismissed *He vel a queur* as inscrutable. Anticipating more strangeness than the song delivers, Dobbins not only misread chords and missed identifying the folia, he also let the *b*♮′ in the first phrase of the *haute-contre* stand against the B♭ in the bass without editorial remark. To put it bluntly, the unexpectedness of the *chansons turcquesques* seems to have short-circuited the textual criticism at which Dobbins otherwise excelled.

Dobbins noted nothing "strange" about *Tal lissi man / Dalışman*, where—fair enough—hearing the *maḳām* Beyātī would have required reading past the diatonic straitjacket of Tessier's chordal harmonies. But we need not leave off here, for Yousefi's rendition of the melody, with its half-flat second scale degree, affords two critical moves, making audible the *maḳām*, as already discussed, but also aligning these songs with Renaissance attempts to recover the microtonal singing of ancient Greeks. Here too, a Mediterranean perspective opens up alternative readings with direct relevance to Tessier's collection.

In southern France, in Toulouse, Anthoine de Bertrand employed the enharmonic genus in his chansons to recreate the ravishing effects of ancient music, while in Ferrara and Rome, Nicola Vicentino railed against the limits of diatonicism in *L'antica musica ridotta alla prattica moderna* (1555).[116] Accounts of these experiments generally frame them as expressions of Renaissance neo-Platonism, but we should note that Vicentino took inspiration both from ancient Greek music and contemporary song traditions. In his characterization, all the peoples of the world sing with microtones.[117] Hence the invention of his famous *archicembalo* with its division of the octave into thirty-one parts, which he developed to better match these idiomatic styles of singing:

> Tutti potranno porre in musica il suo modo di cantare con i gradi della divisione del nostro strumento, che con la musica che hora s'usa, non si può scrivere alcuna canzone Franzese, ne Tedesca, ne spagnuola, ne Ungara, ne Turca, ne Hebrea ... si che con questa nostra divisione havremo accommodato tutte le nationi del mondo, che potranno scriver i loro accenti e comporli à quante voci à loro parerà.[118]

> [All nations represent their own way of singing by means of the steps found in the division of my *archicembalo*. But with the music in use nowadays it is not possible to write French, German, Spanish, Hungarian, Turkish, or Hebrew songs. ... This is why I have devised my division, which allows all nations of the world to write with their own accents and to compose in as many voices as they like.]

Had Tessier employed Vicentino's microtonal compositional method and enharmonic notation, he could have indicated the half-flat second scale degree of the *maḳām* Beyātī, if *Tal lissi man / Dalışman* was actually based on it, but the larger point is that the very invention of the *archicembalo* and experiments with subtle divisions of the octave are symptomatic of an urge among polyphonists to defy the constraints of diatonicism and develop genres of vernacular polyphony keyed more directly to the idioms of various tongues. Tessier's polyglot *Airs et villanelles Fran. Ital. Espa. Suice. et Turcq.* achieves linguistically what Vicentino aspires to harmonically.

Comparing Tessier's printed song to performances of it by Yousefi and others stands as a strong reminder that we also know very little about how French *airs* were performed at the time. Star singers such as Lambert de Beaulieu or Estienne Le Roy would have employed pitch, rhythm, diction, and ornament affectively, and to presume that they stuck to printed parts denies the declamatory aesthetic of this largely monodic genre. Yousefi's interpretation may radically defamiliarize songs once imagined as plodding choral renditions, but it has much in common with that of Le Poème Harmonique, whose recording of *Tal lissi man / Dalışman* opens with percussion and a solo viol. The gambist employs wide vibrato in places, a sprinkling of mordents, and adds slides to falling intervals. When the singer enters, voice and viol celebrate an Ottoman aesthetic of melodic heterophony and mixed timbres. Even in the final section of four-part harmony, the singers' balance favors the melody, still doubled by viol, as if to create a sound musically at sea, half-way to Algiers, someplace between Dalışman and Tessier.

In the end, Vicentino's assessment of how inadequately diatonic notation represents songs in any vernacular—Turkish or French—is doubtless truer than we realize. With so little information about contemporary attitudes toward the four-voice versions of *airs* that churned from commercial presses, there is every reason to be skeptical that Tessier's printed songs would represent the performances of professional lutenist-singers much more accurately than they would those of *ʿāşıḳs*. What Claudio Monteverdi meant by the "canto alla francese" that he heard in Spa in 1599 remains as much a mystery as the "pleasing effect" of the tremolo chords produced by the Arab instrumentalist he heard at Mantua around 1604.[119]

If this essay has worked to connect the *chansons turcquesques* with the French, Italian, Todesca, and Spanish songs in Tessier's collection, it is with the aspiration that they might inspire more attention to musical difference, not less. The surprise they have elicited in the past—"deux airs turcs!"—can be redirected toward undoing notions of European culture as a coherent whole: the clean appearance of white mensural notation, standardized and employed throughout Europe, may have facilitated the printing and transmission of repertoires, yes, but the *chansons turcquesques* should not now be integrated into a history of pan-European polyphony standing behind the "rise" of a Western musical canon of universal, timeless appeal. On the contrary, the critical turns incited by these songs—toward histories of mobility, oral transmission, cross-cultural study of lyric traditions, microtonality, and performance as research—can disrupt histories that ignore ethnic complexity within Europe itself and privilege polyphonic composition and written texts over the lyric performances that inspired them.

Finally, learning to hear Franco-Ottoman relations in the *chansons turcquesques* should provoke resistance to labels like "turquerie," a term shot through with imperial imaginings of the Orient as Europe's feminized Other: decadent, sexualized, weak, and in need of Western governance. Trade capitulations facilitated French consumption of imported goods while diplomacy and travel heightened interest in Arabic and the practices of Islam, but—as Nicholas Dew has underscored in his study of what he calls "baroque Orientalism"—despite the aspirations of Louis XIV to establish an Eastern empire, the French could not compete with the dominant powers of the age: the Ottoman, Safavid Persian, Mughal, and Qing empires.[120]

As long as we allow Orientalism to frame studies of early modern music with presumptions of Western cultural hegemony, songs like Tessier's *chansons turcquesques* will continue to be positioned as precursors of the post-Enlightenment ideologies described by Edward Said. Orientalism is an old critical move, one that allows scholars to reinforce anachronistic boundaries between Europe and its cultural Others by keeping "Turks" safely confined to the stage, draining meaning from lyrics, capturing the Ottoman voices behind Tessier's songs in falsifying quotation marks ("pseudo-Turkish"), and allowing Western imperialism to continue assimilating cultural artifacts to a colonial view of the world, unchecked by scholarly critique. Early modern studies are uniquely positioned to define alternative critical approaches, if we listen a little more closely to the sources.

Notes

* With very special thanks to Cemal Kafadar, Judith Haug, and Mehmet Sanlıkol for their tireless responses to my queries and invaluable comments and corrections. My work truly would not have been possible without their support and the assistance of numerous musicians, especially Ozan Karagöz, Payam Yousefi, Dimitri Psonis, and Dr. Sanlıkol. Judith, Cemal, Alex Robinson, and Emily Wilbourne all read drafts of this essay and their feedback improved it considerably. Warm thanks also to Suzanne Cusick and especially Bonnie Gordon for inspiring discussions during our stays in Florence in 2017.

1. See Villamont, *Les voyages*, 101v. The *patron* was Candido di Barbari (see Braudel, *Mediterranean*, 2:563).

2. Villamont, *Les voyages*, 102r, "qui avoient faict apporter espinettes, luts, cistres & autres instruments au son desquels nous passions souvent le temps."

3. Ibid., 104r–v. The crew was sizable, as the main mast held thirty sailors (104v).

4. Yerasimos, "Voyageurs européens," 99, and Isom-Verhaaren, *Allies with the Infidel*, 165–79.

5. See Yerasimos, "Voyageurs européens," 94, and Jensen, "The Ottoman Turks," 462–63.

6. Armstrong and Weiss, "Introduction: France and the Early Modern Mediterranean," 1.

7. For this critique of Braudel, see ibid., as well as Greene, "Beyond the Northern Invasion," and Miller, "The Mediterranean."

8. Judging from the polyglot dictionary in Palerne, *Peregrinations*, 522–54, the "moresque" used by Villamont was a dialect of Arabic.

9. See Dakhlia, *Lingua franca*, 15–17, and Dursteler, "Speaking in Tongues," 67–74, for helpful definitions of *lingua franca*.

10. Bakhtin, *Dialogic Imagination*, 68.

11. Villamont, *Les voyages*, 261r, "tant ceste ville est habitee & peuplee de toutes les nations qui sont au monde, à cause du grand commerce qui s'y faict des Indes, & de toute l'Asie, Affrique & Europe."

12. On the gifts of organs and their reception, see Wright, "Turning a Deaf Ear," 5, 18–19.

13. "Ayant eu cest heur de succer quelq[ue]fois le doux Nectar de ces doctes pucelles, & d'estre admis en leurs vergers plus delicieux de France, d'Italie, d'Espagne, d'Allemagne et Arabie, mesme ay en iceux recueilly un assez bon nombre des plus belles fleurs" (1604). For the publication history of the 1604 edition and its two dedications, see Tessier, *Œuvres complètes*, ed. Dobbins, li–lii.

14. See the biography in Tessier, *Œuvres complètes*, ed. Dobbins, xii–xv, and Brooks, "Tessier's Travels in Scotland and England," on Charles' contacts in England.

15. Dobbins, "Les airs de Charles Tessier," 142.

16. Robinson, "Musique et musiciens," 203–5, believes Tessier was probably engaged at the court, but not in a steady position (that is, not a musician "ordinaire").

17. Palerne, *Peregrinations*, 4. The Turkish song in Palerne's collection has the incipit "Brey aramber" (Palerne, *Poésies*, 179). For later transcriptions of Ottoman and Safavid songs (with notation), see Wright, "Turning a Deaf Ear," 152–55; Du Loir, *Voyages* [1654], 154–55, which includes a Dervish hymn; and Muḥammadī, *Musical Souvenirs*, 13–16, on a Persian song in the travelogue of Jean Chardin (1643–1713).

18. Subrahmanyam, "Connected Histories," 762.

19. Savary de Brèves, *Relation des voyages*, "Traicté faict en l'annee mil six cents quatre," 23.

20. On the negotiations of 1536 and capitulations of 1569, 1581, and 1604, see Jensen, "The Ottoman Turks," 456, 461–62, 466, and 469–70, and, for the period to 1560, Barthe, *French Encounters with the Ottomans*.

21. Isom-Verhaaren, *Allies with the Infidel*, chapter 4.

22. This plan for a French king of Poland seems to have originated with the Ottomans. See Charrière, *Négotiations*, 4:73 n. 1. According to a French dispatch dated March 28, 1573, Selim II sent a *çavuş* to Poland to secure Henry's election (AAE MD Turquie, vol. 4, fols. 209r–212r).

23. Tessier, *Œuvres complètes*, ed. Dobbins, lxii; idem, "Les airs de Charles Tessier," 142–43.

24. Robinson, "Musique et musiciens," 206.

25. See McGowan, *L'art du ballet de cour*, 254–61.

26. For non-French *airs* written for court performances, see Guillo, *Pierre I Ballard et Robert III Ballard*, 1:691–98. The earliest was probably written for the *Ballet de la Folie* (1614). Most date from 1645 or later.

27. Boësset, *Airs de cour ... treizième livre*, 9v–12r. For an overview, see McGowan, *L'art du ballet de cour*, 149–53, plates XVII–XXI. Also see Ravelhofer, *The Early Stuart Masque*, especially 232–36 and 252–53 for an excellent account of ethnicity on stage in this and other productions.

28. Louis XIII played a Persian scholar in the Turkish scene with his gentlemen; all sang or recited French verse, see Bordier, *Grand bal de la douairière de Billebahaut*, 17–23.

29. Prunières, *Le ballet de cour*, 177.

30. Bordier, *Grand bal de la douairière de Billebahaut*, 39. McGowan, *L'art du ballet de cour*, 153.

31. On Delfin, see Le Vassor, *Histoire du règne de Louis XIII*, 501. Corsica and Sardinia were transit points in the Mediterranean slave trade. For a Sardinian convert to Islam who rose to high ranks, take note of Hasan Aga, Barbarossa's lieutenant in Algiers, who led an embassy to France in 1562 (table 2).

32. Bordier, *Grand bal de la douairière de Billebahaut*, 53. Another recit (ibid., 33) for characters from Greenland or Friesland resembles neither language.

33. For the biographical outlines, see Frajese, "Andreini, Francesco."

34. Scala and Andrews, *The* commedia dell'arte *of Flaminio Scala*, 19–30, and Jaffe-Berg, Commedia dell'arte *and the Mediterranean*, 50–3, 88–91. Giovan Battista Andreini's *La Sultana* (Paris, 1622), has lines in *lingua franca* and Turkish for the Sultana and includes songs in Spanish, Slavic, or Turkish, "if she [the player] knows some" (62).

35. On reading such "sonic records," see Wilbourne, "*Lo schiavetto* (1612)."

36. Tessier, *Œuvres complètes*, ed. Dobbins, lxii–lxiii.

37. Durosoir, *L'air de cour en France*, 45, also see p. 35, "turc!"

38. Vaisse, "Charles Tessier, Carnets d'un voyageur," 44–45 with translation by Mary Pardoe at 16.

39. By contrast, see Salvatore, "Parodie realistiche," a brilliant study of Afro-Mediterranean speech in the *moresca* and "realistic" parodies.

40. "... un parcours épicé, goûteux et polyglotte," R. Ma., Review, "Charles Tessier, Carnets de voyages."

41. Tessier, *Carnets de voyage*, 24.

42. Usually these pen names are given in the last stanza: these stanzas may have been mixed up.

43. See Elçin, *Akdeniz'de ve Cezâyir'de Türk halk şâirleri*, 8.

44. Some vowel sounds in modern Turkish (which is used to transcribe Ottoman poetry from Arabic script), such as the "ı" of "katılayım" ("ɯ" in IPA), and some consonants, such as the "k" of "ki" ("c" in IPA), have no equivalents in modern French, Italian, or Spanish: the inconsistency of Tessier's orthography suggests that it was difficult to transcribe them (for instance, the phoneme "gö" is spelled "queur," "geau," and "guie"). That said, where French and Italian offer contrasting orthographies for the same sound, such as the "ş" of "yoldaşlar" and "yoldaş" ("ʃ" in IPA), Tessier's version uses equivalents of modern French spellings "c" and "ch" ("ol da celar," "ol dacch"), though "Dalışman" is spelled with "ss" (Italian

would be "sc"). In one place where Italian offered a sound not used in (modern) French—the "dʒ" sound of "cefa" and "cihanı"—Tessier's lyrics employ non-Italian spellings ("gie far" and "chi ha hin").

45. For generic definitions, see Haug, *Ottoman and European Music in ʿAlī Ufuḳī's Compendium, Monograph,* 208–12 and 351–67. The line-lengths of the *chansons turcquesques* fall outside those of the *türkī*s transmitted in the later seventeenth-century compendium of ʿAlī Ufuḳī (8-, 11-, and 15-syllable lines [ibid., 355–56]), but quatrains and cinquains ending with refrains are common stanza types (ibid., table 8.7), as are rhyme schemes that shift from stanza to stanza. Also see Şenel, "Ottoman *Türkü,*" 199–201.

46. On such spots in Constantinople, see Andrews and Kalpaklı, *Age of Beloveds,* 63–73.

47. On the performance of *türkī*s at court, see Haug, *Ottoman and European Music in ʿAlī Ufuḳī's Compendium, Monograph,* 352–53.

48. The *Serai Enderum* survives in a number of seventeenth-century copies, among which is a French translation, US–Ch Ms. Fr. 103 of Houghton Library at Harvard University. On the provenance of this copy, see Koval, "'Ottoman Secrets'."

49. See Haug, *Ottoman and European Music in ʿAlī Ufuḳī's Compendium, Monograph,* 212–13 on the *ʿāşıḳs,* and 417–19 on the *çöğür.*

50. US–Ch Ms. Fr. 103, fols. 89v–90r.

51. See Atıl, "Haydar Ra'is."

52. According to Savary de Brèves, *Relation des voyages,* 359–60, in 1600, the garrison of Algiers numbered 10,000 soldiers with 6000 Janissaries governing the city of 100,000. Dalışman, the *nom de plume,* may mean "diver."

53. On the ubiquitousness of enslavement, see Andrews and Kalpaklı, *Age of Beloveds,* 237–50. "Thus, at the higher levels of society, everybody (even the kuls) owned slaves, men made love to slaves, and everybody was in some degree dominated by slaves" (238).

54. On love and violence, see ibid., chapter 8.

55. See, for instance, Andrews, Black, and Kalpaklı, *Ottoman Lyric Poetry,* 107–9, and Goldberg, "*Romeo and Juliet*'s Open Rs," 225–26 on Shakespeare's "dark lady" sonnets.

56. Andrews and Kalpaklı, *Age of Beloveds,* 292.

57. Hamilton, "François Savary de Brèves."

58. Wright, "Turning a Deaf Ear," 161.

59. See Weiss, *Captives and Corsairs,* 14, 12.

60. Ghobrial, *The Whispers of Cities,* 17.

61. One important research initiative is the French Laboratoire d'excellence "Religions et Sociétés dans le Monde Méditerranéen," which is spearheading research into subjects such as Mediterranean humanism, Byzantine diplomacy, and more.

62. Weiss, *Captives and Corsairs,* 10.

63. I am grateful to the team at the Sefâretnâmes—Ottoman Embassy Reports Edition at the Don Juan Archiv Wien for their assistance. For seventeenth-century French understandings of Ottoman titles (*āġā, çavuş,* and so forth), see Rouillard, *The Turk in French History,* 670–72. Here and in table 2, where relevant, I use names and titles as given in the sources.

64. On Mahumet, see Charrière, *Négotiations,* 3:175–84.

65. Baudier, *Inventaire de l'histoire générale des Turcz,* 441–42.

66. I rely here on Jensen, "The Ottoman Turks," 466–67.

67. Charrière, *Négotiations,* 4:114.

68. Ibid., 4:114–17, and Skilliter, "The Sultan's Messenger," 54–55.

69. Isom-Verhaaren, *Allies with the Infidels,* 180–85.

70. "Relation des ambassadeurs envoyez par le Grand-Seigneur, Empereur des Turcs"; L'Estoile, *Journal,* 1:222. The Venetian ambassador reports 10–12 in the party of Hasan Aga, and we can guess at the same number in that of Ali Aga. Charrière, *Négotiations,* 4:72.

71. L'Estoile, *Journal,* 1:222.

72. See Jensen, "The Ottoman Turks," 461 and 467, and Charrière, *Négotiations,* 2:766–67 for a 1564 letter from the French ambassador pressing for diplomatic gifts.

73. Hathaway, *The Chief Eunuch,* 88–97. Ágoston and Masters, *Encyclopedia of the Ottoman Empire,* 23, 153.

74. Héroard, *Journal,* June 27, 1607. On the captives he liberated see Savary de Brèves, *Relation des voyages,* 353.

75. Savary de Brèves, *Relation des voyages*. Their galleon left Constantinople May 15, 1605 and arrived in Marseille November 19, 1606. Mustafa Aga's presence is attested intermittently in the journal.

76. Héroard, *Journal*, June 27, 1607.

77. See the "Relation au vray de ce qui s'est passé au baisemain de Monsieur de Salagnac Ambassadeur pour le Roy en Levant le premier Mars 1605," AAE MD Turquie, vol. 2, fols. 36r–39r.

78. L'Estoile, *Journal*, 3:310.

79. Ibid.

80. Norton, "Iconographs of Power," 340–41.

81. See Gürkan, "Mediating Boundaries," 120–24.

82. On the dragomans, see ibid., 111–16.

83. AAE MD Turquie, vol. 2, fols. 53r–62r.

84. In 1569, Olivieri was signing as "truchement et interprete du Roy"; under Henry III he received a salary ("Comtes de dépenses de Henri III," 433).

85. See the biography in Skilliter, "The Sultan's Messenger," 52–54.

86. Gürkan, "Mediating Boundaries," 111, 124–25.

87. For the order of ceremonies, see "Traitement fait en France au chiaoux que l'Empereur des Turcs envoya au roi Henri IV en 1607," AAE MD Turquie, vol. 10, pièce 2, fols. 37r–38v. "Puis mettant une seconde fois le genoüil en terre il [the *çavuş*] baisa le bord du manteau de sa M.[té] et luy ayant presenté la lettre du G.[d] Seigneur, il fit sa harangue a haute voix en sa langue. Cette harangue fut interpretée par l'Interprete du Roy, et sa M.[té] luy repondit par des paroles d'honesteté qui luy furent interpret[é]es par le même trucheman."

88. Dew, *Orientalism in Louis XIV's France*, 24–25.

89. See Daston and Park, *Wonders and the Order of Nature*, 100–108, 193–95.

90. Charrière, *Négotiations*, 2:460.

91. The French ambassador Jean de la Vigne confirmed: "sans point de faulte il y a quelques esclaves turcqs en votre royaume et en vostre court, mesmement quelques femmes." Charrière, *Négotiations*, 2:459.

92. In 1558, Diane de Poitiers relinquished those of her enslaved Muslims that had not converted—number unknown—but not the Christian converts. See Charrière, *Négotiations*, 2:459.

93. Skilliter, "Catherine de' Medici's Turkish Ladies-in-Waiting," 194.

94. McGowan, *Dance in the Renaissance*, 149, and Coulas, *Henri II*, 357–58.

95. Rothman, "Contested Subjecthood," 428.

96. Wilbourne, "'... la curiosità del personaggio': 'il Moro' on the Mid-Century Operatic Stage."

97. Pacifici, "Luigi d'Este, Cap. XV, Gli ultimi anni," 16, 23.

98. Daston and Park, *Wonders and the Order of Nature*, 101.

99. Héroard, *Journal*, January 29, 1606.

100. See Rothman, "Contested Subjecthood," and Savary de Brèves, *Relation des voyages*, 344–45, on captive boys as young as two, three, and four being circumcised, "made Turk" by force, and kept for sex in Algiers.

101. "Houja" may be the Turkish "houda": Lord, God, or master. For the Greek, alternative interpretations include: *Krya kai* (κρύα καὶ, cold and) for Criaqué and *Christé* (Χριστέ, vocative of Christos, Christ) for christa. "Chinchin" remains indecipherable. My thanks to Théodora Psychoyou and Cemal Kafadar for their renderings and Judith Haug for suggesting that the lyrics were more Greek than Turkish.

102. The Turkish words for *galère* (*caterga*), *noir* (*cara*), *flèche* (*oc*), *vingt-six* (*igrimi alti*) are provided with French translations in Palerne, *Peregrinations*, 522–35; *esclave* is given as *hiaser* (m.) and *haliac* (f.).

103. Contreras, *Les estranges avantures*, 236–45.

104. Said, *Orientalism*, 54.

105. Haug, *Ottoman and European Music in ʿAlī Ufuḳī's Compendium, Monograph*, 322–23. On the relevance of *maḳām*s and *uṣūl*s to *türkī*s, see ibid., 359, and Feldman, "The Musical 'Renaissance' of Late Seventeenth Century Ottoman Turkey," 100.

106. See Reinhard, "Ist die türkische Volksmusik über die Jahrhunderte konstant geblieben?," 224 and the discussion in Haug, *Ottoman and European Music in ʿAlī Ufuḳī's Compendium, Monograph*, 365–66 and 429–32.

107. The syllables represent drumming patterns in which düm = a flat stroke with the dominant hand, tek and te = striking with the ring finger near the rim, and ke = striking with the index finger of the non-dominant hand near the rim.

108. US-Ch Ms. Fr. 103, fols. 88v–89r.

109. Classroom demonstration at Harvard University, October 23, 2018. Judith Haug (personal correspondence, December 8, 2019), agrees that Ṣōfyān is a more plausible identification.

110. Tessier, *Œuvres complètes*, ed. Dobbins, lxiii.

111. Dimitri Psonis, who performed with Jordi Savall at I Tatti during the "Music in the Mediterranean Diaspora" conference in May 2017, agreed with Yousefi that Beyātī was the most likely *maḳām* for *Tal lissi man / Dalışman*. On the relative frequency of Beyātī, Nihāvend, and Ḥüseynī in the repertoire transmitted by ʿAlī Ufuḳī, which Sanlıkol factored into his assessment, see Haug, *Ottoman and European Music in ʿAlī Ufuḳī's Compendium, Monograph*, 233–38.

112. For the *maḳām* Beyātī as characterized by ʿAlī Ufuḳī and Cantemir, see Haug, *Ottoman and European Music in ʿAlī Ufuḳī's Compendium, Monograph*, 247–48, and Wright, *Demetrius Cantemir*, 134–35.

113. Tessier, *Œuvres complètes*, ed. Dobbins, lxiii. "This *turquerie* has a square repetitive rhythm and limited melody with strange mode and cadences–g-F, g-D, F-C, g-A & a-D."

114. It was reprinted in 1570, 1572, 1573, 1575, and 1580.

115. In La Grotte's collection, the major third is common in final sonorities; for a song that begins as a folia in G minor and ends in F, see *Las! je n'eusse jamais pensée*.

116. See Vaccaro, "Les Préfaces d'Anthoine de Bertrand," and Vicentino, *L'antica musica*.

117. Wright, "Turning a Deaf Ear," 157–58, notes that Charles Perrault (1688) linked "Oriental" melodic refinement with ancient music, aptly adding "one might have expected such open-minded responses" from Vicentino and Monteverdi.

118. Vicentino, *L'antica musica*, 85v. I thank Daniel Walden for drawing this passage to my attention.

119. See Ossi, *Divining the Oracle*, 111–12, on "canto alla francese", and Monteverdi, *Letters*, ed. Stevens, 412–17, on the Arab instrumentalist.

120. Dew, *Orientalism in Louis XIV's France*, 6–9.

Bibliography

Archival Sources

AAE CP Turquie: France, Archives diplomatiques du ministère des Affaires Étrangères, Correspondance Politique et documents divers, Turquie (133 CP).

AAE MD Turquie: France, Archives diplomatiques du ministère des Affaires Étrangères, Mémoires et Documents, Turquie (50 MD).

Manuscript Sources

US–Ch Ms. Fr. 103: Cambridge, MA, Harvard University, Houghton Library, Ms. Fr. 103

F–Pn Ms. Turc 292: Paris, France, Bibliothèque nationale de France, Ms. Turc 292

Printed Sources

Ágoston, Gábor, and Bruce Masters. *Encyclopedia of the Ottoman Empire*. New York: Facts On File, Inc., 2008.

Andreini, Giovan Battista. *La Sultana*. Paris: Nicolas de La Vigne, 1622.

Andrews, Walter G., and Mehmet Kalpaklı. *The Age of Beloveds: Love and the Beloved in Early-Modern Ottoman and European Culture and Society*. Durham: Duke University Press, 2005.

Andrews, Walter G., Najaat Black, and Mehmet Kalpaklı. *Ottoman Lyric Poetry: An Anthology*. Expanded edition. Seattle and London: University of Washington Press, 2006.

Armstrong, Megan C., and Gillian Weiss. "Introduction: France and the Early Modern Mediterranean." *French History* 29 (2015): 1–5.

Atıl, Esin. "Haydar Ra'is [Haydār Ra'īs; Haydar Reis; Nigari; Reis Haydar]." Grove Art Online. www.oxfordartonline.com, accessed August 18, 2019.

Bakhtin, Mikhail. M. *The Dialogic Imagination: Four Essays*, ed. Michael Holquist; trans. Caryl Emerson and Michael Holquist. Austin: University of Texas Press, 1981.

Barthe, Pascale. *French Encounters with the Ottomans, 1510–1560*. Transculturalisms, 1400–1700. Abingdon, Oxon, and New York, NY: Routledge, 2016.

Baudier, Michel. *Inventaire de l'histoire générale des Turcz*. Rouen: Clement Malassis, Louys Oursel, Jacques Besongne, 1641.

Boësset, Antoine. *Airs de cour avec la tablature de luth d'Antoine Boesset, treizième livre*. Paris: Ballard, 1626.

Bordier, René. *Grand bal de la douairière de Billebahaut, ballet dansé par Sa Majesté*. Paris: Imprimerie du Louvre, 1626.

Braudel, Fernand. *The Mediterranean and the Mediterranean World in the Age of Philip II*, trans. Siân Reynolds. 2 vols. New York: Harper & Row, 1972.

Brooks, Jeanice. "Tessier's Travels in Scotland and England." *Early Music* 39 (2011): 185–94.

Chalcondyle, Laonicus, et al. *Histoire générale des Turcs, contenant l'Histoire de Chalcondyle, traduite par Blaise de Vigenaire ... et continuée jusques en l'an 1612 par Thomas Artus et en cette édition par le sieur de Mezeray jusques en l'année 1661*. Paris: Sebastien Cramoisy, 1662.

Charrière, Ernest. *Négociations de la France dans le Levant, ou correspondances, mémoires et actes diplomatiques*. 4 vols. Paris: Imprimerie Impériale, 1848–1860.

"Comtes de dépenses de Henri III, 1580–1588." In *Archives curieuses de l'histoire de France depuis Louis XI jusqu'a Louis XVIII*, ed. M. L. Cimber and F. Danjou. Series 1, vol. 10:427–33. Paris: Beauvais, 1836.

Contreras, Jerónimo de. *Les estranges avantures contenans l'histoire merveilleuse des amours extremes d'un chevalier de Sevile dit Luzman*, trans. Gabriel Chappuys. Lyon: Benoit Rigaud, 1580.

Coulas, Ivan. *Henri II*. Paris: Fayard, 1985.

Dakhlia, Jocelyne. *Lingua franca*. Arles: Actes Sud, 2008.

Daston, Lorraine, and Katherine Park. *Wonders and the Order of Nature, 1150–1750*. New York: Zone Books, 2001.

Dew, Nicholas. *Orientalism in Louis XIV's France*. Oxford: Oxford University Press, 2009.

Dobbins, Frank. "Les airs de Charles Tessier." In *Poésie, musique, et société: l'air de cour en France au* XVIIe *siècle*, ed. Georgie Durosoir. Pp 135–53. Sprimont: Mardaga, 2006.

Du Loir. *Les voyages du sieur Du Loir*. Paris: Clouzier, 1654.

Durosoir, Georgie. *L'air de cour en France, 1571–1655*. Liège: Mardaga, 1991.

Dursteler, Eric R. "Speaking in Tongues: Language and Communication in the Early Modern Mediterranean." *Past & Present* 217 (2012): 47–77.

Elçin, Şükrü. *Akdeniz'de ve Cezâyir'de Türk halk şâirleri*, Türk Kültürünü Araştirma Enstitüsü, yayınları 78. Seri IV; sayı A. 23. Ankara: Türk Kültürünü Araştirma Enstitüsü, 1988.

L'Estoile, Pierre de. *Journal de Henri III, de Henri IV et de Louis XIII*. 4 vols. Collection complète des mémoires relatifs à l'histoire de France, 45–48. Paris: Foucault, 1825–1826.

Feldman, Walter. "The Musical 'Renaissance' of Late Seventeenth Century Ottoman Turkey: Reflections on the Musical Materials of Ali Ufkî Bey (ca. 1610–1675), Hâfiz Post (d. 1694) and the 'Marâghî' Repertoire." In *Writing the History of "Ottoman Music,"* ed. Martin Greve. Istanbuler Texte und Studien 33. Pp. 87–138. Würzburg: Orient-Institut Istanbul, 2015.

Frajese, Franca Angelini. "Andreini, Francesco." In *Dizionario Biografico degli Italiani*. http://www.treccani.it/enciclopedia/francesco-andreini_(Dizionario-Biografico)/, accessed May 5, 2019.

Ghobrial, John-Paul A. *The Whispers of Cities: Information Flows in Istanbul, London, and Paris in the Age of William Trumbull*. Oxford: Oxford University Press, 2013.

Goldberg, Jonathan. "*Romeo and Juliet*'s Open Rs." In *Queering the Renaissance*, ed. Goldberg et al. Pp. 218–35. Durham: Duke University Press, 1993.

Greene, Molly. "Beyond the Northern Invasion: The Mediterranean in the Seventeenth Century." *Past & Present* 174 (2002): 42–71.

Guerrero, Francisco. *El viaje de Hierusalem*. Valencia: herederos de Juan Navarro, 1590.

Guillo, Laurent. *Pierre I Ballard et Robert III Ballard, imprimeurs du roy pour la musique (1599–1673)*. Centre de Musique Baroque de Versailles. 2 vols. Sprimont: Mardaga, 2003.

Gürkan, Emrah Safa. "Mediating Boundaries: Mediterranean Go-Betweens and Cross-Confessional Diplomacy in Constantinople, 1560–1600." *Journal of Early Modern History* 19 (2015): 107–28.

Hamilton, Alastair. "François Savary de Brèves." In *Christian-Muslim Relations 1500–1900*, ed. David Thomas et al., accessed October 25, 2019. doi:http://dx.doi.org/10.1163/2451-9537_cmrii_COM_28372.

Hammer-Purgstall, Joseph. *Geschichte des Osmanischen Reiches, Grossentheils aus bisher unbenützten Handschriften und Archiven*. 10 vols. Pest: C. A. Hartleben, 1827–.

Hathaway, Jane. *The Chief Eunuch of the Ottoman Harem: From African Slave to Power-broker*. Cambridge and New York: Cambridge University Press, 2018.

Haug, Judith I. *Ottoman and European Music in ʿAlī Ufuḳī's Compendium, MS Turc 292: Analysis, Interpreta-*

tion, Cultural Context. Monograph. Schriften zur Musikwissenschaft aus Münster 25. Münster: Readbox Unipress, 2019.

Haug, Judith I. *Ottoman and European Music in ʿAlī Ufuḳī's Compendium, MS Turc 292: Analysis, Interpretation, Cultural Context. Volume 1: Edition, Volume 2: Critical Commentary*. Schriften zur Musikwissenschaft aus Münster 26. Münster: Readbox Unipress, 2020.

Héroard, Jean. *Journal de Jean Héroard sur l'enfance et la jeunesse de Louis XIII (1601–1628)*. Paris: Didot, 1868.

Işıksel, Güneş. "Haci Murâd (Agi Morato): An Elusive Dignitary Active in the Second Half of the Sixteenth Century." *Osmanlı Araştırmaları / Journal of Ottoman Studies* 47 (2016): 249–63.

Isom-Verhaaren, Christine. *Allies with the Infidel: The Ottoman and French Alliance in the Sixteenth Century*. London: I.B. Tauris & Co. Ltd., 2011.

Jaffe-Berg, Erith. Commedia dell'arte *and the Mediterranean: Charting Journeys and Mapping "Others."* Transculturalisms, 1400–1700. Farnham, Surrey and Burlington, VT: Ashgate, 2015.

Jensen, De Lamar. "The Ottoman Turks in Sixteenth-Century French Diplomacy." *The Sixteenth Century Journal* 16 (1985): 451–70.

Koval, Sarah. "'Ottoman Secrets': Alī Ufkî's Musical Intervention into Seventeenth-Century Ottoman-European Discourse." Unpublished typescript, 2018.

La Grotte, Nicolas de. *Chansons de P. de Ronsard, Ph. Desportes, et autres (1580)*, ed. Jane A. Bernstein. The Sixteenth Century Chanson 15. New York: Garland, 1992.

Le Vassor, Michel. *Histoire du règne de Louis XIII, Roi de France et de Navarre, tome cinquième*. Amsterdam: Chatelain, 1751.

Ma[chart], R[enaud]. Review, "Charles Tessier, Carnets de voyage, Le Poème Harmonique, Vincent Dumestre (direction)." *Le Monde*, January 8, 2007.

McGowan, Margaret M. *L'art du ballet de cour en France, 1581–1643*. Collection Le Chœur des Muses. Paris: Éditions du Centre National de la Recherche Scientifique, 1963.

McGowan, Margaret M. *Dance in the Renaissance: European Fashion, French Obsession*. New Haven and London: Yale University Press, 2008.

Miller, Peter N. "The Mediterranean and the Mediterranean World in the Age of Peiresc." In *The Sea: Thalassography and Historiography*, ed. Peter N. Miller. Pp. 251–76. Ann Arbor: University of Michigan Press, 2013.

Monteverdi, Claudio. *The Letters of Claudio Monteverdi*, trans. Denis Stevens. Cambridge and New York: Cambridge University Press, 1980.

Muḥammadī, Muḥsin. *Armaghān-i ṭarab: Naghmah'nigārī'hā-yi mūsīqī-i Īrān az Ṣafavīyān tā Mashrūṭah = Musical Souvenirs: European Transcriptions of Persian Music (1600–1910)*. Tehran: Mu'assasah-yi Farhangī–Hunarī-i Māhūr, 2015.

Norton, Claire. "Iconographs of Power or Tools of Diplomacy? Ottoman *Fethnames*." *Journal of Early Modern History* 20 (2016): 331–50.

Ossi, Massimo. *Divining the Oracle: Monteverdi's Seconda Prattica*. Chicago: University of Chicago Press, 2003.

Pacifici, Vincenzo. "Luigi d'Este, Cap. XV, Gli ultimi anni." *Atti e memorie della Società Tiburtina di Storia e d'Arte* 27 (1954): 16–72.

Palerne, Jean. *Les peregrinations du S. Jean Palerne, … où est traicté de plusieurs singularités et antiquités remarquées és provinces d'Egypte, Arabie … Terre Saincte, Surie, Natolie, Grece*. Lyon: Jean Pillehotte, 1606.

Palerne, Jean. *Poésies de Jean Palerne Forézien*, ed. Auguste Benoît. Paris: Pillet et Dumoulin, 1884.

Pedani Fabris, Maria Pia. *In nome del Gran Signore: inviati ottomani a Venezia dalla caduta di Costantinopoli alla guerra di Candia*. Miscellanea di studi e memorie 30. Venice: Deputazione Editrice, 1994.

Prunières, Henry. *Le ballet de cour en France avant Benserade et Lully*. Paris: Éditions H. Laurens, 1914.

Ravelhofer, Barbara. *The Early Stuart Masque: Dance, Costume, and Music*. Oxford and New York: Oxford University Press, 2006.

Reinhard, Ursula. "Ist die türkische Volksmusik über die Jahrhunderte konstant geblieben?" In *IV. Milletlerarası Türk Halk Kültürü Kongresi Bildirileri*. 3: Halk Müziği Oyun, Tiyatatro, Eğlence. Pp. 213–25. Ankara: Feryal Matbaası, 1992.

"Relation des ambassadeurs envoyez par le Grand-Seigneur, Empereur des Turcs, vers le roy Henry III." In *Archives curieuses de l'histoire de France depuis Louis XI jusqu'a Louis XVIII*, ed. M. L. Cimber and F. Danjou. Series 1, vol. 10:171–74. Paris: Beauvais, 1836.

"Religions et Sociétés dans le Monde Méditerranéen." http://www.labex-resmed.fr, accessed January 6, 2020.

Robinson, Alexander. "Musique et musiciens à la cour d'Henri IV (1589–1610)." PhD diss., Université Paris-Sorbonne, 2015.

Rothman, E. Natalie. "Contested Subjecthood: Runaway Slaves in Early Modern Venice." *Quaderni Storici* 47 (2012): 425–41.

Rouillard, Clarence Dana. *The Turk in French History, Thought, and Literature (1520–1660)*. Études de littérature étrangère et comparée 13. Paris: Boivin, 1941.

Said, Edward W. *Orientalism*. New York: Knopf Doubleday, 2014.

Salvatore, Gianfranco. "Parodie realistiche: Africanismi, fraternità e sentimenti identitari nelle canzoni moresche del Cinquecento." *Kronos* 14 (2011): 97–130.

Savary, François, Seigneur de Brèves. *Relation des voyages de Monsieur de Brèves ... ensemble un traicté faict l'an 1604 entre le Roy Henry le Grand et l'Empereur des Turcs, et trois discours dudit Sieur, le tout recueilly par le S. D. C.* Paris: Nicolas Gasse, 1628.

Scala, Flaminio, and Richard Andrews. *The* commedia dell'arte *of Flaminio Scala: A Translation and Analysis of 30 Scenarios*. Lanham, MD: Scarecrow Press, 2008.

Şenel, Süleyman. "Ottoman *Türkü*." In *Writing the History of "Ottoman Music,"* ed. Martin Greve. Pp. 195–209. Istanbuler Texte und Studien 33. Würzburg: Orient-Institut Istanbul, 2015.

Setton, Kenneth M. *The Papacy and the Levant, 1204–1571*. Vol. 4, *The Sixteenth Century from Julius III to Pius V*. Memoirs of the American Philosophical Society 162. Philadelphia: American Philosophical Society, 1984.

Skilliter, Susan A. "Catherine de' Medici's Turkish Ladies-in-Waiting: A Dilemma in Franco-Ottoman Diplomatic Relations." *Turcica* 7 (1975): 188–204.

Skilliter, Susan A. "The Sultan's Messenger, Gabriel Defrens; An Ottman Master-Spy of the Sixteenth Century." *Wiener Zeitschrift für die Kunde des Morgenlandes* 68 (1976): 47–59.

Subrahmanyam, Sanjay. "Connected Histories: Notes towards a Reconfiguration of Early Modern Eurasia." *Modern Asian Studies* 31 (1997): 735–62.

Tessier, Charles. *Airs et villanelles Fran. Ital. Espa. Suice. et Turcq. mises en musique à 3. 4. & 5. parties par le Sr. Charles Tessier*. Paris: la veufve R. Ballard et Pierre Ballard son fils, 1604.

Tessier, Charles. *Carnets de voyages*. Le Poème Harmonique, dir. Vincent Dumestre. Paris: Alpha Classics, 2006.

Tessier, Charles. *Œuvres complètes: chansons, airs, villanelles*, ed. Frank Dobbins. Collection "Épitome musical." Turnhout: Brepols, 2006.

Unat, Faik Reşit. *Osmanlı Sefirleri ve Sefaretnameleri*. Ankara: Türk Tarih Kurumu Basımevi, 1987 [1968].

Vaccaro, Jean-Michel. "Les Préfaces d'Anthoine de Bertrand." *Revue de musicologie* 74 (1988): 221–36.

Vaisse, Damien. "Charles Tessier, Carnets d'un voyageur"/"A man and his travels," trans. Mary Pardoe. Pp. 12–17; 40–45. Liner notes to Tessier, *Carnets de voyages*.

Vicentino, Nicola. *L'antica musica ridotta alla moderna prattica*. Rome: Antonio Barre, 1555.

Villamont, Jacques de. *Les voyages du seigneur de Villamont, Chevalier de l'ordre de Hierusalem, Gentilhomme du pays de Bretaigne*. Paris: Claude de Montr'oeil et Jean Richer, 1595.

Weiss, Gillian. *Captives and Corsairs: France and Slavery in the Early Modern Mediterranean*. Stanford: Stanford University Press, 2011.

Wilbourne, Emily. "*Lo Schiavetto* (1612): Travestied Sound, Ethnic Performance, and the Eloquence of the Body." *Journal of the American Musicological Society* 63 (2010): 1–43.

Wright, Owen. "Turning a Deaf Ear." In *The Renaissance and the Ottoman World*, ed. Anna Contadini and Claire Norton. Pp. 143–65. Farnham, Surrey and Burlington, VT: Ashgate, 2013.

Wright, Owen. *Demetrius Cantemir: The Collection of Notations; Volume 2: Commentary*. New York: Taylor and Francis, 2017.

Yerasimos, Stéphane. "Voyageurs européens en Palestine ottomane au XVIe siècle (1517–1600), essai de bibliographie." *Revue d'Études Palestiniennes* 11 (1984): 77–104.

Yirmisekiz Mehmet Çelebi. *Le paradis des infidèles: relation de Yirmisekiz Çelebi Mehmed efendi, ambassadeur ottoman en France sous la Régence, traduit de l'ottoman par Julien-Claude Galland*, ed. Gilles Veinstein. Paris: F. Maspero, 1981.

Latin Musical Practices in the Greek Isles: Mapping Early Modern Confessional Plurality in the Eastern Mediterranean*

Théodora Psychoyou

Exordium: a very long coexistence

Beyond the village of Melanes, in the mountains of Naxos island, at the end of a dirt road a couple of kilometers long, present-day travelers will come upon an abandoned palace in an idyllic setting (see figure 1). This building, constructed between 1679 and 1683, was used as a resort by Jesuit monks. It is a place of meditation and reflection, located in a verdant valley, far away from Chora, the main city of Naxos. Built from the debris of an earlier ducal residence and financed by the family of Robert Saulger, this monastery quickly came to be called a "palace" owing to its splendor.[1] Its many rooms include bedrooms, guest quarters, laundry rooms, kitchens, stables, an impressive pigeon loft, and a beautiful loggia overlooking the valley. Even in decay, one can appreciate the palace's former magnificence during its more prosperous days. At the same time, however, the extreme state of its dilapidation is symptomatic of a broader ruin that runs far deeper than the visible erosion of cultural heritage. If I begin here, with the material fate of this Jesuit monastery on a middling island in the Eastern Mediterranean, it is to signify the historiographic fate with which it is conjoined, one that has effaced the unique histories of musical hybridity in this part of the sea. These processes of loss and degradation continue apace, they are still with us, and any essay designed—as this one—to address the past must also confront this present.

Evidence for music-making in this context is extremely fragile, but not entirely absent. Having fortuitously come across a book of seventeenth-century Italian music many years ago, in the early 2000s, at the Jesuit monastery of Tinos island, I first became intrigued by the complexity of musical practices in the Catholic communities of early modern Greece.[2] The curiosity initially piqued by this source (and all that it conveys) has been reactivated recently thanks to a larger research project that I was invited to join, concerning religion and sociability in the Mediterranean,[3] mainly in antiquity and the Byzantine era, as well as the activities of the International Musicological Society study group "Mediterranean Music Studies," which was created in 2016.

Fig. 1. The "Jesuit palace" at Melanes, Naxos

At this preliminary stage of research, far-reaching questions loom large: What musical practices arose in these zones of encounter, fusion, and cultural crossing? How does music evince the cosmopolitanism of the Eastern Mediterranean and the trade routes between Europe and the Levant, North and South, East and West, between Genoa, Venice, and Rome on one side, and Smyrna, Constantinople, Damascus, and Jerusalem on the other, exactly where Ottoman and Christian forces were disputing the extent of their dominions (see figure 2)?[4] This field of inquiry is potentially vast, and in order to circumscribe it, I follow the lead suggested by the book I saw on Tinos all those years ago and focus on the Jesuit environment.

Latin has been a permanent presence in the Greek area since the Roman Empire and throughout its history. It evolved into a "Catholic presence" after the East-West Schism of 1054 and was strongly implanted following the fourth crusade (1204) during the time known as *Latinokratia*, *Frangokratia*, or *Venetokratia*, when crusader states were established in the territories of the disintegrating Byzantine Empire. Venetians ruled mainly in the islands, while continental Greece came under Ottoman rule with the conquest of Constantinople

Fig. 2. Michel Servet, "Tabula nova Graeciae, Sclavoniae, & Bulgariae," in *Claudii Ptolemaei Alexandrini geographicae enarrationis, Libri Octo*, Stanford Libraries, David Rumsey Map Center, David Rumsey Map Collection

in 1453. Thus, the Jesuit missionaries that were deployed in Greece during the Counter-Reformation landed in a strongly multi-confessional environment, one that was already highly Christian, mainly Orthodox but also, in some areas, Catholic, though under Venetian and not Roman governance, the whole situated in a largely Ottoman part of the sea.[5]

This chapter proposes an overview of (what it is possible to know about) musical practices linked to Catholic devotion in the Greek isles during the seventeenth century, and more specifically in the Jesuit post-Tridentine sphere of influence. To date no study has been dedicated specifically to this topic,[6] even if

Fig. 3. Southern Greece, the Archipelago and Crete: detail from *Carte de la Grèce dressée sur un grand nombre de mémoires anciens et nouveaux [...] par G[uillaume] de l'Isle*, Paris and Amsterdam. Princeton University Library

some research is presently underway:[7] my own investigation is still in its early stages, but its potential outcomes are promising. Moreover, the field seems ready now for collaborations across institutions and the pursuit of more ambitious interdisciplinary projects that might combine different disciplinary approaches: musicology, history, ethnology and historical anthropology, religious history, and ethnomusicology are all implicated in the analyses that follow.

My contribution here considers the Cycladic area (shown in figure 3), and mainly the situation on the island of Tinos, a setting that permits a good overview of a variety of source materials (including those of the Jesuit collections that are today more or less centralized in Athens). These sources are remarkable for their very disunity and hybridity, and in this respect, they aptly represent music, ritual, and political life throughout the Archipelago. Described in 1686 as *archipelagus turbatus*, the "troubled archipelago,"[8] it was the site of intense confessional, commercial, geopolitical, and cultural "missions" emanating from near and far, and any first impressions of homogeneity collapse as soon as one scratches the surface. Geography is a defining feature of the Cyclades, and it makes each of the islands unique. My goal in the following pages it to produce an initial cultural and social history with specific focus on religion; my method in the musical investigation is microhistorical and based in particular on the materiality of certain documents, in particular those found in Tinos, but also on the oral or improvised practices discernable from them. Indeed, working as it does along the margins of musicological perspectives that more regularly privilege polyphonic and highly authored music, this cultural survey draws attention to modest non-elite environments identifiable in the hybrid and popular use of language by the unlettered; it also grapples with hybrid expressions of faith and devotional practices—hybrid in both confession and language—and, consequently, the corresponding music-making. In sum, music on the islands is mixed in ways keyed to the specificity of these places, at once remote and linked, a string of interconnected sites of mobility and exchange.

In a musical environment largely characterized by orality, one needs to consult several types of sources in order to understand the devotional and liturgical practices that enlisted music in cross-cultural contexts, since the effects of acculturation appear in various ways. The most important and spectacular set of sources employ *Frangochiotika*, also known as *Frangolevantinika*, a written transliteration of spoken Greek using a Latin alphabet, which was employed in a consequential manuscript corpus of hymns and other music-related documents, as well as in a printing tradition that reached from Venice to Smyrna and endured into the nineteenth century.

Jesuits in Greece: context and challenges

Greek lands were for the most part majority Orthodox, but also, in some specific territories, very Latin (or "Latinized"), and this since the early Christian era. This made the circumstances of Jesuit missionization in Greece rather singular compared to other expeditions of the order, since in Greece the Jesuits deployed to lands that were already Christian, if not Catholic; in this respect, the situation was perhaps similar to the one they encountered in the 1630s in Ethiopia.[9] That said, there were several missions within continental Europe that aimed to reinforce and consolidate Catholic presence: the Jesuit colleges in France can be considered in analogous terms, especially during the religious wars—as missions designed to secure Catholic belief in places under threat.

Obviously, these missions raise issues of power and influence. In the case of Jesuits, tensions over imbalances of power primarily concerned struggles between Venice and Rome, much more so than religious battles between Christians and the Ottomans or the contests pitting the Eastern Church (Greek Orthodox) against the Western Church (Latin and Roman Catholic). Also, it is more appropriate to speak first of the *Latin* church, which became *Catholic* only later. This tension seems quite clear in the case, typically, of Crete, where the Jesuit mission failed to take root because of the strong rivalry between Rome and Venice: it was not the Orthodox nor the Ottomans but the Venetians who hindered the Jesuit settlement project in Crete. Indeed, in 1588 Jesuits established a college and a convent in Candia (the capital of Crete, now called Heraklion) near the thirteenth-century Catholic basilica of St. Mark. In 1606, however, they were expelled from all the Venetian territories, including Crete, as a result of the *Guerra dell'Interdetto*, a major dispute between Venice and the Papal Curia.[10] The Jesuit ban was finally lifted in 1657, whereupon they returned to Venetian territories, but by then reestablishing their mission in Crete proved impossible, since Candia was already under siege by the Ottomans.[11]

Being Greek and Latin at the same time is not an absurd oxymoron but an organic condition, one linked to the original status of the Byzantine Empire, which was the Roman Empire of the East or, beginning in the period of Roman antiquity, the Roman Empire in Greek lands. From the early Christian era until the eighth century, the Greek islands (mainly Ionian and Cyclades) belonged to the bishopric of Rome, and not to that of Constantinople. With the arrival of the crusaders, two centuries later, and Venetian rule, Greece entered a new phase of "Latinity" within the context of a long continuum.[12]

From a historiographical point of view, this mixed past created—classically—an identity issue that affects everything from religious denomination to national identity. Indeed, the questions I am posing here regarding the various practices and modalities of the Latin communities (which also pertain to Hebrew and Ottoman communities) and especially the questions of their interaction, have not been thoroughly investigated (or not at all, in the case of the musical expressions of their interaction). Of course, this very long period has already been treated by historians, beginning in the nineteenth century and with increasing frequency in recent years.[13] But many of these histories have been marked by ideologies of national, ethnic, and confessional identity: within Greece the national narrative has privileged the representation of an Orthodox nation, and Greece is surrounded by countries that built their nationalistic narratives on fictionalized connections with a glorious indigenous past.[14] Approaching the subject of Latinity in Greece therefore requires an especially critical reading of the secondary literature. Identifying these very contemporary concerns further illuminates the stakes of this investigation, for in going beyond ideological projections and macroscopic schemata that can be wholly anachronistic, we can challenge past representations of impermeable cultural and geographical entities, and thus of national and confessional entities, with new histories of cross-cultural encounters and exchanges.[15] The challenges raised by island-based histories in the Mediterranean, such as those addressing the highly cosmopolitan environments of Crete, Sicily, or Cyprus (which continues to be a site of geopolitical struggle), are particularly emblematic in this regard.[16]

Another important issue relating to Greek historiography, beyond questions of religious diversity, concerns the degree of continuity in Greek culture from antiquity to the foundation of Greece as a nation-state in 1830. These debates color the controversies that surrounded the foundation of the new state, which were tinted with nineteenth-century nationalisms: Jakob Philipp Fallmerayer's controversial theory[17] claimed total racial discontinuity between ancient and modern Greeks as bloodlines were replaced during and after the decline of the Western Roman Empire by those of the Arvanitic (Albanian), Aromanian, Slavic, and Turkish peoples. Hardly a disinterested outsider, Fallmerayer's theory exuded disdain for modern Greeks and was motivated by a geopolitical struggle in which Austro-Hungarian powers endorsed Ottoman domination of Greece and sought to shore up the Ottoman Empire as a counterbalance to the menace of Imperial Russia in the region. Fallmerayer was also reacting to the very intense philhellenism of European romantics, who viewed the 1821 Greek revolt against Ottoman rule as a return to antique virtue. (It is not by chance that Lord Byron died at Missolonghi in 1824 during the Greek revolution of independence.) In contrast to Fallmerayer's ideology of annexation, the vision of the Greek and Oriental lineage described by Victor Hugo in the preface to *Les Orientales* (1829) sounds more measured, with concerns that proved prescient given the carnage that befell Europe in the decades that followed: "For empires as well as for literatures, perhaps soon the East is called to play a role in the West. [...] Old Asian barbarism may not be as devoid of superior men as our civilization wants to believe."[18] Finally, we should see in Fallmerayer's position a Western appropriation of Greek antiquity that transformed nineteenth-century art, culture, and historiography.[19] The idea that classical culture found its ultimate expression in Western Europe subsequently fed early twentieth-century German nationalism and justified a logic of appropriation according to which the German nation was the true heritor of an ancient legacy (and not the Greeks, since they were no longer racially connected to the ancient peoples that had inhabited those places). Thus, Leni Riefenstahl's German propaganda documentary *Olympia* (1938) adopted and reproduced classical antique aesthetics in a spectacular example of this racially charged brand of German Hellenism.[20]

Fallmerayer's ideas elicited intense reaction from various scholars of the newly established Greek state and precipitated a new historiography aiming to demonstrate continuity:[21] scholars sought to provide definitive proof of the links between modern Greeks and ancient Greek civilization, a movement exemplified by the official *National History* of Constantin Paparrigopoulos of 1860–1874.[22] Thus, two quite opposite elements, Orthodoxy and Antiquity, have been used to forge, over the past 150 years, a representation of Greek identity that leaves little room for characteristics (religious or linguistic) that lie outside the canonized norms. This explains in part why so little attention has been devoted to the subject of music in Catholic circles in Greece. Of course, contemporary Greek historiography has moved away from this binary vision, but these ideologies continue to mark public debates and the collective unconscious to this day. Thus, Greek Jews, Catholics and Pomaks, or Slavophones (Orthodox or not), numerically in the minority, are also minoritized by a Hellenity that, in its monolithic unity, has left them little space. Indeed, well beyond the Archipelago, reactions to this "unbearable similarity of the other"[23] are evident in histories of the Balkans and, from there, have impoverished the representation of identities and cultural plurality in both the European past and present.

My initial survey of this relatively uncharted material ran in all directions and raised various issues. Foremost was the question of language: on the one hand, liturgical ceremonies in the Greek environment were generally celebrated by Italian or French clergy (in Latin), yet several sorts of devotional ceremonies employed the local vernacular modern Greek. This crossing between Latin and Greek created a very specific expressive mode that required quite a bit of contextual analysis to fully comprehend. Secondly, the situations for which we have evidence of music-making were of sometimes quite different status and function: musical practices overlap with the ritual practices of various faiths, devotional practices that might be more personal, and the social practices typical of weddings, funerals, and local festivities. Locality emerges as a highly significant factor, which means that any broader assessment needs to begin island by island and in the end, facts may not add up to a regional whole. For instance, the situation on Tinos—which was connected to the Cretan sphere of influence—was not the same as that on Syros, Naxos, or Santorini, all of which lay outside the Venetian orbit, making them quite different from Crete, and so on. Finally, the question—or the problem—of written sources of music requires piecing together musical content from fragmentary documentary evidence usually lacking musical notation.

This last matter of primary sources merits a preliminary review, since the sources and archives are far from uniform in preservation and accessibility. Each island, with its unique economic situation, spheres of influence, and repertoires, not only presents specific cases: the quantity and state of the sources that have come down to us vary widely from place to place in the Archipelago. For instance, the Jesuit archives of the Ionian islands of Corfu and Zante were destroyed in tragic circumstances (severe bombings in Corfu during the winter 1940–41; devastating earthquakes in Zante, Ithaca, and Cephalonia in August 1953). There is an old archive at the central Jesuit library in Athens, which brings together parts of the libraries of several Jesuit settlements (primarily those of Athens, Syros, and Tinos). But historical archives also remain in place locally as well, at the archbishopric of Tinos, and in other less-explored places, especially on the islands of Syros, Naxos, Chios, and Crete. Finally, as already mentioned, the Jesuits were but one force of Catholicism in Greece during the early modern era, so eventually it will be necessary to move beyond Jesuit archives altogether. But for the purposes of this inquiry, focusing on the Jesuits permits us to restrict the scope of this initial study in a coherent way that allows for the consideration of relatively similar contexts and optimal use of surviving documentation.[24]

In the following sections, I evaluate four different categories of source material: travel literature and memoirs, hymns and chants in modern vernacular Greek (and transliterated into *Frangochiotika*), plays in Greek (in the post-Tridentine context), and finally some sources with music notation.

Travel literature and memoirs

A vast corpus of travel literature survives from the early modern period,[25] as well as several mission reports and memoirs. These texts contain extensive descriptions of archaeological sites as well as accounts of local customs both religious and secular, any remarkable thing, such as the state of the volcano on Santorini island, which remains astounding to this very day (figure 4), or even beliefs about the existence of *vrykolakas* (a sort of revenant or vampire) and other supernatural phenomena.[26]

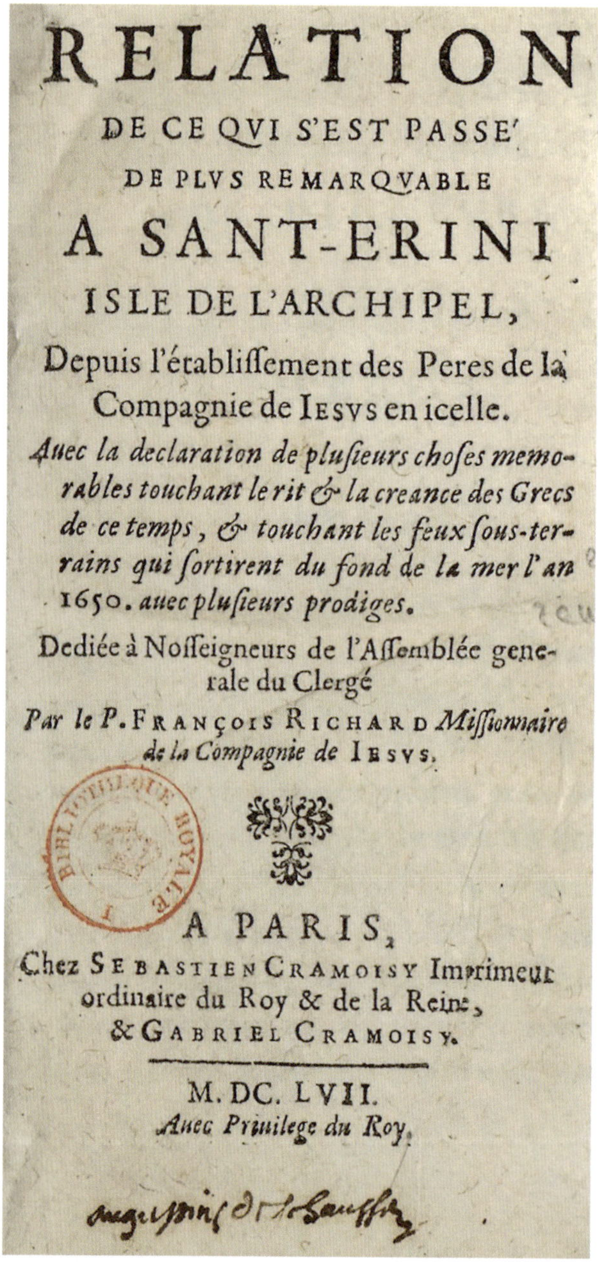

RELATION

DE CE QVI S'EST PASSE'
DE PLVS REMARQVABLE
A SANT-ERINI
ISLE DE L'ARCHIPEL,
Depuis l'établiſſement des Peres de la Compagnie de IESVS en icelle.

Auec la declaration de pluſieurs choſes memorables touchant le rit & la creance des Grecs de ce temps, & touchant les feux ſous-terrains qui ſortirent du fond de la mer l'an 1650. auec pluſieurs prodiges.

Dediée à Noſſeigneurs de l'Aſſemblée generale du Clergé

Par le P. FRANÇOIS RICHARD *Miſſionnaire de la Compagnie de* IESVS.

A PARIS,
Chez SEBASTIEN CRAMOISY Imprimeur ordinaire du Roy & de la Reine, & GABRIEL CRAMOISY.

M.DC.LVII.
Auec Priuilege du Roy.

Fig. 4. François Richard, *Relation de ce qui s'est passé de plus remarquable à Saint-Erini* (Paris, 1657): "Report of the most remarkable things that happened in Sant-Erini, island of the Archipelago [i.e. Santorini, also called Thera], since the establishment of the Fathers of the Society of Jesus. With notification of many memorable things concerning the rite and the belief of the Greeks of our time [i.e., not the Greeks of Antiquity, as understood by default], and touching the underground fires that came out of the bottom of the sea in the year 1650, with several wonders"

Among the most significant descriptions of the Archipelago are the writings of the Jesuit fathers François Richard (1657)[27] and Robert Saugé (1698),[28] and those of the travelers Jean de Thévenot (1664),[29] Antoine Des Barres (1678),[30] and Joseph Pitton de Tournefort (1717).[31] Unsurprisingly, the two Jesuits comment in more detail on religious, devotional, historical, and cultural issues; as for the lay travelers, their approach is generally more descriptive, empirical, and ethnographic. Others, finally, focus on archaeological observations—such as Jacob Spon, in his writings about continental Greece.[32]

The mission reports, such as that of Fleuriau d'Armenonville from 1695, are systematic accounts of the denominational situation of several communities, and they chart the deployment of missionaries from one island to another. What marks these reports (and perhaps biases them) is that the Greek Orthodox are considered schismatics and—by the same logic—efforts to convert them are depicted as a peaceful and passionate battle. If the Turks (or even the Jews) were seen by Catholic missionaries as infidels—unbelievers who were nonetheless "people of the book"—Greeks and Latins seem to have viewed each other through a prism of reciprocal heresy. Thus, conversion scenes of Orthodox Greeks becoming Catholic were considered victories *ad majorem Dei gloriam*: "On voyoit de tous côtez des troupes de penitens qui alloient d'Eglise en Eglise psalmodiant d'un ton lugubre, & déchirant leurs corps à coups de discipline" [There were troops of penitents on all sides going from Church to Church, chanting in a dismal tone, and tearing their bodies with thrashings].[33] As is evident from this passage, these missives include passing remarks that allow us to gather significant information about singing and music practices.

Alongside the printed reports and memoirs, a corpus of manuscript letters and mission reports is slowly coming into view as increasing numbers of documents are identified, cataloged, and edited.[34] I have been able to locate several Jesuit reports in Roman archives[35] and the Lazarist archives of Thessalonica;[36] in addition to mission reports, the archives of the Capuchin Library-Archive in Paris may also hold useful information.[37]

From these documents one can glean, from a phrase or sentence here or there, a little information concerning musical practices, in particular those accompanying religious feasts and lamentations for the dead. Thus, Robert Saulger describes in detail how the *Mirologitres*—professional female mourners—wail for the deceased, from the deathbed to the tomb, something that shocked him for its excessive manifestation of pain in "dismal songs," large gestures, grimaces, pathetic cries, and "contortions." Glimpsing in the excesses of this "Christian nation" the vestiges of its idolatrous antique past, the Jesuit likened these women gathered around the coffin to "real furies of hell," similar to the "ancient Bacchantes."[38] In a similar vein, he describes dancing in popular public balls as morally suspect, especially when it involved women:

> Tous les Grecs des Isles, & sur tout les femmes, ont une passion furieuse pour les danses publiques. Dés la veille des fêtes un peu solennelles, particulièrement si c'est du Patron de quelque Eglise de l'Isle, on les voit tous arriver par bandes des lieux les plus éloignez, & danser tant que la nuit est longue dans la grande place de l'Eglise. Les Dames de qualité qui peuvent sortir ces jours-là, y viennent à cheval partagées en plusieurs brigades, & précédées de musettes & de tambours, qui annoncent de loin leur arrivée. Les Missionnaires font ce qu'ils peuvent pour empêcher ces assemblées.[39]
> [All the Greeks of the Islands, and especially women, have a furious passion for public dances. By the eve of any solemn feast, especially if it is of the Patron of any Church of the island, we see them all come in groups from the most remote locations and dance all night in the main church square. Ladies of quality who can go out on these days, arrive on horseback, divided into several brigades and preceded by musettes and drums, which announce their arrival from afar. Missionaries do their best to prevent these assemblies].

Since musical information like this is scattered throughout these texts, musicologists will need to review them with specific categories in mind in order to collect references in a systematic way. As suggested by the foregoing examples, life events (marriage, baptism, death), religious feasts, and social activities will doubtless be fruitful subjects for research.

Hymns and chants in *Frangochiotika*

Definition and functions

In the course of my initial survey of the field, an important corpus of sources emerged that reflects devotional practices, potentially sung, which are specific to "Latin" (i.e., Catholic) communities in the Archipelago. They are written in vernacular Greek (the nineteenth-century term is "demotic Greek"), as opposed to ancient Hellenistic Greek, and this is significant, since the use of the spoken vernacular is marked in post-Tridentine Catholic evangelism as a strategy of missionization, not just in the Archipelago but also in France, Italy, and the Americas. The sources in vulgar Greek are distinctive because a large portion of them, in manuscript as well as print, are written in a transliteration of spoken Greek that employs the Latin alphabet. This Latinized spelling of Greek was known at the time as *Frangochiotika* or, later on, *Frangolevantinika*: its use has been largely attested in the Aegean islands, and especially on the island of Chios, hence the term of *Frangochiotika*. The use of the word *Frangolevantinika* is likely a little posterior, given that Smyrna, on the Anatolian coast—the "Levant"—became a center of book production using this form of writing in the nineteenth century; the Latinate transliteration of Greek by the "Francs" (the West Europeans[40]) probably owed to the fact that while they did learn to speak Greek, they had difficulties learning Greek spelling and script, and so they opted for a phonetic version in a familiar alphabet.[41] Indeed, *Frangochiotika* (or *Frangolevantinika*) refers exclusively to the written aspect of the language, the spoken version of it being ordinary vernacular Greek.[42] Of course, this vernacular Greek, distinct from ancient Greek, came to include vocabulary from Italian, French, Turkish, and even Arabic, but it is not a *lingua franca* in the sense of the western Mediterranean *sabir*, nor is it a specific dialect, such as the Calabrese *grecanico* or the Venetian *greghesco*,[43] which was a Greco-Venetian dialect that can be found in *commedia dell'arte* scenarios and polyphonic songs printed in Venice.

To summarize, two elements are at play in the linguistic issues raised by *Frangochiotika*: the use of vernacular spoken Greek by the Roman Catholic clergy (the "Latins," as they were known), which stood in contrast to the practices of the Greek Orthodox Church (the "Greeks"). The Orthodox Church was and remains to this day very strongly attached to the original language of the New Testament, which was written in the *Koine* Greek language (ancient Hellenistic Greek): continuing to use the ancient Greek New Testament mobilizes every possible theological, philosophical, symbolic, and political stake that might be linked to its singularly privileged connection to the original *Logos/Verbum*, even as its distance from spoken Greek imbues the "Church language" with a dimension of authority. Then as now, Latin was the official language of the Catholic Church, yet when Jesuits used modern Greek in para-liturgical, devotional, and pedagogical contexts, it facilitated the transposition of an entire arsenal of Latin texts into the local language of their parishioners, allowing the missionaries to stand out as more welcoming than the Orthodox Church and to fulfill the mandates of the Catholic Reformation with its rejection of distant authority in favor of greater proximity to the faithful. The simplicity and expressiveness of effective language was central to the ideals of the Catholic Reform.

In other words, *Frangochiotika* can be traced to the integration of modern Greek in Catholic devotion, which coincided with the missions that were launched in the wake of Tridentine reforms. In 1590 the Jesuits settled on the

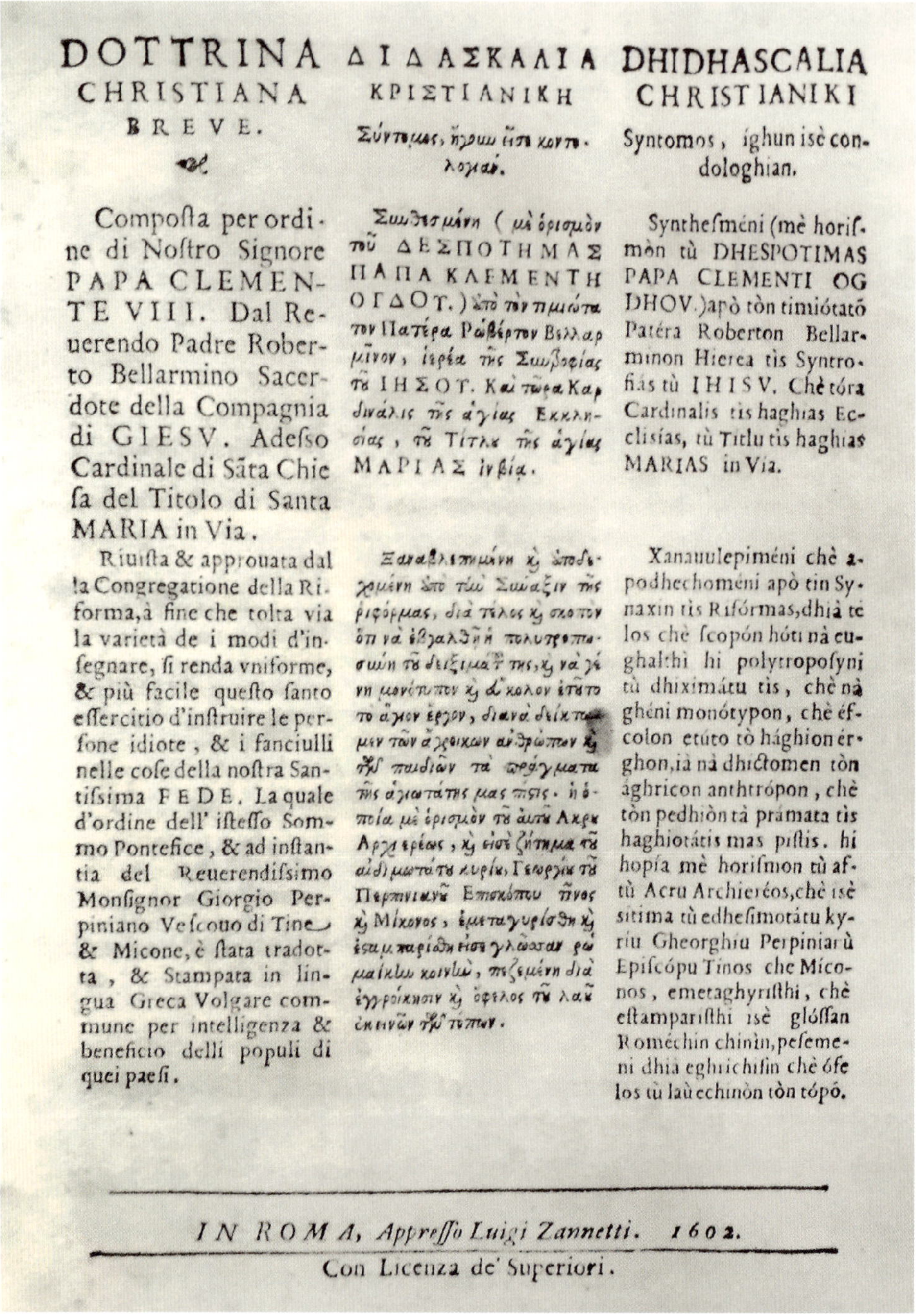

DOTTRINA CHRISTIANA BREVE.

Compoſta per ordine di Noſtro Signore PAPA CLEMENTE VIII. Dal Reuerendo Padre Roberto Bellarmino Sacerdote della Compagnia di GIESV. Adeſſo Cardinale di Sãta Chiesa del Titolo di Santa MARIA in Via.

Riuiſta & approuata dal la Congregatione della Riforma, à fine che tolta via la varietà de i modi d'inſegnare, ſi renda vniforme, & più facile queſto ſanto eſſercitio d'inſtruire le perſone idiote, & i fanciulli nelle coſe della noſtra Santiſsima FEDE. La quale d'ordine dell' iſteſſo Sommo Pontefice, & ad inſtantia del Reuerendiſsimo Monſignor Giorgio Perpiniano Veſcouo di Tine & Micone, è ſtata tradotta, & Stampata in lingua Greca Volgare commune per intelligenza & beneficio delli populi di quei paeſi.

ΔΙΔΑΣΚΑΛΙΑ ΚΡΙΣΤΙΑΝΙΚΗ

Σύντομας, ἤγουν εἶσε κοντολογιαῖς.

Συνθεσμένη (μὲ ὁρισμὸν τοῦ ΔΕΣΠΟΤΗ ΜΑΣ ΠΑΠΑ ΚΛΕΜΕΝΤΗ ΟΓΔΟΥ.) ἀπὸ τὸν τιμιώτατον Πατέρα Ῥωβέρτον Βελλαρμῖνον, ἱερέα τῆς Συνοδείας τοῦ ΙΗΣΟΥ. Καὶ τώρα Καρδινάλις τῆς ἁγίας Ἐκκλησίας, τοῦ Τίτλου τῆς ἁγίας ΜΑΡΙΑΣ ἐν βίᾳ.

Ξαναβλεπημένη καὶ ἀποδεχομένη ἀπὸ τὴν Σύναξιν τῆς ῥιφόρμας, διὰ τέλος καὶ σκοπὸν ὅτι νὰ ἐβγαλθῇ ἡ πολυτροπωσύνη τοῦ δειξιματός της, καὶ νὰ γένη μονότυπον καὶ εὔκολον εἰς τοῦτο τὸ ἅγιον ἔργον, διὰ νὰ δείχνωμεν τῶν ἀγροίκων ἀνθρώπων καὶ τῶν παιδίων τὰ πράγματα τῆς ἁγιωτάτης μας πίστις. ἡ ὁποία μὲ ὁρισμὸν τοῦ αὐτοῦ Ἄκρου Ἀρχιερέως, καὶ εἰς ζήτημα τοῦ αἰδεσιμωτάτου κυρίου Γεωργίου τοῦ Περπινιανοῦ Ἐπισκόπου Τήνος καὶ Μίκονος, ἐμεταγυρίσθη καὶ ἐσταμπαρίσθη εἰς γλῶσσαν ῥωμαίκην κοινὴν, πεζεμένη διὰ ἐγγροίκησιν καὶ ὄφελος τοῦ λαοῦ ἐκείνων τῶν τόπων.

DHIDHASCALIA CHRISTIANIKI

Syntomos, ighun isè condologhian.

Syntheſméni (mè horiſmòn tù DHESPOTIMAS PAPA CLEMENTI OGDHOV.) apò tòn timiótatō Patéra Roberton Bellarminon Hierea tis Syntrofiás tù IHISV. Chè tóra Cardinalis tis haghias Ecclisías, tù Titlu tis haghias MARIAS in Via.

Xanauulepiméni chè apodhechoméni apò tin Synaxin tis Rifórmas, dhià tè los chè ſcopón hóti nà eughalthi hi polytropoſyni tù dhiximátu tis, chè nà ghéni monótypon, chè éfcolon etúto tò hághion érghon, ià nà dhictomen tòn ághricon anthrópon, chè tòn pedhiòn tà prámata tis haghiotátis mas piſtis. hi hopía mè horiſmon tù aftù Acru Archieréos, chè isè sitima tù edheſimotátu kyríu Gheorghíu Perpiniarū Epiſcópu Tinos che Miconos, emetaghyriſthi, chè eſtampariſthi isè glóſſan Roméchin chinìn, peſemeni dhià eghrichiſin chè óſe los tù laù echinòn tòn tópó.

IN ROMA, Appreſſo Luigi Zannetti. *1602.*

Con Licenza de' Superiori.

Fig. 5. The *Dottrina Christiana* of Bellarmino, translated into modern Greek by Matteo Karyofilis, and financed by Giorgio Perpiniano, bishop of Tinos and Mykonos. The text is presented in three columns, in Italian, Greek, and *Frangochiotika* (Rome, 1602)

island of Chios, where they opened a school that immediately enrolled two hundred and fifty students, mostly Orthodox.[44] Vincent Castagnola of Chio, a Jesuit, translated the *Doctrina Christiana* of Jacopo Ledesma into vernacular Greek and had it printed with both Greek and Latin characters in Rome in 1595.[45] Some years later, in 1602, the *Dottrina Christiana* of Bellarmino was printed in three different forms, including both *Frangochiotika* and Greek (see figure 5). Similarly, several Catholic devotional books and catechisms, initially produced in Latin, were translated into Greek, some of them in *Frangochiotika* (or combining both Greek and Latin scripts). From 1595 to the end of the eighteenth century, the Jesuits produced approximately seventy such editions in Greek.[46]

Eugène Dalleggio, who has produced a bibliography of Greek books printed in Latin characters, explains that the popular term *Frangochiotika* (φραγκοχιώτικα), which does not figure in any dictionary, likely comes from the enthusiasm the people of Chios displayed for Greek books printed in Latin characters. That said, it is important to note that this was not a new invention: the use of Latin letters to write in Greek dates to Roman antiquity, and of course we all know the case of *Kyrie eleison, Christe eleison* at the very least, but there are many more examples of transliteration beyond this isolated phrase in the Mass Ordinary.[47] The originality of *Frangochiotika* is in fact double: one factor is the length of the texts, which far surpass a few words or sentences in Greek. These are whole books. The other, most important point is that the books and documents in *Frangochiotika* are transliterations of texts in the modern Greek dialect. By adopting Greek words in their works, these Latin authors established an "orthography" of Greek in the Latin alphabet in the early modern era.[48]

This practice supported a pedagogical project. As explained by Niki Papaïliaki-Gamelon:

> the missionaries, although they did not exercise a monopoly on education, revolutionized the educational landscape of Greek territories with the introduction of print in teaching and their liberal distribution of small catechisms. This is the main difference between the missionary school and the Greek school. While the pupils in Greek schools focused on learning ancient Greek, missionary pupils learned vernacular Greek and foreign languages.[49]

These missionaries settled on various islands of the Archipelago and from the end of the sixteenth century they founded schools in Syros, Tinos, Naxos, Serifos, Santorini, Paros, and Chios. They did not attempt to convert the students

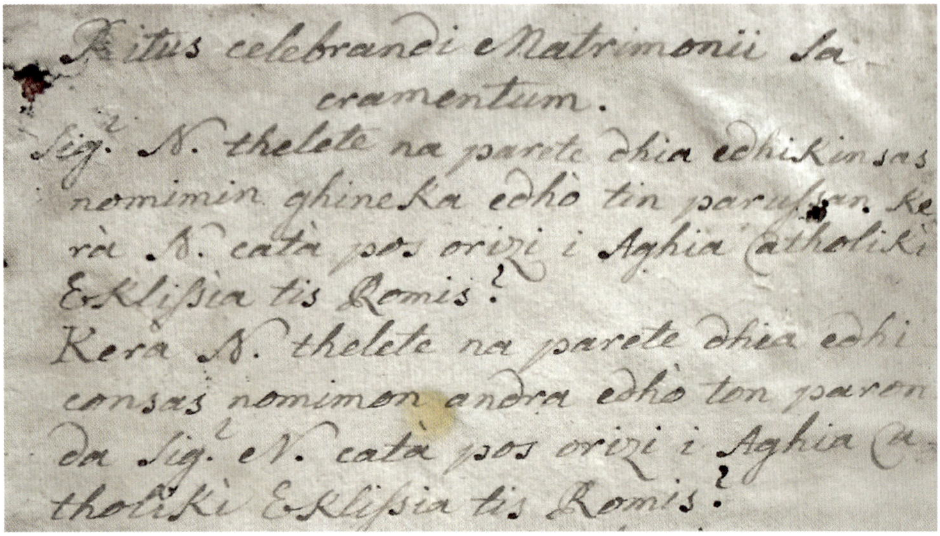

Ritus celebrandi Matrimonii Sa
cramentum.
Sig.r N. thelete na parete dhia edhikinsas
nomimin ghineka edhò tin parusan ke
rà N. catà pos orizi i Aghia Catholiki
Eklissia tis Romis?
Kerà N. thelete na parete dhia edhi
consas nomimon andra edhò ton paron
da Sig.r N. catà pos orizi i Aghia Ca-
tholiki Eklissia tis Romis?

Fig. 6. "Ritus celebrandi Matrimonii sacramentum," manuscript note inserted in a *Rituale romanum* (Venice: Pezzana, 1748), copy in the Jesuit library of Athens, shelfmark 064/542

who came to their schools, but they did effectively proselytize indirectly, since their exemplary morality, the high quality of education they provided, and the foreign languages and vernacular Greek they taught to the children enhanced their prestige. Consequently, beginning in the last decades of the sixteenth century, the number of Catholic inhabitants in the Aegean islands increased significantly. The flagship of this development was Syros, which already had a strong base of Catholicism and then became a Catholic island. Half of the villages of Tinos were Catholic, and thousands of residents of Naxos, Paros, and Santorini also became Catholic, though they remained in the minority. Thus, the Catholic pastoral and educational missions in Greece, starting with the Cycladic islands, eventually created a religious linguistic field distinct from that of the Patriarchate of Constantinople, which to this day persists in maintaining the language of the New Testament, as already mentioned. This missionary Greek output therefore clarifies the religious context of *Frangochiotika* even as it shows how it was largely imposed by Roman Catholics in their desire to teach in a "natural language."[50] Of course, these missions find an echo in projects located in Rome itself, such as the Stamperia orientale Medicea, the Tipografia poliglotta, and so forth.[51] And, from an even broader perspective, all of these educational and evangelical missions, which deployed new tools and new pedagogies, participated in the modern process of the circulation of knowledge, and—paradoxically—ended up contributing to the secularization of the modern world.[52]

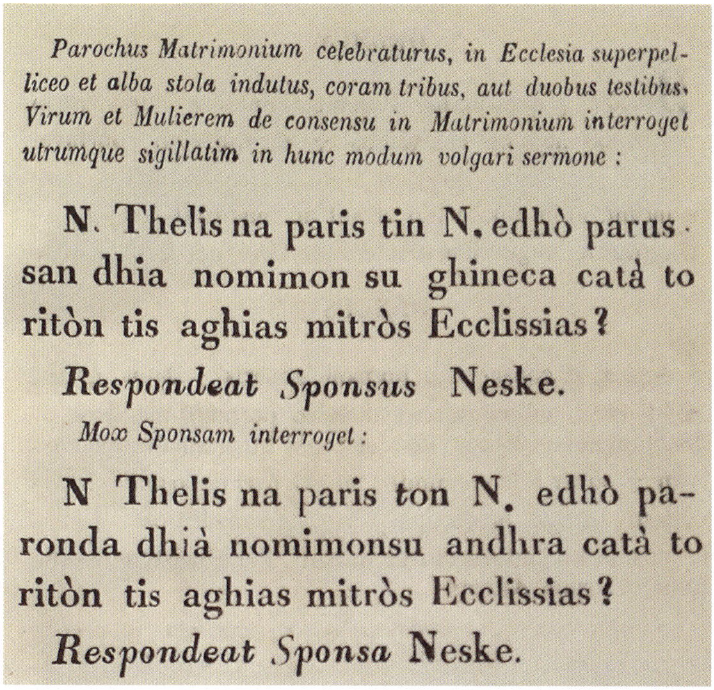

Parochus Matrimonium celebraturus, in Ecclesia superpelliceo et alba stola indutus, coram tribus, aut duobus testibus. Virum et Mulierem de consensu in Matrimonium interroget utrumque sigillatim in hunc modum volgari sermone :

N. Thelis na paris tin N. edhò parus. san dhia nomimon su ghineca catà to ritòn tis aghias mitròs Ecclissias?

Respondeat Sponsus Neske.

Mox Sponsam interroget :

N Thelis na paris ton N. edhò paronda dhià nomimonsu andhra catà to ritòn tis aghias mitròs Ecclissias?

Respondeat Sponsa Neske.

Fig. 7. *Ritus celebrandi matrimonium sacramentum juxta consuetudinem ecclesiae Tenensis* (Galata Constantinopoleos, 1849): [Celebration rite of the marriage sacrament according to the custom of Tinos island]

Sources in Frangochiotika

An important corpus of devotional texts, hymns, and dramatic works was produced in the vernacular by missionaries in Greece, some of them in *Frangochiotika* and some of them (especially the dramatic works) in Greek characters. One purpose of these books was surely to assist church personnel, who needed to be able to function in a language they had not mastered. In the eighteenth-century manuscript note shown in figure 6, the priest has used phonetic spellings to write out the vows he needed to say in order to celebrate a wedding. In this case, the Latin transcription acts as a script for a vocal performance, privileging pronunciation over any sort of letter-perfect transcription. The Greek version is a translation of the Roman rite, originally in Latin, the title of which has been retained:

> "*Ritus celebrandi Matrimonii sacramentum.* Sig. N. thelete na parete dhia edhikin sas nomimin ghineka edhò tin parusan Kerà N. catà pos orizi i Aghia Catholiki Eklissia tis Romis? Kerà N. thelete na parete dhia edhikon sas nomimon

Figs. 8–9. *Canti ed Inni in Greco volgare*. Archives of the Catholic archbishopric of Tinos at Xinara, ms. pp. 44–45 and 2–3

andra edho ton paronda Sig.r N. catà pos orizei i Aghia Catholiki Eklissia tis Romis?"

[*Celebration Rite of the Marriage Sacrament.* Signor N. do you want to take as your own legal wife Lady N, present here, according to the rules of the Sacred Catholic Church of Rome? Lady N., do you want to have as your own legal husband Sigor N., present here, according to the rules of the Sacred Catholic Church of Rome?]

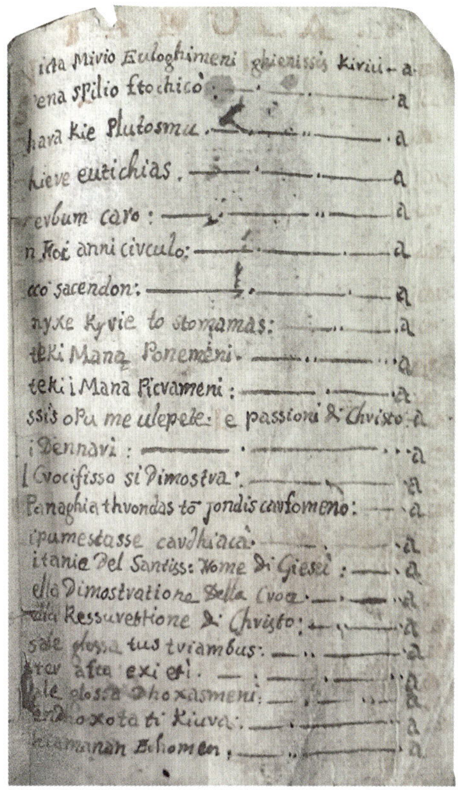

Fig. 10. *Canti ed Inni in Greco volgare,* Archives of the Catholic archbishopric of Tinos, ms. p. 123 ("Tabula": Table of Contents)

A small pamphlet containing the entire wedding office was printed in 1849 (in Constantinople) specifically for the rite of the church of Tinos. Most of the texts are in Latin (psalms, prayers, etc.) but the consent dialogue between spouses is in the vernacular (figure 7). The proximity between the manuscript and the printed versions is striking. There are several differences between the two versions, but the consistencies in both content and graphic design reflect the dissemination of a standardized Greek version, at least at the scale of the island (which has about thirty Catholic parishes). In the nineteenth century, printed versions like the one shown here also indicate the answers to be given by bride and groom: "Respondeat Sponsus (Sponsa) Neske" [The spouse answers yes of course].

The Archives of the Catholic archbishopric of Tinos at Xinara hold several rare documents worthy of further investigation, including the late seventeenth-century manuscript collection of *Canti ed Inni in Greco volgare* shown in figure 8. This manuscript compendium contains mainly songs and hymns in Greek written in *Frangochiotika,* along with some prayers in Latin;[53] as is usual in this genre, there are texts but no musical notation. The use of vernacular Greek locates the register of these songs and hymns at the most popular level of devotion, something underscored by the abundant illustrations, such as the

Tinos ms. *Frangochiotika*	Restitution of the Greek version	Restitution of a more literal transcript	Translation
TABULA	TABULA	TABULA	TABLE
Nicta Mirio Euloghimeni Ighienissis Kiriu	Νύχτα μυριοευλογημένη η γέννησις Κυρίου	Nychta myrioeuloghemeni i genissis Kyriou	In a very blessed night, the Birth of the Lord
Sena spilio ftochikò	Σ'ένα σπήλαιο φτωχικό	S'ena spileo phtochiko	In a humble cave
Chara Kie Plutosmu	Χαρά και πλούτος μου	Chara kai Ploutos mou	My joy and my wealth
Chiere eutichias	Χαίρε ευτυχίας	Chaire eutychias	Rejoice in happiness
Verbum caro	Verbum caro	Verbum caro	*The Word [was made] flesh*
In hoc anni circulo	In hoc anni circulo	In hoc anni circulo	*In the ending of the year*
[...]			

Table 1. Table of Contents of the *Canti ed Inni in Greco volgare*

crucified Christ and Virgin Mary shown in the margins alongside the texts on this opening. These "*versi della Madona*," as mentioned in the Italian header of these pages, consist of a strophic prayer to the Virgin Mary under the Cross, in *Frangochiotika*. The two previous pages provide other *versi* on the same theme, preceded by an instruction for the prayers, in Italian as well, which indicates that the strophes should be sung: "Questi versi si hano da cantare avanti l'Altare della Madona tutti inginochioti" ("These verses have to be sung before the Altar of the Madonna, all kneeling"). As a whole, the book follows the Temporal cycle, beginning with the Nativity, but it also contains some local hymns, such as a "rain prayer."[54] Many titles and other indications are in Italian, which sheds light on the identity of the copyist and his linguistic and cultural background.

At the bottom of page 2, the manuscript bears the ex-libris of Bernardo Scordialo (figure 9). The presence of the Scordialo family in Tinos is documented from 1615 to 1718, after which they can be sighted in Naxos.[55] Thus, the book can be dated to the very end of the seventeenth century or the beginning of the eighteenth century. We can also see, in this example, that the iconography either illustrates the text in a literal way (the Nativity scene in a small cave, "S'ena spilio ftochicò" [in a humble cave]), or adds popular pastoral characters to the margins, such as the flute player depicted on page 3 (but not mentioned in the accompanying poem).

This manuscript contains a table of contents at the end (figure 10), which proves key to understanding some characteristics of the method used in the *Frangochiotika*. In order to clarify some of its details, table 1 transcribes the table of contents and sets it alongside a reconstruction of the original Greek and a more "orthodox" transliteration, with a translation into English as well.

The first feature to remark is that the original transliteration is phonetic and—more precisely—a phonetic transcription based on Italian pronunciation. For example, the diphthong "ου" is represented phonetically by "u," thus the pronoun "μου" is transcribed "mu" (and not "mou"), and "Κυρίου" becomes "Kiriu" (and not "Kyriou"). The Greek words are sometimes separated incorrectly: "Mirio euloghimeni" should be one word, but given that it is a long composite term, this may not be relevant here. Conversely, some words are joined together when they should remain separate, as in "plutosmu" or "ighenissis." The whole ensemble works well from the phonetic perspective and provides an accurate script, but the copyist obviously has not entirely mastered Greek syntax. Finally, it is worth stressing the richness and the beauty of this rare and unpublished collection of "hymns and songs" in modern Greek, with its very popular devotional style and simple and tender expression.

In sum, documents like these witness the prevalence of post-Tridentine Catholic pastoral work, which mobilized popular forms of devotion and created new types of poetry, facilitated access to the written and learned world via oral traditions, and accelerated the subsequent dissemination of such texts, in part through the development of an atypical editorial tradition employing *Frangochiotika*. This material production and the spiritual programs it supported did not stand alone, but ran alongside a parallel tradition that sometimes used *Frangochiotika* as well: the corpus of Cretan epic and dramatic poetry and other forms of neo-Hellenic literature that emerged in Crete in the wake of Italian humanism.

Early modern Greek theater

The island of Crete was under Venetian rule from 1211 to 1669. During the sixteenth and seventeenth centuries, the *regnum Candiae*[56] was one of the most prosperous islands of the Mediterranean, a crossroads of East and West that produced numerous scholars, including philologists, as well as painters, musicians, and composers, who traveled not only to Venice, but also to Central and Western Europe.[57] The most famous example is that of the Cretan painter Domenico Theotocopoulos (1541–1614), *El Greco*, who was educated and lived in Crete to the age of twenty-six, when he left for Italy and finally Spain; equally exemplary is the classicist Markos Mousouros (1470–1517), a leading

Greek philologist and editor in Venice, who was born and trained in Heraklion, before becoming a pupil of the Greek scholar Janus Lascaris in Venice. Similar life trajectories pertain for musicians as well, such as Francesco Londariti (d. 1572), a Cretan composer, singer, and hymnographer also known as *il Greco*, whose path took him to the island of Tinos, before he moved on to Venice and Munich, and finally returned to Crete; his output includes three polyphonic masses and more than eighty motets and madrigals.[58] Other less famous musicians include the Cretan Francesco de Laudis,[59] who sojourned in Venice and Munich as well, and the Cypriot Orthodox monk, singer, and theorist Hieronymous "Tragoudistes" (i.e., "singer"), who spent nine years as a student in Italy, three in Venice as a pupil of Gioseffo Zarlino and six at the University of Padua.

Crete was the main center of early modern dramatic poetry in vernacular Greek, a place where a bi-confessional society—Orthodox and Catholic—developed a bilingual literature in Italian and Greek that stands as a unique expression of Renaissance and Baroque culture, distinct both in its production and its social reach.[60] The most striking social feature is the large number of literate readers across all social classes in Crete, a phenomenon that owed largely to the existence of numerous private teachers of Latin and classical Greek on the island, whose schooling proved more organized and systematic than education provided by ecclesiastical institutions.[61] A valuable overview of the services offered by these teachers and their clientele can be gained from the archival collection "Notai di Candia," of the Archivio di Stato di Venezia.[62] It contains various contracts between masters and families, including a dozen contracts concerning music lessons. Sometimes the contractual agreement outlines the program of study with a precise deadline for its completion, as in a contract between Tibaldo from Venice and Francisco Venerio, both inhabitants of Candia, signed July 6, 1532. Tibaldo agrees to teach his pupil how to play lute and specifically how to perform "twelve balli and all the modern saltarelle" within a year.[63] Overall, these private students are both Catholic and Orthodox, and contracts are in Latin, Italian, or Greek.

While private instruction predominated, some institutions did provide various sorts of free education, primary and secondary (but no higher), such as the "Greek school" founded in Candia by the Cardinal Bessarion and controlled throughout the sixteenth century by the "unionists," who defended the reunification of Catholics and Orthodox; in the same city was the school of the Catholic Archdiocese, a seminary for Catholic priests. Similar schools had been established in the dioceses of Rethymno and Chania. Education was also provided free of charge in the large Catholic monasteries of Candia, such as the public school in the Franciscan monastery of St. Francis, where the Cretan Petros Philargis studied as a boy, going on to a brilliant ecclesiastical career in Italy and election as Pope Alexander V (1409–1410).[64] Finally, students could receive a free education in the schools of the Dominican monastery of St. Peter in Candia, the Orthodox Sinaitic monastery of St. Catherine in the same city, which is said to have been attended by the later patriarchs of Constantinople Meletius I Pegas (1549–1601) and Cyril Loukaris (1572–1638), and other micro-schools of Orthodox and Catholic monasteries elsewhere on the island. The programs were far less formal than those of the Jesuit colleges and less organized than the *ratio studiorum*: the educational result was thus more random and depended on the personality and charisma of individual teachers.[65]

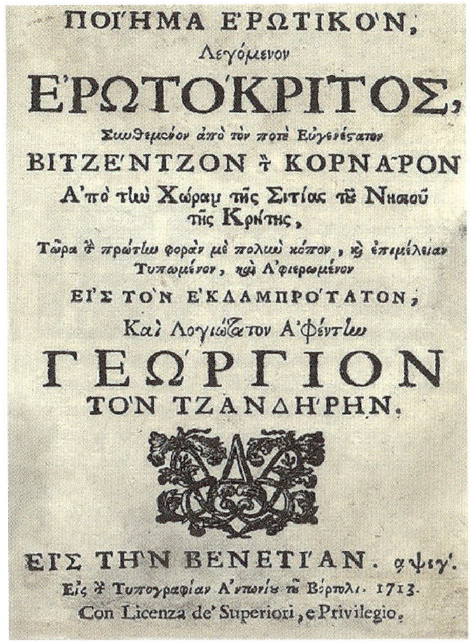
ΠΟΙΉΜΑ ἘΡΩΤΙΚΌΝ,
Λεγόμενον
ἘΡΩΤΟΚΡΙΤΟΣ,
Συνθεμένον ἀπὸ τὸν ποτὲ Εὐγενέστατον
ΒΙΤΖΕΝΤΖΟΝ τὸν ΚΟΡΝΑΡΟΝ
Ἀπὸ τὴν Χώραν τῆς Σιτίας τοῦ Νησιοῦ
τῆς Κρήτης,
Τώρα τὴν πρώτην φορὰν μὲ πολλὺν κόπον, καὶ ἐπιμέλειαν
Τυπωμένον, καὶ Ἀφιερωμένον
ΕἸΣ ΤῸΝ ἘΚΛΑΜΠΡΟΤΑΤΟΝ,
Καὶ Λογιώτατον Ἀφέντην
ΓΕΏΡΓΙΟΝ
ΤῸΝ ΤΖΑΝΔΗΡΗΝ.
ΕἸΣ ΤῊΝ ΒΕΝΕΤΙΑΝ. αψιγ'.
Εἰς τὴν Τυπογραφίαν Ἀντωνίου τοῦ Βόρτολι. 1713.
Con Licenza de' Superiori, e Privilegio.

Fig. 11. Title-page of the first printed edition of *Erotokritos* [ca 1590–1610], a romance of more than 10,000 lines by Vincenzo Cornaro (Venice, 1713): "Erotic poem, named Erotokritos" ("Ποίημα ερωτικόν, λεγόμενον Ερωτόκριτος")

Venice deployed several measures to mitigate the distinctions between conquerors and conquered, which favored syncretism by allowing the Greek-Byzantine tradition to meet Latin-Italian practices in creative formulations. These encounters were reinforced by the fact that from the middle of the sixteenth century onwards, hundreds of Cretans traveled to the great universities of Northern Italy for higher education, especially the University of Padua, one of the oldest in the world. It is estimated that during the period 1500–1700, at least a thousand Cretans studied law or medicine at Padua, which became the "alma mater" not only of Cretans, but of the entirety of Venetian-occupied and Ottoman-occupied Greece. When these students—including those who studied elsewhere in the Italian peninsula—returned to their homeland, they brought along important elements of the Italian culture in which they had been immersed.[66] In this way, Crete became part of the European learned community, enjoying an impressive intellectual flourishing (and a unique cultural identity founded on this East-West syncretism). Three academies of letters, sciences,

Η' ΘΥΣΙ'Α
ΤΟΥ' ΑΒΡΑΑ'Μ,
Ι'ΣΤΟΡΙ'Α ΨΥΧΩΦΕΛΕΣΤΑ'ΤΗ,
Ευγαλμένη από τ' Α'γίαν Γραφήν,
Συνθεμένη παλαιά διά Στίχων απλών,
Καί τώρα πάλιν εις χάριν των Ευσεβών,
Καί Φιλαρέτων με πολλήν επιμέλειαν διορθωμένη, και μετατυπωμένη.
Εις τ' ΒΕΝΕΤΙ'ΑΝ, αψιγ'.
Παρά Νικολάω τω Σάρω, 1713.
Εις τ' Τυπογραφίαν Α'ντωνίου τω Βόρτολι,

Fig. 12. Title-page of *The Sacrifice of Abraham* (Venice, 1713): "The sacrifice of Abraham, a story most beneficial for the soul" ("ψυχωφελέστατη")

and the arts, modeled on Italian academies, contributed significantly to this development: the Academy of Vivi in Rethymno, the Stravaganti Academy in Candia, and the Sterili Academy in Chania.[67]

Cretan literary output was significant, and it has attracted numerous studies by scholars of neo-Hellenic literature. Indeed, taken as a whole, the story of Cretan literature during the time of Venetian rule is one of the most intensively investigated chapters in the history of modern Greek literature.[68] The output includes a large number of epic and dramatic poems that intersect with Italian and even some French literary traditions in explicit ways. The most famous poem, still popular today through an oral tradition in song, is the epic romance *Erotokritos* by Vitsentzos Kornaros (or Vincenzo Cornaro), in vernacular Greek (figure 11). *Erotokritos* is composed of fifteen-syllable rhyming couplets, a form that matches the meter and rhyme scheme used in the Cretan folk songs known as *mantinades*;[69] thus, several couplets from *Erotokritos* were taken up as *mantinades* and entered popular lyric traditions as songs.

While the dramatic corpus has been well studied by scholars, little research addresses the circumstances of performance or approaches the repertoire from the disciplinary perspective of theater studies. The most notable exception in this regard is Walter Puchner's pioneering book *Greek Theater Between Antiquity and Independence* (2017), which is an invaluable resource even though it does not focus on performance practice *per se*. As of this writing, no studies have been devoted to questions concerning the presence (or not) of music in plays, or the kinds of music that might have been heard in the theater. I will not review in detail the history of early modern Cretan theater and dramatic poetry, but it is nonetheless useful to mention some emblematic examples.[70]

The corpus includes two tragedies, seven or eight pastoral dramas, eighteen intermedia, three comedies, and one religious drama, *The Sacrifice of Abraham*, the title-page of which is shown in figure 12. This poem, usually attributed to Vincenzo Cornaro, relies on contemporary Italian models, and particularly the poem *Lo Isach* by Luigi Groto, published in 1586. The Greek play was first published in Venice; indeed, after the fall of Constantinople, in 1453, Venice was the main center of Greek editions. *Erophili* by Georgios Chortatsis, the most popular Cretan tragedy, was printed in Venice in 1637 and followed by several reprints, while Cornaro's *Erotokritos*, which circulated in manuscript throughout the seventeenth century, was printed in Venice for the first time 1713. These three titles are the most famous and influential examples of late Renaissance Cretan literature, but there are many more. Only now is Cretan theater slowly being integrated into scholarship on broader European trends in dramatic poetry of the time.[71]

No music sources survive for these plays, but *Erophili* has several indications implying the use of music, while *The Sacrifice of Abraham*, since it follows several dramatic conventions of post-Tridentine Jesuit theater, arguably might have adopted its musical conventions as well: by analogy with contemporary religious dramas in Latin or the vernacular and their connections to musical theater, *The Sacrifice of Abraham* could be likened to Italian oratorios. It would not be surprising to discover that similar features of performance were developed for these neo-Hellenic dramatic poems, including musical interludes at the very least, if not more. Recent studies of theater beyond Crete have focused on moral pieces based on subjects drawn from the Old and New Testaments that were performed in Jesuit schools connected to the Society's missions in Constantinople and the Archipelago, which were staffed by French and Italian missionaries. With the suppression of the Jesuit order in 1773, this theatrical tradition ended. According to Walter Puchner, the rediscovery of this Baroque past has marked

> an entirely new episode in Modern Greek theatre history which was unknown before 1970, and which adds ten new dramatic texts written between 1640 and the first decades of the eighteenth century to the annals of Modern Greek literature. Together these texts provide many new details about theatrical performances between 1580 and 1750. The investigation started with the sale of a miscellaneous codex from Chios by auction at Sotheby's & Co. in London in 1973 and ended with the publication of eight dramatic texts in a critical edition at the turn of the new millennium, with a supplemental investigation on school performances of religious theatre on the Greek islands of the Aegean Sea in 2005.[72]

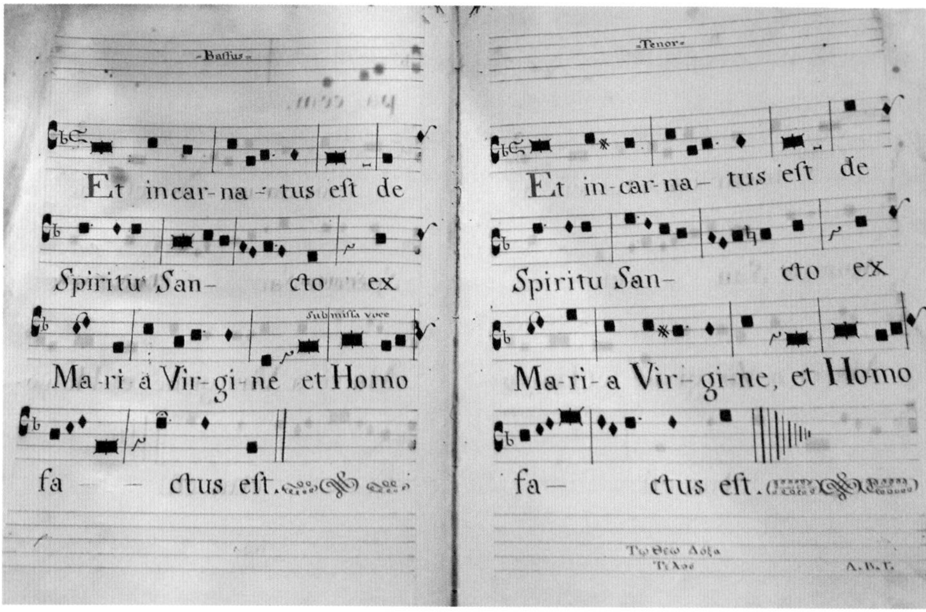

Fig. 13. "Et incarnatus. Ton. V. 2bus vocibus," plainsong-style melody with a voice in parallel thirds. Archives of the Catholic archbishopric of Tinos, Ms. 4181/19 IX.203

With this new information, a musicological evaluation of the corpus needs to be initiated, notwithstanding the fact that the music from Jesuit colleges and similar devotional environments has been lost owing to the ephemeral nature of the performances and, probably, the kinds of music that were used.[73] The evidence that we do have survives mainly in the form of stage directions indicating that the plays were generally accompanied by musical instruments; this is the case for *The Tragedy of St. Demetrius*, an anonymous but well-documented five-act tragedy with four comic interludes performed on Naxos island in 1723.[74] Unfortunately, the critical edition and reconstruction ignore the music, which remains challenging to reimagine; further musicological research promises to yield a more holistic understanding of historical performance practices and the interaction of music and spoken drama in these plays.

Sources with musical notation

As of this writing, the only early modern Greek sources known to contain musical notation are books of liturgical chant. The Jesuit collections in Athens and Tinos conserve many antiphoners and liturgical books dating from the sixteenth to the eighteenth century, most of which are printed editions, principally from Venetian presses.[75] These sources also include many hymns and processional songs, in *Frangochiotika* and in Greek, that are designated as "chants" even though the music is missing, which is fairly predictable, since this music did not require notation in order to be sung.

From the island of Tinos, we are fortunate to have a corpus of local melodies that are still sung today (a preliminary inventory of which has recently been published).[76] They witness extensive parody and paraphrase of the sort that commonly occurs when hymns are sung to pre-existing melodies. A sung tradition that combines the legacies of both Byzantine and Gregorian chant persists as well, in addition to which it is possible to find examples of Italian melodies that were imported to Tinos by Capuchin Franciscan monks, as well as French music brought by Lazarist monks from Paris, whose books were translated into Greek. All this creates a unique mix of Byzantine and Latin elements that vary according to the origins, training, and personal trajectories of the various missionaries.

More recently, I have had the good fortune to discover several interesting musical sources in the archives of the Catholic archbishopric, at Xinara on Tinos island. This archive holds a very significant collection of liturgical books as well as pedagogical manuals and philosophical, historical, and literary texts that come from Catholic parishes all around the island. Important as it is, the materials have not yet been thoroughly cataloged; they can be difficult to access, and preservation is uneven.[77] Among the printed liturgical books, I discovered manuscripts that attest to practices of improvising polyphony in a sort of two-part *falsobordone*. For example, a manuscript choirbook of plainsong masses, mostly monophonic, contains some two-voice settings as well (see figure 13). The bass part is on the left-hand side of the opening and the tenor part on the right: while the two parts generally move in parallel motion, principally in thirds, some remarkable features break the regularity of parallel intervals (such as the chromaticism in the middle of the second line of the tenor part). We can also see the initials of the anonymous copyist ("A.B.Γ"), and the phrase indicating the end of the manuscript in Greek: "Τῳ Θεῳ Δόξα Τέλος" ("In the Glory of God, The End"). The provenance of the manuscript and use of the Greek alphabet testifies to that fact that the copyist must have been Greek, which suggests that local musicians appropriated Roman Catholic plainsong, sang it in *falsobordone*, and sometimes transcribed this practice as well. Although several textual sources in the archives of the Catholic archbishopric of Tinos attest to the coexistence of Byzantine Greek, vernacular Greek, and Latin readings and prayers—which witnesses the syncretism of Catholic and Orthodox traditions—none of the rare written music sources explicitly transmit Byzantine musical traditions. More research is required and at a larger scale that includes written musical sources of the Orthodox communities of the island.

Conclusion: Ancients, Moderns, and "Others"

As we have seen, the ancient history and cultural fluidity of the Greek area have characterized its historiographic physiognomy for centuries: the area was perceived by early modern travelers and commentators through the prism of its classical heritage, both in that present and in the trajectory it established toward the "modern" futures imagined by Catholic reformers and all those who espoused a secular and binary conception of time opposing Ancients to Moderns. Thus, the reception of Greece was "contaminated" in an entirely unique way by interest in antiquity.[78] This Renaissance historicism was counterbalanced by the pragmatism of missionaries in the field and their empirical management of the realities particular to the time and places of their efforts to convert non-believers and heretics. In other words, there is an awareness, for Western commentators, of antiquity and the legacies of classical Greek civilization that offsets the sense of alterity: what is going on now, in these same lands, may be an echo of ancient Greece.

These tensions frame the chapter on music in Charles Perrault's *Parallèle des Anciens et des Modernes*, a scholarly project that championed the cause of the Moderns and is characteristic of that Querelle as a whole. One of the paradoxes of music for participants in the debate was the absence of ancient sources. Unlike sculpture, architecture, literature, and philosophy, where the heritage of the Ancients was attested by numerous monuments of human creation, musical evidence was scarce and difficult to interpret. At the same time, Platonic and Aristotelian accounts of ancient music attributed exceptional ethic and moral properties to it, bordering on the wondrous, making it difficult to sideline from consideration.

Seeking to establish objective criteria for their comparisons, the Moderns identified polyphony as the central attribute of Modern music that made it different from the monophonic or homophonic music of the Ancients. Polyphony, which was not used in ancient Greece, became an emblem of historical progress and the evolution of musical language, coming to represent a superior form of art. That blunt dichotomy is evident in Perrault: relying on the Moderns' ideal of continuous progress, Perrault asserts that the monophonic music-making practiced by "Orientals," including contemporary Greeks, Turks, and Persians, must be close to that of the Ancients, whereas Western Europeans, who employ polyphony, are the Moderns. In a preview of imperialist

"West and the Rest" oppositions, he lumps together Greeks with Turks and Persians (and elsewhere we can find similar comparisons with the use of monody by the Iroquois):[79] the real point is that polyphony is unique to "a part of Europe." Nevertheless, for Perrault, this difference does not mean, de facto, that the Moderns are superior to the Ancients and those without polyphony; rather, his point of view is subtler:

> L'Abbé. La Musique des Anciens est encore aujourd'huy la Musique de toute la Terre, à la reserve d'une partie de l'Europe. Cela est si vray qu'à Constantinople mesme ils ne connoissent point encore la Musique à plusieurs parties. [...] M$^{r.}$ de Guillerague avoit des Laquais & des Valets de chambre qui joüoient tres-bien du Violon, & qui composoient une bande complette. Lorsqu'ils joüoient quelques-unes de ces belles Ouvertures d'Opera, qui nous ont charmez tant de fois, les Turcs ne pouvoient les souffrir, traittant de charivary le meslange des parties auquel ils ne sont pas accoûtumez. [...] Mais afin que vous ne croyiez pas que je fasse injustice aux Orientaux ny aux Anciens, je vais leur accorder tout ce qu'ils peuvent souhaiter de nous; je vais avoüer que comme ils n'ont cultivé que le chant seul, ils y ont peut-estre rafiné plus que nous: l'oreille des Orientaux s'offense de certains sons peu reguliers, que nous souffrons pour n'y estre pas assez délicats.[80]
>
> [The Abbot. The Music of the Ancients [i.e. monophony] is still today the Music of the whole Earth, except for a part of Europe [which has polyphony]. This is so true that even in Constantinople they are not yet acquainted with music in several parts. [...] Mr. de Guillerague had lackeys and chamber valets that played the violin very well and formed a full band. When they played some beautiful Opera overtures, which have charmed us so many times, the Turks could not endure them, hearing as pandemonium the combination of parts, to which they are not accustomed. [...] But to prevent you from thinking that I am being unfair to the Orientals or the Ancients, I will accord to them all they could wish from us; I will admit that since they have exclusively cultivated solo singing, they have perhaps refined it more than we: the ears of Orientals are offended by some irregular sounds, which we endure because we are not delicate enough.]

Perrault underscores the intrinsic value of this musical alterity: it arises not because musicians of the Levant ignore the learned practice of polyphony (the distinctive signature of the Moderns, used as a measure of the evolution of musical language and thought), nor because monody and melodic heterophony lack subtlety and high virtuosity deserving of attention. Rather, it is a continuation of the Music of the Ancients, a parallel tradition that might be revealing of classical values and therefore worthy of study in its own right. The push-and-pull between progress and historicism and between assimilation and alterity marked the musicological quests of the Latins in Greece as well, for they swiftly abandoned the fantasy of discovering new polyphonic musical sources there, similar, for instance, to Francesco Londariti's polyphonic masses and motets:[81] even if Londariti is rightfully considered by several scholars to be the first Greek composer of Western polyphony, it is also true that his works were not primarily aimed at a Greek public.

Going forward, we must set aside the desire to write Greece into a music history privileging polyphonic composition and instead embrace alternatives: we must open our ears and horizons to a completely different sound environment, mobilizing different kinds of sources, and listening for practices that are not central to the written polyphonic repertoires of the Western European Renaissance and Baroque. Indeed, for modern scholars, studying music in Greece and the Latinate musical practices of the Eastern Mediterranean requires confronting oral, memorized, and improvised musicking, and this in turn requires a methodological turn toward historical ethnomusicology and musical anthropology; recordings and living traditions should be considered as part of this research, since they allow us to think beyond the literalness of texts and recover a broader understanding of the practices that texts might (and might not) have supported in the past. Moreover, even if we discover similar and comparable situations on several of the islands or in a number of the continental cities with a strong Catholic presence, there are too many variables to support a single monolithic or homogeneous history: the Ionian islands, Cyclades and the Archipelago, Crete, Rhodes, and Cyprus are each tremendously different, and the continent—Patras, Monemvasia, Negroponte, Thessalonica, Constantinople, Smyrna—also presents highly local conditions and diverse modes of circulation and influence. Ultimately, we must aggregate microhistories of syncretism and transculturation whose terms and parameters are multiple, in order to comprehend the blurred identities—especially religious—that are so central to Greek history, which was far from uniform and consistently Orthodox. At the same time, language, in its plasticity, in its permeability, remains a vital witness to cultural and religious entanglements. The quarrels over the Greek language in the eighteenth, nineteenth, and twentieth centuries, between supporters of the *Katharevousa* ("purified Greek") and demotic Greek result from the enduring tension between the canons of classical and contemporary practices, whether the Greek language of the seventeenth or that of the twenty-first century. Whether the debate centers on the continuity of language in the Orthodox liturgy and its transformations in practice or the musical practices emanating from oral transmission, the tensions are by now age-old.

Even as the emerging history of these transmissions and transformations stands to challenge vertical and diachronic narratives of "Hellenic" continuity from Classical Greece through Byzantium, another historiography to be reckoned with concerns horizontal relationships with the musical heritage shared by Greece, the Balkans, and Anatolia, which reveal complementary patterns of transmission and exchange. If these commonalities have yet to be fully discovered, it may owe in part to the way identifying shared heritage can provoke antagonisms along ethnic, linguistic, and confessional lines. Consequently, microhistorical research is all the more valuable for the way it short-circuits the latent nationalism of these broader comparativist patterns in order to observe phenomena per se in their context.

Going forward, the history of demotic Greek and its musics stands out as a fruitful and necessary field of investigation. The transcription and charting of concordances among the manuscript sources and other items in the archives, especially the various Italian liturgical books, will likely provide more specific evidence, and this research should be pursued, for even if to date there is no significant proof of polyphonic or *concertante* styles of music-making, the social activities involving an array of musics is amply attested both directly and implicitly. While the monodic liturgical practices are those of the Church of Rome, the proper ceremonies as well as the para-liturgical and devotional practices—even profane in the case of Crete—already allow us to glimpse an alternative sonic and artistic universe, one full of underlying references that in part borrow from Western music and poetry but are also unique. It is a confessional space full of post-Tridentine practices assimilated in syncretic forms, marked in particular by alternative uses of the Greek language and hybrid ritual forms and social practices. In sum, for those who seek to place artistic, confessional, and linguistic mobility at the center of their studies, future musicological research in Grecian lands and islands will amply repay the scholars who undertake it.

Notes

* I would like to express my gratitude to Fr. Sebastian Freris, librarian of the Jesuit library in Athens, and Fr. Markos Foscolos, archivist of the Archdiocese of Tinos and Naxos in Xinara (Tinos island), for their kind welcome, their documentary help, and their availability, and to Prof. Kate van Orden for her stimulating reactions to my work.

1. Robert Saulger or Saugé (Paris, 1637–Naxos, 1709) is mainly known for his *Histoire nouvelle des Ducs et autres Souverains de l'Archipel, avec les descriptions des principales îles, et des choses remarquables qui s'y voient encore aujourd'hui* (Paris, 1698), which has been, for a long time, one of the only sources on the history of the Duchy of Naxos, and the habits, customs, and notable happenings of the time.

2. Since first seeing this book in the early 2000s, I have not been able to relocate it, since the Monastery at Loutra has in the meantime reorganized its small museum and no one has been able to provide leads as to its whereabouts.

3. See the Laboratoire d'excellence research group "Religions et Sociétés dans le Monde Méditerranéen."

4. Several studies examine the geopolitical and cultural issues of this area; for a recent overview of the Ottoman presence in the Mediterranean from the perspective of Western cartographic representations of the Turkish, see Brummett, *Mapping the Ottomans*. On Greek areas in particular, see Davies and Davis, eds., *Between Venice and Istanbul*.

5. On the Jesuits in Greece, see Roussos-Milidonis, *Ιησουίτες στον ελληνικό χώρο (1560–1915)* [*Jesuits in the Greek space (1560–1915)*].

6. Although it concentrates on later periods, see the important study of Valdramidou, "Η Καθολική μουσική παράδοση στην Σύρο και στην Τηνο" ["The tradition of Catholic music on Syros and Tinos"], drawn from her unpublished Masters thesis of 1997.

7. A new project devoted to Cretan Byzantine chant, directed by Flora Kritikou (Athens University) and Vassa Kontouma (EPHE, Paris) is currently in development: "Le Chant Ecclésiastique en Crète vénitienne aux XVIe et XVIIe siècles [ChECret]." It is pathbreaking in its joining of Byzantine musicology with Western medieval musicology, as, unfortunately, these fields rarely communicate.

8. Enderlin, *Archipelagus Turbatus, Oder Deß Schönen Griechen-Lands, verwüstete und Erödete Wasser-Felder*.

9. For a musical assessment of the Ethiopian mission, see Damon-Guillot, "Toucher le cœur des schismatiques. Stratégies sonores et musicales des jésuites en Ethiopie, 1620–1630."

10. On the terms of the Venetian Interdict see Sarpi, *Storia dell'Interdetto*, a text that represents the Venetian point of view in a highly controversial context. It is dated 1607 but was published posthumously. On the stakes of the Interdict see Hermann de Franceschi, "Antijésuitisme, modernité politique et juridictionalisme vénitien."

11. On the results of this rivalry between Venice and Rome in Greece, see Foscolos, "Οι πρώτες εγκαταστάσεις Ιησουϊτών στον ελληνικό χώρο. Προβληματισμοί και εμπόδια" ["The first Jesuit establishments in Greece. Concerns and obstacles]," and Roussos-Milidonis, [*Jesuits in the Greek space*], 74–76.

12. For a generous account of the Latin presence in the Cycladic Islands and its persistence long after they had passed under Ottoman control, see Slot, *Archipelagus turbatus: Les Cyclades entre colonisation latine et occupation ottomane c. 1500–1718*.

13. See Finlay, *Greece under Othoman and Venetian Domination*.

14. See Kohler, "Naissance de l'historiographie grecque moderne," and Herzfeld, *Ours Once More: Folklore, Ideology and the Making of Modern Greece*.

15. See the stimulating essay of Herzfeld, *Anthropology through the Looking-Glass*, and Hamilakis, *The Nation and its Ruins*.

16. On the new perspectives gained from an island-centered approach, see Greene, *A Shared World: Christians and Muslims in the Early Modern Mediterranean*.

17. Fallmerayer, *Geschichte der Halbinsel Morea während des Mittelalters. Teil 1: Untergang der peloponnesischen Hellenen und Wiederbevölkerung des leeren Bodens durch slavische Volksstämme*.

18. "Au reste, pour les empires comme pour les littératures, avant peu peut-être l'Orient est appelé à jouer un rôle dans l'Occident. Déjà la mémorable guerre de Grèce avait fait se retourner tous les peuples de ce côté. Voici maintenant que l'équilibre de l'Europe paraît prêt à se rompre ; le *statu quo* européen, déjà vermoulu et lézardé, craque du côté de Constantinople. Tout le continent penche à l'Orient. Nous verrons de grandes choses. La vieille barbarie asiatique n'est peut-être pas aussi dépourvue d'hommes supérieurs que notre civil-

isation le veut croire." [For empires as well as for literatures, perhaps soon the East is called to play a role in the West. Already the memorable Greek war has turned all peoples to this side. Now the balance of Europe seems ready to break; the European *status quo*, already worm-eaten and fractured, cracks on the side of Constantinople. The whole continent looks to the East. We will see great things. Old Asian barbarism may not be as devoid of superior men as our civilization wants to believe]. Hugo, *Les Orientales*, preface.

19. Concerning the stakes of Hellenism, in France and Germany, for the history of art, see also Passini, *La fabrique de l'art national*.

20. This discursive mechanism is common, and still deployed today by far-right, white supremacist, and other hate groups; the online platform "Pharos: Doing justice to the Classics," documents and responds to appropriations of Greco-Roman antiquity by hate groups (generally by exposing the errors, omissions, and distortions that underpin misleading interpretations of ancient material).

21. See Veloudis, *O Jakob Philipp Fallmerayer*... [*Jakob Philipp Fallmerayer*].

22. Paparrigopoulos, *Ἱστορία τοῦ Ἑλληνικοῦ Ἔθνους* [*History of the Greek nation*]. For an analysis, see Puchner, "Introduction: Imagined Community?" in *Greek Theatre*, 1–12.

23. I borrow this expression from the author and scholar Gazmend Kapllani, whose identity is caught between Albania and Greece; he argues that the late twentieth-century "clash of civilizations" in the Balkans has not been provoked by differences, but rather by the unbearable similarity of "the other."

24. The "Institute of humanist studies," with the support of the Jesuit library in Athens, has produced important studies of Catholicism in early modern Greece; see especially Roussos-Milidonis, [*Jesuits in the Greek space*], and Freris, "Βιβλία Ιησουιτών στα Ελληνικά" ["Books by Jesuits in Greek"].

25. Although we lack any systematic index, travel literature is ample and has been well-studied. See the bibliography of sources compiled by the Centre de Recherche sur la Littérature des Voyages (http://www.crlv.org/). For two useful anthologies on Greece with thematic indexes and mention of music and dance, see Simopoulos, *Ξένοι Ταξιδιώτες στην Ελλάδα* [*Foreign travelers in Greece*], especially volumes A2 (1500–1700) and B1 (1700–1780), and Vingopoulou, *Le monde grec vu par les voyageurs du xvi*[e] *siècle*.

26. Travelers and missionaries such as Robert Saulger, Jean Thévenot, François Richard, or Joseph Pitton de Tournefort all mention the *vrykolakas*.

27. Richard, *Relation de ce qui s'est passé de plus remarquable à Saint-Erini*.

28. Saulger, *Histoire nouvelle des Ducs et autres Souverains de l'Archipel*.

29. Thévenot, *Relation d'un voyage fait au Levant*.

30. Des Barres, *L'estat présent de l'Archipel*.

31. Tournefort, *Relation d'un voyage du Levant*.

32. Spon, *Voyage d'Italie, de Dalmatie, de Grèce et du Levant*.

33. Fleuriau d'Armenonville, *Estat des missions de Grèce*, 225–26.

34. See especially Roussos-Milidonis, *Ιησουίτες στον ελληνικό χώρο (1560–1915)* [*Jesuits in the Greek Area (1560–1915)*].

35. Portier S.J., *Relation de ce qui s'est passé aux Missions Volantes*; edited by Roussos-Milidonis, *Η Τουρκοκρατούμενη "Ελλάδα" μέσα από ανέκδοτα έγγραφα Ιησουιτών* [*Ottoman-Occupied "Greece" through Unpublished Jesuit Documents of the 17th and 18th Centuries: 1. The Greek Archipelago*], 33.

36. Carton I.XXI in the Lazarist Archives of Thessalonica contains about 25 documents and reports concerning Jesuit activities. See Roussos-Milidonis, ibid. 61.

37. See Papaïliaki, *Aspects de la mission catholique auprès des Grecs de l'Empire ottoman*.

38. Saulger, *Histoire nouvelle des Ducs et autres Souverains de l'Archipel*, 386–88.

39. Ibid., 385–86.

40. Initially this term referred to crusaders, and then, by extension, the Catholics.

41. Mansel, *Levant: Splendour and Catastrophe on the Mediterranean*, 166.

42. Similarly, in some regions of Central Anatolia, especially the provinces of Karaman and Cappadocia, Turkish-speaking Greek-Orthodox Christians (the "Karamanlides") used "Karamanlidika," a form of Turkish written in the Greek alphabet. The first known printed example is a translation in Turkish of a Greek text by the Patriarch Gennadius II Scolarios, included in a 1584 edition by Martin Cursius: *Turcograeciae Libri Octo: Quibus Graecorum Status Sub Imperio Turcico, in Politia et Ecclesia*. Like *Frangolevantinika* in the nineteenth century and up to 1922, editions in *Karamanlidika* multiplied and presented an astonishing variety of content, including grammars, Turkish-Greek dictionaries, historical and literary works, and even ancient authors (see Evangelia Balta, *Karamanlidika Legacies*).

43. On the Venetian *greghesco*, see Coutelle, *Le Greghesco*.

44. Amántos, *Τα γράμματα εις την Χίον κατά την Τουρκοκρατίαν* [*Letters in Chios island from during Ottoman occupation*], 7.

45. Ledesma, *Διδασκαλία Χριστιανική / Didaskalia christianiki*. This catechism, originally written in Spanish, was translated into several languages, including vernacular Greek. In this edition, the Greek text is presented in two versions: with Greek characters and transliterated using the Latin alphabet. See Freris, "Βιβλία Ιησουιτών στα Ελληνικά" ["Books by Jesuits in Greek"], 70–71.

46. Ibid., 51–144.

47. For other examples of Greek in the Latin liturgy see Wanek, "Missa graeca: Mythen und Fakten um griechische Gesänge in westlichen Handschriften," and Memelsdorff, "Cantus grecus. Greek liturgy *more latinorum*."

48. See Dalleggio, "Bibliographie analytique d'ouvrages en grec imprimés avec des caractères latins," 389.

49. Papaïliaki-Gamelon, "Livres de catéchismes et pratiques scolaires des missionnaires français en Grèce au XVIIe siècle," 146

50. Ibid.

51. See Pizzorusso, "Tra cultura e missione: la Congregazione *de Propaganda Fide* et le scuole di lingua araba nel XVII secolo."

52. See *Missions d'évangélisation et circulation des savoirs, XVIe-XVIIIe siècles*.

53. Markos Foscolos, archivist of the Archdiocese of Tinos and Naxos in Xinara, is preparing a critical edition of this manuscript.

54. "Preghiera de l'aqua. O Kirie mu eftexame," *Canti ed Inni in Greco volgare*, ms., Tinos, pp. 104–6. Litanies for rain are quite common in the Archipelago, since water can be scarce, even today. Travelogues often mention these processions; Jean de Thévenot, in his chapter on the island of Chios, explains that every Spring the different communities each process in a set order: "the Turks first, then the Greeks, then the Latins, then the Jews." Thévenot notes that "les Turcs se mettent fort peu en peine lesquelles de toutes ces prieres sont exaucées, pourveu qu'ils ayent ce qu'ils demandent" [the Turks are very little troubled about which of all these prayers will be answered, provided they get what they ask for]. Thévenot, *Relation d'un voyage fait au Levant*, 186.

55. Florakis, *Οικόσημα Τήνου* [*Coats of Arms of Tinos Island*].

56. Candia is the medieval name of Heraklion, the capital of Crete.

57. See Geanakoplos, "The Cretan Role in the Transmission of Greco-Byzantine Culture to Western Europe via Venice."

58. On Londariti, see especially Panagiotakes, *Φραγκίσκος Λεονταρίτης* [*Franghiskos Leontaritis*].

59. Very little is known about Francesco de Laudis; for a critical edition of music by Londariti and de Laudis, see Bamichas, *Δυτική μουσική στην βενετοκρατούμενη Ελλάδα. Κρήτη (Candia)* [*Western Music in Venetian Greece. Crete (Candia)*].

60. The Ionian islands (mainly Corfu, Zante, Cephalonia), were also under Venetian rule: they were situated closer to Italy and enjoyed a more stable geopolitical environment. Corfu is the only Greek island that never fell under Ottoman rule; Crete fell in 1669, after the twenty-year siege of Candia (1648–1669), which ended the former poetic, theatrical, and artistic movements on the island.

61. On the educational system in Crete, see Panagiotakes, *El Greco: The Cretan Years*, 67–70, and idem, "Η παιδεία κατά τη Βενετοκρατία" ["Education during the Venetian rule"].

62. See especially Panagiotakes, "Μαρτυρίες για τη μουσική στην Κρήτη κατά τη Βενετοκρατία" ["Testimonies about music in Crete during the Venetian occupation"] and Maltezou, *Venetiae quasi alterum Byzantium. Όψεις της ιστορίας του Βενετοκρατούμενου Ελληνισμού: Αρχειακά τεκμήρια* [*Venetiae quasi alterum Byzantium. Aspects of the history of Venetian-occupied Hellenic space: Archival sources*].

63. Archivio di Stato di Venezia, Notai di Candia, b. 167 (Demetrio Marà), fols. 76–76v, edited by Panagiotakes, see "Μαρτυρίες για τη μουσική στην Κρήτη κατά τη Βενετοκρατία" ["Testimonies about music in Crete during the Venetian occupation"], 74–5.

64. On Petros Philargis see Geanakoplos, *Byzantine East and Latin West*.

65. Panagiotakes, "Η παιδεία κατά τη Βενετοκρατία" ["Education during the Venetian rule"], 172–75.

66. Vitti, Mario, "Η ακμή της Κρητικής Λογοτεχνίας καί το Ευρωπαϊκό Σύνολο (ΙΣΤ'-ΙΖ' αι.)" ["The heyday of Cretan Literature and the European Ensemble (16th-17th centuries)"].

67. On Cretan academies see Panagiotakes, "Έρευναι εν Βενετία. ΙΙ. Περί της Ακαδημίας του Χάνδακος και

της πνευματικής ζωής εν Κρήτη κατά τον 16ον και 17ον αιώνα" ["Researches in Venice, II: About the Academy of Candia and the intellectual life in Crete during the 16th and 17th centuries"].

68. The bibliographic overview provided by Walter Puchner is state-of-the-art; see Puchner, *Greek Theatre*, 152–72.

69. A *mantinada* (pl. *mantinades*) is a pair of fifteen-syllable rhymed verses, often improvised and sung; this art of musical declamation has been very popular in Crete for centuries (an equivalent would be verse in *ottava rima*, employed by Boccaccio and still popular in Tuscany as a genre of improvised lyric).

70. On the history of Cretan theater see Puchner, *Greek Theatre*, 112–72.

71. The publication of *Literature and Society in Renaissance Crete*, ed. Holton, brought Cretan theater to the attention of international academic circles. This European perspective is underlined by Jean-Laurent Savoye in his critical edition and French translation of *Erophili* (*Érophili de Georges Chortatsis; tragédie crétoire de la Renaissance*), as well as by Puchner, *Greek Theatre*, 153.

72. Puchner, *Greek Theatre*, 196.

73. It is important to recall that practically all Jesuit theatrical music from such a well-documented place as seventeenth-century Paris is lost as well (with the exception of the manuscript score of *David et Jonathas* by Marc-Antoine Charpentier and some manuscript dance suites collected by Philidor).

74. On *The Tragedy of St. Demetrius*, see Varzelioti and Puchner, "Αναστηλώνοντας μια θεατρική παράσταση" ["Restituting a Theater play"].

75. This assessment is incomplete, as I have not yet been able to access all of the Jesuit archives in Greece and, as far as I know, the older holdings have not yet been completely cataloged.

76. Valdramidou, "Η Καθολική μουσική παράδοση στη Σύρο και στην Τήνο" ["The Catholic music tradition in Syros and Tinos"].

77. Many have been collected by Markos Foscolos, a Catholic priest and historian who is native to Tinos and has been of invaluable assistance to my research.

78. See Irving, "Ancient Greeks, World Music, and Early Modern Constructions of Western European Identity."

79. Claude Perrault, "De la musique des Anciens", 359.

80. Charles Perrault, *Parallèle des Anciens et des Modernes*, 265–68.

81. Panagiotakes, *Φραγκίσκος Λεονταρίτης* [*Franghiskos Leontaritis*].

Bibliography

Primary Sources

Manuscript

Canti ed Inni in Greco volgare, ms., Archives of the Catholic archbishopric of Tinos.

[Plainsong Masses]. Archives of the Catholic archbishopric of Tinos, Ms. 4181/19 IX.203.

Portier, Jacques Xavier, S.J. *Relation de ce qui s'est passé aux Missions Volantes depuis le 23 juillet 1700 jusqu'au 18 janvier 1701* [March, 1701]. Rome, Archivum Romanum Societatis Jesu, Ms. Gallia 105, fols. 353–420.

Printed

Chortatsis, Georgios. *Τραγωδία ονομαζόμενη Ερωφίλη* [*Tragedy named Erophili*]. Venice: Antonios Ioulianos, 1637; *Érophili de Georges Chortatsis; tragédie crétoire de la Renaissance*, ed. Jean-Laurent Savoye. Paris: Honoré Champion, 2013.

Crusius, Martin. *Turcograeciae Libri Octo: Quibus Graecorum Status Sub Imperio Turcico, in Politia et Ecclesia, Oeconomia et Scholis*. Basel: Leonardus Ostenius, Sebastianus Henricpetrus, 1584.

Des Barres, Antoine. *L'estat présent de l'Archipel*. Paris: Claude Barbin, 1678.

[Enderlin, Jacob]. *Archipelagus Turbatus, Oder Deß Schönen Griechen-Lands, verwüstete und Erödete Wasser-Felder*. Augsburg, Jacob Enderlin, 1686.

Fleuriau d'Armenonville, Thomas-Charles. *Estat des missions de Grèce présenté à nosseigneurs les archevesques*. Paris: Antoine Lambin, 1695.

Hugo, Victor. *Les Orientales*. Paris: J. Hetzel, 1829.

Ledesma, Jacobus. *Διδασκαλία Χριστιανική. Εις την οποίαν ο διδάσκαλος [sic] ερωτά, και ο μαθητής απηλογάται [...] / Didaskalia christianiki, is tin opian o Didaskalos erota, che o mathitis apilogate [...]*. Roma: Luigi Zannetti, 1595.

Perrault, Charles. *Parallèle des Anciens et des Modernes, où il est traité de l'Astronomie, de la Géographie, de la Navigation, de la Guerre, de la Philosophie, de la Musique, de la Médecine, etc. Cinquième et dernier Dialogue*. Paris: Jean-Baptiste Coignard, 1697.

Perrault, Claude. "De la Musique des Anciens." In *Essais de physique*. Vol. 2. Pp. 335–402. Paris: Jean-Baptiste Coignard, 1680.

Richard, François. *Relation de ce qui s'est passé de plus remarquable à Saint-Erini*. Paris: Sébastien Cramoisy, 1657.

Ritus celebrandi matrimonium sacramentum juxta consuetudinem ecclesiae Tenensis. Galata Constantinopoleos: typis S. Benedicti, 1849.

Sarpi, Paolo. *Istoria dell'Interdetto* [Venice, 1606]. Modern edition in *Istoria dell'Interdetto e altri scritti editi ed inediti*, eds. M. D. Busnelli and G. Gambarin. 3 vols. Bari: Laterza e figli, 1940.

Saulger, Robert. *Histoire nouvelle des Ducs et autres Souverains de l'Archipel*. Paris: Etienne Michallet, 1698.

Spon, Jacob. *Voyage d'Italie, de Dalmatie, de Grèce et du Levant*. Lyon: Antoine Cellier, 1678.

Thévenot, Jean de. *Relation d'un voyage fait au Levant*. Paris: Louis Bilaine, 1664.

Tournefort, Joseph Pitton de. *Relation d'un voyage du Levant, fait par ordre du Roy*. 2 vols. Paris: Imprimerie Royale, 1717.

Secondary Sources

Amántos, Constantin. *Τα γράμματα εις την Χίον κατά την Τουρκοκρατίαν 1566–1822 (Σχολεία και λόγιοι)* [*Letters in Chios island from during the Ottoman Occupation, 1566–1822 (Schools and Scholars)*]. Piraeus: Pherousès, 1946.

Balta, Evangelia ed. *Karamanlidika Legacies*. Istanbul: The Isis Press, 2018.

Bamichas, Pyrros. *Δυτική μουσική στην βενετοκρατούμενη Ελλάδα. Κρήτη (Candia). Francesco Londariti (c 1518–1572)—Francesco de Laudis (?): Opera omnia* [*Western Music in Venetian Greece. Crete (Candia). Francesco Londariti (c 1518–1572)—Francesco de Laudis (?): Opera omnia*]. Athens: Panas Music/Papagrigoriou-Nakas, 2015.

Brummett, Palmira. *Mapping the Ottomans: Sovereignty, Territory, and Identity in the Early Modern Mediterranean*. Cambridge: Cambridge University Press, 2015.

Castelnau-l'Estoile, Charlotte de, Marie-Lucie Copete, Aliocha Maldavsky, and Ines G. Županov, eds. *Missions d'évangélisation et circulation des savoirs, XVIe-XVIIIe siècles*. Madrid: Casa de Velázquez, 2011.

Centre de Recherche sur la Littérature des Voyages. http://www.crlv.org, accessed March 29, 2020.

"Le Chant Ecclésiastique en Crète vénitienne aux XVIe et XVIIe siècles [ChECret]: transferts culturels et façonnement des identités dans l'espace méditerranéen à l'époque moderne," dir. Flora Kritikou and Vassa Kontouma. https://www.efa.gr/index.php/en/recherche/programmes-de-recherche/chant-ecclesiastique, accessed September 9, 2019.

Coutelle, Louis. *Le Greghesco. Réexamen des éléments néo-grecs des textes comiques vénitiens du XVIe siècle*. Thessalonica: Society of Macedonian Studies, 1971.

Dalègre, Joëlle. *Venise en Crète, Civitas venetiarum apud Levantem*. Paris: Presses de l'Inalco, 2019.

Dalleggio, Eugène. "Bibliographie analytique d'ouvrages en grec imprimés avec des caractères latins." *Μικρασιατικά χρονικά* [*Chronicles of Asia Minor*] 9 (1961): 385–499.

Damon-Guillot, Anne. "Toucher le cœur des schismatiques. Stratégies sonores et musicales des jésuites en Ethiopie, 1620–1630." *Le Jardin de Musique—Revue de l'association Musique ancienne en Sorbonne* 6 (2009): 65–99.

Davies, Siriol, and Jack Davis, eds. *Between Venice and Istanbul: Colonial Landscapes in Early Modern Greece*. Athens: American School of Classical Studies at Athens, 2007.

De Franceschi, Sylvio Hermann. "Antijésuitisme, modernité politique et juridictionalisme vénitien." In *Les Antijésuites. Discours, figures et lieux de l'antijésuitisme à l'époque moderne*, ed. Pierre-Antoine Fabre and Catherine Maire. Pp. 265–90. Rennes: Presses universitaires de Rennes, 2010.

Fallmerayer, Jakob Philipp. *Geschichte der Halbinsel Morea während des Mittelalters. Teil 1: Untergang der peloponnesischen Hellenen und Wiederbevölkerung des leeren Bodens durch slavische Volksstämme*. Stuttgart and Tübingen: J.G. Cotta'schen Buchhandlun, 1830.

Finlay, George. *Greece under Othoman and Venetian Domination*. Edinburgh and London: William Blackwood and Sons, 1854.

Florakis, Alekos E. *Οικόσημα Τήνου* [*Coats of Arms of Tinos Island*]. Athens: Erinni, 2001.

Foscolos, Markos. "Οι πρώτες εγκαταστάσεις Ιησουϊτών στον ελληνικό χώρο. Προβληματισμοί και εμπόδια" ["The first Jesuit establishments in Greece. Concerns and obstacles"]. *Σύγχρονα βήματα* [*Modern steps*] 77 (1991): 29–60.

Freris, Sebastian. "Βιβλία Ιησουιτών στα Ελληνικά" ["Books by Jesuits in Greek: Contribution to the Documentation of Greek Jesuit Bibliography"]. *Anno Domini* 4 (2015): 51–144.

Geanakoplos, Deno John. *Greek Scholars in Venice: Studies in the Dissemination of Greek Learning from Byzantium to Western Europe*. Cambridge, MA: Harvard University Press, 1962.

Geanakoplos, Deno John. *Byzantine East and Latin West: Two Worlds of Christendom in the Middle Ages and the Renaissance*. New York: Barnes and Noble, 1966.

Greene, Molly. *A Shared World: Christians and Muslims in the Early Modern Mediterranean*. Princeton: Princeton University Press, 2000.

Hamilakis, Yannis. *The Nation and its Ruins: Antiquity, Archaelogy, and National Imagination in Greece*. Oxford: Oxford University Press, 2007.

Herzfeld, Michael. *Ours Once More: Folklore, Ideology and the Making of Modern Greece*. Austin: University of Texas Press, 1982.

Herzfeld, Michael. *Anthropology through the Looking-Glass: Critical Ethnography in the Margins of Europe*. Cambridge and New York: Cambridge University Press, 1987.

Holton, David, ed. *Literature and Society in Renaissance Crete*, Cambridge: Cambridge University Press, 1991.

Irving, David R. M. "Ancient Greeks, World Music, and Early Modern Constructions of Western European Identity." In *Studies on a Global History of Music: A Balzan Musicology Project*, ed. Reinhard Strohm. Pp. 21–41. Abingdon, Oxon, and New York: Routledge, 2018.

Kohler, Denis. "Naissance de l'historiographie grecque moderne." In *Philologiques I, Contribution à l'histoire des disciplines littéraires en France et en Allemagne au XIXe siècle*, ed. Michel Espagne and Michael Werner. Pp. 279–309. Paris: Éditions de la Maison des Sciences de l'Homme, 1990.

Maltezou, Chrysa A., ed. *Venetiae quasi alterum Byzantium. Όψεις της ιστορίας του Βενετοκρατούμενου Ελληνισμού: Αρχειακά τεκμήρια* [*Venetiae quasi alterum Byzantium. Aspects of the history of Venetian-occupied Hellenic space: Archival sources*]. Athens: Institute of Hellenic Culture, 1993.

Mansel, Philip. *Levant: Splendour and Catastrophe on the Mediterranean*. New Haven: Yale University Press, 2010.

McKee, Sally. *Uncommon Dominion: Venetian Crete and the Myth of Ethnic Purity*. Philadelphia: University of Pennsylvania Press, 2000.

Memelsdorff, Pedro, "Cantus grecus. Greek liturgy *more latinorum* in the Codex Faenza 117." In *Mondo latino e civiltà bizantina: Musica, arte e cultura nei codici del '400*, ed. Antonio Lovato and Dilva Princivalli. Pp. 203–24. Padua: CLEUP editrice, 2014.

Panagiotakes, Nikolaos. "Έρευναι εν Βενετία. ΙΙ. Περί της Ακαδημίας του Χάνδακος και της πνευματικής ζωής εν Κρήτη κατά τον 16[ον] και 17[ον] αιώνα" ["Researches in Venice, II: About the Academy of Candia and intellectual life in Crete during the 16th and 17th centuries"]. *Θησαυρίσματα* [*Treasurings*] 5 (1968): 58–105.

Panagiotakes, Nikolaos. "Η παιδεία κατά τη Βενετοκρατία" ["Education during the Venetian rule"]. In *Κρήτη: ιστορία και πολιτισμός* [*Crete: History and Civilization*], ed. N. Panagiotakes. 2 vols. Heraklion: Editions of the Local Union of Cities and Villages of Crete, 1988.

Panagiotakes, Nikolaos. *Φραγκίσκος Λεονταρίτης. Κρητικός μουσικοσυνθέτης του δέκατου έκτου αιώνα. Μαρτυρίες για τη ζωή και το έργο του* [*Franghiskos Leontaritis. Cretan composer of the sixteenth century. Evidence of his life and works*]. Venice: Library of the Hellenic Institute of Byzantine and Post-Byzantine Studies, 1990.

Panagiotakes, Nikolaos. "Μαρτυρίες για τη μουσική στην Κρήτη κατά τη Βενετοκρατία" ["Testimonies about music in Crete during the Venetian occupation"]. *Θησαυρίσματα* [*Treasurings*] 20 (1990): 9–169.

Panagiotakes, Nikolaos. *El Greco: The Cretan Years*. London and Surrey: Centre for Hellenic Studies, King's College London and Routledge, 2009.

Papaïliaki Niki. "Aspects de la mission catholique auprès des Grecs de l'Empire ottoman: archives grecques inédites des Capucins de Paris (XVIIe-XVIIIe siècles)." PhD thesis. Paris: EPHE, 2009.

Papaïliaki-Gamelon, Niki. "Livres de catéchismes et pratiques scolaires des missionnaires français en Grèce au XVIIe siècle." In *Pédagogies missionnaires: Traduire, Transmettre, Transculturer*, ed. Hugues Didier and Madalena Larcher. Pp. 137–46. Paris: Karthala, 2012.

Paparrigopoulos, Constantin. *Ἱστορία τοῦ Ἑλληνικοῦ Ἔθνους* [*History of the Greek nation*]. Athens: S. Paulidou, 1860–1874.

Passini, Michela. *La fabrique de l'art national: Le nationalisme et les origines de l'histoire de l'art en France et en Allemagne (1870–1933)*. Paris: Éditions de la Maison des Sciences de l'Homme, 2012.

"Pharos: Doing justice to the Classics," hosted by the Department of Greek and Roman Studies at Vassar College. http://pages.vassar.edu/pharos/, accessed October 10, 2019.

Pizzorusso, Giovanni. "Tra cultura e missione: la Congregazione *de Propaganda Fide* et le scuole di lingua araba nel XVII secolo." In *Rome et la science moderne: Entre Renaissance et Lumières*, ed. Antonella Romano. Pp. 121–52. Rome: Publications de l'École française de Rome, 2008.

Puchner, Walter. "Jesuit Theatre on the Islands of the Aegean Sea." *Journal of Modern Greek Studies* 21 (2003): 207–22.

Puchner, Walter. "The Forgotten Fiancée: From the Italian Renaissance Novella to Modern Greek Fairy Tales." *Fabula* 51 (2010): 201–16.

Puchner, Walter. *Greek Theatre between Antiquity and Independence: A History of Reinvention from the Third Century BC to 1830*. Cambridge: Cambridge University Press, 2017.

Laboratoire d'excellence RESMED: Religions et Sociétés dans le Monde Méditerranéen, Sorbonne Université http://www.labex-resmed.fr, accessed March 29, 2020.

Roussos-Milidonis, Markos. *Ιησουίτες στον ελληνικό χώρο (1560–1915)* [*Jesuits in the Greek Area (1560–1915)*]. Athens: KEO Editions, 1991.

Roussos-Milidonis, Markos. *Η Τουρκοκρατούμενη "Ελλάδα" μέσα από ανέκδοτα έγγραφα Ιησουιτών του 17ου και 18ου αιώνα: 1. Το Ελληνικό Αρχιπέλαγος* [*Ottoman-Occupied "Greece" Through Unpublished Jesuit Documents of the 17th and 18th Centuries: 1. The Greek Archipelago*]. Athens: KEO Editions, 2002.

Simopoulos, Kyriakos. *Ξένοι Ταξιδιώτες στην Ελλάδα* [*Foreign Travelers in Greece*]. 5 vols. Athens: Stachy, 1970–1976.

Slot, B. J. *Archipelagus turbatus: Les Cyclades entre colonisation latine et occupation ottomane c. 1500–1718*. 2 vols. Leiden: Nederlands Instituut voor het Nabije Oosten, 1982.

Valdramidou, Eleni. "Η Καθολική μουσική παράδοση στη Σύρο και στην Τήνο" ["The Tradition of Catholic Music on Syros and Tinos"]. *Analecta Catholica* 2 (2013): 103–59.

Varzelioti, Gogo, and Walter Puchner. "Αναστηλώνοντας μια θεατρική παράσταση: η παράσταση του 'Αγίου Δημητρίου' στις 29 Δεκεμβρίου 1723 στη Νάξο και οι συντελεστές της" ["Restituting a Theater Play: The Performance of Saint Demetrius on 29 December 1723 on Naxos and Its Contributors"]. *Παράβασις* [*Parabasis*] 3 (2000): 123–66.

Veloudis, Giorgos. *Ο Jakob Philipp Fallmerayer και η Γένεση του Ελληνικού Ιστορισμού* [*Jakob Philipp Fallmerayer and the Birth of the Greek Historicism*]. Athens: Mnimon, 1982.

Vingopoulou, Ioli. *Le monde grec vu par les voyageurs du xvi*e *siècle*. Athens: Institut de Recherches Néohelléniques, 2004.

Vitti, Mario. "Ή ακμή της Κρητικής Λογοτεχνίας καί το Ευρωπαϊκό Σύνολο (ΙΣΤ'-ΙΖ' αι.)" ["The heyday of Cretan Literature and the European Ensemble (16th-17th centuries)"]. In *Πεπραγμένα του Γ' Διεθνούς Κρητολογικού Συνεδρίου* [*Proceedings of the 3rd International Cretological Congress*]. Vol. 2. Pp. 371–77. Athens: [Ministry of Culture and Sciences], 1974.

Wanek, Nina Maria. "Missa graeca: Mythen und Fakten um griechische Gesänge in westlichen Handschriften." In *Menschen, Bilder, Sprache, Dinge. Wege der Kommunikation zwischen Byzanz und dem Westen 2: Menschen und Worte*, ed. F. Daim, Chr. Gastgeber, D. Heher and C. Rapp. Pp. 113–26. Mainz: Schnell & Steiner, 2018.

Layers of Song: Migrations, Identities, and Synagogue Music in Corfu, Greece

Francesco Spagnolo

Avec ma gueule de métèque
De Juif errant, de pâtre grec
De voleur et de vagabond ...
Georges Moustaki (aka, Giuseppe Mustacchi,
Alexandria, Egypt, 1934–Nice, France, 2013), *Le métèque* (1969)[1]

Jews of varied geographical origins from across the Mediterranean diaspora settled on the island of Corfu beginning in the thirteenth century, living there without interruption until the Second World War. Over time, these immigrants created a small yet highly diverse community composed of Greek, Italian, Sephardic, and (to a lesser extent) Ashkenazi groups, each characterized by distinct cultural and ritual identities. With increasing frequency, peaking in the nineteenth century, Corfuan Jews also left the island seeking trade opportunities and better living conditions elsewhere, settling across the Mediterranean, and in Europe and the United States. By maintaining family and communal ties with Corfu, and at times returning to live there, they became the protagonists of a numerically small but culturally significant Corfuan "micro-diaspora" that continues to the present day beyond Corfu itself.[2]

The Jewish migratory waves that reached Corfu over time spawned the establishment of several religious congregations, each following different ritual customs, practiced at times in distinct synagogue buildings, as well as in syncretic ritual settings. In Jewish liturgical terms, the community thus featured several main constituencies, each inspired by a different multi-layered "ritual identity." An older Greek community, which followed the ancient *romaniyoti* ritual of Greece and Byzantium, was joined by refugees from Apulia (Puglia), in Southern Italy, who followed the ancient Italian (*italiyani*) rite, and who had reached Corfu after the expulsion from Spain and Spanish-ruled Southern Italy. Members of the cosmopolitan Sephardic mercantile elites of Venice, Livorno, Salonica (Thessalonica) and beyond, whose ritual affiliations were

Western-Sephardic, or "Spanish-Portuguese," also settled on the island, along with Ashkenazi merchants. The languages spoken in the community included Greek, Judeo-Apulian (or *pugliso*),[3] local variants of the Venetian dialect (or *corfioto*) and, eventually, modern Italian. Over time, the different constituencies congregated in four distinct synagogues, following Greek, Apulian, Italian, and Spanish rites. Only one synagogue building remains on the island today.

The multi-layered, diasporic dimensions displayed by these Jewish groups are traceable in the various strains of liturgical and para-liturgical music, transmitted over centuries by oral tradition. A principal source of information documenting the liturgical repertoires sung by Corfu's Jews are a poignant series of archival field recordings collected in the twentieth century, following the quasi-total annihilation of the community during the Holocaust. These were made in Corfu itself, in Italy, and in Israel between 1956 and 1972, by Israeli musicologists Leo Levi (1912–1982) and Amnon Shiloah (1928–2014), and are preserved in the National Sound Archives of the National Library of Israel in Jerusalem.[4] Additional information can be gleaned from an array of written sources, ranging from community records (in Venetian, Italian, and Hebrew), liturgical manuscripts (in Hebrew), and news items that appeared in the local Jewish press, which was established in the nineteenth century by Italian rabbinic authorities.[5] Our ability to reconstruct aspects of Corfu's Jewish liturgical music yields a broader understanding of the cultural networks that characterize the history of this community, beyond the realms of either music or liturgy themselves. As indicated by Edwin Seroussi, the "performance of prayers in the synagogue has always been a locus for the public display of communal identity, the representation of its aesthetic ideals, and the construction and exposition of its historical memory."[6] Articulated across the annual cycle of Jewish liturgy, texts sung and recited in the synagogue and in Jewish homes reflect the panoply of languages and musical cultures that have intersected on the island of Corfu for several centuries. In turn, the study of these musical repertoires—which involves the investigation of the interaction of musical and linguistic elements—prompts a reconsideration of Jewish diasporic cultures, well beyond Corfu itself.

Written sources that document the Jewish liturgies of Corfu include manuscript prayer books and community records, as well as the records of a rabbinic *querelle* on liturgical music dating from the mid-eighteenth century, recorded in manuscript and print (most manuscript sources are kept in the libraries of Columbia University and the Jewish Theological Seminary). Ethnographic sources on the rituals of Corfu include literary descriptions found in the nineteenth-century Jewish press published locally in Italian, as well as the aforementioned archival field recordings. A combined analysis of these sources that concentrates on the distinctive linguistic and musical features of the liturgy reveals the intricate cultural relations and exchanges that occurred among these Jewish groups and the surrounding cultures, both established and transient. Such analysis also suggests that liturgy itself eventually became a forum in which differences could be negotiated and cultural identity could shift, in order to accommodate the evolving needs of the community, as it faced a variety of challenges, namely, the need to establish a unified political representation vis-à-vis local political authorities, the relationship with other communities across the Jewish diaspora, and the issues of mobility and displacement that characterized the fate of the community as it confronted modernity.

Even if it is focused on a place that is territorially Greek, research into the music and rituals of the Jewish communities in Corfu constitutes, in essence, a chapter of the broader study of the nexus between music and synagogue life among Italian Jews from the early modern period to the present, and must thus be approached as a transregional and transnational cultural phenomenon. Both Leo Levi, whose field recordings documented the state of Jewish liturgical music among the Jews of Corfu in the 1950s, and Israel Adler (1925–2009), whose research unearthed precious literary sources on a musico-liturgical disputation within the Jewish community of Corfu in the middle of the eighteenth century,[7] addressed Corfu in conjunction with Italian musical activities. Many of the sources documenting Corfu's liturgical traditions are indeed intimately connected with Italian Jews, while, at the same time, they also display distinctively cosmopolitan traits that connect them to the global dimensions of the Jewish diaspora. Such traits lay at the intersection of the history of the geographic origins of the members of the Corfu community with the multi-layered dimensions of their local ritual identities, as expressed in the realm of liturgical music.

The broad diasporic connections that characterize the Jewish community of Corfu largely result from the peculiar history of its formation.[8] In 1147, Corfu was visited by the Jewish traveler, Benjamin of Tudela (1130–1173), who in his travelogue mentioned having met only one Jewish resident. The Venetian Republic subsequently ruled the island uninterruptedly from 1386 to 1797. During the initial phase of the Venetian rule, the community comprised mostly Greek (*romaniyoti*) and Venetian (Italian and Sephardic) Jews. In the earlier decades of the sixteenth century, a new Jewish group migrated to Corfu from Puglia, following their expulsion from the Kingdom of Naples. This migration was an after-effect of the mass expulsion of Jews from Catholic Spain in 1492. The latter, although it is broadly defined as a phenomenon that impacted the history of "Sephardic" Jews, greatly disrupted Jewish life across the Italian peninsula as well. In the aftermath of the Napoleonic wars, Corfu was ruled by France (1797–1799, and 1805–1815). After the Congress of Vienna (1815), the island became a British protectorate, until it was annexed to Greece in 1864. In 1855, when the British financier and philanthropist Moses Montefiore (1784–1885) visited the island, the community numbered 4,000 people. At its demographic height, in 1863, Corfu's Jewish population reached 6,000 residents, or 9.23 percent of the total population. In the second half of the nineteenth century, the Jewish press of Corfu produced *Cronaca Israelitica* (1861–63), in Greek and Italian; *Mosé* (1878–1885) in Italian; and the Zionist *O Israilitis Khronoghrafos* (1899–1901) in Greek. In the late nineteenth century Corfuan Jews also became the protagonists of a statistically irrelevant but culturally significant diaspora of their own that scattered across the Mediterranean (mainland Greece, Egypt, Palestine, Italy), Europe (France and England), and the United States (especially New York City). Anti-Jewish incidents that occurred under Greek rule—including riots in 1864 and a Blood Libel in 1891—brought survivors to Italy (Ancona, Trieste, and Milan), Manchester (where they were among the founders of the local Spanish and Portuguese synagogue, Sha'are Tefillah, in the early 1870s), and New York City (where a Greek congregation, Kehila Kedosha Janina, established in the 1920s on the Lower East Side of Manhattan, included the Corfuan arrivals). Around 1,800 Jews were deported to Auschwitz in 1944, leaving less than two hundred survivors. Many of the remaining residents moved to Israel, where most of the ethnographic documentation concerning their musical rituals was collected and investigated beginning in the 1960s.[9] Of the four synagogues built on the island, only one remained after the Second World War.

The diasporic character of the community was further enhanced by the varied origins of its rabbinic leaders. Throughout the history of the community, Sephardic rabbis from across the Mediterranean were a constant presence: Yehudah Bibas (ca. 1789–1852, of Gibraltar or Morocco) was Rabbi in Corfu between 1831 and 1852; and Israel Mosheh Hazzan (1808–1862 or 1863, of Izmir and Jerusalem) followed him between 1853 and 1857 (after serving as the Chief Rabbi of Rome). Ashkenazi rabbis from Central and Eastern Europe also traveled to Corfu seasonally, brought there by the harvesting of *etrogim*, the citrons used ritually during the Festival of Sukkot. Italian rabbis exercised particularly strong authority within the community, playing a pivotal role in the nineteenth century: Isacco Raffael Tedeschi (1826–1908, of Ancona), Giuseppe Emmanuel Levi (1823–1887, of Fossano, Piedmont), and Alessandro da Fano (1847–1935, of Florence) held rabbinic chairs between 1865 and 1900; they were followed by Nathan Levy (1869–1943, of Alsace), a graduate of the seminary in Paris, who was Rabbi of Corfu until 1902, and Gustavo Calò (1879–1956, of Florence), who held the post between 1907 and 1918. Their leadership greatly affected liturgical music: the influence of the modernizing brand of synagogue music developed in the Sephardic-Portuguese community of Livorno and from there transmitted throughout Italy, was thus felt across local ritual denominations.[10]

The intersecting geographic origins and ritual identities of Corfu's Jewish community constitute a compelling case study in the epistemology of the Jewish diaspora, one that has largely defied explication. Embedded as they are in an extremely diverse cultural microcosm, the rituals of the Jewish communities of Corfu have presented an almost insoluble conundrum to those who have attempted to describe them across the normative Ashkenazi/Sephardic binaries that often characterize Jewish Studies.[11] While this might be surprising—after all, the very notion of "diaspora" is foundational to Jewish cultures—it also represents, perhaps, a particularly significant "statement of need" when it comes to the relevance of the interrelated notions of migration and displacement and their significance to redefinitions of culture *tout court*.[12] Most histories of the Corfuan Jewish settlement, which came to the attention of scholars in the late nineteenth century, refer to its "two communities," namely, the Greek and the Italian "Università," which represented local Jews in the Venetian Republic through separately appointed rabbis and political emissaries.[13] However, descriptions of the composition of Corfu's Jewry quickly become incoherent, if not outright confused, when scholars attempt to reconcile the Greco-Italian duality with the multiplicity of rituals and traditions present on the island, and thus with its complex migratory history and layers of Jewish diasporas.

On the one hand, it could be argued that such confusion—equally present in scholarship on history, literature and music—may very well stem from the ambiguity of the Hebrew acronym, ק"ק (or *q"q*), which may indicate either an organized Jewish body of self-government (*qehillah qedoshah*, or "holy community"), or a self-selected ritual community (*qahal qadosh*, or "holy congregation"). In Hebrew sources, the various aggregations of Jews in Corfu are referred to with this acronym, and its meaning remains vague, since it may have referred to: communities of faith expressing a certain type of ritual identity in their liturgy; or, instead, formally organized "political" entities that represented their constituents beyond liturgy itself; or both, i.e., the intersection of mingled ritual identities within a single organizational structure. On the other hand, however, this scholarly impasse—recognized already by Leo Levi in his study of Italian Jewry (itself just as culturally diverse and just as perplexing for scholars)—can also be seen as symptomatic of a certain scholarly inability to confront the fluidity of Jewish cultural life. This impasse is particularly evident in all scholarly attempts to describe Jewish ritual diversity on the basis of written records alone, without comparing them to ethnographic evidence and musical sources documenting oral traditions. Levi openly stigmatized the work of musicologists he defined as "Ashkenazi scholars" (who were, for the most part, Israeli scholars educated in Germany), who failed to make sense of the "typically Italian symbiosis of liturgical customs."[14] This symbiosis, which I propose to describe as a "liturgical *koiné*," or lingua franca, allowed the Jews of Italy—and the Jews of Corfu with them—to share (and at times merge) texts, melodies, and liturgical customs from communities that identified with distinct Italian, Ashkenazi and Sephardic liturgical traditions even while living in close proximity to one another for centuries.[15]

A liturgical *koiné* analogous to that of the Italian mainland formed on a smaller but equally complex scale in Corfu, where it fostered dynamic relationships among different forms of synagogue ritual. Given their composite cultural landscape, it is not surprising that mapping liturgical differences and identities in Corfu has proven arduous for the scholars who attempted to describe them based on written sources alone. The 1906 *Jewish Encyclopedia* included a highly informative entry on Corfu—penned by Richard Gottheil (1862–1936, of New York) and M. Caimi (of Athens). It opens with a rather puzzling statement regarding the ritual identity of the Jews on the island:

> [Corfu]. Most northerly of the Ionian Islands. The native Jews of Corfu fall into three distinct divisions of different origin (Greek, Spanish, and Apulian) and belonging to different epochs. There was formerly also a fourth division, that of the Levantines, the greater part of whom apparently became merged into the Italians. [...] The Greek synagogue is the oldest on the island. Until recently it differed somewhat from the others in its liturgy, and the ministers officiating in Greek still preserve that nasal chant peculiar to the Greco-Oriental preachers. The Greek Jews, who were absorbed by the more numerous Apulians, forgot their language, but have retained characteristic words and phrases. [...] Spanish Jews [...] emigrated to Corfu at the end of the fifteenth and during the sixteenth century [and] united with the Apulians, who came at the same time or a little

> later, to form the Apulian or Italian congregation. [...] The Greeks, who now constitute the majority of the Jewish population, speak the despised Apulian dialect, while the Apulians have generally adopted the more refined Venetian.[16]

The diasporic taxonomy presented by these scholars clearly reflected a certain inability to reconcile Greek and Apulian groups with the broader—inapplicable—division of Sephardic Jewry into those from the Iberian West (or "Spanish") and the Ottoman East (or "Levantine") of the Jewish Mediterranean. Alas, the "distinct divisions" (three, four, or five, if we count the "Italians") posited by the *Jewish Encyclopedia* are not further clarified by the entry on Corfu that appeared a century later in the *Encyclopaedia Judaica*:

> During the 16th century there were two congregations in Corfu, that of the Romaniots who preserved the ancient Byzantine rite (known as *Minhag Korfu*), and that of the Italians. In the course of time the Italian community was enlarged by Jews from Apulia, Spanish exiles, Portuguese Marranos, and Ashkenazim, who ultimately adopted the Sephardi rite. [...] Relations between the two communities did not always run smoothly. The Romaniot community enjoyed special privileges and objected to the right of permanent residence being granted to the Italians. [...] Each of the communities had two "overseers" (*syndikoi*), two *kashrut* supervisors, and two *parnasim*. In 1563 the traveler Elijah of Pesaro reported that the Italians constituted the majority of the Jewish colony in Corfu. They imposed their language on all the Jews of the island, most of whom spoke the Apulian dialect interlaced with Greek words.[17]

This overview, too, leaves one wondering how many communities, or at least distinctive ritual identities, actually made up the complex cultural mosaic of the Jewish group in Corfu. An official report by the Center for Jewish Art of the Hebrew University of Jerusalem, following two expeditions led by the Center in the summer of 2001 and the spring of 2002, further complicates the layout of Corfu's ritual *koiné*:

> Unlike other communities in Greece, most of the Jews of Corfu followed the Italian tradition. [...] The Jewish communities living in Corfu, the northernmost island in the Ionian Sea, were divided into three main congregations. Each prayed in its own synagogue and conducted different customs and rites. Out of the three synagogues, only the Greca synagogue, conducting the Romaniot [*sic* for *romaniyoti*] rite, remains. The members of the Scoula [*sic* for Scuola] Italiana

originate in Venice and Spain, Jews who prayed in the Scoula [*sic*] Corfiuty [*sic*] were from Sicily. The Greca synagogue is built within the former Jewish quarter, which at present is inhabited by local Greeks. Although the basic liturgy and customs in this synagogue were Romaniot, the members of the community absorbed the Italian culture and combined it with their own Greek culture. Their Italian Jewish tradition is noticeable in the shape and style of the ritual objects as well as in the structure of their synagogue.[18]

The conundrum emerging from these surveys foregrounds the ways in which research on Corfu's Jewish ritual identities illustrates a dilemma central to all studies of music and migration: how can static categories account for the fluidity of diasporic culture?

This issue had been raised already in an 1891 article by J. A. Romanos, the scholar who pioneered investigation into Corfu's Jewish communal history, who pondered:

> One wonders from whence this group of men arrived in Hellenic lands [...]. The answer to this question is quite complicated. [...]. [Following their expulsion from Spain and the Kingdom of Naples,] a numerous colony of Jews arrived from Apulia and greatly influenced the Jews already settled in Corfu, imposing upon them the language of Apulia, which they still speak today mixed with Greek words, in a jargon that is hardly intelligible to Italians or Greeks. [...]. Many of these unfortunate individuals found refuge in Corfu in 1540, and established a synagogue together with earlier Spanish refugees, which is still called the synagogue of Apulia and Spain, to distinguish it from the Greek synagogue. It is to this era that the division between Italian and Greek Jews in Corfu can be dated.[19]

Accepting standard assumptions about the geography of the Jewish Diaspora thus leaves us wondering where Corfu actually is (or was, while Jews inhabited it): Greece? Italy? An extension of Venice's mercantile empire and the politics of its ghetto? Or, again, a condensed version of the Sephardic Diaspora in its broadest implications (including Iberia, Italy, North Africa, and the Eastern Mediterranean)? All of the above? Such geo-spatial questions arise from the fact that Jewish liturgical spaces are often particularly dense and multi-layered, as the case of Corfu seems to demonstrate. Any given liturgical variant may represent the integration of several geographical locations and the related diasporic cultures originating from them. Although it will never resolve these questions about the movements of people and transformations of ritual practice, studying liturgical music can reveal dynamics of ritual identity within this composite Jewish group that texts alone may not.

A prime example of the interlaced ritual languages—the liturgical *koiné* of Corfuan Jews—can be gleaned from a detailed "ethnographic" report published as an anonymous letter (signed by a "gentleman" known only by the initial, "Z.") in the first issue of Corfu's Italian Jewish periodical, *Mosé: Antologia Israelitica* (1878). The author described, with an authority based on his own familiarity with (Italian) synagogue rituals and musical repertoires, his experience during the Festival of Shavuot in Corfu two years before (May 28–30, 1876). The overall portrait that emerges from this vivid description is one of extreme ritual fluidity, in which liturgical traditions, musical materials, and architectural spaces are shared among different groups.

A Festival of Shavuot in Corfu

Dear Friend,

I landed happily in Corfu at around 2pm on Saturday the 27th, with the ferry that had left Brindisi on midnight of the previous day.

In another letter I will describe to you the wonderful landscape that this city offers from the sea; its beautiful sights; its wonderful fortresses, which look like giants rising from the sea to guard the city; the famous esplanade (a lovely gathering point for its residents at all times of the year); as well as its narrow streets, some of which even have steps, since they are so steep and perpendicular to the hills, etc.

What I really wish to describe to you in this letter is, instead, the Festival of Shavuot, which started on Sunday evening, and is celebrated here in a unique way, at least when compared to the customs of our communities in P[iedmont]. On the first night, I went to the Main Temple (known as *Italian Temple*), where there is an excellent choir. Even though the prayer service had not yet started, it was already very crowded. At that time, without any formalities, and almost in a private manner, the *hekhal* [Torah Ark] was opened by the *shamash* [caretaker], to be closed again only after *minchah* [Afternoon Service] on the second day [of the Festival].

The balustrade was decorated with alternating silver candelabra and vases filled with flowers. Even the holy scrolls [of the Hebrew Bible], which here are kept in richly decorated cases, were crowned with carnations.

The rose, which typically decorates our synagogues on this Festival, has given its place here to carnations and lilies. When it was time to sing the prayers, the

Rabbi was invited by the masters of ceremonies to leave his seat, and to sit next to the *hekhal* [Torah Ark], where a line of chairs had been set. He was soon flanked by the heads of the community, by the elders, and by other prominent community members. The synagogue was overflowing with Jewish synagogue-goers, and with non-Jewish visitors. The heat was stifling, but, luckily, one of the masters of ceremonies allowed me to sit next to a window, through which blew a refreshing breeze. The synagogue has only one nave, flanked by small arcades supported by small columns, upon which rest the Ladies' galleries. The *hekhal* is beautiful and richly decorated, all in mahogany, but it is disproportionately big in comparison with the size of the room. The altar (*tevah*) is also made of mahogany, but it is more finely made [than the Ark], and it is situated across the room, away from the Ark. The *'arvit* [Evening Service] celebration lasted for about an hour. The choir sang beautifully various songs, the best of which was in my opinion an *hashkivenu* [evening blessing] by Maestro Giuseppe Penso, of Livorno. The choir sings without [instrumental] accompaniment, and it receives the pitch by the Head Chorister, Mr. Leone Mustacchi, a talented tenor.

The following morning, I made sure to get to my place on time, but I found that it had already been taken by others. Except for the Rabbi and the community council members, no one here has a set place in the synagogue. However, I was soon directed to another seat, which was reasonably comfortable.

I truly enjoyed listening to *min ha-metzar* [Ps. 118] by the immortal Giacomo Meyerbeer, and *atah horeta lada'at* [liturgical poem], and *mizmor ledavid* [Ps. 29]. I did not enjoy at all, however, the interruption, at *hallel*, for auctioning off the *mitzvoth* [liturgical honors]. I expressed my disgust to a gentleman sitting next to me, about how the synagogue that just moments before was permeated by such intensity had now taken on the aspect and noise of a secular place. The gentleman seemed to agree with me, but he said that what was at stake was the financial well-being [of synagogue life], which prompts even the most Orthodox and God-fearing among the congregants to close their eyes where it would be necessary to have two sets of them, if they were available.

I meant to add more to this when I was interrupted by the sale of flower-throwing.

– What is this? I asked my kind interlocutor.

– Just wait and see. Don't you see, up on the baluster on the left, above the *hekhal*, two silver containers filled with flower petals? I heard that the first five flowers have been bought for ten Francs, and the others for five.

In the meantime, the choir began singing the *atah horeta lada'at*. Then, the Torah scrolls were taken out of the Ark, still enclosed in their golden cases, and the sacred procession moved slowly towards the altar. At each step, a good-looking young man sprinkled the scrolls with a rain of flowers, which spreads a sweet fragrance all around. This "rain" continues also when the scrolls are raised (*hagbaah*), when, after the case is opened, the Torah is exhibited to the adoration of the faithful. In this solemn moment, during which the choir is silent, the entire congregation is bent in front of that most sacred object, softly reciting words of thanks and praise.

In the morning, until the *'amidah* [Standing Prayer], the congregational leaders sit again in front of the Ark.

The Morning Service started at 7am, and lasted until 10am.

At 11:30, the synagogue reopens for *minchah*. A line of youngsters, most of them pupils of the Talmud Torah [Jewish day school], begin reciting the Book of Ruth and the *azharot* [didactic liturgical poem for Shavuot] assisted by one of the teachers, following a traditional and not displeasing chant. Each text is followed by a translation in the vernacular. Meanwhile, the synagogue starts to become crowded, the heads and the prefects of the other synagogues also arrive, and the choir takes its place. The liturgy begins with some hymns for the Festival, set to music by Maestro Wolf, followed by Solemn Blessing of the King and the Royal Family [*ha-noten teshu'ah*...]. The latter is preceded by a beautiful *lekhu neranenah* [Ps. 95], followed by a commendable *haleluyah halelu el be-qodsho* [Ps. 150]. The *ha-noten* [*teshu'ah*...] is a true masterpiece, by Maestro Tivoli. All pieces were performed extremely well.

Minchah did not feature any remarkable events. I learned later that the ceremony was going to be repeated on the following day, but not in the Italian Temple, and instead in the Greek one, so called because it belongs to the Greek community, which is more ancient than the Italian one, since its existence dates back to time immemorial.

Therefore, I went to the Greek synagogue on the second day. The room is small and crowded, and many congregants have to stay downstairs by the entrance. Both the *hekhal* and the *tevah* [altar] deserve a mention for the ancient decorations. The same liturgy took place here as well, and here, too, the *hekhal* was left open at all times, turned during those two days into a richly decorated small temple. Here, too, the throwing of flowers was sold off for a good sum, and performed as in the other Temple. Services were shorter, since there is no choir; the Cantors are accompanied and assisted by other assistant-cantors, or *mesaye'im*.

The choir then moved to this Temple on the second day, where the Blessing of the King was repeated in the same way as the previous day. At the end of *minchah*, after the singing of a few hymns, the *hekhal* was solemnly closed.

Thus, without much form, but with fullness of sentiment, I too close this letter and embrace you with my heart.

Z.

Corfu, June 1, 1876

P.S. I would like to add that, aside from the two Temples I have mentioned, there are two more: one is beautiful and large, known as New Temple, and the other is small, known as *Medrash*; both are extensions of the Italian synagogue.[20]

The whole of this extraordinary first-hand anonymous testimony—however "tainted" by a reformist, or modernizing, agenda (as revealed in the anonymity of the "letter" itself)—helps clarify a few facts about the complex liturgical exchanges among the different Jewish groups in Corfu. Many of these traits, which provide us with a first-hand account of the fluidity of the Jewish ritual *koiné* of the island's diasporic community, can be further corroborated by the evidence of archival field recordings.

The musico-liturgical repertoires of both the Italian and the Greek synagogues in Corfu, as described by the anonymous nineteenth-century author, specifically share the following traits:

1. A well-established practice of choral music, performed by one choir (directed by Leone Mustacchi, a tenor), was shared between Italian and Greek congregations over the two days of the Festival.[21]
2. Music of composers known in the repertoire created, collected, and circulated by the Spanish-Portuguese community of Livorno throughout the nineteenth century was part of the local repertoires. This included compositions by the Livornese musician Giuseppe Penso,[22] and by "the immortal" Giacomo Meyerbeer (1791–1874; the piece was drawn from the collection *Zemirot Yisrael*, issued in 1847–1864 by the French synagogue composer Samuel Naumbourg, 1817–1880), whose works are found in nineteenth-century music manuscripts from Livorno and other Italian communities under Livornese influence.
3. Local repertoires also included music by composers from the Ashkenazi Jewish community of Trieste, where Corfuan Jews had settled and with which they maintained ongoing connection: Augusto Tivoli (1809–1886) and "Maestro Wolf" (Samuele Wolf) were both active there during the nineteenth century.
4. The liturgical use of *targum* (or *a calco* translation of scriptural texts in the course of synagogue rituals),[23] expressed by the chanting of the Book of Ruth and the *azharot* (Hebrew liturgical poems enumerating the 613 commandments includ-

ed in the Hebrew Bible) in the Apulian vernacular during the Afternoon Service of the First Day of Shavu'ot in the Italian synagogue (*Tempio italiano*) is well documented in archival field recordings of both liturgical and para-liturgical materials, made during the second half of the twentieth century by Leo Levi.[24]

Corfu's liturgical *koiné*, in which Greek, Apulian, Sephardic, and Italo-Venetian Jews shared musical and liturgical traits across their respective ritual spaces, was likely propelled by the modernizing effect of the "Sephardic" music imported from Livorno, either directly or via Italy, and its difference from the more consolidated pre-existing practices of earlier immigrants to the island. The Livornese repertoire had been in formation since the late 1700s.[25] A century later, interpolation of these new repertoires with the older "traditions" created a truly unified sound, that of a wide-ranging "Sephardic"—or Mediterranean—big tent, where Jews of different denominations could all come together, at least in part, without completely letting go of their traditional differences. That process was not easy, and it came at a cost. This is apparent in a series of harsh disputes, such as those over the introduction of choral music that exploded in Corfu in the 1750s. As Simonsohn and Adler discovered, this eighteenth-century *querelle* involved the "Italian" and "Greek" rabbis of Corfu, as well as numerous rabbinic authorities in Italy, the Balkans, and the Middle East.[26] New information shows that the rabbinic courts failed to resolve the dispute, and eventually consular authorities of the Republic of Venice had to adjudicate.[27] We do not know how these authorities viewed the cultural complexity of Corfu's Jewish community, and are left to imagine that they may have experienced a puzzlement similar to that of the Jewish Studies scholars who tried to untangle the threads of Corfu's ritual life in much later times. Manuscript records suggest that, once the various Corfuan constituencies realized that they were subject to Venetian authority, they attempted to lessen their mutual differences, and presented themselves as part of "only" two constituencies: Italian and Greek. Over a century later, however, the divergences between the two (or three, or four) communities could be negotiated in real time by sharing musical and liturgical resources from each of the communities involved, performing them as a "traditional" anthology of sorts, comprised of historical and contemporary musical repertoires from across an increasingly scattered diaspora.

Notes

1. Moustaki, *Le métèque*: "With my features of a stranger [metic], a wandering Jew from a Greek father, a thief and a rogue...." All translations my own.

2. On the earlier settlements, see Zeldes, "Jewish Settlement in Corfu"; on nineteenth- and twentieth-century development, see Catalan, *Evraikì, una diaspora mediterranea.*

3. On *pugliso*, see Sermoneta, "Testimonianze letterarie" (with annotated texts from manuscript sources: 147–68).

4. Levi conducted several sessions of ethnographic field recordings with informants from Corfu, all kept at the National Sound Archives (NSA) of the National Library of Israel. An unnamed informant, possibly Chayyim Menachem, in Corfu, was recorded in July of 1956 (NSA Y0189); Isacchetto Gesuà was recorded in two sessions, in Corfu in 1956 (NSA Y0188) and in Jerusalem on October 10, 1966 (NSA Y0498, Y0499, and Y0500); members of the Eliyahu (or, in Italian, Elia) family were recorded at their home in Ramat Gan in 1963 (NSA Y0226), and again during the week of Passover in 1966 (NSA YC00034); on February 2, 1963, Kol Israel (Israel's public radio) broadcast a program about Corfu, hosted by Levi (NSA YC02560, Gerson-Kiwi collection). Two examples from the 1963 broadcast were transcribed and discussed by Edith Gerson-Kiwi in an attempt to trace their origin to Calabria (Gerson-Kiwi, "Vocal Folk-Polyphonies," 16–25, examples 9–10). Additional recordings made by Levi in Ancona, Trieste, and Milan also include Corfuan materials. Between August 2–19, 1970, ethnomusicologist Amnon Shiloah conducted additional fieldwork in Corfu with one of Levi's informants, Chayyim Menachem (NSA YC00274, YC00275, YC00276, and YC00324) as well as with another informant, named Yosef Vital (NSA YC00305 and YC00341). Some of the melodies collected by Levi and Shiloah were transcribed and published by Isaac Levy (see Levy, *Antología*).

5. Spagnolo, "La stampa periodica ebraica."

6. Seroussi "Singing Modernity," 164.

7. Adler, *La pratique musicale savante*, 116–22. Israel Adler's discovery of these rabbinic sources was announced that same year by Shlomo Simonsohn (Simonsohn, "Some Disputes on Music in the Synagogue," see especially n. 26).

8. Fleming, *Greece: A Jewish History*.

9. Levi, "Tradizioni liturgiche"; Gerson-Kiwi, "Vocal Folk-Polyphonies"; Shiloah, *Greek-Jewish Musical Traditions*.

10. See Seroussi "Livorno."

11. Efron, *The Jews: A History*, 213.

12. See for example Boyarin and Boyarin, *Powers of Diaspora*.

13. An extant seventeenth-century manuscript presenting each congregation before the Venetian authorities (Columbia University Libraries Ms. X893 Z8 v.3 no. 6, *Università Italiana della Sinagoga Corfiota Aborigine contro Università della Sinagoga Corfiota Greca*, 1674) offers an example of the Italian-Greek dichotomy expressed through both text and visual elements.

14. Levi, "Le due più antiche trascrizioni musicali."

15. Spagnolo, "Musiche in contatto."

16. Gottheil and Caimi, "Corfu," 269.

17. Marcus and Kerem, "Corfu," 221–22.

18. Amar, "Tracing the Roots of Greek Jewry," 12, 15–16.

19. Romanos, "Histoire de la communauté de Corfou," 63.

> On se demande d'où vient, au milieu de la terre hellénique, ce groupe d'hommes qui ont des caractères si particuliers et quelle est leur histoire. La réponse à cette question est assez difficile. [...] [pp. 68–69] Environ un demi-siècle plus tard [after the expulsion from Spain, 1492], une colonie juive bien plus nombreuse vint d'Apulie et exerça une si grande influence sur les Juifs déjà établis à Corfou, qu'elle leur imposa la langue d'Apulie, qu'ils parlent encore aujourd'hui avec un mélange de mots grecs, ce qui a produit un jargon difficile à comprendre et par les Italiens et par les Grecs. [...] Beaucoup de ces malheureux ce réfugièrent à Corfou en 1540, et y fondèrent, en commun avec les anciens réfugiés espagnols, une synagogue, qu'on appelle encore aujourd'hui synagogue d'Apulie et d'Espagne, pour la distinguer de l'ancienne synagogue grecque. C'est de cette époque que date la division des Juifs à Corfou en italiens et en grecs. L'organisation de la communauté juive était à peu

près semblable à celle des chrétiens. Chacune des deux synagogues avait deux syndics (Memunnim), deux surveillants et deux gérants (Parnasim); elle constituait un corps à part, qui avait son conseil présidé par les syndics. Lorsqu'on avait à délibérer sur des intérêts communs, les deux conseils se réunissaient et délibéraient ensemble. Les syndics étaient élus par les confrères des synagogues, convoqués à cet effet, chaque année, par le Provéditeur vénitien en son palais.

20. Z., "Una festa di Sciabuot a Corfù."

Caro Amico, Sono sbarcato felicemente a Corfù verso le due pomeridiane di sabbato 27, col vaporino, che partì da Brindisi alle 12 della notte precedente. Ti scriverò in altra mia del magnifico panorama che presenta sul mare questa città; de' suoi varii punti bellissimi; de' suoi meravigliosi forti che paiono giganti usciti dal mare per mettersi a guardia della città; della famosa *Spianata*, simpatico ritrovo della cittadinanza in tutte le stagioni dell'anno; e anche de' suoi viottoli, di cui alcuni muniti persino di gradinata, tanto sono ripidi e perpendicolari ecc. ecc. Quello di cui voglio darti con questa mia ragguaglio è della festa di *Sciabuot*, che succedeva appunto la sera di domenica, e celebrata qui in modo tutto particolare, almeno se confrontiamo cogli usi delle nostre Comunità del P.^e [Piemonte]. Mi portai dunque fino dalla prima notte nel Tempio maggiore, detto *Tempio italiano*, ove funziona un buonissimo coro; e sebbene non fossero incominciate ancora le preghiere esso era affollatissimo. In quel momento si apriva senza alcuna solennità, dirò così in forma privata dal bidello, l'*Echal*, il quale non doveva chiudersi che dopo la *Minchà* del secondo giorno. La Balaustrata era coperta con alternazione di candelieri d'argento e vasi d'argento carichi di fiori. Anche i sacri Rotoli, [p. 134] che qui stanno chiusi entro ricchissime custodie, erano incoronati di garofani. Qui a *Sciabuot* la rosa, ornamento dei nostri Templi in tale solennità, ha già ceduto il suo impero ai garofani e ai gigli. Giunta l'ora d'intuonare le preghiere, il Rabbino veniva invitato da Maestri di cerimonie a lasciare la cattedra e andarsi a sedere davanti l'*Echal* ov'era disposta una fila di sedie. Esso era tosto fiancheggiato dai Capi della Comunità e da vecchi ed altri rispettabili personaggi. Il tempio rigurgitava di fedeli e di curiosi; il caldo era soffocante, ma fortunatamente uno dei cerimonieri mi ha fatto prendere posto vicino ad una finestra d'onde spirava un balsamico venticello. Il Tempio ha una sola navata fiancheggiata da piccoli portici sorretti da pilastrini su cui poggiano le gallerie delle Signore. E' bello e ricco l'*Echal*, tutto mogano, ma troppo grande e sproporzionato alla dimensione locale. Anche di mogano, ma di lavoro più minuto e più grazioso, è la tribuna (*Tevà*), posta dirimpetto dall'altra estremità della Sala.—La cerimonia dell'*Arvit* durò circa un'ora. Il coro cantò egregiamente diversi pezzo, il migliore dei quali mi parve un *Aschivenu* del M.° Giuseppe Penso di Livorno. Il coro canta senza accompagnamento, e riceve l'intonazione dal Capo-coro, signor Leone Mustacchi, abile tenore. L'indomani non mancai di portarmi per tempo al mio posto, che però trovai occupato da altri; giacché fuori del Rabbino e dei capi delle Comunità qui nessuno ha un posto fisso nei Templi; ma me ne venne subito indicato un altro abbastanza comodo. Mi piacque molto il *Min Ametzar*, dell'immortale Meyerbeer; l'*Atà Orhèta* e il *Mizmor Ledavid*. Non mi è però piaciuta l'interruzione che successe all'*Allel* per la vendita delle Mitzvot. Espressi ad un gentilissimo signore mio vicino questo mio disgusto, con cui il Tempio che presentava tanto raccoglimento pochi istanti prima, avesse ora preso l'aspetto e il frastuono di un luogo profano. Quel signore mostrò dividere il mio [p. 135] avviso intorno alla sconvenienza dell'uso, ma ci va di mezzo, diss'egli, la quistione finanziaria, la quale anche ai più ortodossi e timorati di Dio fa spesso chiudere gli occhi dove sarebbe necessario aprirne quattro se si avessero. Voleva soggiungere, ma ne fui trattenuto perché sentii esporre in vendita il getto dei fiori.

– Che cosa è ciò? domandai al mio gentile interlocutore.

– Aspetti e saprà. Non vede là sulla balaustrata dell'*Echal*, a sinistra, quelle due guantiere d'argento piene di foglie di fiori? ho sentito che i primi cinque fiori furono acquistati per dieci franchi, i secondi per cinque.

Ma intanto il coro aveva intuonato l'*Atà Orhèda*; sono estratte le Bibbie, però chiuse nelle loro auree buste e il sacro corteo muove lentamente verso la Tribuna. Un giovine ben messo fa cadere ad ogni passo sui sacri rotoli lungo il breve tragitto una pioggia di fiori che spande all'intorno soavissima fragranza. Questa pioggia continua pure nel momento dell'elevazione (הגבה) quando aperta la custodia la *Torah* viene esposta all'adorazione dei fedeli. Momento questo solenne, in cui tace il coro, e tutta la popolazione curva dinanzi a quell'oggetto santissimo, mormora a bassa voce parole di ringraziamento e di laudi. Anche il mattino sino al momendo della *Hamidà* i magnati prendono posto dinanzi all'*Echal*. L'uffiziatura del mattino cominciata alle sette terminava alle dieci. Ma alle undici e mezzo il Tempio si riapre per la preghiera di *Minhà*. Una schiera di giovanetti, per la maggior parte alunni del Talmud Torah, assistiti da uno dei maestri, comincia la recita del libro di *Rut* e delle *Atzarot* [*sic* for *azharot*] con una cantilena tradizionale non disaggradevole. Ogni testo è seguito da traduzione in lingua volgare. Intanto il tempio va popolandosi; i capi ed i prefetti degli altri Templi ivi pure convengono; il coro è al suo posto. Si esordisce con alcuni inni relativi alla festività, musicati dal M.° Wolf; poi ha luogo la benedizione [p. 136] solenne del sovrano e della reale famiglia. Questa è preludiata da un bellissimo לכו נרננה; segue un ammirabile הללויה הללו אל בקדשו. L'הנותן poi è un vero capolavoro del M.° Tivoli e tutti i pezzi sono stati assai bene interpretati. La *Minhà* non presentò nulla di rimarchevole. Seppi che la stessa cerimonia doveva ripetersi il giorno seguente, ma non più nel Tempio italiano, sebbene nel Tempio greco, così detto, perché appartenente alla Comunità greca, più antica di quella Italiana, datando la sua legale esistenza da tempo immemoriale. Volli dunque il secondo giorno andare al Tempio greco. L'aula è angusta pel molto consorso; molti sono costretti rimanere a basso nell'atrio. Meritano attenzione pel loro lavoro antico tanto l'*Echal*, quanto la *Tevà*. Anche qui lo stesso cerimoniale, anche qui l'*Echal* sempre aperto e convertito per quei due giorni in un tempietto riccamente ornato. Anche qui il getto dei fiori fu comperato ad un buon prezzo, ed eseguito come nell'altro Tempio. Le funzioni per altri qui durarono meno non essendovi coro; e gli Oratori sono accompagnati ed assistiti da altri oratori o coadiutori מסייעים . Il coro si portò poi lo stesso giorno in corpo in questo Tempio ove si è ripetuto, collo stesso ordine e colla stessa precisione, l'uffiziatura del giorno precedente per la benedizione del Sovrano. Senonché terminata la *Minchà* si procedette previo il canto di alcuni inni alla solenne chiusura dell'*Echal*. E così senza alcuna solennità di forma, ma colla pienezza degli affetti, chiudo io pure questa lettera e col cuore ti abbraccio. Z. Corfù 1 Giugno 1876.

P.S. Per non mancare a nessun debito aggiungo che oltre ai due Tempi che ho indicato ce ne sono ancora altri due; di cui l'uno bello e grande, detto il Tempio nuovo, e l'altro più piccolo, detto Medrash tutti e due succursali del Tempio italiano.

21. One descendant of the prominent Corfu Jewish family, Mustacchi, was the French singer-songwriter Georges Moustaki (born Giuseppe Mustacchi in Alexandria, Egypt, to Jewish parents from Corfu).

22. For manuscript sources with synagogue compositions by Giuseppe Penso (who was also active in Livorno as an opera composer), see *Musica sacra di Livorno ridotta da Moise Ventura*, Mus Add 6; *Shabbat: Musica sacra ridotta in chiave di violin da Ernesto Ventura*, Mus Add 7; and *Shirim le-yamim noraim u-le-yom tov. Canti sacri per i Giorni Penitenziali e Festivi raccolti da Ernesto Ventura*, Mus Add 8, all in the Birnbaum Collection of Jewish Music, Klau Library, Hebrew Union College, Cincinnati; and Untitled Ms. Mus. Coll. Casale 2, [ca. 1875], National Library of Israel, Music Department. (Moise Ventura was Chief Cantor of Livorno, 1845–1920.)

23. On *targum* and its liturgical use, see Bernard Grossfeld and S. David Sperling, "Translations: Ancient Versions" in Sarna, "Bible," 588–95.

24. See for example recordings NSA Y0188, featuring excerpts sung by Isacchetto Gesuà, including Hebrew and Pugliso versions of Mishnah Sanhedrin 10; and NSA Y0034, including a multilingual version of the Passover Haggadah as sung by the Elia (Eliyahu) family of Ramat Gan, Israel, in Hebrew, Aramaic, Pugliso, Venetian, and Italian.

25. Seroussi, "Livorno."

26. Simonsohn, "Some Disputes on Music in the Synagogue in Pre-Reform Days," and Adler, *La pratique musicale savante*. Some sources of the *querelle* had already been noted by David Benvenisti and Hayyim Mizrachi (see Benvenisti and Mizrachi, "Sources").

27. See *pesaq 'al nigun ḳeri'at shema' be-nigun ba-'ir qorfu* (Rabbinic ruling on the use of melody for the singing of the Shema' in the city of Corfu), 1753, 35 leaves: paper; 15 × 21 cm., Ms. X893 Sh354: manuscript written on paper in Hebrew Oriental script. "A response regarding a new custom in Corfu, to say Shema with a tune. The response was written by Hayyim Shabtai ha-Cohen and Eliyahu ben Menahem ha-Cohen. The response received written approvals (in Hebrew and Italian) from Gatenio Benvenist, Yosef ibn Goya of Safed, Yitsḥak ha-Lev of Salonika, and Yaakov Refa'el Hizkiyah ben Avraham Yisrael Hazak of Padua." I am grateful to Michelle Chesner, Norman E. Alexander Librarian for Jewish Studies at Columbia University, for bringing this manuscript to my attention.

Bibliography

Adler, Israel. *La pratique musicale savante dans quelques communautés juives en Europe aux XVIIe et XVIIIe siècles.* Paris–The Hague: Mouton, 1966.

Amar, Ariella. "Tracing the Roots of Greek Jewry." *Newsletter. Center for Jewish Art, The Hebrew University of Jerusalem.* 16 (Winter 2004): 12–19.

Benvenisti, David, and Hayyim Mizrachi. "Sources for the History of the Jewish Community of Corfu." *Sefunot: Studies and Sources on the History of the Jewish Communities in the East* 1 (1957): 303–14.

Boyarin, Jonathan, and Daniel Boyarin. *Powers of Diaspora: Two Essays on the Relevance of Jewish Culture.* Minneapolis and London: University of Minnesota Press, 2002.

Catalan, Tullia. *Evraikì, una diaspora mediterranea da Corfù a Trieste.* Trieste: Museo della Comunità ebraica di Trieste Carlo e Vera Wagner and La Mongolfiera Libri, 2013.

Efron, John M., Steven Weitzman, and Matthias B. Lehmann. *The Jews: A History.* 2nd ed. Boston: Pearson, 2014.

Fleming, Katherine Elizabeth. *Greece: A Jewish History.* Princeton: Princeton University Press, 2010.

Gerson-Kiwi, Edith. "Vocal Folk-Polyphonies of the Western Orient in Jewish Tradition." *Yuval: Studies of the Jewish Music Research Centre* 1 (1968): 169–93; 16–25.

Gottheil, Richard, and M. Caimi. "Corfu." In *The Jewish Encyclopedia*, ed. Isidor Singer and Cyrus Adler. Vol. 4:269–73. Funk and Wagnalis: New York, 1906.

Levi, Leo. "Tradizioni liturgiche, musicali e dialettali a Corfù (colla trascrizione di tre canti)." *Rassegna Mensile di Israel* 28/1 (January 1961): 20–31.

Levi, Leo. "Le due più antiche trascrizioni musicali di melodie ebraico-italiane." In *Scritti sull'ebraismo in memoria di Guido Bedarida.* Pp. 105–48. Florence: Tipografia Giuntina, 1966 (reissued in Leo Levi, *Canti tradizionali e tradizioni liturgiche. Ricerche e studi sulle tradizioni musicali ebraiche e sui loro rapporti con il canto cristiano 1954–1971*, ed. Roberto Leydi and Giacomo Baroffio. Lucca: Libreria Musicale Italiana, 2002.

Levy, Isaac. *Antología de liturgia Judeo-Española / Antologyah shel chazanut sefaradit.* Jerusalem, 1964-1980.

Marcus, Simon, and Yitzchak Kerem. "Corfu." In *Encyclopaedia Judaica*, ed. Michael Berenbaum and Fred Skolnik. 2nd ed. Vol. 5:221–23. New York: Macmillan Reference USA, 2007.

Moustaki, Georges. *Le métèque.* New York: Peters International, 1969.

Romanos, J. A. "Histoire de la communauté de Corfou." *Revue des Etudes Juives* 23 (1891): 63–74 (transl. from the original Greek, *Hestia* 31(1891): 369–74, 385–88, 401–03).

Sarna, Nahum M., et al. "Bible." In *Encyclopaedia Judaica*, ed. Michael Berenbaum and Fred Skolnik. 2nd ed. Vol. 3:572–679. New York: Macmillan Reference USA, 2007.

Sermoneta, Giuseppe (Joseph Baruch). "Testimonianze letterarie degli ebrei pugliesi a Corfù." *Medioevo romanzo* 15 (1990): 139–68, 407–37.

Seroussi, Edwin. "Livorno: A Crossroads in the History of Sephardic Religious Music." In *The Mediterranean and the Jews. Society, Culture and Economy in Early Modern Times*, ed. Elliot Horowitz and Moises Orfali. Pp. 131–54. Ramat-Gan: Bar-Ilan University Press, 2002.

Seroussi, Edwin. "Singing Modernity: Synagogue Music in Nineteenth- and Early Twentieth-Century Italy." In *Acculturation and Its Discontents: The Jews of Italy from Early Modern to Modern Times*, ed. David Myers and Peter Reill. Pp. 164–82. Toronto: University of Toronto Press, 2008.

Shiloah, Amnon. *Greek-Jewish Musical Traditions.* Folkways FE 4205, 1978.

Simonsohn, Shlomo. "Some Disputes on Music in the Synagogue in Pre-Reform Days." *Proceedings of the American Academy for Jewish Research* 34 (1966): 99–110.

Spagnolo, Francesco. "La stampa periodica ebraica come fonte per la ricostruzione della vita sinagogale nell'Italia dell'Emancipazione." *Materia Giudaica* 9 (2004): 265–73.

Spagnolo, Francesco. "Musiche in contatto: Le tradizioni ebraiche in Italia nelle registrazioni di Leo Levi, questioni metodologiche e prospettive di ricerca." In *Musica e Religione. EM. Annuario degli Archivi di Etnomusicologia della Accademia Nazionale di Santa Cecilia.* Pp. 83–107. Rome: Squilibri 2006.

Z., "Una festa di Sciabuot a Corfù." *Mosè: Antologia Israelitica* 1 (June 1878): 133–36.

Zeldes, Nadia. "Jewish settlement in Corfu in the aftermath of the expulsions from Spain and southern Italy, 1492–1541." *Mediterranean Historical Review* 27 (2012): 175–88.

ISTANBUL: Dimitrie Cantemir, 1673–1723*

Jordi Savall

At the time of Dimitrie Cantemir (1673–1723), the city which stands at the crossroads of the continents of Europe and Asia, ISTANBUL for the Ottomans and CONSTANTINOPLE for the Byzantines, already marked a veritable high point in history. Despite the memory and very palpable presence of the old Byzantium, it had become the true heart of the Muslim religious and cultural world. An extraordinary melting-pot of peoples and religions, the city has always been a magnet for European travelers and artists. Cantemir arrived in the city in 1693, aged twenty, initially as a hostage and later as a diplomatic envoy of his father, the ruler of Moldavia. He became famous as a virtuoso of the tanbur, a kind of long-necked lute, and was also a highly-regarded composer, thanks to his work Kitābu ‹İlmi'l-Mūsīḳī (*The Book of the Science of Music*), which he dedicated to Sultan Ahmed III (1703–1730).

Such is the historical context of our project on "Dimitrie Cantemir's The Book of the Science of Music and the Sephardic and Armenian musical traditions," in which we have aimed to present the "cultivated" instrumental music of the seventeenth-century Ottoman court, as preserved in Cantemir's work, in dialogue and alternating with "traditional" popular music, represented by the oral traditions of Armenian musicians and the music of the Sephardic communities who had settled in the Ottoman Empire in cities such as Istanbul and Izmir after their expulsion from Spain. In Western Europe, our cultural image of the Ottoman Empire has been distorted by the Ottoman Empire's long bid to expand toward the West, blinding us to the cultural richness and, above all, the atmosphere of tolerance and diversity that existed in the Empire during that period. As Ştefan Lemny points out in his interesting book on *Les Cantemir*, "in fact, after taking Constantinople, Mahomet II spared the lives of the city's Christian population; what is more, a few years later he encouraged the old aristocratic Greek families to return to the district known as Fener or Phanar, the hub of the former Byzantium."[1] Later, under the reign of Süleyman—the Golden Age of the Ottoman Empire—contacts with Europe intensified on a par with the development of diplomatic and trade relations. As Amnon Shiloah reminds us in his excellent book *Music in the World of Islam*: "Although Venice established a permanent diplomatic mission in Istanbul toward the end of the fifteenth century, the treaties concluded in 1543 between Süleyman and the 'King of the Christians,' François I of France, were the most significant factor in increasing opportunities for deeper and more meaningful cultural interaction. It is noteworthy that on the occasion of the treating signing, François I sent Süleyman an orchestra as a sign of friendship; guest performances by the newly arrived musicians seem to have inspired the creation of two new rhythms: *frenkcin* (12/4) and the *frengi feri* (14/4)."[2]

From 1601, the Patriarchate of the Orthodox Church, the rallying point for the Greek aristocracy proceeding from all corners of the Empire—from the islands in the Aegean, the Peloponnese, Europe, and Asia Minor—finally became established in the Phanar district, where the old aristocratic Greek families had settled after the fall of Constantinople. Thus, thanks to the presence of this Greek community, the ancient Byzantine capital continued to be the seat of the Orthodox Church throughout the Empire. In this sense the Patriarchate's Academy, or Great School, was crucial in ensuring cultural hegemony. Based on his reading of Cantemir, Voltaire listed the disciplines taught at the Academy: ancient and modern Greek, Aristotelian philosophy, theology, and medicine: "In truth," he wrote, "Demetrius Cantemir reiterates many old myths; but he could not have been mistaken about the modern monuments he saw with his own eyes, or the Academy where he himself studied."[3]

Dimitrie Cantemir's *Book of the Science of Music*, which has served as the historical source for our recording, is an exceptional document in many ways; first, as a fundamental source of knowledge concerning the theory, style, and forms of seventeenth-century Ottoman music, but also as one of the most interesting accounts of the musical life of one of the foremost Eastern empires. This collection of 355 compositions (including nine by Cantemir), written in a system of musical notation invented by the author, constitutes the most important collection of sixteenth- and seventeenth-century Ottoman instrumental music to have survived to the present day. I first began to discover this repertory in 1999, during the preparation of our project on Isabella I of Castile, when our friend and colleague Dimitri Psonis, a specialist in Oriental music, suggested an old military march from the collection as a musical illustration of the date commemorating the conquest of Constantinople by the Ottoman armies of Mahomet II.

A year later, on our first visit to Istanbul to give a concert with Montserrat Figueras and Hespèrion XX, when we visited the Yapı Kredi Cultural Centre, our friends in Istanbul, Aksel Tibet, Mine Haydaroglu and Emrah Efe Çakmak, gave us a copy of the first modern edition of the music contained in Dimitrie Cantemir's *Science of Music*.[4] I was immediately fascinated by the music in the collection and by the life of Cantemir, and I subsequently set about studying both the music and the composer in order to learn about a culture which, despite its proximity, seems remote to us as a result of sheer ignorance. I was determined to find out more about the historical and aesthetic context with a view to embarking on an interesting project. Six years later, during the preparation of our Orient-Occident project, I selected four magnificent *maḳāms* which gave the project a new dimension in that it was the only Oriental music to come not from an oral tradition, but from a contemporaneous written source. Finally, in 2008, as a natural continuation of our original project on the dialogue between East and West, we succeeded in bringing together an exceptional group of musicians from Turkey (oud, ney, kanun, tanbur, lyra, and percussion) together with musicians from Armenia (duduk, kemençe and ney "Beloul"), Israel (oud), Morocco (oud), Greece (santur and morisca), and our principal specialist soloists in Hespèrion XXI, with whom we have prepared and carried out this recording. I would like to take this opportunity to express to them all my heartfelt gratitude, since without their talent and knowledge this project would never have been possible.

To begin with, we had the difficult task of selecting about ten pieces out of a total of 355 compositions, choosing the most representative and varied pieces from among the *maḳāms* which struck us as being the most beautiful, although we are aware that this preference was influenced by our Western sensibility. After this "bewildering" choice, we had to complete the pieces chosen for the Ottoman part with the corresponding taksim, or preludes, improvised before each *maḳām*. At the same time, we had also selected Sephardic and Armenian pieces for the Sephardic repertoire: we chose music from the Ladino repertory preserved in the communities of Izmir, Istanbul, and other regions of the former Ottoman Empire, while for the Armenian repertoire we selected the most beautiful of the various pieces proposed by the Armenian musicians Georgi Minassyan (duduk) and Gaguik Mouradian (kemençe).

Nowadays, all of this music is probably performed very differently from the way it was at the time of Cantemir. Therefore, in our quest for other possible performance techniques, we had to rely on various accounts, often written by European travelers, which describe the specific characteristics of Ottoman music during those historical periods and provide a series of interesting considerations on musical performance, practice, instruments, court orchestras, and military bands, as well as the ceremonies of the mystical confraternities. One such account is that of Pierre Belon in 1553, who remarks on the Turks' extraordinary skill at making bow and lute strings from gut, which "are more common here than in Europe," adding that "the Turks have four sorts of guitars and lutes, and many people can play one or another type, which is not the case in France and Italy."[5] He also mentions the existence of a great variety of flutes, remarking on the wonderfully sweet sound of the miskal (panpipe), although in 1614 the Italian traveler Pietro Della Valle wrote that the sweetness of the instrument "does not match that of the long flute [ney] of the Dervishes."[6] Around 1700 Cantemir himself observed in his *History of the Growth and Decay of the Othman Empire*: "It will perhaps seem strange to the *European* Reader to see the study of so noble an art [i.e. music] prais'd by me in a Nation accounted barbarian by all *Christendom*."[7] He concedes that barbarism may have reigned during the period when the Empire was being forged, but remarks that, "when a cessation of war allow'd the Arts of Peace, to be cultivated, they so far departed from their former fierceness, and became so civiliz'd, that scarce any signs of their ancient Barbarousness now appear."[8] He concludes with the following words, which must have come as a shock to his European readers: "I may certainly venture to say, that the *Turkish* Musick for metre and proportion of words is more perfect than any *European*, but withal so hard to be understood, that in the spacious City of *Constantinople* where resides the greatest Court in the World, among so many Musicians and Lovers of Musick, you will scarce find above three or four, who thoroughly understand the grounds of this art."[9]

(Translated by Jacqueline Minett)

Notes

* An earlier version of this essay was published with the recording *ISTANBUL: Dimitrie Cantemir, 1673–1723*. Hespèrion XXI, dir. Jordi Savall. [Bellaterra, Spain]: AliaVox [2009], AVSA9870. I would like to thank Amnon Shiloah, Ştefan Lemny, and Ursula and Kurt Reinhard for their research and analysis on the history, music, and the period, which I have used in documenting some of the sources in my commentary.

1. Lemny, *Les Cantemir*, 60, "De fait, après la prise de la ville, Mahomet II avait épargné la vie des habitants chrétiens. Bien plus, quelques années après, il avait encouragé le retour des vieilles familles aristocratiques grecques dans le quartier nommé Phanar, ou Fener, vestige de l'époque byzantine."

2. Shiloah, *Music in the World of Islam*, 89.

3. Voltaire, *Essai sur les mœurs*, ch. XCI, p. 4135. "J'avoue que Démétrius Cantemir a rapporté beaucoup de fables anciennes; mais il ne peut s'être trompé sur les monuments modernes qu'il a vus de ses yeux, et sur l'académie où il a été élevé."

4. Cantemir, *Demetrius Cantemir: The Collection of Notations*, ed. Wright.

5. Belon, *Les Observations*, 454, "Elles y sont plus frequentes qu'en Europe, dont pouvons bien donner la raison: c'est, que les Turcs ont de quatre sortes de guiternes & Luts, desquelz plusieurs sçavent sonner ou des uns ou des autres, ce que n'avient pas en France, n'en Italie: car peu de gens des villages se entremeslent de jouer du Lut, ou de Guiterne."

6. Della Valle, *Viaggi*, 50, letter from Constantinople dated October 25, 1614, "però di dolcezza di suono non arriva ai flauti dei dervisei di gran lunga."

7. Cantemir, *History of the Growth and Decay of the Othman Empire*, 151.

8. Ibid.

9. Ibid., 151–2.

Bibliography

Belon, Pierre de. *Les Observations de plusieurs singularités et choses mémorables, trouvées en Grèce, Asie, Judée, Egypte, Arabie et autres pays étrangers, rédigées...par Pierre Belon.* 2nd ed. Paris: chez Hierosme de Marnef, & la veufve Guillaume Cavellat, 1588.

Cantemir, Dimitrie. *Demetrius Cantemir: The Collection of Notations*, edited and with commentary by Owen Wright. 2 vols. SOAS Musicology Series 1. London: School of Oriental and African Studies, University of London and Aldershot, Hampshire: Ashgate, 1992–2000.

Cantemir, Dimitrie. *History of the Growth and Decay of the Othman Empire* [*Historia incrementorum atque decrementorum Aulae Othomanicae*], trans. N. Tindal. London: James, John, and Paul Knapton, 1734.

Della Valle, Pietro. *Viaggi di Pietro Della Valle Il Pellegrino.* Turin: Fontana, 1843.

Lemny, Ştefan. *Les Cantemir, L'aventure européenne d'une famille princière au XVIIIe siècle.* Paris: Complexe, 2009.

Reinhard, Kurt, and Ursula Reinhard. *Musik der Türkei.* 2 vols. Taschenbücher zur Musikwissenschaft 95–96. Wilhelmshaven: Heinrichshofen, 1984.

Shiloah, Amnon. *Music in the World of Islam: A Socio-cultural Study.* Detroit: Wayne State University Press, 1995.

Voltaire. *Essai sur les mœurs et l'esprit des nations.* In *Voltaire: Oeuvres complètes.* Paris: Arvensa Editions, 2013.

PART II

Into Italy, Out of Italy

'... la curiosità del personaggio': 'il Moro' on the Mid-Century Operatic Stage

Emily Wilbourne

> About the Moor, I supplicate the good grace of Your Highness to help me have him, since as much as I esteem his talent, even more am I banking on the novelty of his character; given that here in Venice it will be new, and never before seen, that which perhaps is considered ordinary there [in Florence]; and if the good grace of the Prince Cardinal were to favor me in this, I would send him a similar voice, or perhaps a better one.[1]

On October 14, 1662, the opera impresario Vettor Grimani Calergi wrote to Prince Mattias de' Medici, requesting the Moorish singer who belonged to the Cardinal Prince Giovan Carlo de' Medici (Mattias' brother) for the coming season in Venice. Above and beyond the Moor's talents as a singer, Grimani professed interest in his novelty: perhaps merely "ordinary" in Florence, "il Moro" would be "new, and never before seen" on the Venetian stage. Indeed, Grimani promised to send a singer of equal or better talent to replace the Moor, emphasizing that the combination of his voice and his Black face was a stronger draw than his voice alone. While this letter seems not to have borne immediate fruit, just over a year later Grimani mentioned the Moor again, insisting that he "set out" for Venice.[2] That he did eventually arrive and perform in the 1663/64 Venetian season is documented in yet another letter, this by the famous castrato-turned-diplomat Atto Melani, who wrote that, "the Moor has not had much chance to bring honor upon himself, because he has had a very small role in this second opera."[3] These letters have become widely available only recently, with Sara Mamone's publication of the *carteggio* of Mattias in 2013, though knowledge of the Cardinal's opera-singing Moor has floated around musicology, art history, and theater studies for some time, surfacing in particular in work on the Pergola theater, where "il Moro" sang regularly during the period 1657–1663.

I stumbled upon these letters as part of a larger project about race and representation on the seventeenth-century operatic stage. My initial reaction was that of astonishment: not only to find a Black singer performing on the centrally important stages of La Pergola (in Florence) and S.S. Giovanni e Paolo (in Venice), but also to realize what little impact his Blackness has had on musicological literature—this despite a relative wealth of visual, poetic, musical, and descriptive sources, many of which are transcribed or reproduced in the secondary literature. As is frequently the case for performers and other little-studied individuals of the period, the available material is confusing and at times contradictory; such circumstances are only exacerbated when the individual concerned is largely identified by a racial moniker. Though preliminary, my work in the archives begins to shed light on the rather tangled nexus of slavery, race, and performance in mid-seventeenth-century Italy. Modern scholarship has struggled to account for Black characters and for Black lives in early modern Europe, however placing this particular Black singer front and center stage promises to give the discussion some historical specificity and to produce avenues with which to think about race and representation in terms that reach beyond "exoticism" or "orientalism" in order to trouble the presumed whiteness of European music making.

1.

Perhaps the biggest point of confusion in the secondary literature on "il Moro" concerns his name. This has immediate consequences for the ease with which he can be traced in both secondary and primary sources, and the confusion quickly bleeds into the loaded question of whether this singer was a salaried servant or an enslaved person. In many sources (primary and secondary) he is merely "il Moro."[4] Françoise Decroisette, however, a theater historian who has worked on La Pergola and on the singers of Cardinal Giovan Carlo, calls him Giovanni Buonaccorsi;[5] an identification echoed by Sara Mamone in several publications in 2003, though Mamone spelled his name "Bonaccorsi."[6] Even this seeming agreement provides no clarity, however, since Mamone cites Decroisette as the source of the identification, and Decroisette cites a list of *salariati* employed by Giovan Carlo, which Mamone herself published in a modern transcription that shows the name "Gio Bonaccorsi," but no mention that he was or was called "il Moro" (see table 1). Indeed, by 2013, Mamone had identified the designation "il Moro" with a different singer, Giovanni Michele de Bar.[7]

Principio del servizio	*Nome*	*Cariche*	*Provvisione*
14 settembre 1651	Gio Bonaccorsi	musico di camera	scudi 4

Table 1. Extract from "Ruolo dei provvisionati del Serenissimo Principe Cardinale Giovan Carlo di Toscana, provvisioni il mese," ASF, *Mediceo del Principato*, 5358, cc. fols. 756r–758r, as transcribed in Sara Mamone, ed., *Serenissimi fratelli principi impresari* (2003), as document 1, p. 6

Paul Kaplan, an art historian, has identified "il Moro" with the Black singer depicted by Baldassare Franceschini detto il Volterrano in the *Ritratto di suonatore di liuto con cantore moro,* naming him "Giovannino Moro" based on a description of the painting in Filippo Baldinucci's *Notizie* of 1682: "Giovannino his [Cardinal Giovan Carlo's] Moor, a decent enough *musico,* in the act of singing."[8] Consistent across the board is the name "Giovanni" or a derivative thereof, which perhaps accounts for some of the confusion, predicated on the assumption that enslaved individuals would have been baptized with the names of their owners (in this case, Giovan Carlo de' Medici), though were that the case, our "Moro" would have the surname "Medici," not "Buonaccorsi" or "de Bar." More accurately, documentary sources indicate that enslaved people and religious converts of all stripes were typically baptized with the names of their sponsors, which in the case of the enslaved were frequently but not always their owners.[9] Certainly, while 4 scudi a month is not a particularly generous salary, its presence in Mamone's transcription would suggest that "Gio Bonaccorsi" was not enslaved at the time; Kaplan, too, has argued that "il Moro" was not enslaved, citing small payments (of around 1 scudo) documented in the account books of the Camera del Granduca.[10] Importantly, however, the published transcription of Giovan Carlo's *provvisioni* is inaccurate on a number of counts, and the information it contains clarifies several points, for which see table 2.

Principio del serv:io	*Nomi del servitori*	*Cariche*	*Provisione il mese*	
			Dal Tesoriore	*Dalla Camera*
14 sett. 1651	Gio: Buonaccorsi Moro	Musico di Camera	Vitto, e vestito	Sc.-.4.- [=4 lire]

Table 2. Extract from "Ruolo dei provisionati del Serenissimo Principe Cardinale Gio: Carlo di Toscana," ASF, *Mediceo del Principato,* 5358, c. fol. 757 v; my transcription

From this list, which was compiled in 1663 after the death of Giovan Carlo, we can clearly identify "Gio: Buonaccorsi" as "il Moro," and note that he should indeed be considered an enslaved person.[11] Instead of a salary of 4 scudi a month, he received his food and clothing, and a small allowance of 4 lire a month—far too little to be anything more than pocket money.[12] The only other person on this list of 143 *provvisionati* who is "paid" in food and clothes is Gio: Antonio Gaeta *mutolo,* or "Mute," a person who was very much considered to be a possession of the court, with little-to-no autonomy over his life. Armed with a name, I was also able to trace a death record: "Gio: Buonaccorsi Turco Battezzato buried in S. Felice in Piazza" on August 15, 1674.[13] Though sparse, this death record confirms that "Buonaccorsi" is a baptismal name, not a family name—suggesting that he was brought to Italy under conditions of slavery, rather than being born there to parents who were enslaved or themselves descendants of enslaved individuals —and that at the end of his life he was still close enough to the Medici to be buried in the parish church of the Palazzo Pitti.

I do not know how old Buonaccorsi was when he died or how old he was in 1651 when he entered Giovan Carlo's service. His first documented opera performance, however, was in 1657, nearly six years later, giving him ample time to have studied singing within Giovan Carlo's household. Certainly, by the early 1660s we can assume that Buonaccorsi was an integral part of music making at the court, not least because of Grimani's promise to send a "voice" to replace him in his absence (suggesting that his voice would be sorely missed), but also because so many of the mid-century Florentine operas include a Black character (see table 3): of the Florentine operas performed between the opening of La Pergola in 1657 and Giovan Carlo's death in 1663, three have surviving cast lists mentioning "il Moro," a contemporary description of a further performance calls out one of the characters as a "moorish valet," and three more include a moor in the list of characters, including one (*Scipione in Cartagine,* 1657) that was staged at the Cocomero theater, not La Pergola. We thus have seven surviving libretti (six of which are by Gio: Andrea Moniglia, a member of Giovan Carlo's court) and three surviving scores (two by Jacopo Melani, and one by Francesco Cavalli). I also think it probable that Buonaccorsi performed as the personification of Africa in Moniglia and Domenico Anglesi's horse ballet, *Il mondo festeggiante,* staged at the Palazzo Pitti for the Medici wedding of 1661. Anglesi was also on payroll to Giovan Carlo; the music is unfortunately lost.

In all cases where the music does survive, the moor's part is scored for soprano. Melani, who was on the *ruolo* of Prince Mattias de' Medici, served as singing teacher to at least one of Giovan Carlo's young singers and can be assumed to have had a good grasp of the capacities of the Florentine performers.[14] In each of his two surviving scores for La Pergola the Moor's music is written for soprano (cleffed as C1 and C2, respectively), ranging from *b* to *d''* (a tenth higher).[15] Both Black characters, Monello and Iolao, get a short aria in common time for their first entrance followed by a ritornello; Iolao has a brief B section in triple time and then repeats the opening two lines to conclude. Music also survives for the role of Alindo, in Cavalli's *Hipermestra,* also notated in C1. While the opening line of Alindo's music is set as much as a third higher,

Year	*Title*	*Librettist*	*Composer*	*Black character or role*
1657, rev. 1661	*Il potestà di Colognole*	Gio: Andrea Moniglia	Jacopo Melani	Moro Monello
1657	*Scipione in Cartagine*	Anon	Anon (music lost)	Caralì Moro schiavo su le navi Romane
1658	*Il pazzo per forza*	Gio: Andrea Moniglia	Jacopo Melani (music lost)	Moretta, Zingara
1658	*L'Hipermestrà*	Gio: Andrea Moniglia	Francesco Cavalli	Alindo
1659	*Il vecchio balordo*	Gio: Andrea Moniglia	Jacopo Melani (music lost)	Caralì, moro, schiavetto
1661	*Ercole in Tebe*	Gio: Andrea Moniglia	Jacopo Melani	Iolao, moro servitore di Teseo
1661	*Il mondo festeggiante* (balletto a cavallo)	Gio: Andrea Moniglia	Domenico Anglesi (music lost)	Personification of Africa
1663	*Amore vuole ingegno*	Gio: Andrea Moniglia	Jacopo Melani (music lost)	Moro

Table 3. Musical-theatrical works with an identifiably Black character performed in Florence 1657–1663

the rest of the part is firmly notated within the same range.[16] The consistent tessitura of this repertoire suggests very strongly that it was written for castrato. Baldinucci's citation (from 1682) of Buonaccorsi as both "musico" and "Giovannino" is also suggestive on this front, as diminutives were common for castrati and the term *musico* was frequently though not exclusively used to indicate the castrato voice type.[17] We should also note that in at least one instance, "il Moro" played a female character, and while music for the gypsy character, Moretta, does not survive, it too was presumably scored for soprano.

If Buonaccorsi were not Black, if he were not enslaved, the question of whether or not he was a castrato would be largely academic. After all, at the time most serious male singers were. (Of the six male singers among Giovan Carlo's *provvisionati*, only one—Carlo Righenzi—sang tenor, and none bass or baritone).[18] Still, Buonaccorsi's Black body complicates the already gray morality of pre-pubescent castration. Whose decision was it anyway? And what did Buonaccorsi himself make of it (both before and after the operation)? These are important questions to ask, even if we do not have answers, and even while the evidence remains partly speculative. Not only does Buonaccorsi's Black body force attention to the ways in which the violence of slavery and the violence of castration cohere in their instrumentalization of the human body, Buonaccorsi-as-castrato makes Western music itself integral to his being in the world. It makes of him a serious singer—where I mean serious both in the sense of professional, not casual, and in the sense of "serious" as opposed to the term "comic." For any singer, a castrato voice opened a larger range of dramatic roles and an expanded access to elevated musical repertoires, including chamber cantantas and sacred music. Castration was an investment in a melophilic future.

The soprano voice of Gio: Buonaccorsi is something that modern scholarship needs to take seriously: his (Black) body labored in the production of this music, and the ease with which his body was absorbed into the material production of operatic music and the facility with which his enslaved Black body slipped down unmarked into the footnotes of music history is a methodological warning. Historiographically we need to find a language that can account for Buonaccorsi's centrality and thus for the central importance of racial difference to the monument of European opera. The roles Buonaccorsi played are far from the only Black roles in opera of the time. What would it mean to take the roles of slaves and servants seriously?

2.

Castrato or not, the Black roles of the Florentine stage are closely delimited. With the exception of the Egyptian gypsy, the moors of these mid-century libretti are all servants or slaves—effectively replicating onstage the role that Buonaccorsi played in "real life" for the Medici court. Typically, the Black character appears in only one or two scenes, often in dialogue with a stuttering hunchback servant. Comparing scenes across multiple works, it is fascinating how closely these excerpts adhere to the system of stock characters that (public) opera inherited from the *commedia dell'arte*—even in this private and lavishly funded context where we might imagine greater liberties were accorded.[19] The stuttering servant was played by the Cardinal's comic tenor Carlo Righenzi, where the pitch of his voice and the comedy of his part are tightly related. Righenzi and "il Moro" shared scenes in *Il potestà di Colognole, Il vecchio balordo, Ercole in Tebe*, and *Amore vuole ingegno*: evidently the two singers—or the librettist, Moniglia, who wrote all four libretti—had a schtick that exploited Buonaccorsi's dark complexion as a surprise for Righenzi's character, leading to Buonaccorsi's mis-recognition as supernatural or inhuman. The two passages that follow are extracts, not the full scenes, but they show a shared reliance on whiteness as a visual norm.[20]

Interestingly, while Blackness and its presumed abnormality function here as comic punchline, vocally and linguistically Buonaccorsi/Moro/Iolao is far more adept than Righenzi/Desso/Sifone. These Black characters speak excellent Italian, and in contrast with the destructive, dehumanizing sounds of stuttered speech, Buonaccorsi/Moro/Iolao articulates the action and responds in a logical

DESSO, MORO	Oste, oste, oste, Porta un lume.	Innkeeper, innkeeper, innkeeper! Bring a light!
MORO	Per certo Facciam a non c'intendere. Per il vero comprendere, Rispondi, chi è l'oste, tu o io?	Clearly We are making it so we don't understand each other, So that we really understand, Respond: Who is the innkeeper, you or me?
DESSO	I-, i-, i-, io ...	I-, I-, I-, I...
MORO	Se dunque L'oste tu sei, perché Domandi il lume a me?	Well then, If you are the innkeeper, Why are you asking me for a light?
DESSO	... Io non son oste.	... I am not the innkeeper.
MORO	E nemmen io.	Well, me neither.
DESSO	Ma vedo una lanterna. Lascia ch'io ti discerna.	Ok, I see a lantern. Let me take a look at you.
	(Piglia la lanterna lasciata da Anselmo.)	*(He takes the lantern left by Anselmo.)*
MORO	Guarda pur quanto vuoi. Ma tu chi sei?	Look all you want. But who are you?
DESSO	Il diavolo.	The devil!
MORO	Il diavolo, sicura.	The devil, for sure!
DESSO	O-, o-, o-, o-...	O-, o-, o-, o-...
MORO	Per la mia vita rendere, Gambe mie, voi sappiatemi difendere.	In order to save my life, Legs, you'd better know how to defend me!

Example 1. Taken from Gio: Andrea Moniglia, *Il potestà di Colognole* (perf. 1657), II, xi

SIFONE	Per tro-, trovare Alceste vò cercando per tutto oh, che paese bru-, bru-, bru-	To f-, find Alceste I am searching everywhere Oh, this place is ug-, ug-, ug-
IOLAO (MORO)	In queste parti e come Per qual strana occasione arrivasti Sifone che fai, non mi conosci? Guardami, chi son io	In these parts, and how? For what strange reason does Sifone arrive? What are you doing? Don't you recognize me? Look at me! Who am I?
SIFONE	bru-, bru-, bru- bru-, bru-, bru-, brutto. Ohimè, un Demonio, ohimè	ug-, ug-, ug- ug-, ug-, ug-, ugly. Oh no, a demon, oh no!
IOLAO (MORO)	Di che paventi? Iolao son' io.	Why are you so scared? It is me, Iolao!
SIFONE	È quando sei venuto nella patria di Pluto?	And when did you arrive in the land of Pluto?

Example 2. Taken from Gio: Andrea Moniglia, *Ercole in Tebe* (perf. 1661), III, vi

fashion to events around him (in the extract from *La podestà*, for example, Desso thinks Moro a *diavolo* because of his Black skin, but Moro thinks Desso a *diavolo* because grammatically speaking he claims to be one: Q. "But who are you?" A. "The devil!").[21] Indeed, had Righenzi/Desso/Sifone known Buonaccorsi/Moro/Iolao was Black from his voice or speech alone, there would have been no surprise at seeing his face.

This neutral, "Italianate" voice, however, is not consistent across all of the roles under discussion. In reference to the character of Caralì in Moniglia's *Il vecchio balordo*, Decroisette writes, "this figure of the moor is typical in the dramas of Moniglia, who gives him an exotic, macaronic language, dominated by a final ù, by the substitution of *b* for *p*, by the use of infinitive verbs, and by the omission of grammatical articles."[22] The two excerpts just discussed make it clear that the "exotic" Black voice is not necessarily typical of Moniglia's dramas. Where it is deployed (in the travesty role of the Gypsy Moretta, and as the enslaved Black laborers in the anonymous *Scipione in Cartagine* and Moniglia's *Il vecchio balordo*—both characters coincidently enough are called Caralì) the characters concerned are noticeably less elevated—less educated, more comic—and specifically singled out as recent immigrants. The linguistic deformations of this slaves' *gergo* are remarkably consistent with *moresche* texts stretching back into the previous century, which as Gianfranco Salvatore has shown, incorporate the speech patterns of enslaved communities.[23] Across this audible axis of dialect and signification we can recognize a contemporary distinction whereby the role of galley slave and court servant are markedly different, even when both individuals might well be Black, Muslim or recent convert, and literally enslaved.

I include here an excerpt from the anonymous libretto for *Scipione in Cartagine*, in which the slave jargon given to the Moor is particularly dense. In the scene directly proceeding this one, Caralì learned that Scipione has liberated all the slaves; this scene is Caralì's song of celebration. Given the heavily marked Italian, the deliberate grammatical errors, and the use of both foreign and dialect words, the translation offered here is necessarily partial.[24] I have made no attempt to reproduce the errors in the English text.

Though the score of this opera does not survive, the poetic meter of this scene suggests an introductory recitative followed by two verses of aria. Direct reference is made to the life of the galley slave—No longer will they have to eat ship's biscuit!—while the names of Caralì's fellow slaves are recognizably ethnic, even Ottoman. The refrain cites the traditional Arabic greeting: "As-salāmu'alaykum," or "Peace be upon you," possibly with the word "Allah" or "in sha Allah" ("God willing") tacked on the end. The "Italian" text reflects

CARALÌ	O Quanto star contentu Baes miù andar, Marmorata trovar; Legressa grandu Diù, O fatma core miù.	Oh, how happy I am, To return to my country To find my beloved; How generous the great God, O, Fatima, my love.
1	Camarata nesciumù, Non biscottu mansgiar, Non corbasciù tuccar; Tenimu libertà; Scibiona gentilisco Fasito carità; *Salamalech Ikallà, Ikallà.*	Leave the cabin, We will not eat ships' biscuit, Nor be touched by the whip, We hold our liberty; Noble Scipione Has done us this good deed; *Peace be upon you, God willing!*
2	Ber chistu ligramente Frofalla, & Ebrahin, Corcùt, Dragùt, Selin, Soliman, Mustafà, Ballar, e ghimberì. Sonar, Alì, Cassa, *Salamalech Ikallà, Ikallà.*	For this happily, Frofalla, and Ebrahin, Corcùt, Dragùt, Selin, Soliman, Mustafà, Dance and [with] cymbals, Play, Alì, Cassa. *Peace be upon you, God willing!*

Example 3. Taken from Anon, *Scipione in Cartagine* (perf. 1657), I, xv

precisely the final ù as described by Decroisette, as well as the transposed *p*/*b* (see, for example, Scipione's name, which is rendered as "Scibiona"). In example 4 we see the same *gergo* used by the Caralì character in *Il vecchio balordo* in conversation with a stuttering servant, Piero (played by Righenzi), who in this opera, is not shocked by the slave's Black skin, having assumed his Blackness from the beginning of the interaction.

There is a stark contrast between Moro/Iolao's sophisticated courtly polish and the lower register of Caralì's dialogue. One interpretation (and my own initial assessment) would see this contrast as indicative of the varieties of Black representation (and perhaps differences of Black experience)—court retainer/galley slave—and also as documenting the breadth and flexibility of Buonaccorsi's stock character type. Something I found in the archives, however, undermines this second point.

I have looked at some length for the baptismal records of "Gio: Buonaccorsi Turco Battezzato," and although that search has as yet been unsuccessful, I have found a considerable number of records for other Medici-owned slaves. One in particular stood out. The records of the Pia Casa dei Catecumini are fascinating because the priests were required to interview and transcribe the responses of would-be converts to certify that the conversion was genuine and that the convert understood the basic tenets of Catholicism. Here is a section of one of these interviews, dated July 21, 1657:

> My name is Caralì; I do not know the name of my father, and I was born in Barbary, in Zeila [a coastal city in present-day Somalia], of the race of Granadians, to be 16 years old, to live in Florence, and being on the sea, the boat where I found myself was captured by Captain Flaminio, who brought me to Livorno and gave me to Prince Mattias.[25]

On August 1, "Caralì, moor from Barbary of the race of Granadians, aged approximately 16 years old," was sponsored for baptism by the Most Serene Prince Mattias of Tuscany, although it was Andrea Pellegrini, his *cappellano*, who stood up for the prince at the ceremony. Caralì took the baptismal name "Mattia Medici."[26]

It seems likely to me that the thickly accented Caralì roles were taken by Caralì (an ex-galley slave), rather than by Buonaccorsi. If so, we are dealing with two opera-singing Black Medici slaves, not just one, which elegantly explains the characterological dichotomy between "Caralì" and "Moro/Iolao." Elsewhere, the documents attest that by 1657 Caralì had been in Florence for four years.[27] Captured at sea, therefore, at the tender age of twelve, Caralì was

PIERO	Schia, schia, schia, schia, schiavetto Caralì, mo, mo, morino vien qui.	Sl, sl, sl, sl, little slave Caralì, Mo, mo, little moor, come here.
CARALÌ	Salamalecch', dù star Badruna.	Peace be upon you, where is my master?
PIERO	Or ora ve, ve, verrà.	Na, now He co, co, comes.
CARALÌ	Ber ti star sciamatù. Dicir pipa tabaccu avir?	For you Have been called. Say, He wants pipe tobacco?
PIERO	Vi, vi, vi, vino vuol essere.	W-, w-, w-, wine It has to be.
CARALÌ	Biager vinù, si donar libertà, e non bibir, io campar non putir.	To like wine, To have the freedom of it, and not to drink I could not bear it.
PIERO	Ti, ti diletta questo paese?	You, you like This country?
CARALÌ	Multo golentieri son schiavù; ma sciamar Anselma signura.	Very much I am a slave; but I call Anselmo master.
PIERO	Come spesso ti da, danno? di?	How often Does he gi-, gi-, give it to you?
CARALÌ	Non bastuna ber mi. Non bastuna ber mi.	He never beats me. He never beats me.
PIERO	Ecco che viene.	Here he comes!

Example 4. Taken from Gio: Andrea Moniglia, *Il vecchio balordo* (perf. 1659), II, xiv

deemed young enough (and presumably handsome enough) to be taken to court and given to a prince. Caralì himself may have spoken the slave jargon represented in these libretti (whether at his arrival in 1653 or throughout his life) or known—through intimate experience—how to effectively perform it.

I—like Decroisette, Kaplan, and surely all modern scholars who had thought about the situation at all—had assumed there to be but one singing Black slave. Caralì (later Mattia Medici) reminds us that the "cortigiani di basso servizio," the buffoons, jesters, moors, and dwarves of early modern courts were engaged in performance and in music making that has largely been lost. What is unique about Buonaccorsi and Caralì is not that they made music—for many Black Europeans clearly made music—but that they performed in the high-cultural form of opera, which has allowed some level of documentation to survive.

3.

Yet if Caralì's historical existence militates against Buonaccorsi's exceptionalism, Grimani's letter would seem to argue for it, declaring as he does that Buonaccorsi's character would be "new, and never before seen" on the Venetian stage. Of the two operas staged by the Grimani at S.S. Giovanni e Paolo in 1663/64, the first was *La Rosilena* by Aurelio Aureli and Giovanni Battista Volpe *detto* Rovettino. The music is unfortunately lost, but the libretto includes a character that seems custom made for Buonaccorsi: "Ergisto Moro servo d'Ariadeno."[28] The second had a libretto by Nicolò Minato and music by Cavalli; the work was *Scipione affricano*.[29] The explicit confluence of an opera set entirely on African soil with this rare Italian singer of African descent would seem a unique opportunity to confront the tangled nexus of race and representation—if it was not for Buonaccorsi's reported "piccolissima parte," and the pressing question of which role Buonaccorsi took.

Jennifer Williams Brown, who is close to completing an edition of *Scipione affricano*, has suggested that Buonaccorsi could have played the small role of the Sibyl—noting that the comic servant Lesbo runs away at the sight (thus echoing the behavior of the comic servant Desso)—probably double cast with the page and an onstage musician, each of whom sing only a line or two.[30] While to modern sensibilities the obvious casting for a Black singer in *Scipione affricano* would be as one of the African characters (imagine Buonaccorsi, for just a moment, in the celebrated castrato role of Siface, king of the Massessuli), Grimani and his peers obviously thought otherwise. As the (Black) page, as a (Black) musician, as a (Black) Sibyl, Buonaccorsi's performance once again confirms the representational associations of Black skin and servitude. Ironically,

Buonaccorsi's presumed role as the Black pageboy points up not only a European obliviousness to Africa, but also the thoroughly normalized presence of Afro-Europeans within Italian society, such that Blackness and servant can be virtually synonymous—so typical of contemporary culture that even within representations of Africa, the Black presence is unremarkable.

In this context it is worth invoking a letter from castrato singer Giovanni Antonio Cavagna to the Venetian impresario and librettist Giovanni Faustini in 1666. This letter is regularly cited as indicative of a singer's ability to negotiate their role; it is notable here for the casual reference to Blackface costuming: "Two things alone worry me, the first, is the need to sing in a Black moor's mask, a thing that I no longer do, and which I did not realize [was necessary] until after I read the third act."[31] It is not clear whether Cavagna is objecting to singing in a mask, or to singing the role of a moor, but it is clear that he once did so, perhaps regularly. It would seem then that the "novelty" of "il Moro's" *personaggio* was less about his Black face than about his Black body.

Despite Atto Melani's faintly damning assessment of Buonaccorsi's debut Venetian season, it is worth considering a continued role for Buonaccorsi in the Grimani theater and elsewhere. In 1665, the Grimani staged Aureli and Andrea Mattioli's *Perseo*, which includes a whole slew of Ethiopian and Mauritanian characters, some of whom are servants, as well as a remake of Giulio Cesare Sorrentino and Francesco Provenzale/Cavalli/Mattioli's *Ciro*, which includes the character "Fatama Mora, Schiava [di Cleopilda], vestita da Zingara," which would have been a perfect role for Buonaccorsi who had previously played a Gypsy Moretta on at least one occasion.[32]

4.

I am hopeful that more details of the lives and the music making of Gio: Buonaccorsi and Caralì-Mattia Medici will come to light, yet even the sources we have give us food for thought. Cavagna's "Maschera da Moro" and sources like Ruccellai's description of *L'Hipermestra*, which marks as Black (as "Moro valletto") a role that textually can be presumed white, raise the possibility that any servant or slave role could have been understood to represent racial difference, performed by Black singers or white singers in Blackface. Similarly, the presence of Gio: Buonaccorsi and Cavalì-Mattia Medici, along with a host of other Moors, Turks, and slaves at the Medici court, make clear how normalized racial and religious slavery was in early modern Italy. The representation of Black slaves was no more or less exoticist than was court life itself. Black slaves were not an imagined, fantasized representation symbolizing something allegorical, but a reflection of the mundane, day-to-day co-existence of white and Black Europeans. Furthermore, the two very different onstage characters—of "Caralì," galley slave, and "Iolao/Moro," court retainer (not to mention the Black Egyptian gypsy, not discussed in this brief essay)—are a forceful reminder not to collapse the Black Italian experience into a single "type."

Like Cavagna—who did not realize a "Black moor's mask" was necessary until he got to the third act—scholars have failed to recognize the presence of race in the written sources. Still, if we take Black singers and Black roles seriously, we can get beyond the mere "curiosità del personaggio," and work toward a better understanding of the foundational place of race in seventeenth-century Italian performance.

Notes

The initial version of this paper, as given at the Music in the Mediterranean Diaspora conference at I Tatti in May 2017, was based on material that was already available—in print, facsimile, or online. I have since begun archival work in Florence, and the current version of the text takes some new information into account. I would like to thank Queens College in the City University of New York for a Scholar Incentive Award; and the Harvard University Center for Renaissance Studies, I Tatti, Florence, for a fellowship during the year 2017–2018 and for the invitation to the initial conference; without this support the research that underlies this paper would not have been possible. I am also indebted to Paul Kaplan and Jennifer Williams Brown, who both shared pre-publication versions of their own work and engaged in ongoing conversations about the implications of my archival finds, and to Francesca Fantappiè for the time she spent helping me make sense of the Medicean account books.

1. "Del Moro, io supplico la benignità di Vostra Altezza farmelo avere, poiché sì come stimo la sua virtù altretanto fo capitale della curiosità del personaggio; già che qui a Venezia sarà nuovo, e non più veduto; che costì forse sarà stimato ordinario; e quando la benignità del Principe Cardinale mi volesse far grazia, io le manderei voce simile, e forse migliore." Vettor Grimani Calergi to Prince Mattias de' Medici, October 14, 1662, ASAF *Mediceo del Principato*, 5487, Registro di riscontri di pagamenti; lettere di segretari e auditori (1632–1663), fol. 666. Transcribed in Mamone, ed. *Mattias de' Medici serenissimo mecenate* as lett. 1590, p. 796.

2. "Già è tempo, ch'il Moro s'incamini a questa volta, che perciò potrà Vostra Altezza restar servita ordinarle, che se ne venga." Grimani to Mattias, November 9, 1663, I-Fas *Mediceo del Principato*, 5477, Diversi, con minute di risposta (1662–1663), fol. 175r. Transcribed in ibid., as lett. 1625, p. 814.

3. "Il Moro non ha avuto troppo campo di farsi onore, perché ha avuto pochissima parte in questa seconda opera." Atto Melani to Mattias de' Medici, February 16, 1664, I-Fas *Mediceo del Principato*, 5478, Diversi, con minute di risposta (1662–1664), fols. 427r–28r. Transcribed in ibid., as lett. 1636, pp. 818–19.

4. This is true for the musicological literature, see for example, Weaver and Weaver, *A Chronology of Music*.

5. See Decroisette, "Un exemple d'administration," 81 n. 17; "I virtuosi del Cardinale," 85; Moniglia, *Il vecchio balordo*, 149.

6. See Mamone, ed. *Serenissimi fratelli principi impresari*, XXXVI, XXXVII; and Mamone, "Most Serene Brothers-Princes-Impresarios," 4.8.

7. See the index to Mamone's *Carteggio di Giovan Carlo de' Medici*.

8. "... dipoi gli rappresentò in un quadro un giovanetto staffiere di sua Corte, con Giovannino suo moro, che fu assai buon musico, in atto di cantare." The mention of the picture comes as part of a section describing works made by Volterrano for the Cardinal Giovan Carlo de' Medici around 1662, which begins on the previous page, see Baldinucci, *Notizie de' professori del disegno*, 400. There are several other visual sources that relate to "Giovannino" Moro, none of which are discussed in this essay (for reasons of space). For a discussion of and reproduction of costume drawings for operas including his character, Moro Monello, see Massar, "Costume Drawings by Stefano della Bella," 243–66, 297–317.

9. I came to this conclusion myself on examination of the baptismal records kept by the Baptistry of S. Giovanni in Florence (available online, http://archivio.operaduomo.fi.it/battesimi/); other scholars have made a similar point, see Marconcini, "Una presenza nascosta," 104; Wipertus, "Le baptême des musulmans esclaves," 9–181.

10. Of the other singers on the list, Antonio Riviani was paid the most, at 16 scudi per month, and the young girls seemingly the least, at 2 or 3 scudi per month. See also, Kaplan, "Giovannino Moro." He cites I-Fas *Camera del Granduca,* 28b (1656–1657), fols. 17r, 43v.

11. The document is in the same hand as and cross-referenced with another document in the same *filza* entitled, "Ruolo dei Cortigiani del Ser(enissi)mo Car(dina)le Gio: Carlo, à quali doppo la morte di S.A.Ill(uminissi)mi doveva dargli impiego," I-Fas *Mediceo del Principato,* 5358, fols. 728r-29r. In that second document, "Moro" is assigned a charitable handout of 8 scudi in recognition of the death of his owner but is not dismissed from service to the family.

12. In the conversion equivalency at the time, 1 scudo = 7 lire; 1 lire = 20 soldi; 1 soldo = 12 denari.

13. I-Fas *Arte di Medici e Speziali, Registro dei morti della città di Firenze,* 260, fol. 141r.

14. For Melani's presence on Mattias' rolls, see Mamone, *Carteggio di Mattias de' Medici,* lett. 1103–1004. Alessandro and Jacinto Melani were also on Mattias' rolls during the late 1650s, see I-Fas *Mediceo del Principato,* 5417, cc. fols. 942–43. Bartolomeo Melani is listed as a singer in Giovan Carlo's household in I-Fas *Mediceo del Principato,* 5358. For the reference to Jacopo as a singing teacher, see *Carteggio di Giovan Carlo de' Medici,* lett. 803.

15. I have not seen the original score of *Il Podestà,* only the Leve edition of 2005, but I thank Jennifer Williams Brown for information regarding the cleffing. The other Melani score has been published in facsimile, see Melani, *Ercole in Tebe.* Moro Monello sings from *c'* to *d''* (a ninth); Iolao sings from *b* to *d''*.

16. Francesco Cavalli, *L'Hipermestra* (Biblioteca Nazionale Marciana, Venice; Codex Contarini 3621654), II, 18, fols. 78r–79v. My enormous thanks to Judy Tsou, for copying this music for me from the microfilm at UW. The score itself is highly illegible, but Alindo's part seems to range from *c'* to at least *f''* (possibly *g''*) above the staff; the top notes appear only in the first line of music, after that the range stays below *d''* with a possible *e''* in the last phrase. Brown has noted that the Venice score is Cavalli's own pre-production original, composed several years before the actual performance, and almost certainly modified at some point.

17. Also, it is notable that both Buonaccorsi and Antonio Riviani (a castrato) are listed as "musico da camera" in the list of *provvisionati* discussed earlier.

18. Alongside Antonio Riviani, a known castrato, and Buonaccorsi, the list includes Francesco Leonardi (soprano), Carlo Righenzi (tenor), Vincenzo Oliviviani (soprano) and Bartolomeo Melani (contralto). The list also includes six female singers, three *donne,* three *fanciulle*: Donna Lucia Coppa, Angela Socii fanciulla, Donna Lisabetta Falbetti Nacci, Francesca Chiarelli fanciulla, Donna Leonora Falbetti Ballerini, and Luisa Massai fanciulla. See I-Fas *Mediceo del Principato,* 5358, fol. 757v.

19. Wilbourne, *Seventeenth-Century Opera.*

20. The libretti translations that follow are mine, although modern edition of the libretto and an English translation of the first example is provided by Leve along with his published score, see Melani, *Il potestà di Colognole.*

21. On the topic of musical stutters, see Wilbourne, "Demo's Stutter," 659–63. For a discussion of the animalistic noises of mute characters in relation to noble Black characters, see "*Lo Schiavetto* (1612)."

22. "[Q]uesta figura di moro è abituale nei drammi di Moniglia, che gli dà un linguaggio esotico maccaronico, dominato dalla ù finale, dalla sostituzione di -p- in -b-, dall'uso degli infinitivi verbali, e dalla soppressione degli articoli." See the editorial apparatus to Moniglia, *Il vecchio balordo,* 149.

23. Salvatore has traced Kanuri words in portions of *moresche* texts that were previously assumed to be nonsense syllables, see Salvatore, "Parodie realistiche."

24. I would like to extend my thanks to Riccardo Strobino and Giuliano Mori for their help deciphering the jargon incorporated into this text and the following.

25. "Io mi chiamo Caralì, non so il nome di mio padre, e sono nato in Barberia a Zeila di razza di Granatini, esser d'anni 16. abitare in Firenze et essendo in mare fu preso il legno dove mi ritrovavo dal

Cap. Flaminio, il q(ua)le mi condusse a Livorno e mi dono al S.r Princ(ip)e Mattia." ACAF *Pia Casa dei Catecumini*, 2, August 21, 1657; the papers in this *filza* are unnumbered though ordered chronologically. I have left in place the grammatical inconsistencies of this text. It is not clear whether the scribe recorded errors that Caralì himself made (the unconjugated verbs are suggestive on this front), or whether the infinitive verbs indicate a notational shorthand in which "he declares himself" has been omitted.

26. I-Fd *Registri Battesimali*, Maschii, register 51, fotogram 236, August 1, 1657.

27. ACAF *Pia Casa dei Catecumini*, 2.

28. Aurelio, *La Rosilena*.

29. Details of both productions are listed in Appendix 1 of Glixon and Glixon, *Inventing the Business of Opera*, 333. The Glixons note that the dedication of *La Rosilena* is dated January 4, 1664, and that of *Scipione affricano* February 9 (thus *La Rosilena* is the "first" opera, and *Scipione affricano* the "second").

30. Personal communication, January 18, 2018. See also Cavalli, *Scipione affricano*, ed. Brown.

31. "Due cose sole mi spaventano, l'una, di dover cantar con la Maschera da Moro, cosa non più usata da me, et non mai compresa che doppo haver letto il terzo atto... " Rosand states that the letter is about Cavagna's role in Giovanni Faustini and Pietro Andrea Ziani's *Alciade* (initially scheduled for the 1666 season, but postponed until 1667); "The role in question was probably that of Megaristo, Alciade's servant," see p. 239, and n. 61. Transcribed as doc. 16 in Appendix 3A, Correspondence and Documents, Venice, Archivio di Stato: Scuola grande di San Marco, busta 188:37, in Rosand, *Opera in Seventeenth-Century Venice*.

32. The production schedule is listed by Glixon and Glixon, *Inventing the Business of Opera*, 333. For the list of "intervenienti," see Aurelio, *Perseo*; note that the list of characters identifies Fatama as "schiava d'Elmera (slave to Elmera)," however the libretto text itself makes it clear that Fatama is enslaved to the character Cleopilda, an Egyptian princess.

Bibliography

Archival Sources

AAI (Archivio dell'Accademia degli Immobili, Firenze)
  Archivio storico, 1.7, 1.14, 1.17

ACAF (Archivio della Curia Arcivescovile di Firenze)
  Pia Casa dei Catecumini, filza 2

I-Fas (Archivio di Stato di Firenze)
  Arte di Medici e Speziali, Registro dei morti della città di Firenze, n.260
  Camera del Granduca, filza 28b
  Mediceo del Principato, filze 5358, 5417, 5477, 5478, 5487

I-Fd (Archivio del Opera del Duomo di Firenze)
  Registri Battesimali, maschii, reg. 51

I-Fn (Biblioteca Nazionale di Firenze)

Printed Sources

Anon. *Scipione in Cartagine, dramma musicale; Fatto rappresentare da gli Accademici Sorgenti, nel loro Teatro, sotto la protezzione del Sereniss. e Reverendiss. Princ. Card. Gio: Carlo di Toscana*. Florence: Gio: Anton Bonardi, 1657.

Aurelio, Aureli. *La Rosilena, drama per musica*. Venice: Francesco Nicolini in Spadaria, 1664.

Aurelio, Aureli. *Perseo, dramma per musica*. Venice: Francesco Nicolini, 1665.

Baldinucci, Filippo. "Decenn. V. della Part. I. del sec. V. dal 1640. al 1650." In *Notizie de' professori del disegno da Cimabue in qua*. Florence, 1682.

Cavalli, Francesco. *L'Hipermestra*. Biblioteca Nazionale Marciana, Venice; Codex Contarini 3621654.

Cavalli, Francesco. *Scipione affricano*. Edited by Jennifer Williams Brown. Forthcoming.

Decroisette, Françoise. "Un exemple d'administration des théâtres au XVIIème siecle: Le théâtre de la Pergola à Florence (1652–1662)." In *Arts du spectacle et histoire des idées: Recueil offert en hommage à Jean Jacquot*. Pp. 73–90. Tours: Publications de la Société des amis du Centre d'Études Supériures de la Renaissance, 1984.

Decroisette, Françoise. "I virtuosi del Cardinale, da Firenze all'Europa." In *Lo "spettacolo maraviglioso." Il Teatro della Pergola: l'opera a Firenze*, ed. Marcello de Anglis, Elvira Garbero Zorzi, Loredana Maccabruni, Piero Marchi and Luigi Zangheri. Ufficio Centrale per i Beni Archivistici. Florence: Pagliai Polistampa, 2000.

Glixon, Beth, and Jonathan Glixon. *Inventing the Business of Opera: The Impresario and his World in Seventeenth-Century Venice*. Oxford: Oxford University Press, 2008.

Kaplan, Paul H.D. "Giovannino Moro." Unpublished conference paper as given at "Staging Africans: Race and Representation in Early Modern European Theaters," Columbia University, October 23, 2015.

Mamone, Sara, ed. "Most Serene Brothers-Princes-Impresarios: Theater in Florence under the Management and Protection of Mattias, Giovan Carlo, and Leopoldo de' Medici." *Journal of Seventeenth-Century Music* 9 (2003): http://sscm-jscm.org/jscm/v9/no1/mamone.html.

Mamone, Sara, ed. *Serenissimi fratelli principi impresari: Notizie di spettacolo nei carteggi medicei. Carteggi di Giovan Carlo de' Medici e di Desiderio Montemagni suo segretario (1628–1664)*. Florence: Le Lettere, 2003.

Mamone, Sara, ed. *Mattias de' Medici serenissimo mecenate dei virtuosi. Notizie di spettacolo nei carteggi medicei. Carteggio di Mattias de' Medici (1629–1667)*. Florence: Le Lettere, 2013.

Marconcini, Samuela. "Una presenza nascosta: Battesimi di 'turchi' a Firenze in età moderna." *Annali di Storia di Firenze* 7 (2012): 97–121.

Massar, Phyllis Dearborn. "Costume Drawings by Stefano della Bella for the Florentine Theater." *Master Drawings* 8 (1970):243–66; 97–317.

Melani, Jacopo. *Ercole in Tebe*. New York: Garland Publishing, 1978.

Melani, Jacopo. *Il potestà di Colognole*, ed. James Leve. Middleton, WI: A-R Editions, 2005.

Moniglia, Giovanni Andrea. *Il pazzo per forza, Dramma civile rusticale, Fatto rappresentare in Musica, Da gl'illustriss. Sig. Accademici Immobili Nel loro Teatro, Sotto la protezione del Sereniss e Reverendiss. Principe Cardinale Gio: Carlo di Toscana*. Florence: per il Bonardi, 1659.

Moniglia, Giovanni Andrea. *Delle poesie dramatiche di Giovann'Andrea Moniglia, Accademico della Crusca, Parte prima*. Florence: Vincenzio Vangelisti, 1689.

Moniglia, Giovanni Andrea. *Il vecchio balordo*, ed. Françoise Decroisette. Biblioteca Pregoldoniana. Venice: Lineadacqua, 2014.

Rosand, Ellen. *Opera in Seventeenth-Century Venice: The Creation of a Genre*. Berkeley: University of California Press, 1991.

Rudt de Collenberg, Wipertus H. "Le baptême des musulmans esclaves à Rome aux XVIIe et XVIIIe siècles. I. Le XVIIe siècle." *Mélanges de l'Ecole française de Rome. Italie et Méditerranée* 101 (1989): 9–181.

Salvatore, Gianfranco. "Parodie realistiche: Africanismi, fraternità e sentimenti identitari nelle canzoni moresche del Cinquecento." *Kronos* 14 (2011): 97–130.

Weaver, Robert Lamar, and Norma Wright Weaver. *A Chronology of Music in the Florentine Theater 1590–1750*. Detroit Studies in Music Bibliography. Detroit: Information Coordinators, 1978.

Wilbourne, Emily. "Demo's Stutter, Subjectivity, and the Virtuosity of Vocal Failure." *Journal of the American Musicological Society* 68 (2015): 659–63.

Wilbourne, Emily. "*Lo Schiavetto* (1612): Travestied Sound, Ethnic Performance, and the Eloquence of the Body." *Journal of the American Musicological Society* 63 (2010): 1–44.

Wilbourne, Emily. *Seventeenth-Century Opera and the Sound of the Commedia dell'arte*. Chicago: University of Chicago Press, 2016.

Alla [vera] spagnola: Hearing Spain and Playing Guitar in Early Modern Italy

Cory M. Gavito

In May of 1609, Giuseppe Faccone, working as a talent scout for the Duke of Mantua, Vincenzo Gonzaga, sent the following news to Mantua regarding his brother's pursuit in Naples of a talented nineteen-year-old singer: "My brother told me that for a while he has been following the progress of a Neapolitan girl who has all of these qualities: she plays the harp excellently and sings from the book all kinds of madrigals with such confidence that there is no other singer who can surpass her."[1]

As is now well known, this force of nature was Adriana Basile, who months later became the superstar of the Mantuan court. Monteverdi ranked her voice even above Francesca Caccini's. The beauty of her voice, however, was not for Faccone the most impressive statistic of her musicianship: "And what is even better" he goes on to say, "she plays the guitar very well and sings *alla spagnola* (in the Spanish manner), and in such a pairing that between the Italian and Spanish [songs] she knows more than three hundred works by heart."[2]

As impressive as this dimension of Basile's musical talent might have been for Faccone and others fortunate enough to have heard her sing and play these songs, I would like to pose a few questions about this account that direct us first to the practical and formative nature of Basile's musicianship, and second to the nature of her repertory, namely guitar songs *alla spagnola*. I want to ask if her talent alone suffices in explaining how Basile could have memorized such an extensive repertory before the age of twenty. Was there something about her repertory of guitar songs that facilitated memorization? Are we misguided in understanding her repertory as a "repertory" per se—a body of composed works learned, studied, organized, and compiled expressly for the purpose of performance? I will suggest that we might better understand the musical abilities of Basile by instead thinking of her "three hundred works" as a practice or an idiom, a mode of knowledge, a way of doing, and one in which the Spanish guitar and an Italian concept of Spanishness (*alla spagnola*) were central in defining this practice for her Italian audiences.

In what follows, I examine how Italians cultivated a discourse about Spanish musical identity that sought to materialize the foreign, mysterious, and immaterial elements of Spanish musical practice. The sites that curated this discourse not only include performers like Basile, but also the multitude of amateur "Spanish-guitar singers" who followed in her wake, whose demands to learn the Spanish guitar were met by the guitar tutors issued in great numbers by the Italian music presses starting in the early seventeenth century. In particular, I will show how the authors of these books—by and large Italian maestros of the Spanish guitar—promised readers access to the "true" Spanish manner of playing the guitar, an elusive performance idiom that required the mastery of strumming patterns in *sesquialtera* and hemiola rhythms. In the second part of the chapter I note additional routes through which Italians defined and heard Spain musically, namely in travel literature of the seventeenth century, where writers such as Pietro Della Valle called upon Spanish musical traditions and the Spanish guitar as touchstones for deciphering his musical encounters in Turkey and Egypt. I conclude the chapter by introducing an aspiring guitar singer *alla spagnola* in the making: Caterina Picchena, a precocious thirteen-year-old Florentine musician with Medici ties, whose father tapped his contacts in Madrid for help in satisfying young Caterina's desire to sing and play *alla spagnola*. Ever present in all three contexts is the five-course Spanish guitar, the instrument through which Italians came to know Spanish music since its introduction to the peninsula in the sixteenth century. In my investigation the Spanish guitar emerges quite literally as an instrument of mobility, a tool that simultaneously translated and transmitted Spanish musical practices and repertories to Italy, and could even stand in as a reference when assessing musical cultures still further across the Mediterranean.

Conspicuously absent from my discussion will be the voices of Spaniards, the ultimate authorities and the very sources of this ethnically defined musical knowledge. Spanish guitar maestros and composers in the first half of the seventeenth century did not diffuse their methods or repertories of guitar music through the medium of print as the Italians did.[3] The "native" practice of playing the Spanish guitar—in the Iberian Peninsula—was largely physical and oral, hidden in casual, everyday musicianship. As the lexicographer Sebastián Covarrubias put it in 1611: "[In Spain] the guitar is no more than a cowbell, so easy to play, especially in the strummed manner, that there isn't a stable boy who doesn't play guitar."[4] While seventeenth-century Italians were certainly aware of contemporary musical trends in Spain,[5] their enthusiasm for playing and singing *alla spagnola* with the Spanish guitar was managed from within Italy, published in the Italian language, and for Italian readers.

At the heart of it, and somewhat paradoxically, making music in the "Spanish manner," was a simulated encounter with Spanish music as it was practiced in the Iberian Peninsula, hardly surprising given that Spain loomed so large in the Italian imagination from the Treaty of Cateau-Cambrésis (1559) to the War of Spanish Succession at the beginning of the eighteenth century, a period during which Habsburg Spain laid its territorial claims to Sicily, Naples, Milan, Sardinia, and the *Stato dei Presidi*. Musicologists have previously made such claims about the "alla [/in] spagnola" designation that appeared in Italian musical sources in the sixteenth and seventeenth centuries, arguing that the phrase is indicative of the Spanish manner of music-making in the Naples-Rome orbit and not in the Iberian Peninsula (Adriana Basile herself was Neapolitan).[6] Yet the small corrective to the phrase encountered in the sources examined here—"alla <u>vera</u> Spagnola"—is compelling, as it makes an effort to distinguish between two kinds of music-making, one more "Spanish" than the other. This chapter considers the Italian articulation of an authentic, "true" Spanish musical manner within the complex and variegated discourse that Italians cultivated about Spain and Spanish culture during the seventeenth century. Furthermore, the emphasis on Florence in the final part of the chapter places my work in dialogue with the already established (and still growing) scholarly interest in Italo-Iberian cultural affairs in the Italian cities, provinces, states, and republics outside official Spanish management, which included not only diplomatic affairs of state and networks of commercial trade, but also artistic and creative exchange, transmission, and collaboration.

Alla spagnola as oral practice

Before addressing the *alla vera spagnola* phenomenon in more detail, I would like to return briefly to Adriana Basile's "300" that opened this chapter, in order to first introduce and expand the possibilities of what a musical experience *alla spagnola* might encompass.[7] As scholars have already noted, context is crucial for making sense of the label "alla spagnola" found in early modern Italian musical texts and repertories, which at its most fundamental level might indicate simply the presence of a text in Spanish.[8] Giuseppe Faccone makes it clear that *alla spagnola* describes both Basile's manner of performance (singing while playing the five-course Spanish guitar) and the fact that she had memorized this repertory. With these parameters in mind, I want to further ask questions of why and how she could have committed to memory an extensive repertory of guitar songs, which for Faccone was such a fascinating dimension of her musicianship (singing and playing *alla spagnola*).

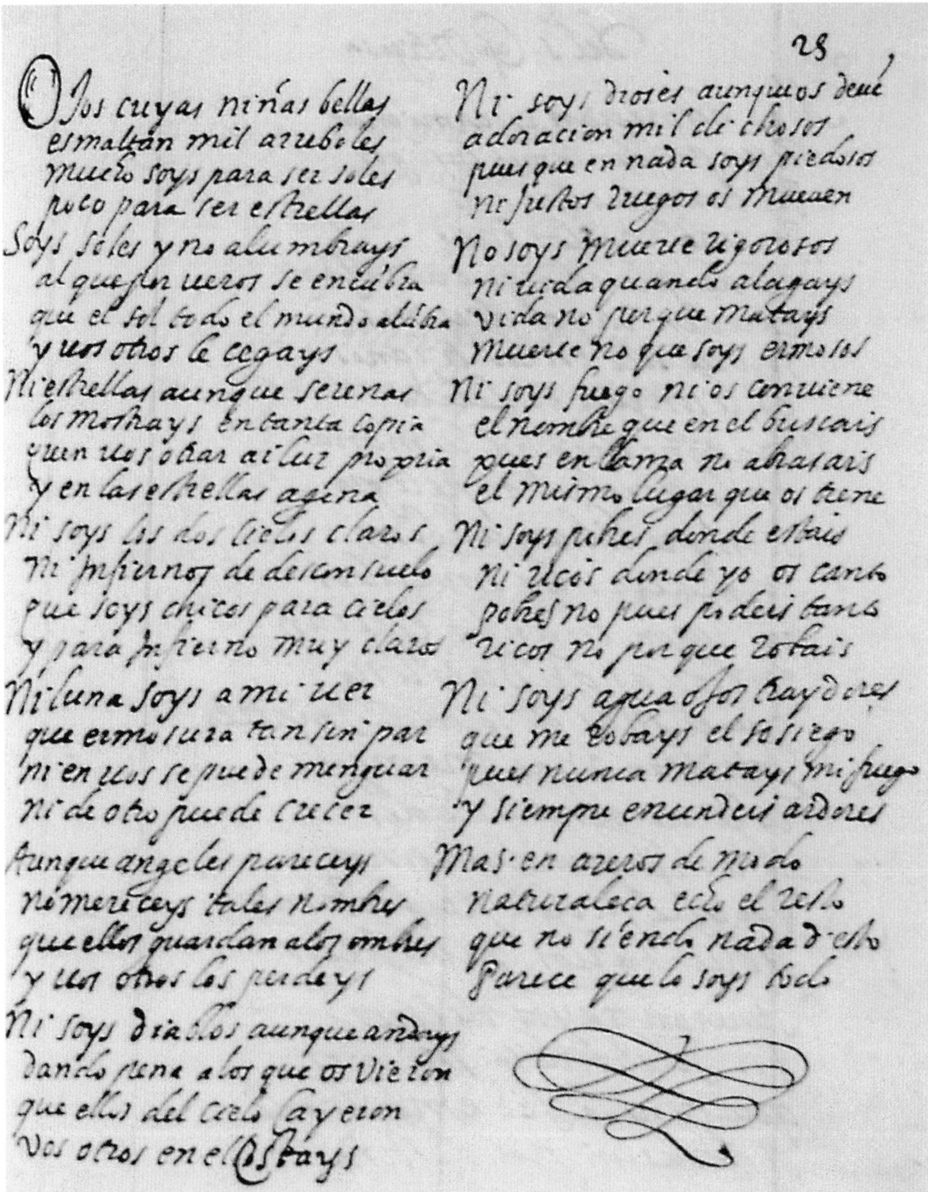

Fig. 1. "Ojos cuyas niñas bellas" from I-Nn. Naples, Biblioteca Nazionale Vittorio Emanuele III, Ms. Mus. XVII.30

Fortunately, documentation survives that can help us answer these questions, and in a way that leads us further into the world where *alla spagnola* performances were common. It may be found in a manuscript of Spanish and Italian poetic texts held in the Biblioteca Nazionale in Naples, Ms. Mus. XVII.30, which is believed to have been compiled in the 1620s and 1630s.[9] A small portion of the texts are scored with *alfabeto* chord notation for the Spanish guitar; none are scored in staff notation. In fact, the manuscript contains two separate collections bound together: the first was compiled for the Duke of Alba and one-time Viceroy in Naples Antonio Álvarez de Toledo; the second portion of the manuscript is believed to have been compiled by or for Adriana Basile and her daughter.[10] Following Benedetto Croce's description of the manuscript in 1900,[11] later scholars continued to note that Basile's portion was added to the earlier first portion, and that the entire manuscript bundle was in her possession sometime prior to 1635.[12] Thus this manuscript may contain some of Basile's performing repertory, perhaps even some of the three hundred songs she was purported to know by heart.

Previous discussions of the manuscript have noted the lack of musical concordances in staff notation for the texts with *alfabeto*, going so far as to question the status of this text a musical source.[13] This observation is inconclusive, however, since it does not take into account the presence of poetic texts *without alfabeto* that appear in other sources with musical notation. One example is "Ojos cuyas niñas bellas," (figure 1) which is also found with *cifras* (numbered guitar chord tablature) in Luis Briçeño's 1626 *Metodo mui facilissimo para aprender a tañer la guitarra* (figure 2). Briçeño sets the text as a "passacalle," a highly stereotyped musical formula of chords, rhythm, and perhaps a melody (or melodies) that, apart from being virtually synonymous with Spanish musical practice,[14] is here unspecified and presumably well-known or easily provided. Is this part of the reason why so many texts in the Naples manuscript are left unnotated, and appear to us—outside this context—as poems to be simply read or recited? And is this why we find in Basile's manuscript songs with *alfabeto* that lack musical concordances in other sources? In other words, were the *alfabeto* songs more difficult to remember, and thus did Basile need to prompt her memory by writing in the guitar chords?

The appearance of this text in Briçeño's guitar tutor provides a way for us to contextualize Basile's 300 within the realm of unwritten practice. As "poesie per cantare" we should be open to the idea, on one hand, that they could have been performed without any musical notation whatsoever because their musical identities were known in the oral tradition. But it also points to hidden or implied forms of knowledge—that is, someone with the training and experience of Adriana Basile could have recognized the text of "Ojos cuyas niñas bellas" as obviously suitable for singing and playing "passacalles," and similarly could have done the same for songs befitting "chaconas," "zarabandas,"

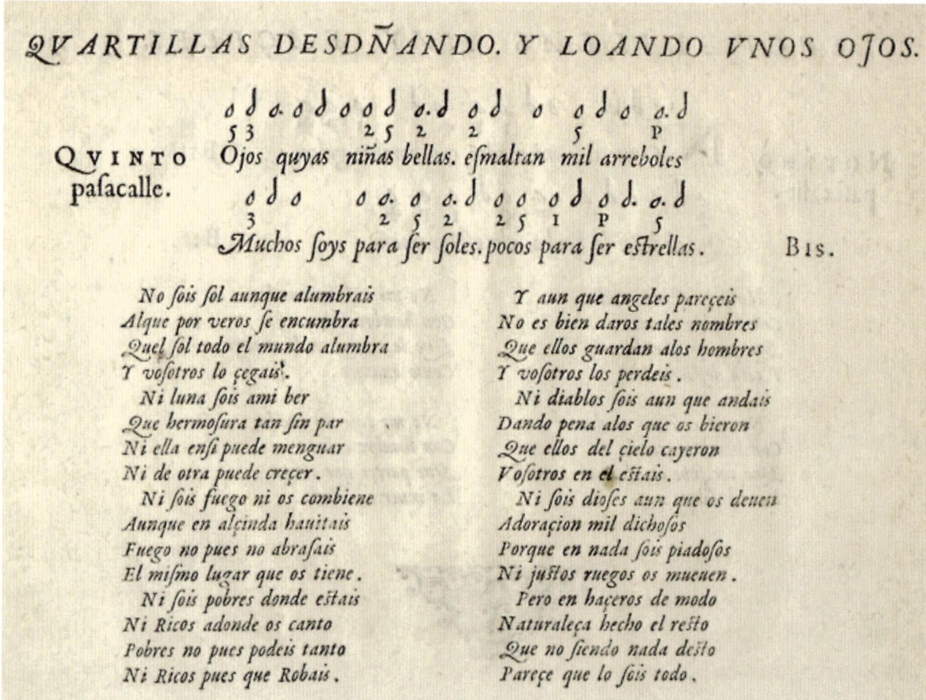

Fig. 2. "Ojos quyas niñas bellas" from Luis Briçeño, *Metodo mui facilissimo para aprender a tañer la guitarra* (Paris, 1636)

"folías" or other musical formulas employed for singing poetry with the guitar.[15] A twentieth-century comparison helpful in relating to this practice is playing and singing "blues," an unwritten musical idiom defined by a general (but flexible) set of musical parameters, which is easily reproducible by those with experience. Just as singers like Muddy Waters and Bessie Smith knew dozens if not hundreds of "blues," how many "passacalles" or "chaconas" did Basile know? Are we supposed to believe that each of Basile's 300 had its own individual and clearly distinctive musical identity? The example of "Ojos cuyas niñas bellas" provides a context for making sense of what Faccone might have admired in Basile's talent for singing with the guitar *alla spagnola*; namely an ability to adapt texts to musical formulas like *passacalles, chaconas*, and *folías*. In this particular case, playing and singing *alla spagnola* might better be understood as a cumulative set of musical skills reflective of unwritten practice rather than the stockpiling of independently "authored" compositions.

Learning to play *alla vera spagnola*

Running parallel to Basile's performing "alla spagnola" was a class of aspiring dilettante musicians in Italy who desired access to the unwritten "secrets" and "true" nature of the *alla spagnola* idiom. This desire to know the true Spanish manner was noted in many Spanish guitar tutors published in Italian, whose authors often expressed purported pressure from esteemed friends and students who wanted to learn guitar songs. Benedetto Sanseverino, for example, in his *Il primo libro d'intavolatura per la chitarra* (1622) announces the following in the introduction: "Having many years of experience—with the present arias and sonatas for the Spanish guitar having been composed for my virtuous amusement, taught to diverse gentlemen in this city, [and] reduced with [their] tablature in the present book—I (having been begged and gently urged by dear friends) have (in order to please them) agreed to publish them in the true manner of playing them and with their [true] meters, which has never perhaps been shown by any others until now, in this very city."[16]

Similarly, Giovanni Ambrosio Colonna, another Milanese guitar maestro, suggests to the readers of his 1637 guitar tutor and anthology that seeking a qualified maestro (one such as himself, undoubtedly) is the best and fastest way to learn to play in the true Spanish manner: "But wishing to be secure in wanting to learn well and in short time, it would be good to be assisted for a while by an intelligent Maestro in order to hold the hand well, play the meters, and play with grace and charm; playing now soft, now loud, in the true Spanish and Neapolitan manner."[17]

Predating Sanseverino's and Colonna's tutors was Girolamo Montesardo's *Nuova inventione d'intavolura per sonare ... la chitarra spagniuola* (Florence, 1606), the earliest pedagogical text for the Spanish guitar published in Italy. In the letter to readers of his book, Montesardo establishes himself as the inventor of a new rule that promises to deliver the secrets of playing the guitar to the uninitiated: "Because many noblemen and gentlemen with whom I've associated all my life have always desired to know how to play the Spanish guitar," writes Montesardo,

> it was necessary—in order to please them—to make a particular [kind] of method, since they not only desired to know how to play this instrument, but they also heartily begged me to invent an easy rule in order to learn to play with [good] meter and measure with help from neither notes nor numbers; and in order for anyone to learn to play the aforesaid instrument, I wanted to publish this ["]new invention of a very easy rule,["] which, anyone on his own—study-

> ing it without help from a Maestro—will be able to play [the guitar] according to the rules that I will teach you, and will quickly be able to do it [according to the rules], which this noble and beautiful skill desires.[18]

And in the dedication to the *Nuova inventione*, Montesardo humbly announces to his patron Francesco Buontalenti his proficiency in playing and singing in the Spanish manner, describing it as a "virtù"—that is a skill or craft, and moreover, a practice desired by Italian gentlemen of discerning taste:

> Being there some days after arriving in Florence, most desirous of hearing and enjoying the singing swans of this most virtuous city, a new Parnassus, and having become enchanted by it all, it seemed necessary to me to make myself known in case there should arise the opportunity (not by my merit but by their grace), at some occasion to please and serve this virtuous Nobility. And despite my other weaknesses, there have been many gentlemen—your Highness in particular—who have been gratified by the playing and singing *alla Spagnola*; so much so that I was so excited by the [favorable] judgment that you expressed, you who are so knowledgeable of this skill [*virtù*] as also of many others accompanied by fine customs and infinite graces.[19]

Thus these tutors take on the role of an advertisement, a calling card promising readers access to learning to play and sing in the true Spanish manner. Moreover, all three maestros agree that learning to play and/or sing "meters" is key to knowing the "true" way of playing *alla spagnola*. Looking to the contents of these tutors we can come closer to identifying what apparently was for many Italian readers an elusive unwritten musical practice, and one defined largely by particularities of rhythm and meter.

Sanseverino is perhaps the most specific about the nature of these "true" meters, on which he elaborated in the preface of his book using examples with rhythmic notation. His biggest concern is differentiating between triple proportions and *sesquialtera* in triple meter. Sanseverino defines *sesquialtera* as a measure of three equal minims in triple time, whereas in "straight" triple proportions a measure is made up of three semiminims. Interestingly absent from Sanseverino's explanation is the common description of *sesquialtera* as three semibreves (or minims) in the time of two, a definition which Praetorius noted in 1619 was held among modern Italians.[20] Instead Sanseverino emphasizes different ways to parse a single measure of *sesquialtera*:

Example 1. "Gagliardas" from Benedetto Sanseverino, *Il primo libro d'intavolatura* (Milan, 1622)

> But the sonatas under the same ternary sign [3] written in *sesquialtera*, that is with minims, will be played by giving three equal strokes per measure at the value of one minim, or by giving six of them at the value of a semiminim, or by giving them one value of the minim and four at the value of the semiminim, as one will find, in fact, that three minims, or rather six semiminims, make up a measure in *sesquialtera*.[21]

Sanseverino's emphasis on the rhythmic division of single measures in *sesquialtera* is further clarified in the examples in the book where *sesquialtera* appears. In the *sesquialtera* Gagliarda in G minor (example 1),[22] for example, the stroke notation and *alfabeto* instruct the player to strum duple groupings of chords in minims across two triple-time measures (noted in the brackets below the groupings). This produces a hemiola effect, and arguably one of the most stereotypical rhythmic gestures of Spanish music of the seventeenth century. I am not interested here in contextualizing Sanseverino's definition of *sesquialtera* within the fraught discourse about *sesquialtera* and hemiola, issues that were debated even in the sixteenth and seventeenth centuries.[23] What is more interesting is that Sanseverino employs the concept of *sesquialtera* to explain how "true" meters work in the strumming patterns found in his Spanish guitar treatise, and furthermore, when readers encounter *sesquialtera* notation

VAGO FIOR DI VIRTV'
DOVE SI CONTIENE IL VERO MODO
PER SONARE LA CHITARRIGLIA SPAGNVOLA,
Con Sonate facili per principianti,
Et per chi sona bene Sonate non più viste,
Raccolte da me Lodouico Monte Bolognese dalla Chitarriglia
CON LICENZA DE'SVPERIORI.
IN VENETIA. Appresso Angelo Saluadori.

Fig. 3. Lodovico Monte, *Vago fior di virtù* (Venice, [n.d.], ca. 1625)

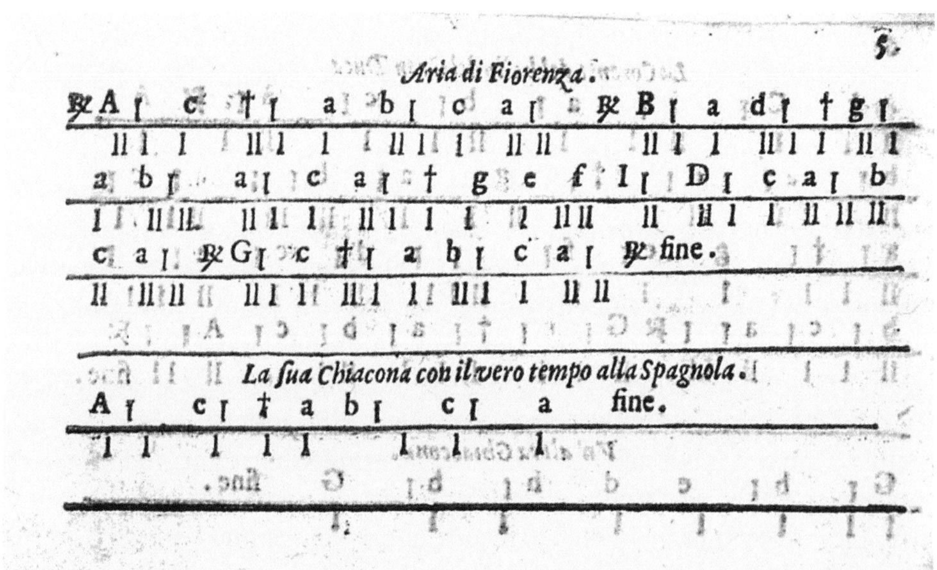

Fig. 4. "Aria di Fiorenza" and "La sua Chiacona con il vero tempo alla Spagnola" from Lodovico Monte, *Vago fior di virtù* (Venice, [n.d.], ca. 1625)

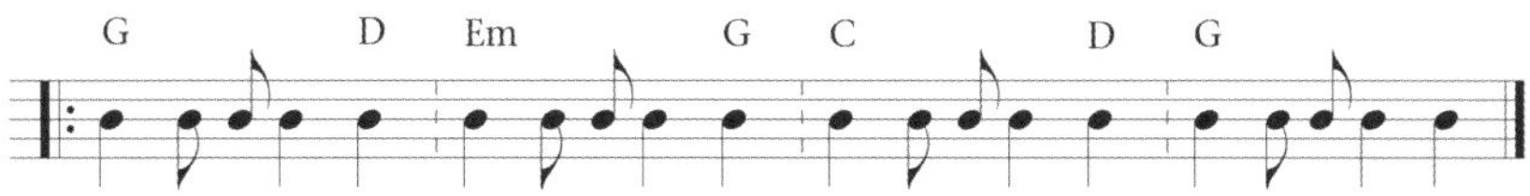

Example 2. "Aria di Fiorenza" from Monte, *Vago fior di virtù* (Venice, [n.d.], ca. 1625)

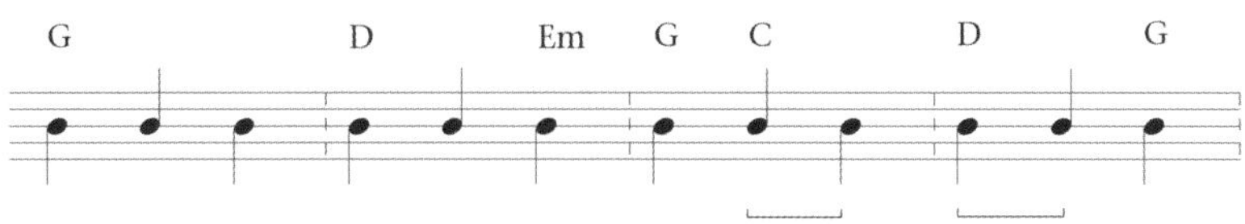

Example 3. "La sua Chiacona con il vero tempo alla Spagnola" from Lodovico Monte, *Vago fior di virtù* (Venice, [n.d.], ca. 1625)

in the book, they do so in passages of hemiola that superimpose duple and triple rhythms.[24] Once mastered, this must have given players a great sense of satisfaction knowing that they had learned the "secrets" of playing the Spanish guitar in the true manner.

The same can be said of other Spanish guitar tutors that promised to deliver the essential character of Spanish rhythms to readers, such as Lodovico Monte's *Vago fior di virtù*, which advertised on the title-page that it contained the true manner for playing the Spanish guitar (figure 3). Monte's book showcases passacaglias, folias, and ciacconas labeled "alla vera spagnola" and featuring dotted notes, syncopations, and hemiola patterns such as those found in Sanseverino's collection (figure 4). The "Aria di Fiorenza" (example 2) and its accompanying "chacona in true Spanish meter" (example 3) is an illustrative case that shows guitarists how to take a straight Italian number and jazz it up in the true Spanish style. Taking the first phrase of the *Aria di Fiorenza*, originally in the key of G and in duple meter, Sanseverino dresses it as a Spanish *chacona* in triple time with chord shifts on the "off beats." This produces a hemiola effect in final IV-V-I cadence of the phrase, transforming the aria's rigid and regular "Italian" rhythm into exciting and complex Spanish rhythmic patterns.

"Di stravaganza di tempi": Pietro Della Valle on Spanish music

Spanish meters and rhythms were of particular interest to Italian writers on musical subjects during the seventeenth century, most notably the Roman travel writer, musician, and scholar Pietro Della Valle, who addressed them in several of his published writings. In his oft-cited essay "Della musica dell'età nostra"—a response to Lelio Guidiccioni on the defense of modern music—Della Valle was explicit about how he acquired knowledge of Spanish meters, a description consistent with the sensitive and detailed manner in which he observed the "native" customs and practices of the Ottoman Empire and Safavid Iran in his epistolary travelogue.[25] Della Valle was careful to archive the transmission of this information, writing that he learned about Spanish meters from his teacher in Naples, Giuseppe Novazio, who himself "da uno Spagnuolo ne aveva avuto prima in Roma" ("first learned about it [Spanish meters] from a Spaniard in Rome.")[26]

Della Valle goes on to specify the idioms of Spanish music whose meters and rhythms were unknown in Italy until the 1640s, the time of his writing:

> Let us leave the Spanish *ciaccone,* the *sarabande,* the *passacagli,* the Portuguese *ciaccotte,* and other such foreign *arie* that for the last little while have greatly enriched the music of *villanelle* and *canzonette* in Rome, by their extravagance of meters and novelty of rhythm that have been unknown to us until now. I have also put down and can publish some Persian, Turkish, Arabic, and Indian songs, very curious and different from ours, and of meters and modes that some have never heard before.[27]

These remarks echo the sentiment of Montesardo, Sanseverino, Colonna, Monte, and other Italian guitar maestros who made public their insider knowledge of playing the guitar and singing *alla vera spagnola.* Extravagant and novel Spanish meters and rhythms were again central to this knowledge, which Della Valle identifies as "foreign," and suggestive of music from across the Mediterranean and points even further east. It should be noted that Della Valle played the *chitarra spagnola* and had his sons instructed in playing it as well, as documented in his letters and financial records.[28] Furthermore, in this quote Della Valle finds it necessary to inform readers about the introduction of Spanish and Portuguese rhythms into contemporary Italian (Roman) musical genres. He finds the appropriation "enriching" due to the complex and unfamiliar effects of these rhythms, which naturally leads him to declare his knowledge of other, even more unusual rhythms and modes found in Eastern music. For Della Valle, Spanish music is at once an interloper and a sonic gateway for accessing the music from distant cultures, an index of both the familiar and foreign.

Similarly, in his epistolary travel discourse Della Valle employed Spanish music as a means for making sense of the foreign music he heard in the Eastern Mediterranean, and in a way that aligns Spanish meters with those he encountered in the Ottoman Empire in particular. In his travel letter to Mario Schipiano from Cairo in March 1616, Della Valle noted the following about the music and dance of local women hired to perform at a Christian Coptic wedding party:

> In sum, their dances don't consist of anything other than natural movements, danced on a carpet covering the ground, and in diverse manners and postures all representing obscene acts, but they are a hundred times more brazen than the Spanish *ciaccone* and *sarabande*, such that, in conclusion, Martial's "Girl from Cádiz" doesn't even compare. And they are danced to by a certain sound and singing, which I will play for [you], Signor Dottore, on the guitar when I return [to Rome].[29]

References to Spain appear three times in Della Valle's description of this musical encounter. First, he selects the Spanish *ciaccona* and *sarabanda* as sources closest in effect to the dances of the Cairene women. Second, in comparing the "brazen" nature of the Egyptian dancers with an example that will resonate with his readership, Della Valle cites a Spanish-themed epigram by the first-century CE Roman poet Martial, himself born in Roman Hispania (modern-day Calatayud). Della Valle cites the salacious epigram CCIII from Martial's fourteenth book, which comments on the arousing choreography of a dancing girl from the coastal city of Cádiz (he provides a footnote to Martial should the reference go unnoticed).[30]

Intriguingly, the guitar is the instrument on which Della Valle promises to translate the music of these foreign dances for Schipiano's Italian ear, providing a third and explicitly aural "Spanish" reference in this account. Perhaps Della Valle considered the guitar most appropriate for handling the job given that these dances of Cairo shared certain qualities with the Spanish *ciaconne* and *sarabande*, guitar dances that he elsewhere praised for their "extravagance of meters and novelty of rhythm." Della Valle also seems to have had a Spanish guitar at his disposal while traveling abroad, as noted in an inventory of items shipped to Rome on his return from the East.[31] Its portability and relative ease of maintenance would have made the instrument a suitable companion for Della Valle's prolonged and extensive peregrinations. Regardless, these layered references to the Iberian Peninsula were clearly designed to evoke "Spanishness" for Della Valle's readers, and in ways that register Spain and Cairo as sites of unusual music and (increasingly) exotic and excessive sexuality.

Della Valle also relied on the Spanish *ciaccona* as an index from which to approximate his experience of a Sufi dervish ritual in Pera (just across the Golden Horn from Constantinople), noting:

> The motion of the feet in their dance is exactly the same as that of the Spanish in their *ciaccone*, which the Moors in Spain must have taught them. But these ones [Sufi], dancing, turn themselves around on one foot, and whoever turns faster, and lasts the longest turning, is the more esteemed man.[32]

In observing how the Sufi dancers of Pera move in the same manner as the Spanish in their *ciaccone*, Della Valle conjectures that the dance was introduced to Spain by way of the historic "Moorish" presence in the Iberian Peninsula. A term fraught with imprecision in late Renaissance Italy, in this context "Mori" (capitalized in the text) most likely denotes the Islamic inhabitants of historic Al-Andalus. That Della Valle also had in mind Black (sub-Saharan) Africans—referred to as "Mori" by many of his early modern contemporaries—is difficult to confirm.[33] Consistently throughout the *Viaggi*, Della Valle employs the term "Moro" with reference to Islamic religious practices and places of worship, often pairing it with "Turchi" (Turks) in the same citation.[34] Della Valle's use of the term "Moro" as a religious label throughout the *Viaggi* might help explain why he chose to invoke the historic "Mori" of Spain when comparing the dancing of Sufi dervishes with the Spanish *ciaccona*.

Nevertheless, what is certain is that in contrast to his description of the sensual dancers of Cairo, here Spanish music and dance for Della Valle act as translators that mediate between an Islamic religious ceremony in Constantinople and the (Catholic) Italian imagination. Again, while Spain stands apart from Italian culture, it is employed as a reference point, as common ground by which Italian readers could understand the cultural practices of the East. These quotations align Della Valle's view of Spain with those of contemporary (Western) Europeans who linked Spain with cultural representations of Islam and North Africa.[35] Granted, the most extreme manifestations of this discourse circulated in English, French, and Dutch anti-Spanish propaganda, but it facilitates the remarkable ease with which Della Valle jumps from Cairo or Constantinople to Spain in recording his experiences abroad.[36] As Barbara Fuchs has recently noted, the conflation of Spain with Islam, North Africa, "Moors," etc., was commonplace in Renaissance Europe; in Italy, for example, she points to the

"Spanish" episodes in Ludovico Ariosto's epic *Orlando furioso*, where "there are no Spanish Christian champions in the poem because Spaniard *means* Moor in the world of the text."[37] At the same time, it is important to note that Della Valle does not go as far as to conflate Spain with the East in these examples ("which the Moors must have taught *them* [Spaniards]"). In articulating the cultural distance between Moors and Spaniards while at the same time emphasizing their proximity, Della Valle is participating in a wider and diverse "intra-European" discourse about Spain in which its cultural identity is situated precariously at the borders between East and West.[38] As a composer and musician, moreover, Della Valle was in the unique position of being able to comment on musical encounters during his travels in the East with one ear toward his subjects and another pointing back home to Italy (with Spain as a mediator).[39]

Caterina Picchena: *Alla spagnola* outside Spanish Italy

The case studies above direct us to Italian encounters with Spanish music that sought to distinguish between the ethnically real and imagined, explicitly so in Spanish guitar tutors, and tacitly in Della Valle's empirical notes about Spanish musical practice. As mentioned earlier, within the larger geopolitical context of the early modern Mediterranean, the circulation of Spanish musical practices in Italy is not surprising, especially in places like Milan and Naples. In fact Vincenzo Giustiniani made such an observation already in 1628, noting that "at that time [ca. 1600] the Spanish guitar was introduced throughout Italy, especially in Naples ... [which] appears to have exiled the lute completely, and has almost succeeded to the point that, like the fashion of dressing *alla spagnola*, it dominates over all other styles in Italy."[40] Yet in Italian territories outside Spanish Italy, the picture becomes less clear, particularly for musicologists,[41] who have lagged behind their historian peers in assessing the transmission of Spanish culture to Italy.[42] Florence has recently emerged among theater historians as a hotbed of *Siglo d'oro* comedy, particularly during the Granducal reign of Ferdinando II de' Medici (1621–1670),[43] who, like his father and grandfather before him, employed a retinue of diplomatic correspondents in Madrid to maintain stable political relations between Tuscany and the Spanish empire.[44] Research in this milieu has revealed the fervent importation and diffusion of Spanish comedy in Florentine theaters and intellectual academies, ushered in by the great success of Giacinto Andrea Cicognini's *Il Don Gastone di Moncada* (1641), which borrowed material from three comedies by Tirso de Molina, Calderón de la Barca, and Lope de Vega.[45] Scholars have also noted, among other events, troupes of Spanish comedians who frequented the city in the 1620s and 1630s,[46] as well as *loas* composed by Spanish Jews to commemorate the 1634 wedding of Ferdinando II de' Medici and Vittoria della Rovere.[47]

Music has largely played a minimal role in historical accounts of Spanish and Tuscan/Florentine relations during this period, a regrettable omission given the abundance of archival sources that document the rich networks of creative exchange between Florence and Madrid.[48] Thanks to digital humanities initiatives like the Medici Archive Project[49] and the recent efforts of archival scholars such as María Teresa Cacho,[50] Maria Grazia Profeti,[51] and Sara Mamone,[52] we can begin to assess the role of music and activities of musicians in the world of Florentine and Spanish diplomacy, affairs of state, and commercial trade during the seventeenth century. One fascinating case that has yet to catch the attention of scholars is documented in the correspondence between the Granducal secretary to Cosimo II de' Medici, Curzio Picchena, and the Medici diplomatic secretary in Madrid, Giulio Inghirami. A focal point of their epistolary exchange in the early 1620s is Picchena's daughter Caterina, who we are told in the following passage is learning to play the Spanish guitar, and to whom Inghirami has promised scores of Spanish songs from Madrid:

> I'm happy above all that Signora Caterina is working to learn to play the Spanish guitar: at your request I will obtain some of the easiest, most beautiful, and most tuneful *canzonette* that circulate in these parts; already I have requested them from the Maestro della Cappella Reale,[53] whom I know, and he promised even others, and so I hope that they will satisfy Signora Caterina and your Lordship, and who knows, even happily so. [...] if the same *canzonette*—or "villancicos" [viglianzzicchi] as they are called here—will be given to me in musical notation as I asked for them, I will send them in the same form; if intabulated I will see to it that this is not so, and will require that it be changed to be intelligible by a maestro, or even better, by a decent enough Florentine maestro who came here last year and today serves in the house of Sig. Presidente di Castiglia.[54]

Caterina's interest in music appears to have been cultivated by her father, himself entrenched within the theatrical and musical activities of the Medici court.[55] From a seventeenth-century account of her life by the Florentine scholar and chronicler Andrea Cavalcanti, written soon after Caterina's death in 1659, we learn that Curzio had Caterina educated in Latin and in music and painting. Cavalcanti recounts that she was well-instructed "nel toccare con maestria diversi musicali instrumenti, nel canto, nel ballo, e nel disegno, nel quale si può in un certo modo dire ella fosse arrivasse molto avanti" (in playing masterfully diverse musical instruments, in singing, in dancing, and in drawing, in which one could say she became very advanced).[56] Such was her talent that Cosimo II himself admired her abilities as a stage performer. In 1621 at the age of 13, she performed for his daughters alongside Francesca Caccini at the Palazzo Pitti.[57] According to Cavalcanti (and other contemporary accounts), in lieu of a musical or theatrical career she led a freewheeling and libertine life, purportedly poisoning the wife of her first husband and pursuing a series of licentious affairs, including one that produced a child and led Caterina to France in search of the father (whom she found and who subsequently robbed her). By 1650 she had been exiled from Florence to Volterra, where according to the seventeenth-century sources she died in the dungeon of one of the towers of Volterra's *fortezza*.[58] The colorful accounts of Cavalcanti and his contemporary chroniclers set into motion recollections of Caterina's life that materialized into the stuff of legend well into the nineteenth century.[59] Despite this, Caterina's close identification with music beyond her teenage years may be recovered by the more recent suggestion that she is the woman seated at the keyboard in the portrait of "Curzio Picchena con la famiglia" on display at the Museo comunale in San Gimignano.[60] From Curzio Picchena's letters, we learn that in addition to relying on his contact with Inghirami in Madrid to satisfy Caterina's interest in learning the Spanish guitar, on one occasion he urged a customs official in Livorno to remain on the lookout among the Spanish vessels arriving at port for a talking parrot for Caterina.[61] These letters ask us to consider the extent to which Caterina's interaction with and even interest in such "Iberian" objects and activities was fostered by Curzio's clerical position within the Medici court, most notably in his relationships with Florentine ambassadors and other administrators involved in foreign trade and affairs.

Nonetheless, in the correspondence cited above between Curzio Picchena and Giulio Inghirami, many precious details emerge that turn our attention to the mobility of musical practices across the Mediterranean navigated once again by the Spanish guitar. One intriguing observation is Inghirami's implication that notation in guitar tablature would have somehow hindered Caterina's access to the music. While Inghirami leaves unclear exactly what kind of Spanish guitar tablature he fears the Spanish maestro might send him—either numbered fretboard tablature or chord tablature—why would Caterina need to have the music notated in the staff if she were learning to play the Spanish guitar? Even if unfamiliar with the technical details of playing from tablature, her status as a beginner—at the time of the letter Caterina was thirteen years old—would make the task of translating music staff notation to the guitar fretboard difficult and cumbersome. Such a process, in fact, runs counter to the basic purpose of tablature since the early sixteenth century, which was to accommodate the mechanical demands and constraints instrumentalists faced while reading music notation.[62]

Inghirami's promise of *canzonette* or "villancicos as they are called here [in Spain]" in music staff notation in order to help Caterina learn the Spanish guitar suggests that Curzio was interested in providing Caterina with guitar songs in Spanish. This might explain Inghirami's worry for their arrival in tablature format; chord tablature *cancioneros*—such as the Naples manuscript of Adriana Basile and the Briçeño print discussed earlier—would have left out too much information for Caterina to make much use of them. Inghirami leaves the impression that he was aware of the particular character and execution of these Spanish songs such that staff notation was required for them to be performed by the uninitiated. This also could explain why he felt that having even a "mediocre" Italian maestro transcribe the tablature into staff notation would be better than leaving the task up to a Spanish maestro. Inghirami's concern might have been that the Spanish maestro's tablature would offer only a sketch of the songs, with at the very least, *alfabeto* or Spanish *cifras*; enough for an experienced Spanish musician fluent in the idiom (or a performer like Adriana Basile) but not for a thirteen-year-old Italian novice at Spanish guitar song.

Curzio Picchena could have easily used his position and experience in the Medici court hierarchy to track down a local player of the Spanish guitar in Florence to help out young Caterina—and perhaps he did. But his correspondence with Inghirami demonstrates that shopping around for local material in Madrid was worth the time and effort, even if it meant ultimately that the musical notation would have to be deciphered by an Italian for Caterina's use. Underscored in this letter is the allure of Spanish "authenticity" reminiscent of the self-promotion evident in the Spanish guitar tutors by Montesardo, Colonna, Sanseverino, and Monte: namely, how to acquire the "true" manner of playing and singing *alla spagnola*. This acquisition of Spanish practice, moreover, was shaped by the prerogatives of Italian authors and expectations of Italian audiences, who perceived it as somewhat mysterious, unstable, unusual, and, of course, foreign. Indeed, if playing and singing in the Spanish manner was something obvious and familiar (as it was in Spain), there would be little reason for authors to distinguish between *alla spagnola* and *alla vera spagnola*. The later phenomenon projects a musical authority defined in cultural terms, one embodied in performers like Adriana Basile and aspired to by students like Caterina Picchena. The Spanish guitar emerges in this discourse as much more than an emblem or representation of Spain and its musical customs; it becomes a vessel of transport for delivering the "true" nature of Spanish music, a mobile agent of Iberian culture that circulated not only in Spanish Italy, but throughout the Italian peninsula and well beyond.

Notes

The research carried out for this chapter was supported by the Melville J. Kahn Research Fellowship (2016–2017) at I Tatti, the Harvard University Research Center for Italian Renaissance Studies in Florence. An earlier version of this chapter was read at the conference "Songs without notes: Exploring avenues of musical transmission and performance in the Early Modern Era," November 8, 2017 at Harvard University, co-sponsored by Harvard and the Real Colegio Complutense, Madrid. Special thanks go out to Álvaro Torrente and Kate van Orden, who offered valuable input on early drafts of the chapter. I thank Aileen A. Feng for her assistance with the English translations of all primary Italian and Latin texts referenced in this chapter. Original language quotations are provided in the endnotes.

1. "Mio fr'ello mi ha detto che un pezzo fa sta su la prattica d'una Napolitana quale ha tutte q'ste qualità: sona di Arpa in eccelenza, e vi canta al libro ogni sorte di madrigali con tal sicurezza che non vi 'è cantante nissuno che la sup[era]re [.]" Giuseppe Faccone (Rome) to Vincenzo Gonzaga (Mantua), May 9, 1609, I-MAa, Archivio Gonzaga 990. Transcribed in Parisi, "Ducal Patronage," 181–82.

2. " [...] e quello che è meglio sona di chitarra beniss.mo e canta a la spagnola, et il tal coppia che tra le Italiani e Spagnole sa più di trecento opera a la mente. è giovane di dicenove anni in circa." Ibid.

3. Valdivia Sevilla, *La guitarra rasgueada,* 140.

4. "... y aora la guitarra no es mas que un cencerro, tan facil de tañer, especialmente en lo rasgado, que no ay moço de cavallos que no sea musico de guitarra." Covarrubias Orosco, *Tesoro de la lengua castellana,* 209.

5. Stein has written on this topic in "The Origins and Character of *Recitado.*" Starting at 4.1, Stein presents an argument for singing "alla spagnola" with some parallels to my own analysis of Adriana Basile, but with reference to only Vincenzo Giustiniani's *Discorso sopra la musica* (1628).

6. Hill, "L'accompagnamento *rasgueado,*" 55–57; Fabris, "Le notti a Firenze," 26.

7. For a survey of the phrase "alla spagnola" as it was encountered in Italian musical sources of the sixteenth and seventeenth centuries, see Zuluaga, "The Five-Course Guitar," 85–94. Zuluaga emphasizes the problematic and variable use of the phrase as a generic label, as in the "villanella alla spagnola," "aria alla spagnola," and "canzonetta alla spagnola." Zuluaga, "The Five-Course Guitar," 85.

8. On such compositions found in late sixteenth-century *villanelle* collections, see Zuluaga, "The Five-Course Guitar," 89–94.

9. I-Nn, Ms. Mus. XVII.30. For a description and inventory of the manuscript, see Croce, "Illustrazione."

10. Baron, "Secular Spanish Solo Song," 24–25.

11. Croce, "Illustrazione," 3.

12. See Baron, "Secular Spanish Solo Song," 25; Cesare Acutis, *"Cancioneros,"* 8–9; Fabris, "Prime aggiunte," 116; and Tyler, *The Guitar and its Music,* 94.

13. See Baron, "Secular Spanish Solo Song," 25, and Zuluaga, "The Five-Course Guitar," 72.

14. On this formula see Hudson, *The Folia,* vol. 3.

15. On this practice see Cavallini, "Sugli improvvisatori"; Griffiths, "Strategies"; and de Zayas, "Il canzoniere."

16. "Havendo io molti anni a dietro, per virtuoso mio trattenimento composte le presente arie, & suonate per la Chitarra alla Spagnuola, & insegnate a diversi Cavaglieri di questa Città; ridotte le poscia con la sua intavolatura nel presente libro, da cari amici pregato, e dolcemente sforzato, ho per compiacerli, deliberato mandarle alle stampe, col vero modo di suonarle, e col suo tempo, da altri forse, in questa stessa Città, fin' hora non mostrato." Sanseverino, *Il primo libro d'intavolatura,* [ii].

17. "Però volendosi assicurare di voler imparar bene, & in breve tempo, saria bene per qualche tempo servirsi da Maestro intelligente per portar bene la mano, & dargli il tempo, & Sonare con gratia, & modestia, toccando hor piano, hor forte, alla vera maniera Spagnola, & Napolitana." Colonna, *Intavolatura di chitarra spagnuola*, 5.

18. "E perche molti Signori, e Gentil'huomini, con li quali ho pratticato tutto il tempo di mia vita hanno sempre desiderato di saper sonare la Chitarra Spagniola, è stato necessario, per compiacerli, di farci un studio particulare; e perche anco non solamente hanno desiderato saper sonare quest'istrumento: ma mi hanno pregato caldamente, ch'io inventassi una Regula facile per impararlo di sonare, con tempo, e con misure; senza aiuto, nè di Note, nè di Numeri; e perche l'impari ogn'uno a toccare il predetto istromento, ho voluto dar in luce questa nuova inventione di Regola facilissima, la quale da se ogn'uno, studiandola senza aiuto di Maestro potrà sonarlo con le Regole, ch'io v'insegnarò, delle quali potrà esser capace presto, che desidera questa nobile, e vaga virtù." Montesardo, *Nuova inventione*, [iii].

19. "Essendo Li giorni a dietro di passaggio a Fiorenza, come desiderosissimo di sentire, e godere li canori Cigni, del nuovo Parnaso di questa virtuosissima Città, & essendone invaghito: mi parve necessario farmi conoscere, acciò s'appresentassi (non per mio merito: ma per loro gratia) alcuna occasione di gradire, e servire a questa virtuosa Nobilità; e frà l'altre mie deboli conditioni, sono stati molto Gentilhuomini, li quali si sono compiaciuti, del sonare, e cantare alla Spagniuola, & in particolare V.S. Molt'Illustre, tanto, che talmente eccitato dal giudicio fattone da lei, intendentissima, così di questa virtù; come anco di molte altre accompagnate di buonissimi costumi, & infinite gratie." Ibid, [ii].

20. Praetorius, *Syntagma musicum III*, 52. For more on the context of this reference within the larger discussion of hemiola and *sesquialtera* during the late sixteenth and early seventeenth centuries, see DeFord, "Tempo Relationships," 35–36.

21. "Ma le suonate che sotto la sodetta ziffera ternaria sono scritte in sesquialtera, cioè con figure de minime si suoneranno con dar tre colpi parimente per battuta del valor d'una minima, o con darne sei del valore della semiminima, o con darne uno del valore della minima, & quattro del valor della semiminima, come in fatti si troverà, che tre minime overo sei semiminime compiscono una battuta della sesquialtera." Sanseverino, *Il primo libro d'intavolatura*, [ii].

22. In all examples I have respelled the *alfabeto* sonorities as modern chord symbols (e.g., Dm = D minor, D = D major). The strumming directions are indicated by the position of the stem attached to the note head; thus a stem above represents an "up" stroke, and a stem below a "down" stroke.

23. See DeFord, "Tempo Relationships," and Michael B. Collins, "The Performance of Sesquialtera."

24. In addition to the Gagliardas, *sesquialtera* notation appears in the "Saltarello di Santino" and the "Saltarello detto della Frascata" of Sanseverino's *Il primo libro d'intavolatura*, pp. 24 and 28.

25. On Della Valle's method of travel description see Brentjes, "Pietro della Valle's Latin Geography," 169–219, esp. 179–85.

26. "E se vogliamo triple, e canzonette alla Napolitana, tanto amate oggi dal Volgo, che son tutte di tempi Spagnuoli, de' quali io presi in Napoli, quando in mia gioventù colà dimorai da cinque anni, assai buona cognizione da Giuseppe Novazio, buon maestro di chitarra, oltre di un poco di lume, che da uno Spagnuolo ne aveva avuto prima in Roma..." Della Valle, "Della musica dell'età nostra," 258–59.

27. "Lasciamo le Ciaccone Spagnuole, le Saravande, i Passacagli, le Ciaccotte Portoghesi, e tante altre arie straniere, che da poco tempo in quà, e di stravaganza di tempi, e di novità di andare hanno in Roma arricchito molto la Musica delle Villanelle, e Canzonette, che prima ci erano ignote. Io ancora ho messo, e posso mettere in luce alcune arie Persiane, Turchesche, Arabiche, e Indiane, e assai curiose, e diverse dalle nostre, e di tempi, e di tuono, che da altri ancora non sono state mai sentite." Ibid, 259.

28. These documents are transcribed in Barbieri, "Pietro della Valle." Della Valle's financial records note purchases of guitar strings (and guitar maintenance) as well as a case (Barbieri, 99–101), and a travel inventory records the shipment of a *chitarra spagnola* to Rome (ibid., 90).

29. "[I]n somma i balli loro non consistono in altro, che in movimenti di vita, fatti in terra sopra un tapeto, in diverse foggie, e diverse posture, tutti rappresentando atti osceni: ma cento volte più sfacciati, che quelli delle Ciaconne, e Sarabande Spagnuole; tali in conclusione: che la Gaditana di Martiale[a] non ci stà per niente; e li fanno a tempo d'un certo suono e canto, che io farò sentire al Signor Dottore, quando tornerò, su la chitara." Letter of March 7, 1616, published in Della Valle, *Viaggi,* 319.

30. Ibid. The epigram from Martial reads: "Puella Gaditana. Tam tremulum crisat, tam blandum prurit, ut ipsum masturbatorem fecerit Hippolytum." Merli, *Marziale. Epigrammi*, 1153. In translation: "Girl from Cádiz; She moved her hips and gyrated in such a way that it would even make Hippolito masturbate."

31. "Inventario degli oggetti appartenenti a Pietro Della Valle il Pellegrino," I-Rvat, Archivio Segreto Vaticano, *Archivio Della Valle-Del Bufalo*, busta 61, fasc. 27. Reference to the inventory is found in Barbieri, "Pietro della Valle," 90.

32. "Il moto de' piedi, ne' lor ballo, è a punto il medesimo che quello degli Spagnuoli nelle loro Ciaccone; che i Mori, nella Spagna, dovettero insegnarlo, ma questi, ballando, si girano sempre attorno sopra un piede; e chi gira più presto, e dura più a girare, è più valent' uomo." Della Valle, Letter of October 25, 1614, *Viaggi*, 63.

33. For a summary of this problematic label in early modern Italy, see Lowe, "Visible Lives," 415–19.

34. Della Valle, *Viaggi*, 290, 400, 421, 467–68, 472. In his 1616 letter from Baghdad (*Viaggi*, 470), Della Valle recounts the arrival of a caravan of a woman named Eustobhà, who he refers to as a "Mora di color nero" (Black Moor [woman]). That Della Valle described Eustobhà as both "Mora" and "di color nero" suggests that he did not consider the term "Moor" to designate skin color.

35. For a summary of this phenomenon see Fuchs, "The Spanish Race," 88–98.

36. Ibid., 94–95.

37. Ibid., 93.

38. I borrow the phrase from Fuchs: "Maurophilia is an unstable and often risky proclivity, which makes its embrace all the more intriguing for a cultural history of the encounters between East and West. Yet that history cannot be separated from intra-European pressures and from the discourses that enlist both race and religion to construct legends of national distinction." Ibid., 98.

39. Such musical detail is absent in the popular travel books in Italian by Francesco Carletti (*Ragionamenti del mio viaggio intorno al mondo*, ca. 1595), Francesco Belli (*Osservazioni nel viaggio*, 1632), and Giovanni Francesco Gemelli Careri (*Viaggi per Europa*, 1693), which further emphasizes the value of Della Valle's observations in the *Viaggi* as particularly sensitive to the cultural practice of music.

40. "Tanto più che nell'istesso tempo s'introdusse la Chitarra alla spagnola per tutta Italia, massime in Napoli ... pare che abbiano congiurato di sbandire affatto il Liuto; et è quasi riuscito a punto, come il modo di vestire alla spagnola in Italia prevale a tutte le altre foggie." Giustiniani, "Discorso sopra la musica," 126.

41. A notable exception is "Spanish" Rome, which figures centrally in the work of Noel O'Regan, especially "Music in the service" and "Historia de dos cuidades." For Spanish-Italian musical contact in Italy outside of Naples and Milan, see Acutis, "*Cancioneros*"; Baron, "Secular Spanish Solo Song"; essays in Lazzi, *Rime e suoni*; Veneziano, *Rime e suoni alla spagnola*; Zuluaga, "The Five Course Guitar"; and Stein, "Three Spaniards."

42. For an overview of Italo-Iberian political, commercial, and military relations in Italian regions outside Spanish Italy, see Murgia, "Conflitti e diplomazia." Among the extensive bibliography on this topic, a few recent essay collections stand out in the field of Italo-Iberian cultural relations outside Spanish Italy: Colomer, *España y Bolonia,* Dandelet, *Spain in Italy,* Herrero Sánchez, *Génova y la Monarquía Hispánica,* Anselmi, *I rapporti tra Roma e Madrid,* and Colomer *Vestir a la española.*

43. On this subject, including an extensive and up-to-date bibliography, see Michelassi, *Il teatro spagnolo a Firenze.*

44. Martelli, "Introduzione al secondo volume," vii-ix.

45. For a summary of this phenomenon see Michelassi, "Introduction."

46. Castelli, "Comici spagnoli a Firenze."

47. Cacho, "Dos loas hispano-hebreas."

48. In addition to Zuluaga, "The Five-Course Guitar," and Fabris, "Le notti a Firenze," see Cacho, "Canciones españolas"; Stein, *Songs of Mortals*, 185–205; idem, "The Origins and Character of *Recitado*"; Profeti, "Spettacoli musicali"; Whitaker, "Florentine Opera comes to Spain."

49. The Medici Archive Project, www.medici.org, accessed December 22, 2018.

50. Cacho, *Manoscritos*; idem, "Italia mira a España"; idem, *Spagna e dintorni.*

51. Profeti, *Commedia e musica.*

52. Mamone, *Serenissimi fratelli*; idem, *Mattias de' Medici.*

53. Most likely Mateo Romero, a.k.a. "Capitán," who served as *maestro de capilla* at the Spanish royal court in Madrid from 1598 until his retirement in 1633.

54. "Mi rallegro sommamente che la Signora Caterina attenda ad imparare a sonar la chitarra spagnuola: io le buscherò in esecuzione del comandamento di V.S. alcune canzonette delle più vaghe e più facili e più ariose che vadino attorno, già le ho chieste al Maestro della Cappella Reale conosciuto mio, nel ha promesse, siccome ancor altri, onde spero che e la Signora Caterina e V.S. resteranno serviti, e chi sa, contenti. [...] se le sudette canzonette, o viglianzicchi che così qui li domandano, mi saranno date in musica, come le ho chieste l'inveirò nell'istessa forma, se intavolate vedrò se questa è come cotesta caso che non sia, la farò ridurre intelligibile costa, da un maestro, o per dir meglio, mezzo maestro di sonare fiorentino, che venne qua li anno passato et hoggi sta in casa del Sig. Presidente di Castiglia." Giulio Inghirami (Madrid) to Curzio da Picchena (Florence), June 6, 1621, I-Fas, *Mediceo del Principato*, busta 4949, fol. 935.

55. On Curzio Picchena's role in assisting with the entertainment festivities for the wedding of Cosimo II de' Medici and Maria Maddalena of Austria, see Carter, "A Florentine Wedding of 1608."

56. Cavalcanti, *Successo della Picchena*, fol. 176r–v, transcribed in Acanfora, "Furini giovane," 58–59. For a slightly varied version of this account, see also *Vita e morte della Caterina Picchena*, I-Fas, *Manoscritti* 166, fol. 199, wherein by virtue of her precocious talent in painting and music, Caterina is lauded as "un altro Buonarotti" (another [Michelangelo] Buonarotti).

57. Curzio Picchena to Caterina de' Medici, February 4, 1621, I-Fas, *Mediceo del Principato*, busta 6108, fol. 1036.

58. For a summary of these accounts see Acanfora, "Furini giovane," 57–59.

59. Most famously serving as the subject of Francesco Domenico Guerrazzi's historical novel *La figlia di Curzio Picchena* (Milan, 1874).

60. Acanfora, "Furini giovane," 60–61.

61. Ottavio Cappelli (Livorno) to Curzio Picchena (Florence), December 30, 1625, I-Fas, *Mediceo del Principato*, busta 2145, fol. 330.

62. Griffiths, "The Lute," 93.

Bibliography

Manuscript Sources

Naples, Biblioteca Nazionale Vittorio Emanuele III (I-Nn)

Ms. Mus. XVII.30

Archival Sources

Florence, Biblioteca Riccardiana (I-Fr)

Ms. 2270. Andrea Cavalcanti, *Successo della Picchena*.

Florence, Archivio di Stato (I-Fas)

Manoscritti

166. *Vita e morte della Caterina Picchena.*

Mediceo del Principato

Vol. 2145. *Governi di Città e Luoghi Soggetti [1601–1627]*, fol. 330. Letter of Ottavio Cappelli to Curzio Picchena, December 30, 1625.

Vol. 4949. *Relazioni con Stati Italiani ed Esteri [1619–1621]*, fol. 935. Letter of Giulio Inghirami to Curzio Picchena, June 6, 1621.

Vol. 6108. *Carteggi dei Principi, delle Granduchesse e delle Principesse [1617–1629]*, fol. 1036. Letter of Curzio Picchena to Caterina de' Medici, February 4, 1621.

Printed Sources

Acanfora, Elisa. "Furini giovane a Roma, le Virtuose delle Arti e un'allieva libertina," *Paragone: Arte* 87–88 (2009): 44–66.

Acutis, Cesare. *"Cancioneros" musicali spagnoli in Italia, 1585–1635*. Pisa: Università di Pisa, 1971.

Anselmi, Alessandra, ed. *I rapporti tra Roma e Madrid nei secoli XVI e XVII: arte diplomazia e politica*. Rome: Gangemi, 2014.

Barbieri, Patrizio. "Pietro della Valle: the 'Esthèr' oratorio (1639) and other experiments in the 'stylus metabolicus.' With new documents on triharmonic instruments." Trans. Ken Hurry. *Recercare* 19 (2007): 73–124.

Baron, John H. "Secular Spanish Solo Song in Non-Spanish Sources, 1599-1640," *Journal of the American Musicological Society* 30 (1977): 20-42.

Brentjes, Sonja and Volkmar Schüller. "Pietro della Valle's Latin Geography of Safavid Iran (1624–1628): Introduction." *Journal of Early Modern History* 10 (2006): 169–219.

Briçeño, Luis. *Metodo mui facilissimo para apprender a tañer la guitarra*. Paris: Pierre Ballard, 1636.

Cacho, María Teresa. "Dos loas hispano-hebreas a Ferdinando II de' Medici." In *Spagna e dintori*, ed. Maria Grazia Profeti. Pp. 7–30. Florence: Alinea, 2000.

Cacho, María Teresa. *Manoscritos hispánicos en las bibliotecas de Florencia*. 2 vols. Florence: Alinea, 2001.

Cacho, María Teresa. "Canciones españolas en cancioneros musicales florentinos." In *Rime e suoni alla spagnola*, ed. Giulia Veneziano. Pp. 83–96. Florence: Alinea, 2003.

Cacho, María Teresa. "Italia mira a España: Manoscritos históricos hispánicos de los siglos XVI y XVII en bibliotecas italianas." *e-Spania: Revue interdisciplinarie d'études hispaniques médiévales et modernes* 24 (2016): http://journals.openedition.org/e-spania/25637

Cacho, María Teresa and Maria Grazia Profeti, eds. *Spagna e dintorni*. Florence: Alinea 2000.

Carter, Tim. "A Florentine Wedding of 1608." *Acta Musicologica* 55 (1983): 89–107.

Castelli, Silvia. "Comici spagnoli a Firenze: notizie e documenti (1621–1639)." *Medioevo e Rinascimento* 11 (1997): 387–94.

Cavallini, Ivano. "Sugli improvvisatori del Cinque-Seicento: persistenze, nuovi repertori e qualche riconoscimento." *Recercare* 1 (1989): 23–40.

Colonna, Giovanni Ambrosio. *Intavolatura di chitarra spagnuola del primo, secondo, terzo, & quarto libro*. Milan: Dionisio Gariboldi, 1637.

Collins, Michael B. "The Performance of Sesquialtera and Hemiola in the Sixteenth Century." *Journal of the American Musicological Society* 17 (1964): 5–28.

Colomer, José Luis and Amadeo Serra Desfils, eds. *España y Bolonia: siete siglos de relaciones artísticas y culturales*. Madrid: Centro de Estudios Europa Hispánica, 2006.

Colomer, José Luis and Amalia Descalzo, eds. *Vestir a la española en las cortes europas (siglos XVI y XVII)*. 2 vols. Madrid: Centro de Estudios Europa Hispánica, 2014.

Covarrubias Orosco, Sebastián. *Tesoro de la lengua castellana o española*. Madrid: Luis Sanchez, 1611.

Croce, Benedetto. "Illustrazione di un canzoniere ms. italo-spagnolo del secolo XVII." *Atti dell'accademia pontaniana* XXX (1900): 1–32.

Dandelet, Thomas, and John Marino, eds. *Spain in Italy: Politics, Society, and Religion, 1500–1700*. Leiden and Boston: Brill, 2007.

DeFord, Ruth I. "Tempo Relationships between Duple and Triple Time in the Sixteenth Century." *Early Music History* 14 (1995): 1–51.

Della Valle, Pietro. *Viaggi di Pietro Della Valle Il Pellegrino*. Venice: Paolo Baglioni, 1667.

Della Valle, Pietro. "Della musica dell'età nostra [16 January 1640]." In Giovanni Battista Doni, *De' trattati di musica... tomo secondo*, ed. Anton Francesco Gori. Pp. 249–64. Florence: [Nella Stamperia Imperiale], 1763.

Fabris, Dinko. "Prime aggiunte italiane al volume RISM B/VII—Intavolature mss. per liuto e chitarra." *Fontes artis musicae* 28 (1982): 103–21.

Fabris, Dinko. "Le notti a Firenze, i giorni a Napoli: gli esordi della chitarra spagnola nell'Italia del Seicento." In *Rime e suoni alla spagnola*, ed. Giulia Veneziano. Pp. 15–34. Florence: Alinea, 2003.

Fuchs, Barbara. "The Spanish Race." In *Rereading the Black Legend: The Discourses of Religious and Racial Difference in the Renaissance Empires*, ed. Margaret R. Greer, Walter D. Mingolo, et al. Pp. 89–98. Chicago: University of Chicago Press, 2008.

Giustiniani, Vincenzo. "Discorso sopra la musica de' suoi tempi [1628]." Transcribed in Angelo Solerti, *Le origini del melodramma*. Pp. 98–128. Turin: Fratelli Bocca, 1903.

Griffiths, John. "The Lute and the Polyphonist." *Studi musicali* 31 (2002): 89–108.

Griffiths, John. "Strategies for the Recovery of Guitar Music." In *Rime e suoni alla spagnola*, ed. Giulia Veneziano. Pp. 59–81. Florence: Alinea, 2003.

Herrero Sánchez, Manuel, ed. *Génova y la Monarquía Hispánica (1528–1713)*. Genoa: Società Ligure di Storia Patria, 2011.

Hill, John Walter. "L'accompagnamento *rasgueado* di chitarra: un possibile modello per il basso continuo dello stile recitativo?" In *Rime e suoni alla spagnola*, ed. Giulia Veneziano. Pp. 35–58. Florence: Alinea, 2003.

Hudson, Richard. *The Folia, the Saraband, the Passacaglia, and the Chaconne*. 3 vols. Neuhausen-Stuttgart: Hänssler, 1982.

Lazzi, Giovanna, ed. *Rime e suoni per corde spagnole*. Florence: Polistampa, 2002.

Lowe, Kate. "Visible Lives: Black Gondoliers and Other Black Africans in Renaissance Venice." *Renaissance Quarterly* 66 (2013): 412–52.

Mamone, Sara, ed. *Serenissimi fratelli principi impresario: notizie di spettacolo nei carteggi di Giovan Carlo de' Medici e di Desiderio Montemagni suo segretario, 1628–1664*. Florence: Le Lettere, 2003.

Mamone, Sara, ed. *Mattias de' Medici serenissimo mecenate dei virtuosi: notizie di spettacolo nei carteggi medicei: carteggio di Mattias de' Medici, 1629–1667*. Florence: Le Lettere, 2013.

Martelli, Francesco. "Introduzione al secondo volume." In *Istruzioni agli ambasciatori e inviati medicei in Spagna e nell' 'Italia spagnola' (1536–1648)*, vol. 2, ed. Francesco Martelli and Cristina Galasso. Pp. vii-xlix. [Rome]: Ministero per i beni e le attività culturali, 2007.

Merli, Elena. ed. *Marziale. Epigrammi*, vol. 2, 2nd ed. Milan: Rizzoli, 1996.

Michelassi, Nicola and Salomé Vuelta García. *Il teatro spagnolo a Firenze nel Seicento*. Florence: Alinea, 2013.

Monte, Lodovico. *Vago fior di virtù, dove si contiene il vero modo per sonare la chitarriglia spagnuola*. Venice: Angelo Salvadori, [n.d.].

Montesardo, Girolamo. *Nuova inventione d'intavolatura per sonare li balletti sopra la chitarra spagniuola*. Florence: Christofano Marescotti, 1606.

Murgia, Giovanni and Gianfranco Tore. "Conflitti e diplomazia negli antichi Stati italiani: la difesa dei confini." In *Spagna e Italia in Età moderna: storiografie a confronto*, ed. Francisco Chacón, Maria Antonietta Visceglia, et al. Pp. 189–222. Rome: Viella, 2009.

O'Regan, Noel. "Historia de dos cuidades: Victoria como mediador musical entre Roma y Madrid." In *Tomás Luis de Victoria y la cultura musical en la España de Felipe III*, ed. Alfonso De Vicente and Pilar Tomás. Pp. 279–300. Madrid: Centro de Estudios Europa Hispánica, 2012.

O'Regan, Noel. "Music in the service of Spanish hegemony in Rome in the early modern period." In *Festival Culture in the World of the Spanish Habsburgs*, ed. Fernando Checo Cremades and Laura Fernández-González. Pp. 245–62. Farnham: Ashgate, 2015.

Parisi, Susan. "Ducal Patronage of Music in Mantua, 1587–1627: An Archival Study." PhD diss., University of Illinois at Urbana-Champaign, 1989.

Praetorius, Michael. *Syntagma musicum III*. Wolfenbüttel: Elias Holwein, 1619.

Profeti, Maria Grazia, "Spettacoli musicali a corte tra Firenze e Madrid: *La selva sin amor* e dintori." In *Rime e suoni alla spagnola*, ed. Giulia Veneziano. Pp. 97–108. Florence: Alinea, 2003.

Profeti, Maria Grazia, ed. *Commedia e musica tra Spagna e Italia*. Florence: Alinea 2009.

Sanseverino, Benedetto. *Il primo libro d'intavolatura per la chitarra alla spagnola*. Milan: Filippo Lomazzo, 1622.

Stein, Louise K. *Songs of Mortals, Dialogues of the Gods: Music and Theatre in Seventeenth-Century Spain*. Oxford: Clarendon Press, 1993.

Stein, Louise K. "The Origins and Character of *Recitado*." *Journal of Seventeenth-Century Music* 9/1 (2003): https://sscm-jscm.org/v9no1.html

Stein, Louise K. "Three Spaniards Meet Italian Opera in the Age of Spanish Imperialism." In *Passaggio in Italia: Music on the Grand Tour in the Seventeenth Century*, ed. Dinko Fabris and Margaret Murata. Pp. 231–347. Turnhout: Brepols, 2015.

Tyler, James and Paul Sparks. *The Guitar and its Music: From the Renaissance to the Classical Era*. New York and Oxford: Oxford University Press, 2002.

Valdivia Sevilla, Francisco Alfonso. *La guitarra rasgueada en España durante el siglo XVII*. Málaga: Universidad de Málaga, 2015.

Whitaker, Shirley B. "Florentine Opera comes to Spain: Lope de Vega's *La selva sin amor*." *Journal of Hispanic Philology* 9 (1984): 43–66.

de Zayas, Rodrigo. "Il canzoniere italo-castigliano di Mateo Bezon." In *Musica a Napoli durante il Seicento: Atti del convegno internazionale di studi, Napoli, 11–14 aprile 1985*, ed. Domenico Antonio D'Alessandro and Agostino Ziino. Pp. 93–103. Rome: Torre d'Orfeo, 1987.

Zuluaga, Daniel. "The Five-Course Guitar, Alfabeto Song and the Villanella Spagnola in Italy, ca. 1590 to 1630." PhD diss., University of Southern California 2014.

Musician, Neapolitan, Migrant: Origins of the Seventeenth-Century Diaspora of Neapolitan Music and Musicians

Dinko Fabris

Musical migrations are but one part of the larger history of the massive movements of peoples across the Mediterranean Sea, a subject sadly in fashion in these times of new epic—and often tragic—migrations. Indeed, it is impossible to study the musics of the Mediterranean without addressing migration, though the inevitable twinning of those subjects can be fraught. Martin Stokes has recently described some problems in post-structuralist Mediterranean music studies (in particular ethnomusicological ones) as follows:

> It is not surprising, then, that the Mediterranean area is the site of a number of powerful fantasies about migrants and migrant culture, in which music [...] has played a particularly important role. Metropolitan north-western Europeans love the idea of these migrating sounds. But they are very unsure about those who travel with them.[1]

Mediterranean mobilities are integral to the history of Western music, both at the level of individual moves and the collective migrations of musicians from one area to another. Not by chance many conferences, international projects, and publications of the last few years have addressed music and migration and even diasporas of musicians across the planet, examining in particular the five centuries from the onset of globalization in the early modern age to present times.[2]

My attention here will be devoted to Naples, a major center of music-making in early modern Europe and one strategically situated at a crossroads of the Mediterranean Sea. The importance of music to Neapolitan identity beginning in the sixteenth century is reflected in the creation of Europe's first public music schools there in the seventeenth century and, later on, in the massive emigration of Neapolitan musicians across the whole of Europe. If we accept the systemic perspective in which, according to Leslie Page Moch, "migration itself is conceived as a socially constructed, self-perpetuating system, that includes home and destination—a responsive system that expands, contracts, and changes according to circumstance,"[3] then Neapolitan musicians belong to the fourth type of the migration posited by Charles Tilly: career migration.[4] In such a scenario, workers move toward employment opportunities through systems established by trades, mercantile networks, armies, and so forth. Tilly defines career migration as distinct from local, chain, and circular migration because "the needs and geography of the hiring institution rather than village contacts or family needs determined the timing and the destination of moves." Of all the various types of migration, career migration tends to precipitate the greatest mobility and result in the most definitive moves, making it a particularly stark case for study.

But it is important to remember that career migration was not unique to Neapolitan musicians. Any textbook on the history of Western music has a chapter devoted to the impressive mobility of Franco-Flemish musicians throughout Southern Europe in the fifteenth and sixteenth centuries, and as early as 1829 François-Joseph Fétis and Raphael Georg Kiesewetter noted the parallels between this southward migration of northern-trained musicians and the second massive diaspora of "Italian" musicians who moved in the opposite direction, from south to north, in subsequent centuries.[5] In 1941 Paul Henry Lang devoted part of a chapter of his influential *Music in Western Civilization* to "The Renaissance Migration of Flemish musicians."[6] Finally, Reinhard Strohm returned to the issue yet again in his pivotal book *The Eighteenth-Century Diaspora of Italian Music and Musicians* of 2001:

> The eighteenth-century musical diaspora has a curious pre-history. The entire seventeenth century must be considered as its preparatory stage ... early cultivation of opera is its main driving force, and the Italian Renaissance its parent source. The music of the Italian Renaissance, however, was nourished by another—perhaps the only other—great musical migration in Western history: the arrival of musicians from the Low Countries in Italy in the fourteenth to sixteenth centuries. Did eighteenth-century Italian musicians somehow 'pay back' what Italy owed to her Northern mentors? Was there something like a macro-historical exchange taking place? This possibility is the more suggestive as the two processes seem to be exactly contiguous: Italian musicians began to cross the Alps in that generation in the late sixteenth century when the Netherlanders ceased to arrive. The two phenomena are of course not related in such a simple way [...] The migration of the 'Netherlanders' to Italy connected the musical cultures of the two most urbanised regions of early modern Europe and

> was triggered by metropolitan courts (the papal court and those of Milan and Naples). Similarly, the seventeenth- and eighteenth-century musical migration corresponded to the rapid urbanisation of the Central and Northern European courts in this period...[7]

More recently, Stanislav Tuksar, has advanced a similar argument:

> These musical-cultural transfer and acculturation processes were part of broader phenomena that occasionally emerged on a continent-wide scale at least from the time of Franco-Flemish migrations to Italian Renaissance princely courts during the fifteenth and sixteenth centuries, and were continued by the impressive Czech musical 'invasion' of the German-speaking countries during the eighteenth century, the Italian 'conquest' during the late eighteenth century, of the musical domain of the Czarist Russia and the modern 'infusion' of Japanese, Korean and Chinese musicians into European and North-American music institutions.[8]

In all of these passages, the migration of Franco-Flemish musicians is compared to a generalized "Italian" diaspora. But even if Italians from all regions spread throughout Europe during the centuries from 1500 to 1800, we should note the great number of musicians who came from Naples and proudly identified themselves as "Napolitani." In spite of the impressive literature of the last fifty or so years devoted to the music of Naples and to Neapolitan composers—especially, but not only, in opera studies—very little research has been carried out on the emigration of Neapolitan musicians per se, despite its scale, duration, and importance to the history of Western music.[9]

Before the creation of the so-called "Neapolitan school," the most eminent music teachers in Southern Italy were Flemish. The long wave of the diaspora from Flanders and Northern Europe arrived in Naples at the height of the splendid Aragonese Age at the end of the fifteenth century: among the dozens of foreign singers and instrumentalists in the Neapolitan royal chapel we find composers such as Bernardus Ycart, Alexander Agricola, and the theorist Johannis Tinctoris. But Flemish masters also arrived in the most remote provinces. In Bari, Jean de Willebroot (Joan Franzese) was chapelmaster at the Basilica di San Nicola from 1535 until his death in 1566,[10] and the celebrated Jacquet Berchem established permanent residence in Monopoli beginning in 1553.[11] Later on Federico Wynant "Fiamengo" dedicated his first book of madrigals (Venice, 1597) to the archbishop of Trani, in Apulia, his employer.[12] Both Roland de Lassus and Philippe de Monte made their professional debuts in Naples, before moving on to international careers at the top musical establishments of the day.[13] In 1586 Jean de Macque arrived in Naples from Rome, entering the service of the Prince of Venosa, the father of Carlo Gesualdo, who was able to refine his musical training with the future Flemish master of the Neapolitan royal chapel.[14]

Given these broad outlines, it may indeed appear—as Strohm put it—that "something like a macro-historical exchange" took place between Flemish and Neapolitan composers at the end of the sixteenth century. And yet, on closer analysis, the situation is not that simple. The growing interest in music in Renaissance Naples was born of a frustration: the loss of the city's rank as the capital of the Aragonese kingdom, a demotion that occurred in 1503 when the town came under the rule of Spanish viceroys. The following decades saw numerous laments for this loss and the resulting demise of the Golden Age of arts and culture, including the dissolution of the largest music chapel in Europe. The Spanish viceroys swiftly forbade the Neapolitan nobles, for fear of revolts, to practice their favorite occupations: the handling of arms and riding horses. By contrast, music was not forbidden, therefore young Neapolitan aristocrats began to cultivate the art of singing, playing instruments, and dancing. Music-making became a means to assert cultural hegemony in the face of their Spanish rulers, and men of letters (such as Sannazaro and the followers of Pontano) revived the ancient musical myth of Partenope, the Siren founder of Naples, to justify the semi-professional musical activities of noblemen.[15] The effects of these choices are evident if one considers the twenty-five or so aristocratic Neapolitan composers active in the period 1530–1630, a number unparalleled in other European cities. The case of Carlo Gesualdo, Prince of Venosa, is only the most famous. For instance, Ferrante Sanseverino, Prince of Salerno and a man considered as something of an alternative sovereign of Naples for much of the century, was at the center of a circle that invented the *canzone villanesca alla napoletana* or *villanella,* a sort of political song using the Neapolitan language as an emblem of group identity. When Sanseverino and his musical entourage were exiled by viceroy Pedro de Toledo after the revolt of 1547, the *villanella* spread across Europe, where it became a light and popular alternative to the madrigal, losing some of its political implications even if still associated with Naples and its language.[16]

Meanwhile, the myth of the Siren Partenope captured the popular imagination of Neapolitans, who believed themselves to be a people destined for music. Giovan Battista Del Tufo, a Neapolitan in exile in Milan around 1588, expressed the sentiment beautifully in these lines on "Neapolitans, true Musicians," from a poem devoted to the city:

> Ne la musica poi,
> oh, che gran cose sentireste voi
> di notte e di giorno, e sopra gli strumenti,
> con mille gran concenti
> darvi cantando con le voci aviso
> de la dolce armonia del paradiso
> [...]
> che nel comporre o nel cantar son tanti
> quelli napolitani dolcissimi cantanti,
> Giosquin, Moral, Giacchetti od Adriani,
> Zerlin, Felippi, Orlandi e Cipriani;
> anzi tutti son buon, perfetti e rari
> per insegnar agl'altri onde vien detta
> la musica perfetta
> [...]
> E tra quei cittadini o cavalieri
> vi son così gentil musici veri,
> tanto nell'arpe e quanto ne le lire,
> che placarebbon de le Furie l'ire...[17]

This self-awareness of being born for music was communicated by Neapolitans to foreign travelers who came to Naples during the seventeenth century, and so the myth spread across Europe of a city where all the inhabitants sang and played in a natural way, perhaps due to the Gulf climate.[18]

But it was not only the myth of Neapolitan musicality that fostered and sustained the migratory waves of Neapolitan musicians who moved throughout Europe beginning in the late seventeenth century. Naples was famed for its public music schools, called conservatories. This Neapolitan invention promoted the idea that the "Neapolitan school" was unrivaled in the training it provided students. The story of this invention is well known: In the early decades of the seventeenth century, Naples experienced such a tremendous surge in population that it became the most populous city in Europe after Constantinople.[19] Of its approximately 400,000 inhabitants, almost 10 percent belonged to religious orders in a capital that had over 500 churches and convents.[20] The potential institutional patrons of sacred music in Naples were innumerable, and music became so important that many charitable institutions, particularly the orphanages (called in Naples *conservatorii*), specialized in providing professional training in music. The oldest of these institutions was the Santa Casa dell' Annunziata, which had been founded to provide dowries to needy girls: here music flourished beginning around 1550. Of the city's dozen male orphanages, four specialized in musical training, which allowed boys without family to find secure jobs in choirs. The increasing level of musical activity in the city created a demand that exceeded the supply of professional musicians formerly trained, in Naples as elsewhere, in religious institutions or the homes of private masters. This soon changed the charitable mission of four Neapolitan conservatories (Santa Maria della Pietà de' Turchini, Santa Maria di Loreto, Sant'Onofrio, and Poveri di Gesù Cristo, each identified in public processions by the color of their wards' robes),[21] which began to accept non-orphaned boys sent by families throughout the kingdom in the hope that they might gain some secure employment during a period of significant economic crisis. Exactly as had happened in Flemish lands during the fifteenth century, the security of a music career was close to that of clerics (not by chance, many musicians, especially singers, were also priests). As early as around 1630, the four conservatories were full of young music students, many of whom were not orphans and whose fees were paid by their families or by noble patrons. If we figure that approximately one hundred new students were admitted every year to each of the four conservatories, the total number, at the end of the seventeenth century, of new professional musicians launched on the public market after eight-to-ten years of instruction was around 4,000. Eventually, demand made it difficult to gain entrance to the conservatories, and families living in the provinces were forced to find new ways to provide their children with quality musical training. The more fortunate boys entered the households of noblemen and rich bourgeois: this was the case in particular for the famous castrato singers, many sent by families from the provinces to Naples (before or after castration) to improve their families' income with the promise of a successful career.[22]

Families from the lower and middle classes used to entrust their children to a well-respected *maestro*, paying him to assure admission to one of the four conservatories. In a special contract signed by the family or their representative, it was specified that a young boy was left in the charge of the *maestro* for a fixed number of years in exchange for which, in addition to an initial payment, the boy promised to give the teacher part of his future earnings. After a period of training, the private pupil was presented to the conservatory where the teacher was employed, and after finishing the full cycle of studies he started his professional career with the continued help of his teacher, who was of course invested in his pupil's success and the eventual financial gains that would fill his own pockets. My reconstruction of this system (very similar to a mafia racket) shows that it was dominated for the entire second half of the seventeenth century by Francesco Provenzale (1632–1704), the most influential Neapolitan composer of his time. Thanks to the benefit of hundreds of students and thanks to the multiple appointments he obtained as chapelmaster in the most highly esteemed religious institutions of the city, Provenzale was able to find positions for many of his pupils, enlarging his income until he became one of the richest musicians of his age.[23]

This process ended by saturating the market for professional musicians during the seventeenth century thanks to the almost industrial levels of production of the four conservatories.[24] The hundreds of churches in the city, its musical institutions, palace establishments, and many confraternities, had all been provided with at least one organist and a few singers, and finally they could not accept more new musicians. For this purely economic reason—a typical motivation for migration—singers, composers, and instrumentalists from Naples eventually spread across Europe in an impressive diaspora. In the first decades of the eighteenth century, the favorite destinations were of course the richest courts and capitals with their free market for music. Gradually the displacement of new masses of musicians, generation after generation, forced the most recently arrived to seek out less-known and increasingly peripheral territories as yet untouched by their contemporaries, until they arrived at the limits of Europe, where the less fortunate or more adventurous embarked for the New World.

As suggested by Reinhard Strohm, two types predominated among the many Italian musicians (including Neapolitans) who organized "self-motivated trips" in order "to do business outside of Italy": "the operisti working in a travelling opera troupe, and the individual virtuosi of certain instruments who gave concerts and joined court orchestras."[25] Neapolitan castrati were among the first to mobilize, with individuals beginning to travel abroad quite early in the seventeenth century.[26] But it was only at the very end of the century that virtuosi such as *Matteuccio* (Matteo Sassani) and *Nicolino* (Nicola Grimaldi) built international reputations with long periods spent abroad.[27] The following generation of migratory Neapolitan castrati are legends of eighteenth-century operatic myth: Carlo Broschi, a.k.a. *Farinelli*, Gaetano Majorana, a.k.a. *Caffarelli*, Giuseppe Millico, a.k.a. *Moscovita*, Giuseppe Aprile, a.k.a. *Scirolino*, and so on. As for the instrumentalists, many Neapolitans made lucrative careers as string players, and it is curious to note that many of them occasionally crossed paths.[28] To the categories articulated by Strohm, we should add a third one: the Neapolitan composers that were invited to produce operas for the most important European theaters or employed as chapelmasters. They were perhaps the most linked to the ideology of their local background, as members of a "Neapolitan School." Since the early Renaissance, musicians traveling across Europe had regularly identified explicitly with their birthplace. But whereas many Northern European musicians presented themselves or were considered "Flemish," no matter what their origins, Italians were more specific. Even musicians living in the Kingdom of Naples indicated the town where they were born, and during the second half of the sixteenth century, printers issued "municipal" collections of music composed by musicians from the same town.[29] Later, though, when the conservatory system in Naples became so successful, even musicians born elsewhere, after completing their training, presented themselves as "Neapolitans": the most obvious case is Pergolesi, a native of Jesi in the Marche region, but there are hundreds of celebrated "Neapolitan" composers born far from Naples.[30] Another extreme case is Vicente Martin y Soler, the Valencian composer known in Vienna at the time of Mozart as "Signor Martini."

The prestige associated with being "Neapolitan," which clearly extended to foreigners who studied in Naples, may provide one explanation for the protectionism of local musicians, who felt threatened by the constant influx of foreigners. Beginning around 1650, the great number of professionals who had been educated in the conservatories decided to create guilds to ensure special privileges and mutual protections that were exclusively for "true" Neapolitans. The most important organization was the Congregazione dei Musici Napoletani (created in 1649), but special privileges for Neapolitans were introduced by many other private or religious institutions as well.[31]

Another typical feature of the "Neapolitan School" was the transmission of musical knowledge from one generation to the next according to established rules.[32] This process started in the third decade of the seventeenth century, when the four conservatories were operating at full capacity. Despite the hundreds of pupils, each institution employed only a few teachers: one master for all wind instruments, one for all string instruments, and a third one that taught both singing and composition (which involved full knowledge of keyboard techniques including figured bass realization and partimento). The singing instructor was the most important staff member at the conservatory, and he was expected to transmit specific rules of composition. Thus began a didactic chain in which each gifted pupil became, in turn, the master of a new generation. The main protagonists of this chain during the seventeenth century (sometimes working in two or more conservatories at the same time) were Giovan Maria Sabino, Giovanni Salvatore, Erasmo di Bartolo (Padre Raimo), Antonio Nola, and especially Francesco Provenzale. Provenzale's pupils Gaetano Veneziano, Gaetano Greco, and Nicola Fago went on to establish a new didactic chain in the eighteenth century that included highly respected composers: Leonardo Leo, Domenico Sarro, Leonardo Vinci, Giambattista Pergolesi, Nicola Porpora, Gaetano Latilla, Niccolò Piccinni, etc. Their work gave rise not only to the establishment of specific teaching methods, but also, progressively, to the codification of stylistic features and compositional formulas that eventually gave the "Neapolitan School" its musical identity. Musicologists are only now fully beginning to recognize the importance of didactic practices such as partimenti in the transmission and formation of compositional technique and style.[33] After eight to ten years of training at conservatory, composers then went on to develop the Neapolitan style in their professional careers, initially in the sacred music they composed for the city's many religious institutions, and subsequently, around 1700, in opera.

The diaspora of Neapolitan composers gradually dissipated in the second half of the eighteenth century, losing its cultural prestige as a natural consequence of a crisis in Naples itself, one created by the massive success of the conservatory system. As future employment prospects for hundreds of students became increasingly uncertain, fewer and fewer students entered the old conservatories. By contrast with the myth of the "Neapolitan School" still widely propagated by musical migrants from Naples, foreign travelers who visited the city expressed growing disillusionment and often described music at the Neapolitan conservatories as in decline during the second half of the eighteenth century.[34] In 1743 the Conservatorio dei Poveri di Gesù Cristo, where Pergolesi studied under Vinci, was closed. At the end of the century, Sant'Onofrio was merged with Loreto, and the remnants of these two conservatories were absorbed into the only one that survives, Pietà dei Turchini, which was renamed Real Collegio di San Sebastiano at the beginning of the nineteenth century. After 1826, the Collegio was transformed into the Conservatorio di San Pietro a Majella, still active today.

Even after the crisis of the local conservatory system and the critiques made by travelers, singers, instrumentalists, and composers educated in Naples continued to circulate throughout Europe and the colonial world. Moreover, the three structural elements of the Neapolitan educational program (solfèges, partimenti, and elaborated counterpoint) became fashionable in the main

European musical capitals: Vienna, London, and Paris. French presses issued several editions of *Solfèges d'Italie* featuring members of the Neapolitan School, and Luigi Cherubini established the Paris Conservatoire Nationale according to the model of Neapolitan singing methods, launching what was then considered the first "modern" conservatory.[35]

Neapolitan musicians abroad tended to reproduce the protection and aid mechanisms they had experienced in Naples during their years of study. Few of them were in fact "Neapolitan" natives: for the most part they came from the different provinces of the kingdom, and their arrival in Naples would have been smoothed by communal organizations of their fellow "foreigners." Since the sixteenth century, these communities had developed forms of assistance for fellow countrymen that could welcome a young person upon arrival from the province and protect him until he entered the world of work through a chain of solidarity. This community welfare might be supplemented by the protections of the noble feudal lords of the territory of origin of the young musician apprentice. The pamphlet *Memorie dell'abate don Bonifacio Pecorone della città di Saponara musico della Real Cappella di Napoli* (published in Naples, 1729) provides many details about these protectionist organizations. The protagonist was born in Saponara (today Grumento Nova, in Basilicata) and started his career in Naples with the help of fellow countrymen and the Sanseverino family, princes of Saponara.

A very similar form of assistance developed in the main cities of Europe where migration led not only musicians but all kinds of citizens from the Kingdom of Naples to settle and establish communities of mutual support. In many cases, Neapolitan ambassadors and their Italian circles provided the most substantial support. But often former viceroys or foreign ambassadors or simple travelers who had been in contact with the Neapolitan environment would, upon returning to their homelands, help the musicians they had met in Naples or their pupils.[36]

Ethnomusicologists have long been engaged with investigating how music contributes to our understanding of migratory phenomena and cultural hybridity. Again in the words of Martin Stokes: "Patriarchal secular nation-state building projects [...] have, in crucial regards, collapsed. Senses of national belonging are now being adjusted to different spatial and temporal orders, in which migrancy is acknowledged, and often seen as a resource rather than a national embarassment."[37] These expanded perspectives have brought the Mediterranean Sea into new focus, with the important result that the Arab Middle East is now being explored within the new field of diaspora studies.[38] History, too, provides compelling cases for analysis, but many still await the anthropological and sociological perspectives traditionally shut off from musical historiographies that tend to concentrate on individuals rather than groups. The collective migrations of Neapolitan musicians that I have been describing offer ample opportunities to reclaim histories of cultural mobility, both migratory and diasporic. As observed by Strohm, Italian displacements during the eighteenth century followed both patterns: many musicians emigrated in "a collective and simultaneous move from and to a specific region," while others dispersed in diaspora, "a 'scattering' of individuals into all directions with no overall pattern." Strohm's solomonic description sees in the moves of Italian musicians both a true "musical diaspora," as well as "an 'emigration,' an almost collective move of Italians, not into specific countries but into all regions of Europe."[39] In this sense, Neapolitan musicians are a prime example of the two kinds of move.

Notes

1. Stokes, "Migrant/migrating music and the Mediterranean," 29–30. The case under consideration by Stokes, an ethnomusicologist and cultural historian specializing in Turkish music, is the ambiguous place of Malta, where Western and Arabic musical influences overlap. Stokes likens the situation to that of the music produced by Turkish immigrants in Europe, especially Germany, and questions basic conceptual categories such as identity and transformation. Also see his earlier contributions as co-editor (with Schulze and Campbell) of *Nationalism, Minorities and Diasporas: Identities and Rights in the Middle East* (1996).

2. I provide an overview and commentary on recent scholarship in "Travellers and Migrants: Musicians around Europe in the Early Modern Age," the introduction to Katalinić, ed. *Music Migrations in the Early Modern Age*, 13–29, to which should be added zur Nieden and Over, eds., *Musicians' Mobilities and Music Migrations in Early Modern Europe*. Major international projects of particular note include: the MUSICI project (2010-2013), which studied foreign musicians active in Venice, Rome, and Naples during the period 1650–1750, and the "Music Migrations project" (MusMig), supported by the European Community Fund HERA, which included scholars from Croatia, Slovenia, Germany, and Poland. The MUSICI project has produced an online database (http://www.musici.eu/index.php?id=3) and two books of conference proceedings: Giron-Panel and Goulet, eds., *La musique à Rome au XVIIe siècle*, and Goulet and zur Nieden, eds., *Europäische Musiker in Venedig, Rom und Neapel*. The MusMig project has also produced an online database (http://www.musmig.eu/database/), as well as the two aforementioned volumes of conference proceedings: Katalinić, ed., *Music Migrations in the Early Modern Age*, and zur Nieden and Over, eds., *Musicians' Mobilities and Music Migrations in Early Modern Europe*.

3. Moch, *Moving Europeans*, 16–17.

4. The four standard migration patterns were described in Tilly, "Migration in Modern European History," 5–14.

5. Kiesewetter and Fétis, *Verhandelingen over de vraag*. This book, published in a bilingual edition, Flemish and German, begins as follows: "Man wird von Jugend auf so sehr an die Vorstellung gewöhnt, alle Musik sey von Italiën aus über Europa verbreitet worden, und die *Italiener* die Lehrer der übrigen Völker in dieser Kunst gewesen, dass man auf eine sonderbare Art überrascht wird, wenn man irgendwo zum ersten Mal erfährt, dass es *Niederländer* waren, welche, zu einer Zeit, wo in Italien und in andern Ländern kaum noch schwache Versuche einer Verbindung mehrerer Stimmen zu einem Harmonischen Gesang

Kunst auftraten [...] und wohl durch anderthalb Jahrhunderte an den Höfen und in den Capellen eben so geschätz und gesucht waren, als es in den uns näher liegenden Zeiten die Italiener nur immer gewesen sind" (p. 1).

6. Lang, *Music in Western Civilizatio*n, chap. 9, section "Migration of Flemish Musicians," 190–94. Lang himself migrated to the United States from his native Hungary (then part of the Austrian empire), but "his immigration was voluntary and enthusiastic" and this "set him apart from the wave of forced emigrants that was about to land on America's shores," especially from Germany (Josephson, "The German Musical Exile and the Course of American Musicology," 12).

7. Strohm, *The Eighteenth-Century Diaspora of Italian Music and Musicians*, xvii. For some remarks of my own that anticipate arguments I pursue in this essay, see Fabris, "Travellers and Migrants: Musicians around Europe in the Early Modern Age,"13–29.

8. Tuksar, "Croatian musicians in Venice, Rome and Naples," 210.

9. For the period before 1800, one of the first sets of studies emerged from a conference I co-organized in Lecce in 1985, proceedings published as Bozzi and Cosi, eds., *Musicisti nati in Puglia ed emigrazione musicale fra Sei e Settecento*. On the subsequent period see Frasca, *Italian Birds of Passage*.

10. See Fabris, "Vita musicale a Bari dal Medioevo al Settecento," 34.

11. In Monopoli, Berchem married Giustina de Simeonibus, member of a noble family, and their daughter Harsilia was born in November 1553, *terminus ante quem* for his arrival in the Apulian town. Even if Berchem was not officially engaged as chapelmaster in Monopoli, he composed and performed music there until his death in 1567. See Morgante, "La cappella musicale del Duomo di Monopoli nel Rinascimento," 27–34; and the Introduction by Galliano Ciliberti to the modern edition of Berchem, *Il primo libro dei madrigali a quattro voci* (1555).

12. Larson and Pompilio, "Cronologia delle edizioni musicali napoletane del Cinque-Seicento," 117.

13. See Larson, "Condizione sociale dei musicisti e dei loro committenti nella Napoli del Cinque e Seicento," 72. Lassus spent the years 1549–1551 in Naples, in the house of Giovanni Battista d'Azzia, marquis of Terza; in the period before 1554, Monte was living in the houses of Cosimo Pinelli and Nardo Antonio Della Porta, teaching among others the young Giovanni Battista Della Porta. Larson also lists Ghiselin Danckerts in the house of Pierluigi Carafa and Giaches de Wert "ragazzo da cantare" (choirboy) in the house of Maria di Cardona. On Wert see MacClintock, "New light on Giaches de Wert."

14. See Lippmann, "Giovanni de Macque tra Roma e Napoli," and D'Alessandro, "Giovanni de Macque e i musici della Real Cappella napoletana," 21–156.

15. See Fabris, *Partenope da Sirena a Regina*.

16. Fabris, "The Role of Solo Singing to the Lute," 133–45.

17. "In music, then / oh, what great things would you hear/ by night and day, and upon instruments, / with a thousand great concerts, / their voices giving you a taste / of the sweet harmony of paradise [...] in composition as in song / those Neapolitans / are most sweet singers, / as they were Josquin [Desprez], Cristobal de Morales, Jacquet [de Mantua] or Adrian [Willaert], / Joseffo Zarlino, Philippe [de Monte], Roland [de Lassus] or Cipriano [de Rore]; all good, indeed perfect and rare / to teach to others whence comes / the perfect music [...] And among those townsfolk or gentlemen / are such true musicians, / on the harp as on the lyre, / as would placate the anger of the Furies [...]." Del Tufo, *Ritratto o modello delle grandezze, delitie e meraviglie della nobilissima Città di Napoli*, 141.

18. See for instance John Evelyn, who noted during his visit to Naples in 1645: "The country people [are] so jovial and addicted to music that the very husbandmen universally play on the guitar, singing and composing songs in praise of their sweethearts, and will commonly go to the field with their fiddle..." (*The Diary of John Evelyn*, 1:239).

19. The first documentary study of the four Neapolitan conservatories was Giacomo, *I quattro antichi conservatorii musicali di Napoli*. Also see Robinson, "The Governor's Minutes of the Conservatory S. Maria di Loreto, Naples"; Del Prete, "La trasformazione di un istituto benefico-assistenziale in scuola di musica"; Olivieri, "Aggiunte a *La scuola musicale di Napoli di F. Florimo*"; Pozzi, "Vita musicale e committenza nei conservatori napoletani del Seicento"; Fabris, *Music in Seventeenth-Century Naples*; and Gjerdingen, "The perfection of craft training in the Neapolitan Conservatories."

20. See Di Maio, *Società e vita religiosa a Napoli nell'età moderna (1656–1799)*.

21. For a brief overview of the foundation and first years of the four Neapolitan conservatories, see Fabris, *Music in Seventeenth-Century Naples*, 26ff. See also Di Benedetto and Fabris, "Naples."

22. The bibliography on Italian castrato singers is huge. Among recent titles: Barbier, *The World of the Castrati*; Freitas, *Portrait of a Castrato: Politics, Patronage, and Music in the Life of Atto Melani*; and Feldman, *The Castrato. Reflections on Natures and Kinds.*

23. Fabris, *Music in Seventeenth-Century Naples*, 66–69, 80, and passim. Updated information in Fabris, "Provenzale, Francesco (Antonio)."

24. For an economic study of the "creative industry" of music in Naples, see Clemente and Del Prete, "Cultural Creativity and Symbolic Economy in Early Modern Naples."

25. Strohm, "Italian Operisti North of the Alps. c.1700-c.1750," in *The Eighteenth-Century Diaspora of Italian Music and Musicians*, 16ff.

26. Donatello Coya, an alto, was the first important Neapolitan castrato of international reputation: in 1628 the viceroy invited him to leave Venice, where he was already famous on theatrical stages, to enter the Neapolitan Royal Chapel, where he served until his death during the plague of 1656.

27. Sassani was first invited to Vienna by the emperor on November 1695, then he passed to Spain in the service of the king. Grimaldi moved first to England in 1708, where in 1711 he performed the title role in *Rinaldo*, Handel's first opera for London. He returned to Naples in 1717, famous and honored with the title of "cavaliere." Both were members of the Royal Chapel, the most important musical institution in Naples.

28. Giovanni Antonio Piani and Angelo Ragazzi served in the same Imperial Chapel where the son of Nicola Matteis was also active; the cello player Salvatore Lanzetti married the daughter of one of the Besozzis, who were virtuoso oboists, while Michele Mascitti's clan exercised considerable influence in the Neapolitan musical scene (his uncle was the virtuoso Pietro Macchitelli, who had helped other members of the family such as Giovanni, Francesco, and Nicola Sabatino to launch their careers). On Neapolitan players of violin and other instruments see Olivieri, *The 'Fiery Genius': The Contribution of Neapolitan Virtuosi.* Giovanni Antonio Piani was better known as Jean-Antoine Des Planes because he started his career in France. In 1704 he was already living in France, but then he spent most of his life in Vienna at the Imperial Court Chapel between 1720 and 1760, where he was the most highly paid instrumentalist. Angelo Ragazzi, after a period in the service of the Royal Chapel in Barcelona, followed Charles VI to Vienna when he became emperor in 1717, remaining in his service until 1722. On his music output see Di Benedetto, "The Sonate a Quattro of Angelo Ragazzi (1736)." Michele Mascitti spent the greater part of his life in Paris after a period of training in Naples with his uncle Pietro Marchitelli. He also visited Germany and the Netherlands. In Paris he published nine books of sonatas between 1704 and 1738, which exerted considerable influence on the next generation of French violin composers. In 1739 he was naturalized as French. See Dean, *The Music of Michele Mascitti.* On the cello tradition and other Neapolitan instrumentalists see Olivieri, "Cello Playing and Teaching in Eighteenth-Century Naples," idem, "Condizione sociale dei musicisti nella Napoli del '700: Pietro Marchitelli," and Fabris, ed., *Gli esordi del violoncello a Napoli e in Europa.*

29. See Piperno, *Gli "Eccellentissimi Musici della Città di Bologna,"* and Fabris, ed., *Gli esordi del violoncello a Napoli e in Europa.*

30. Cerreto, *Della prattica musica vocale, e strumentale*, 154–56, publishes a list of "Nomi de i Musici Napolitani, e Compatrioti, che sono stati in questa città di Napoli dall'anno 1500 infino al dì d'oggi"; several individuals in the list are styled as "per antichità napolitano."

31. On this protectionist attitude see Veneziano, "Strategie di accoglienza nei circuiti professionali. I musicisti 'forestieri' nelle istituzioni napoletane." In addition to the case studied by Veneziano (the musical chapel at the Pio Monte della Misericordia), the same strategy is evident in the discounted admission fees Neapolitans paid to the conservatories, who charged foreigners higher sums.

32. See Gjerdingen, "The perfection of craft training in the Neapolitan Conservatories."

33. Niccolò Piccinni provides information about the typical eight-to-ten-year program of study in the Neapolitan conservatories: students started with solfège (to develop melodic skills), then partimenti (improvisation at the keyboard) and the highest course of counterpoint. See Gjerdingen, *Music in the Galant Style*; idem, "Partimento, que me-veux tu?"; idem, "Images of Galant Music in Neapolitan Partimenti and Solfeggi"; idem, "Partimenti written to impart a knowledge of counterpoint and composition"; Sanguinetti, *The Art of Partimento*; Van Tour, "The lost art of partimento"; idem, *Counterpoint and Partimento: Methods of Teaching Composition in Late Eighteenth-Century Naples*; and Paraschivescu, *Die Partimenti von Giovanni Paisiello Ansätze zu ihrem Verständnis.* A very useful resource is the website managed by Robert Gjerdingen at Northwestern University on Solfeggi and Partimenti: http://faculty-web.at.northwestern.edu/music/gjerdingen/aboutSeries/ aboutSeries.htm.

34. The disillusionment with Neapolitan music is evident in the travelogues of Donatien Alphonse François, marquis de Sade, *Voyage en Italie*, in *Œuvres complètes du Marquis de Sade*; and Burney, "Journey to Naples" in *The Present State of Music in France and Italy*.

35. Among other essays, see Mamy, "L'importation des solfèges italiens en France à la fin du XVIIIe siècle."

36. There are no comprehensive studies of this subject. The specific cases can be drawn from the biographies of the most important musicians: think of the role of Abbot Galiani, a Neapolitan intellectual and diplomat, in Piccinni's call to Paris and Paisiello's to Russia.

37. Stokes, "Migrant/migrating music and the Mediterranean," 35.

38. See especially Ma'oz and Sheffer, eds., *Middle Eastern Minorities and Diasporas*.

39. Strohm, *The Eighteenth-Century Diaspora of Italian Music and Musicians*, xvi.

Bibliography

Barbier, Patrick. *The World of the Castrati: The History of an Extraordinary Operatic Phenomenon*, trans. Margaret Crosland. London: Souvenir, 1997.

Burney, Charles. *The Present State of Music in France and Italy: Or, the Journal of a Tour Through Those Countries, Undertaken to Collect Materials for a General History of Music*. The second edition corrected. London: Becket and Company, J. Robson, and G. Robinson, 1773.

Berchem, Jacquet. *Il primo libro dei madrigali a quattro voci (1555)*, ed. Galliano Ciliberti and Giovanni Rota. Bari: Florestano, 2010.

Bozzi, Detty, and Luisa Cosi, eds. *Musicisti nati in Puglia ed emigrazione musicale fra Sei e Settecento. Atti del convegno di studi di Lecce 1985*. Rome: Torre d'Orfeo, 1988.

Cafiero, Rosa, and Marina Marino, eds. *Francesco Florimo e l'Ottocento musicale*. 2 vols. Reggio Calabria: Jason, 1999.

Clemente, Alida, and Rossella Del Prete. "Cultural Creativity and Symbolic Economy in Early Modern Naples: Music and Theatre as Cultural Industries." In *Cities and Creativity from the Renaissance to the Present*, eds. Ilja Van Damme, Bert De Munck, and Andrew Miles. Pp. 85–104. London and New York: Routledge, 2017.

Cerreto, Scipione. *Della prattica musica vocale, e strumentale*. Naples: Gio. Giacomo Carlino, 1601. Facsimile edition Bologna: Forni, 1969.

D'Alessandro, Domenico Antonio. "Giovanni de Macque e i musici della Real Cappella napoletana." In *La musica del Principe. Studi e prospettive per Carlo Gesualdo*, ed. Luisa Curinga. Pp. 21–156. Lucca: LIM, 2008.

Dean, Robert Henry. "The Music of Michele Mascitti (ca. 1664–1760): A Neapolitan Violinist in Paris." PhD diss., University of Iowa, 1971.

Del Tufo, Giovan Battista. *Ritratto o modello delle grandezze, delitie e meraviglie della nobilissima Città di Napoli* (1588), ed. Olga Silvana Casale. Rome: Salerno Editrice, 2007.

Del Prete, Rossella. "La trasformazione di un istituto benefico-assistenziale in scuola di musica: una lettura dei libri contabili del conservatorio di S. Maria di Loreto in Napoli (1586–1703)." In *Francesco Florimo e l'Ottocento musicale*. 2 vols. 2:671–715. Reggio Calabria: Jason, 1999.

Di Benedetto, Renato. "The Sonate a Quattro of Angelo Ragazzi (1736)." In: *International Musicological Society Congress Report, Copenhagen, 1972*, ed. Henrik Glahn, Søren Sorensen, and Peter Ryom. 2 vols. 1:356–65. Kassel: Bärenreiter, 1974.

Di Benedetto, Renato, and Dinko Fabris. "Naples." In *The New Grove Dictionary of Music and Musicians*, ed. Stanley Sadie, second revised edition. 29 vols. 17:613–30. London: Macmillan, 2001.

di Giacomo, Salvatore. *I quattro antichi conservatorii musicali di Napoli. MDLIII–MDCCC*. 2 vols. (I) *Il Conservatorio di Sant'Onofrio a Capuana e quello di S.M. della Pietà dei Turchini*; (II) *Il Conservatorio dei Poveri di Gesù Cristo e quello di S. M. di Loreto*. Palermo and Milan: Sandron, 1924–1928.

Di Maio, Romeo. *Società e vita religiosa a Napoli nell'età moderna (1656–1799)*. Naples: Edizioni Scientifiche Italiane, 1971.

Evelyn, John. *The Diary of John Evelyn*, ed. Austin Dobson. Cambridge: Cambridge University Press, 2015.

Fabris, Dinko. "Vita musicale a Bari dal Medioevo al Settecento," in *La musica a Bari dalle cantorie medievali al Conservatorio Piccinni*, ed. Dinko Fabris and Marco Renzi, with a contribution by Riccardo Muti. Pp. 19–108. Bari: Levante, 1993.

Fabris, Dinko. "The Role of Solo Singing to the Lute in the Origins of the 'Villanella alla Napolitana,' c.1530–1570." In *Gesang zur Laute*, ed. Nicole Schwindt. Special issue of *Trossinger Jahrbuch für Renaissancemusik* 2 (2002): 133–45.

Fabris, Dinko. *Music in Seventeenth-Century Naples. Francesco Provenzale (1624–1704)*. Aldershot: Ashgate, 2007; repr. London and New York: Routledge, 2016.

Fabris, Dinko. *Partenope da Sirena a Regina. Il mito musicale di Napoli*. Barletta: Cafagna, 2016.

Fabris, Dinko. "Provenzale, Francesco (Antonio)." In *Dizionario Biografico degli Italiani* 85 (2016): www.treccani.it, accessed December 30, 2018.

Fabris, Dinko. "Travellers and Migrants: Musicians around Europe in the Early Modern Age." In *Music Migrations in the Early Modern Age: People, Markets, Patterns and Styles*, ed. Vjera Katalinić. Pp. 13–29. Zagreb: Croatian Musicological Society, 2016.

Fabris, Dinko, ed. *Gli esordi del violoncello a Napoli e in Europa tra Sei e Settecento*. Barletta: Cafagna, 2020

Feldman, Martha. *The Castrato. Reflections on Natures and Kinds*. Berkeley and Los Angeles: University of California Press, 2016.

Frasca, Simona. *Italian Birds of Passage. The Diaspora of Neapolitan Musicians in New York*. Italian and Italian American Studies. New York: Palgrave Macmillan, 2014.

Freitas, Roger. *Portrait of a Castrato: Politics, Patronage, and Music in the Life of Atto Melani*. Cambridge: Cambridge University Press, 2009.

Giron-Panel, Caroline, and Anne-Madeleine Goulet, eds. *La musique à Rome au XVIIe siècle: études et perspectives de recherche*. Rome: École française de Rome, 2012.

Gjerdingen, Robert O. *Music in the Galant Style*, Oxford: Oxford University Press, 2007.

Gjerdingen, Robert O. "Images of Galant Music in Neapolitan Partimenti and Solfeggi." *Basler Jahrbuch für historische Musik-praxis* 31 (2009): 131–47.

Gjerdingen, Robert O. "Partimento, que me-veux tu?" *Journal of Music Theory* 51 (2007): 85–135.

Gjerdingen, Robert O. "The perfection of craft training in the Neapolitan Conservatories." *GATM, Rivista di analisi e teoria musicale* 15 (2009): 26–49.

Gjerdingen, Robert O. "Partimenti written to impart a knowledge of counterpoint and composition." In *Partimento and Continuo Playing in Theory and Practice*, ed. Thomas Christensen, Robert Gjerdingen, Giorgio Sanguinetti and Rudolf Lutz. Collected Writings of the Orpheus Institute 9. Pp. 43–70. Leuven: Leuven University Press, 2010.

Gjerdingen, Robert O. Monuments of Partimenti; Monuments of Solfeggi. Database at http://faculty-web.at.northwestern.edu/music/gjerdingen, accessed December 30, 2018.

Goulet, Anne-Madeleine, and Gesa zur Nieden, eds. *Europäische Musiker in Venedig, Rom und Neapel. Les musiciens européens à Venise, Rome et Naples*. Special issue of *Analecta musicologica* 52 (2015).

Katalinić, Vjera, ed. *Music Migrations in the Early Modern Age: People, Markets, Patterns and Styles*. Zagreb: Croatian Musicological Society, 2016.

Kiesewetter, Raphael Georg, and François-Joseph Fétis, *Verhandelingen over de vraag: welke verdiensten hebben zich de Nederlanders vooral in de 14e, 15e en 16e eeuw in het vak der toonkunst verworven; en in hoe verre kunnen de Nederlandsche kunstenaars van dien tijd, die zich naar Italien begeven hebben, invloed gehad hebben op de muzijkscholen, die zich kort daarna in Italien hebben gevormd?* Amsterdam: Koninklijk-Nederlandsche Instituut, 1829.

Josephson, David, "The German Musical Exile and the Course of American Musicology." *Current Musicology* 69–70 (2005): 9–53.

Lang, Paul Henry. *Music in Western Civilization*. New York: Norton, 1941.

Larson, Keith A. "Condizione sociale dei musicisti e dei loro committenti nella Napoli del Cinque e Seicento." In *Musica e cultura a Napoli dal XV al XIX secolo*, ed. Lorenzo Bianconi and Renato Bossa. Pp. 61–77. Florence: Olschki, 1983.

Larson, Keith A., and Angelo Pompilio. "Cronologia delle edizioni musicali napoletane del Cinque-Seicento." In *Musica e cultura a Napoli dal XV al XIX secolo*, ed. Lorenzo Bianconi and Renato Bossa. Pp. 103–39. Florence: Olschki, 1983.

Lippmann, Friedrich. "Giovanni de Macque tra Roma e Napoli. Nuovi documenti." *Rivista italiana di musicologia* 13 (1978): 243–79.

MacClintock, Carol. "New light on Giaches de Wert." In *Aspects of Medieval and Renaissance Music. A Birthday Offering to Gustave Reese*, ed. Jean LaRue. Pp. 595–602. New York: Norton, 1966.

Mamy, Sylvie. "L'importation des solfèges italiens en France à la fin du XVIIIe siècle." In *L'opera tra Venezia e Parigi*, ed. Maria Teresa Muraro. Fondazione Cini, Studi di Musica Veneta 14. Pp. 67–89. Florence: Olschki, 1988.

Ma'oz, Moshe, and Gabriel Sheffer, eds. *Middle Eastern Minorities and Diasporas*. Brighton: Sussex Academic Press, 2002.

Memorie dell'abate don Bonifacio Pecorone della città di Saponara musico della Real Cappella di Napoli. Naples: Vocola, 1729; ed. with an introduction by Dinko Fabris. Irsina: Giuseppe Barile, 2017.

Moch, Leslie Page. *Moving Europeans: Migration in Western Europe since 1650*. 2nd ed. Bloomington: Indiana University Press, 2003.

Morgante, Domenico. "La cappella musicale del Duomo di Monopoli nel Rinascimento: l'Antifonario del 1532, la prassi esecutiva, i documenti inediti su Jachet de Berchem." *Monumenta Apuliæ ac Japygiæ* 1 (1981): 27–34.

MUSICI. Musicisti Europei a Venezia, Roma e Napoli (1650-1750). www.musici.eu, accessed December 30, 2018.

MUSMIG. Music Migrations in the Early Modern Age: The Meeting of the European East, West and South. www.musmig.eu, accessed December 30, 2018.

Olivieri, Guido. "Aggiunte a *La scuola musicale di Napoli* di F. Florimo: i contratti dei figlioli della Pietà dei Turchini nei protocolli notarili (1677–1713)." In *Francesco Florimo e l'Ottocento musicale*. 2 vols. 2:717–52. Reggio Calabria: Jason, 1999.

Olivieri, Guido. "The 'Fiery Genius': The Contribution of Neapolitan Virtuosi to the Spread of the String Sonata (1684–1736)." PhD diss., University of California, Santa Barbara, 2005.

Olivieri, Guido. "Condizione sociale dei musicisti nella Napoli del '700: Pietro Marchitelli." In *Napoli Musicalissima. Studi in onore di Renato Di Benedetto*. Pp. 45–68. Lucca: LIM, 2006.

Olivieri, Guido. "Cello Playing and Teaching in Eighteenth-Century Naples: F. P. Supriani's *Principij da imparare a suonare il violoncello*." In *Performance Practice: Issues and Approaches*. Pp. 109–36. Ann Arbor: Steglein, 2009.

Paraschivescu, Nicoleta. "Die Partimenti von Giovanni Paisiello Ansätze zu ihrem Verständnis." PhD diss., Universiteit Leiden, 2015.

Piperno, Franco. *Gli "Eccellentissimi Musici della Città di Bologna". Con uno studio sull'antologia madrigalistica del Cinquecento*. Florence: Olschki, 1985.

Pozzi, Raffaele. "Vita musicale e committenza nei conservatori napoletani del Seicento. Il S. Onofrio e i Poveri di Gesù Cristo." In *Atti del XIV congresso della Società internazionale di musicologia: Trasmissione e recezione delle forme di cultura musicale*, ed. Angelo Pompilio, Donatella Restani, Lorenzo Bianconi, and F. Alberto Gallo. 3 vols. 3:915–24. Turin: EDT, 1990.

Robinson, Michael F. "The Governor's Minutes of the Conservatory S. Maria di Loreto, Naples." *RMA Research Chronicle* 10 (1972): 1–97.

Sade, Donatien Alphonse François de [Marquis de Sade]. *Voyage en Italie*. In *Œuvres complètes du Marquis de Sade*. 8:109–457. Paris: Tête de feuilles, 1973.

Sanguinetti, Giorgio. *The Art of Partimento; History, Theory, and Practice*. New York: Oxford University Press, 2012.

Schulze, Kirsten E., Martin Stokes, and Colm Campbell, eds. *Nationalism, Minorities and Diasporas: Identities and Rights in the Middle East*. London: Tauris, 1996.

Stokes, Martin. "Migrant/migrating music and the Mediterranean." In *Migrating Music*, ed. Jason Toynbee and Byron Dueck. Pp. 28–35. London and New York: Routledge, 2012.

Strohm, Reinhard, ed. *The Eighteenth-Century Diaspora of Italian Music and Musicians*. Turnhout: Brepols, 2001.

Tilly, Charles. "Migration in Modern European History." Center for Research on Social Organization, Working Paper 145. Ann Arbor: University of Michigan Press, 1976.

Tuksar, Stanislav. "Croatian musicians in Venice, Rome and Naples during the period 1650–1750." In *Europäische Musiker in Venedig, Rom und Neapel. Les musiciens européens à Venise, Rome et Naples*, ed. Anne-Madeleine Goulet and Gesa zur Nieden. Special issue of *Analecta musicologica* 52 (2015): 193–210.

Veneziano, Giulia Anna Romana. "Strategie di accoglienza nei circuiti professionali. I musicisti 'forestieri' nelle istituzioni napoletane." In *Europäische Musiker in Venedig, Rom und Neapel. Les musiciens européens à Venise, Rome et Naples*, ed. Anne-Madeleine Goulet and Gesa zur Nieden. Special issue of *Analecta musicologica* 52 (2015): 465–84.

Van Tour, Peter. *Counterpoint and Partimento: Methods of Teaching Composition in Late Eighteenth-Century Naples*. Acta Universitatis Upsaliensis, Studia Musicologica Upsaliensia, nova serie 25. Uppsala: Uppsala Universitet, 2015.

Van Tour, Peter. "The lost art of partimento." *Early Music* 41 (2013): 340–41.

zur Nieden, Gesa, and Berthold Over, eds. *Musicians' Mobilities and Music Migrations in Early Modern Europe: Biographical Patterns and Cultural Exchanges*. Mainz Historical Cultural Studies 33. Bielefeld: Transcript, 2017 (open access: www.transcript-verlag.de/978-3-8376-3504-1/musicians-mobilities-and-music-migrations-in-early-modern-europe/?number=978-3-8394-3504-5).

Voi che venist'armati: Plurilingual Singing in Seventeenth-Century Bohemia

Scott Lee Edwards

In the few years preceding the outbreak of the Thirty Years War, the viceregent of Bohemia, Vilém Slavata of Chlum and Košumberk, played a central role in two famously theatrical events in Prague castle with far-reaching implications for the history of music in Central Europe. For the 1617 carnival season, Slavata financed a pro-Habsburg spectacle titled *Phasma Dionysiacum Pragense* ['The Apparition of Dionysians in Prague'] in which he also danced the role of King Ninus of Assyria. Modeled on entertainments at the Florentine and Mantuan courts and performed entirely in Italian, this *ballo sonato, e cantato e ballato* is considered the first sung musical drama based on Italian models to have been staged at the Austrian Habsburg court.[1] The second event occurred a little over a year later on May 23, 1618, when Slavata was hurled with two colleagues from a Prague castle window by members of the Bohemian Estates, who were angered over disagreements with Emperor Ferdinand II when he sought to retract the 1609 Letter of Majesty, which guaranteed them the free exercise of religion. The Estates, comprised primarily of Utraquist members and German-speaking Lutherans, made the ill-fated decision to elect Frederick V of the Palatinate as Bohemian King in 1619. His reign came to an abrupt end but one year later at the Battle of White Mountain, where the imperial forces of Ferdinand II crushed a Bohemian resistance just outside Prague in the span of a few hours. Emboldened by this victory, the Thirty Years War officially began, leaving dissident Bohemians with a choice between two extremes: either convert to Roman Catholicism or flee into exile. According to figures first reported by Slavata, it is estimated that as many as 150,000 Bohemians and Moravians chose the latter option.[2]

This essay considers a book of music produced in Bohemia in 1626, when this human upheaval was at its peak. My primary concern is with the printing in Bohemia of Catholic songs (*laude*) in Italian and the ways they witness the peregrination of Jesuit missionaries and Spanish and Italian troops into Central Europe. But the status of Italian as a musical and religious lingua franca had a long history north of the Alps, and it strengthened significantly in conjunction with a series of sixteenth-century migrations into the Bohemian kingdom from both north and south, ones impelled by the discovery of metal deposits and the transfer of the imperial court of Rudolf II from Vienna to Prague in 1583.[3] Newfound wealth from Bohemian mining spawned whole new royal towns in the sixteenth century, thanks predominantly to an influx of Saxons, who found a welcoming environment of religious toleration.[4] Meanwhile, the arrival of the imperial court in Prague heralded a more international wave of migration: by the end of the sixteenth century the Bohemian capital had doubled in size from the pre-Rudolfine era to an estimated 53,600–70,000 residents, of which a significant share were Italian.[5] These new populations made Bohemia one of the most culturally dynamic areas of Europe, something evident in the songbooks printed there. The market for sacred songbooks in Czech, Latin, and German flourished, led by those produced by the Unity of Brethren, which generated numerous imitations. It was likewise during these decades that Prague witnessed its first domestic production of printed polyphonic music in Latin, Spanish, Italian, and German. Interest in Italian-language music was promoted at the court, where communicating in Italian was an invaluable skill, but it was also embedded in urban culture by an Italian émigré community who made their mark in such fields as stonemasonry, architectural design, and the trade in luxury goods.[6] It was here in Prague where Philippe de Monte, Rudolf's chapelmaster, continued to issue his books of Italian-language music from the Venetian presses, cementing his prominence as the most prolific madrigal composer in all of Europe.

In stark contrast to this burst of music printing in the late sixteenth century, the seventeenth century witnessed extensive waves of emigration that proved detrimental to musical production in Bohemia. When Emperor Matthias transferred the court back to Vienna in 1612, the printing of polyphonic music in Prague came to an abrupt halt and musicians in the Bohemian capital were forced to look elsewhere for work. Eight years later, the printing of songbooks by reformers would similarly cease as Bohemia became mired in military combat, expulsions, and forced religious conversion.

The outbreak of war provoked yet another wave of human displacement: the international mobilization of imperial regiments from Italian territories, the Spanish Netherlands, Bavaria, Poland, and elsewhere, who upended the social fabric as they crisscrossed Bohemia enforcing Habsburg autocracy. The need for Bohemians to find ways to communicate with these new, multilingual cohabitants, which included not only soldiers but the members of their extensive entourages, became a matter of pressing importance, and Latin and

Italian songs became critical media for acquiring new linguistic skills. Singing in Italian was by no means limited to native speakers, but rather served as an important tool through which new languages and, indeed, new ways of thinking could be learned. Addressing this type of singing and the mobilities that accompanied it can expand our understanding of how Italian music in this era traveled across national borders. Historians have traditionally turned their attention to the central role of Italian opera at the Viennese court as primary evidence for both the establishment and preeminence of Italian music in Central Europe in the later seventeenth century. I would, however, argue that this development was already underway in Prague in the sixteenth century, and due to a series of historical and geographical dislocations, its earlier origins have been obscured. Our standard narratives of music history, which are too often based on false images of social fixity and presumptions of linguistic fluency, can be enriched by taking into account the broader histories of migration and cultural mobility through which music so often traveled. Moreover, Italian-language music circulated in a variety of forms, both orally and in print, and not just as seventeenth-century courtly spectacle, or even sixteenth-century madrigals. If we consider the spectrum of Italian speakers in Bohemia during this period—a linguistic culture sustained by various diasporas from the Italian Peninsula but by no means limited to those who spoke fluently—we can imagine the profusion of a much greater variety of Italian musical performance than source materials have so far revealed. This essay concentrates on one example that may speak to this music-making about which we otherwise know so little. Uncovering the oral practices that gave rise to these songs allows us to listen in on a diasporic soundscape at a place and time when music printing had almost ceased, left behind as a dispensable extravagance of the past.

The court's return to Vienna and the outbreak of war appear to have completely decimated the printing of polyphonic music in Bohemia in the years from 1620–1646, with one noteworthy and curious exception: Jan Sixt of Lerchenfels's *Deo opt: max: trino et uni laus, honor, virtus, gloria, triumphus et victoria, qui, justitia & pietate, unionem, non unam: et confoederationem haereticorum pestiferam... dissolvit.* ("To God, the best and greatest, three-in-one, praise, honor, virtue, glory, triumph and victory, who, with justice and piety, dissolved the union as well as the pestilential confederation of heretics...") (RISM A/I L 2036 and S 3563), an effusive celebration in both text and song of Ferdinand II, Eleonora Gonzaga, and Johann Tserclaes, Count of Tilly and commander of the Catholic League, who had just routed the Danish army at the Battle of Lutter on

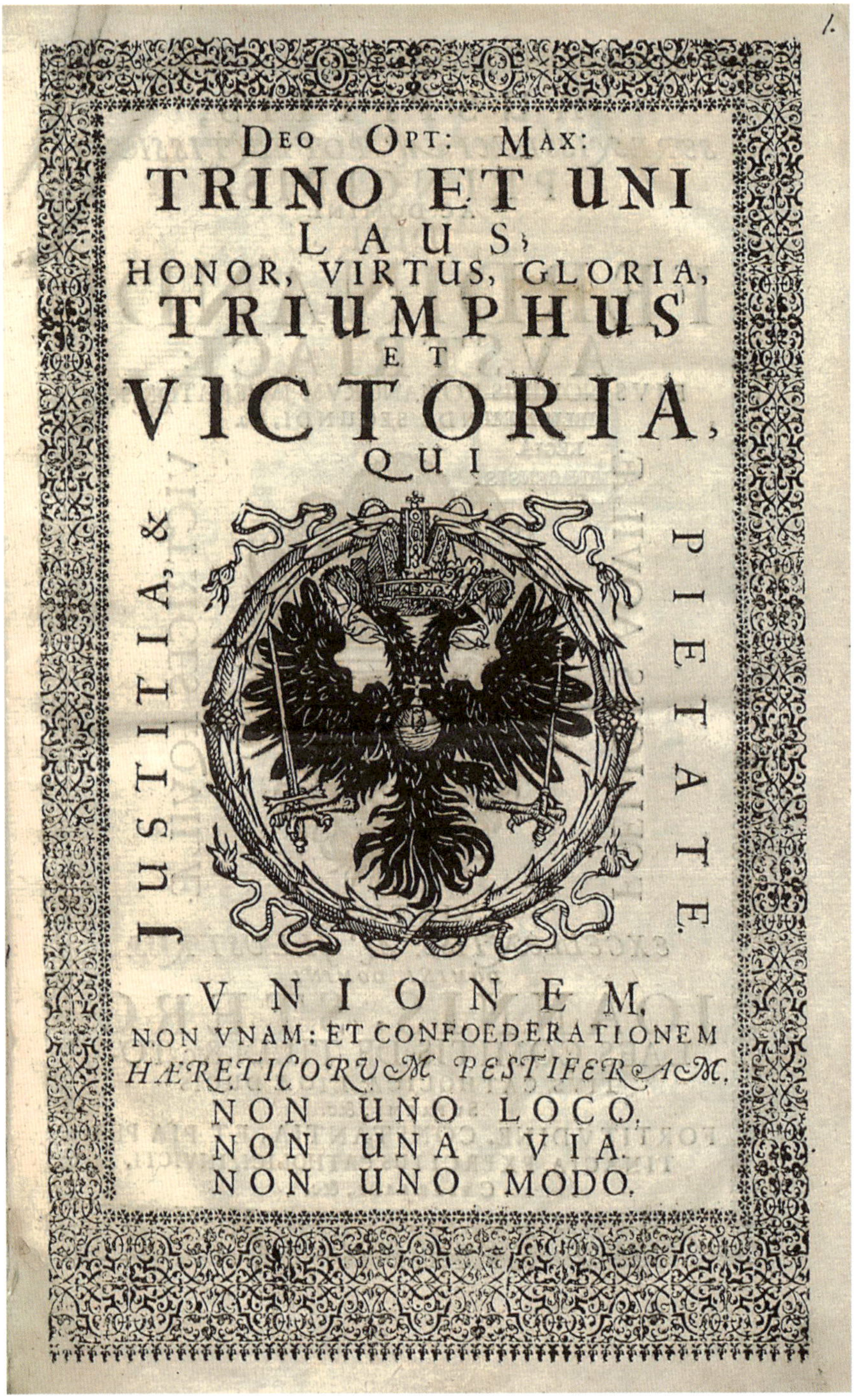

DEO OPT: MAX:
TRINO ET UNI
LAUS,
HONOR, VIRTUS, GLORIA,
TRIUMPHUS
ET
VICTORIA,
QUI
JUSTITIA, & PIETATE.
VNIONEM,
NON VNAM: ET CONFOEDERATIONEM
HÆRETICORUM PESTIFERAM,
NON UNO LOCO,
NON UNA VIA,
NON UNO MODO.

Fig. 1. Jan Sixt of Lerchenfels, *Deo opt: max: trino et uni laus, honor, virtus, gloria, triumphus et victoria...*, fol. [1]r

August 27, 1626.[7] According to the colophon, Sixt published the book less than two weeks later on September 8 at his own printing press in Litoměřice, a royal city in north Bohemia where he served as provost at the collegiate church of St. Stephen. In forty-eight leaves in medium folio,[8] Sixt's enthusiasm for Habsburg authority is matched with eye-catching typography that leaps from practically every page. An initial glance at the opening folios is already bewildering, since a preliminary title-page in the traditional sense cannot be singled out.[9] Rather, the first five folios all bear hallmarks of titles—large font sizes offset by smaller ones, heraldic emblems, decorative borders, centered justification, and aphoristic textual forms, with the one appearance of a date (albeit not in reference to the date of publication, but rather to the victory the print celebrates) appearing at the foot of fol. [2]r.[10] These typographical features immediately evoke a sense of the performative, based on both oral traditions and Sixt's lifelong career in church music. This is immediately evident on the opening title-page, for which Sixt retools the beginning of the processional hymn, *Gloria, laus et honor,* to create a rhythmic declamation pivoting on the rhyme between "gloria" and "victoria" (see figure 1).

The "three-in-one" designation on fol. [1]r, symbolically reiterated by the three heraldic emblems on the opening three pages, defines the overall structure of the print, which is organized to honor its three dedicatees individually, with separate dedications, panegyrics, and musical pieces for each (see table 1). Sixt announces himself only on the title-page fronting the first piece of music (fol. [5]r), a four-voice setting of the *Te Deum*. Here we learn that Sixt served as *puer musicus* in Prague forty-two years prior, that is, in 1584 at the court of Rudolf II, where he would have sung under the direction of Philippe de Monte. In the dedication to Ferdinand II that follows the *Te Deum,* we learn that Sixt composed the setting in Prague in 1590 while still a member of Rudolf's chapel (fol. [21]r). Although my ultimate interest lies in the Italian pieces dedicated to Tilly that comprise the majority of the book, it is worth taking a moment to examine the two sacred Latin settings that precede them. On one hand, they provide a musical complement to the *laude* that frames the whole as moored in monarchic ceremonial. They draw on ideologies advocated by Ferdinand and his commanders to galvanize their armies and, thus, are representative of the sectarian conflicts that brought so many foreigners to Bohemia in the first place. At the same time, it is clear that Sixt chose this music strategically to accommodate a broad public of Catholics and non-Catholics alike, whether of limited musical means or with access to a well-stocked instrumentarium. The variety of musics in the book thus provided scalable musical settings of texts

[1]^{r}	Title-page 1 with imperial double-headed eagle
[1]^{v}	Title-page 2 honoring Ferdinand II and Johann Tserclaes, Count of Tilly with Ferdinand's coat-of-arms
[2]^{r}	Title-page 3 celebrating victory against Christian IV of Denmark with Bohemian lion
[2]^{v}	*Oratio bellica* with two Biblical verses
[3]^{r}	*Acclamationes faustae*
[3]^{v}	Acclamations honoring Ferdinand II and Eleonora Gonzaga
[4]^{r}	*Cantica* honoring the imperial soldiers and Tilly with a *votum ad Deum*, two psalm verses, and additional acclamations
[4]^{v}	*Oratio quam Constantinus magnus Rom: imperator, ipse composuit*
[5]^{r}	Title-page for *Te Deum laudamus, hymnus SS. Ambrosij et Augustini. Harmonia. Quatuor vocum editus a reverendissimo dn. Joanne Sixti a Lerchenfels, Rudolphi II imperatoris, ante annos XXXXII puero musico.*
[5]^{v}–[11]^{r}	Setting of the *Te Deum laudamus* (4vv) in choirbook layout
[11]^{v}	*Parergon ad candidum lectorem*
[12]^{r}–[21]^{r}	Dedication to Ferdinand II
[21]^{v}	Laudatory poem in honor of Ferdinand II by Johannes Seusse, secretary to the Saxon Elector
[22]^{r}–[27]^{v}	Dedication to Eleonora Gonzaga
[28]^{r}	Title-page celebrating the text of the Magnificat
[28]^{v}–[37]^{v}	Setting of the *Magnificat quat[uor] vel octo vocum* (4 or 8vv) in score layout and concluding on fol. 37^{v} with an *Oratio*
[38]^{r}–[40]^{v}	Dedication to Johann Tserclaes, Count of Tilly
[41]^{r}	*Orationes jaculatoriæ sup: Gener: Comitis Tilli*
[41]^{v}–[46]^{v}	*Sonetti italiani, per sonare e cantare, per i valorosi e virtuosi signiori cavagliori*
[41]^{v}–[42]^{r}	Setting of *Lodiamo tutti Dio* (4vv) in score layout
[42]^{v}–[43]^{v}	Setting of *Signior ti benedico* (4vv) in score layout with alternate song, *O peccatore ingrato*, printed underneath
[44]$^{r–v}$	Setting of *Chi vol seguir la guerra* (4vv) in score layout with alternate song, *Voi capitani bravi*, printed underneath
[45]^{r}–[46]^{v}	Four-language *battaglia* titled *Un altro sonetto, a 4. Lingue Della Bataglia di Praga. Per Cantare e Sonare. Sopra, Tutti Venite armati. di Castoldi'* [= Giovanni Giacomo Gastoldi] (5vv) in score layout with stanzas in Latin, Czech, German, and Italian. Includes three additional stanzas for sacred occasions: a Latin song celebrating the Assumption of Mary and two Czech songs celebrating, respectively, the birth and resurrection of Christ
[47]^{r}	*Ad lectores & cantores* with the coat-of-arms and *symbolum* of Sixt
[47]^{v}	Epigram, anagram, and *carmen* honoring Sixt by Jan Václav Caelestinus of Kronenfeld, dean of Litoměřice and canon of Stará Boleslav
[48]^{r}	Anagram and *carmen* honoring Sixt by Matyáš Jiří Černovský of Lerchenfels, dean of Brandýs nad Labem and canon of Stará Boleslav, followed by the colophon: *Litomericii,* I *Typis Domesticis, D. Præpositi, Collegiatæ* I *Ecclesiæ S. Stephani. &c. Anno mundi labentis.* I *M. DC. XXVI. 8. Septemb.*
[48]^{v}	Blank page

Table 1. Outline of the contents of Jan Sixt of Lerchenfels, *Deo opt: max: trino et uni laus, honor, virtus, gloria, triumphus et victoria…* (following the CZ-Kp and D-Mbs exemplars)

whose cross-confessional appeal would act somewhat as a counterweight to the ideologically divisive contents that surround them.

A Habsburg *Te Deum*

The decision to begin with a musical setting composed so long before and to draw attention to its age and pedigree serves not just to highlight the retrospective character of the music and Sixt's career-long engagement in musical composition, but also to trace continuity across the reigns of Rudolf II and Ferdinand II. At once timeless and occasional, the *Te Deum* celebrates both Catholic monarchs even as it refers to Tilly's route of the Danish. Upon receiving news of Tilly's victory, the imperial court in Vienna rejoiced accordingly with the classic hymn:

> I conclude by reporting that the following day, after having received news of the victory against the Danish, the Emperor and Empress walked on foot to [the pilgrimage site of Maria] Hietzing, followed by almost the entire court, especially the foreign ambassadors. That evening when they came in, the French and Venetian residents congratulated His Royal Majesty on account of this victory, but the other ambassadors performed it the next day, at night to be sure, since His Royal Majesty was hunting in Ebersdorf and only came in at dusk. Yesterday, the *Te Deum laudamus* was solemnly sung in the court church of St. Augustine, but on the 6th of September it was sung in all the churches. The cannons were also carried to the bastions and, as a sign of joy, fired all around the city.[11]

Sixt emphasizes the music's retrospective character by printing the setting in traditional choirbook layout with opening historiated initials. The composition is a four-voice *alternatim* setting in lightly imitative polyphony, with the *Te Deum laudamus* intonation printed on both sides of the first opening in mensural notation for choral performance. Sixt avoids flashy technique in favor of concise delivery of the text through short imitative phrases and frequent syllabic declamation. In his dedication to Ferdinand, he offers his own assessment of its style: "If anyone shall perhaps consider its craftsmanship less polished, they ought to attribute this to an age that was proceeding in a simple manner, on a level road, and on a customary path" (fol. [21]r). Conveniently deflecting criticisms of his compositional ability, Sixt turns attention toward issues of musical and political change, setting up the Rudolfine court as emblematic of a less agitated political time, one distinguished by polyphonic simplicity and social stability. Together, these continuities provide reassurance in a time of war as well as justification for Habsburg victory and its potential restoration of peace.

A Gonzaga Magnificat

Sixt's compositional approach to the Magnificat, which he dedicates to Eleonora Gonzaga, is outwardly more modern than that of the *Te Deum*. Laid out in score format, the piece is orchestrated for two choirs, the first consisting of a solo cantus voice accompanied by three viols, which is answered responsorially by a second four-voice choir accompanied by trumpets and organ. Although the orchestration is elaborate, the instruments are not provided separate parts nor is the bass figured, facilitating a reduced performance for four voices as indicated by the header.[12] The setting is chordal and homophonic, albeit with some decoration at the cadences, and the responding choir always repeats the text sung by the soloist. The close connection between this new music and the singing of Czech psalms as espoused by the Unity of Brethren is evident in the CZ-Kp exemplar of Sixt's publication, which is bound with a 1618 edition of the Czech psalter with texts by the Brethren poet Jiří Strejc and settings by Claude Goudimel (Knihopis no. K17540). Like Sixt's Magnificat setting, the music in this folio psalter is laid out in score, and the stylistic similarities that link Sixt's setting to the academic tradition of *musica poetica* serve as a reminder that this music is also somewhat retrospective in nature.[13] Despite the explicit orchestration, designed to highlight the musical resources of Eleonora's court, Sixt's elaboration of what is essentially homophonic writing for four voices indicates the ease with which such music could be flexibly expanded by large ensembles to add pomp to ceremonial occasions.

Inclusion of the Magnificat nods to the high command accorded Mary in the Catholic League. Their charge into battle was led by standards bearing the icon of the Madonna, whom Ferdinand called his "generalissima" and whose image, he believed, would carry more positive connotations than that of the Roman eagle.[14] At the 1620 Battle of White Mountain, Tilly's infamous first victory in the war, the Carmelite priest Dominique de Jésus-Maria, special envoy of Pope Paul V, preached to the soldiers in Italian and French, encouraging them to don a scapular and recite the rosary.[15] With a cry of "Sancta Maria," many of them wrapped rosaries around their arms as they charged forward under Tilly's command, while Duke Maximilian of Bavaria, Charles Bonaventure de Longueval, and the latter's Jesuit confessor retired to sing the *Salve Regina*.[16] Although the *Salve Regina* had been proscribed by Martin Luther, the Magnificat continued to maintain pride of place in Vesper services for both German- and Czech-speaking Lutherans, making the choice of this canticle an especially apt one for a confessionally diverse Central European market.[17] The same is true of the *Te Deum*, which enjoyed widespread acceptance as an enhancement to ceremonial occasions across confessions. Despite the unabashed Roman Catholic and absolutist panegyrics surrounding these works in Sixt's print, his musical choices had broad confessional appeal that made them palatable points of entry to the book's other contents. In conjunction with the Czech psalter included in the CZ-Kp exemplar, for example, the music would have fit well within the repertoire of most Czech-speaking religious communities.

Italian *Laude* for the commander of an international army

Sixt dedicated the bulk of his volume to Tilly, whom he honors with a set of five four-voice *laude spirituali* in Italian and a five-voice *sonnetto battaglia* in four languages accompanied by three alternative strophes for sacred occasions. As Sixt writes in his dedication, he composed these "one might say crude songs in the Italian idiom to praise God and to delight the souls of the entire Catholic army" (fol. [40]v). The use of Italian-texted music to honor the regiments of a field marshal from the Spanish Netherlands may at first seem surprising, but it is important to remember the international make-up of the regiments that Tilly led. A major source of European migration during the Thirty Years War was, of course, the movement of soldiers: Tilly's Catholic League comprised some 30,000 men, while the imperial armies under the command of Albrecht von Wallenstein had a strength of 58,000 by 1626.[18] Further enlarged by the entourage of attendants, chaplains, wives, and children that usually accompanied them,[19] these armies essentially amounted to itinerant cities, whose members repopulated areas vacated by the Protestant exodus.[20] Important to both Tilly and Wallenstein was the fidelity of their armies to the Habsburg and Catholic causes, and given the numbers of heretics in Central Europe, this meant that faithful soldiers were often more reliably enlisted from Spanish and Italian territories. On September 2, 1626, six days before the publication of Sixt's print, Wallenstein was garrisoned with the imperial armies nearby in the Moravian capital of Olomouc. There, he wrote to the emperor that he had dispatched recruitment patents to enlist from Milan two regiments of soldiers, and that he accepted the delay that bringing them over the Alps would cause.[21] The increased presence of Italian-speaking soldiers in the north is signaled by the replacement of the term *Landsknecht* with *Soldateska* in seventeenth-century imperial armies, the same term Friedrich Schiller would later pejoratively use to describe Tilly's and Wallenstein's soldiers in his 1790–92 *Geschichte des Dreißigjährigen Kriegs* ("History of the Thirty Years War").[22] The infiltration of Italian words into military vocabulary during this time, as is evident in this broadsheet etching where *bataglia* is used in place of the German *Schlacht Ordnung* to

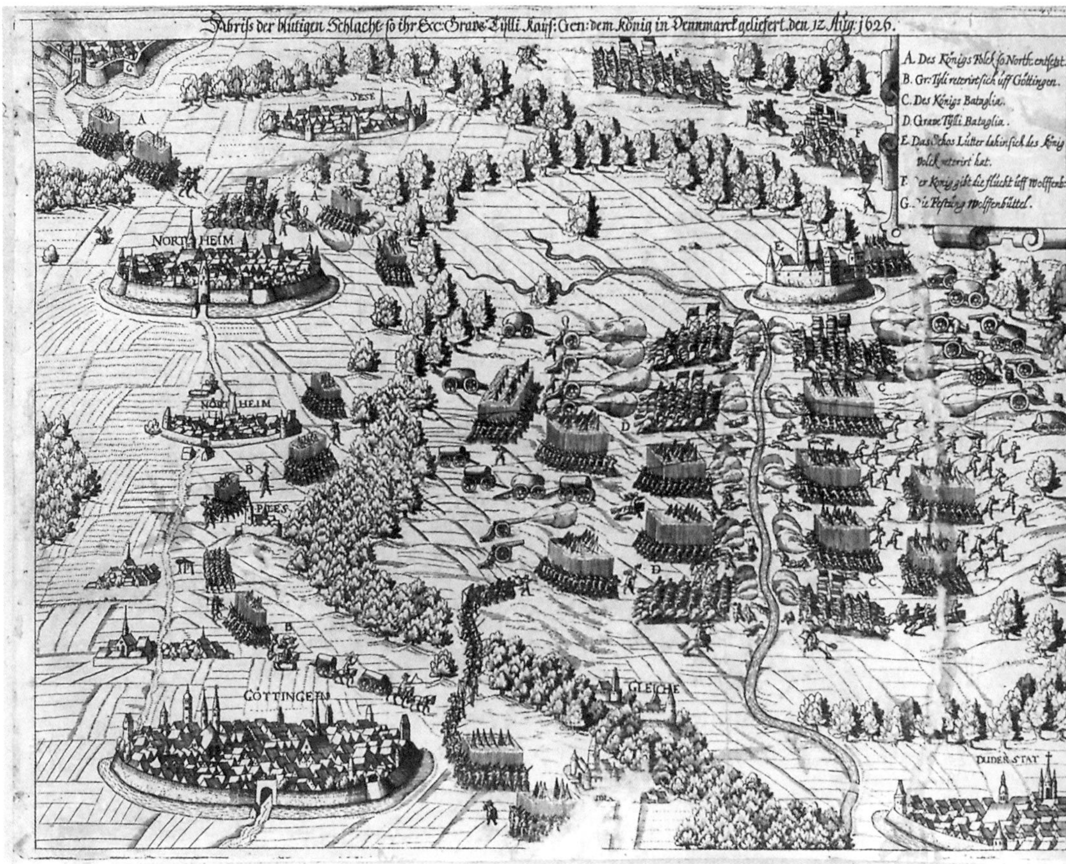

Fig. 2. *Abriss der blutigen Schlacht so ihr Exc. Grave Tÿlli. Kaÿs. Gen. dem König in Dennmarck geliefert den 12. Aug. 1626* [=27 Aug. 1626] (s.l.: s.n., [1626])

describe both the Danish and Catholic armies, was so pervasive that it became the subject of increasing attack by linguistic purists in the 1640s as the war entered its final decade (See figure 2).[23]

Wallenstein, having defeated the army of Ernst von Mansfeld at the battle of Dessau on April 25, 1626, was—at the time Sixt assembled his book—leading a reduced army to Upper Hungary, where he hoped to catch Mansfeld once more as the latter came to the aid of Gábor Bethlen, the Calvinist prince of Transylvania. On route from Dessau, the imperial troops would have passed close to Litoměřice as they journeyed through Olomouc to the Hungarian border. Though Sixt never names Wallenstein, he must have been aware of the march of this military body through northern Bohemia as his book went to press. Sixt identifies himself as Tilly's chaplain, suggesting that he knew through first-hand experience the suitability of Italian *laude* for honoring the Wallonian Tilly in a publication destined for Central European consumption.[24] The themes of these five *laude* suitably address military victory and confrontation with heretical foes. Moreover, the three short homophonic musical settings and simple, repetitive formal structures of the poetry would have been singable by the soldiers on their long marches into battle.

Some of the *laude* were old hits, doubtless familiar to many Italians, for in putting together this collection of "sonetti italiani, per sonare e cantare per i valorosi e virtuosi signiori cavagliori," Sixt culled texts from one or more *laude* anthologies issued by Italian presses, retooled an older *lauda* to celebrate military victory, and found, heard, commissioned, or perhaps composed two *laude* that survive in this print apparently as *unica*. Two of the songs he adapted from other sources, *Signior ti benedico* and *Chi vol seguir la guerra*, were decades-old standards, reprinted multiple times by the Congregazione dell'Oratorio in Rome beginning in 1577, but Sixt's versions outfit them with unique musical settings.[25] Sixt reprints all the stanzas of these two *laude* with only a few minor modifications, but those he makes are significant given their relocation, and underscore the ways these songs were modified to suit new purposes by singers as they traveled. In *Signior ti benedico*, "mio aversario" has been changed to the less windy "il mio nemico," "che mi campo da morte" to the more uplifting "che mi leva da morte," and, curiously, a moment of religious doubt absent in the original has been inserted, by qualifying the "immense charity" of the Lord as something one might occasionally question.[26] Sixt also includes three modifications to the text of *Chi vol seguir la guerra*, one of the most well-traveled *laude* of the age. "Come now! I want to take up again the shield I discarded" suits collectively deployed regiments better than the solitary voice of "Today I want to take up again the shield I discarded." Sixt's version updates the word "slings" with "lead," presumably of the type used for early modern artillery, and in the fourth stanza replaces fear of a peculiar game of "fanciulli, che dican' 'vello, vello'" ("children who say, 'sheepskin, sheepskin'") with fear of "un picciol gioco de fanciulletti, che mi monstran quello [=fuoco e flagello]" ("a small game of little children who show me [fire and scourging]"), a more internationally recognizable form of post-traumatic stress.

More intensively reworked is the first *sonetto* in the book, *Lodiamo tutti Dio*. The original text from which it derives, *Lodate Dio co'l cuor humil, et pio*, is attributed to the fifteenth-century Florentine poet Feo Belcari. In 1563 Giovanni Animuccia published a three-voice version, which subsequently appeared alongside anonymous settings of *Signior ti benedico* and *Chi vol seguir la guerra* in the

2. Venite tutti quanti, Con Fede' e con Amore, Con Himni Sacr'e Canti, Lodiam Nostro Signiore.
3. Cantiamo tutti' insieme, Col' MOSÈ e con MARIA, Che ci fugge, ci tieme, L'Hostil Cavallaria.
4. La VNION e 'sgionta, Dal GEDEONE Pio, E poco men consonta, Lodiamo tutti DIO.
5. Signior Tu desti Palme, A noi de gl'Inimici, Servasti le nostr'Alme, Facendo lor' Mendici.
6. Quanta ne ci fui Gloria, E celebre Vittoria, Che cosi poca Guerra, Getta' il Nemico a Terra.
7. Se ben c'ha dat Affanni, Ma con suoi gravi danni, Poiche fugg'a Disuio, Lodiamo tutti DIO.
8. CHRISTE Bontad'e Vita, Amor senza misura, Vieni darci d'aita, Nella via men' sicura.
9. Tu sei quel Sommo bene, Che tutti n'ha creati, Tutti da mortal pene, Con Tua Morte salvati.
10. O Carità Infinita, Che stesso a noi ti dona, Per Premio è CORONA, Dopo la Fragil Vita.
11. Stampa il Tuo Sant'Amore, E salda Fede' e Viva, Nel fondo al nostro Core, Che Gloria Æterna' arriva.

Example 1. *Lodiamo tutti Dio*

Congregazione dell'Oratorio's *Libro terzo* of 1577.[27] At approximately the same time, another group famously active in promoting the singing of *laude*, the Jesuits, disseminated a paraphrased version of the lyrics through anthologies issued from presses, for example, in Milan (1576), Turin (1579), Macerata (1589), and Brescia (1605), in addition to commissioning an eight-voice setting by Lelio Bertani.[28] The Jesuit version retains much of the text found in *Lodate Dio*, but the removal of two references to love suggests altered priorities in a post-Tridentine world: "Up, gentle souls, get dressed in love" is changed to "Up, gentle souls, lift up your pure hearts"; and "Savor the sounds and songs that are in heaven. Come now, kind lovers!" becomes the less poetic "Savor the sounds and songs that the chosen spirits and saints make in heaven."[29] A critical change is also made to the formal structure. *Lodate Dio* is in the form of a *lauda-ballata* with an asymmetrical two-line refrain ("Lodate Dio / co'l cuor humil, et pio"). In its new guise as *Lodiamo tutti Dio*, it becomes a strophic poem with lines of equal length. Since most of the Jesuit anthologies were printed without music notation, the simplicity of its new strophic form renders it more adaptable to a broad range of performance options and, significantly, ideal for processions.

Sixt's paraphrase of the Jesuit *Lodiamo tutti Dio* streamlines the structure further with revisions that key it more directly to Tilly's victory in battle. He reduces the stanzas to four seven-syllable lines while expanding their number to eleven. After its opening statement, the refrain "Lodiamo tutti Dio" recurs twice in later stanzas, not as a tacked-on addition but integrated within the stanzas themselves, an echo of the song's original design. Beyond the text of the refrain, the first stanza, and the third line of the ninth stanza, all the contents are new. They now sing of the flight of the enemy, the strong union of the Catholic soldiers, and the brevity of the battle that swiftly led to glory and victory. The four-part homophonic setting Sixt devises for the song spotlights the faster pace of his stanzas with two sets of paired phrases, the first, second, and third of which land on F, colored by the arrival of the second phrase on C. Internal phrases are separated by rests, and syllabic declamation moves consistently at the pace of a minim. The absence of harmonic or polyphonic complexity encourages the forward momentum, along with root-position triads placed squarely on the beat (See example 1).

Sixt was involved with the Jesuits from the start of his studies and through them likely gained his first exposure to *laude*, which these Italian-trained missionaries would have brought with them when opening their seminaries in Prague (1556) and Olomouc (1574). Sixt's name appears in 1574 among the list of students enrolled at the Bartholomaeus seminary at the Jesuit collegium

2. Il mio nemico fiero, Delle mie spoglie altiero, Mi hai ferito' e vinto,
   E Poco men ch'estinto, O man pietosa e forte, Che mi leva da morte.
3. A mort'era vicino, Quando d'oglio e Vino, M'ungest'e mi lavasti,
   Ele piaghe ligasti, O benedetta mano, Del bon Samaritano.
4. L'oglio fu l' dolce affetto, De Tuo Paterno petto, E' il vin' il puro sangue,
   Ch'usci da corp'essangue, O charitat'immensa, Pur l'homo non la pensa.
5. Ringratia anima mia, La man potente e pia, Che sana' ogni tua piaga,
   E' ogni tua voglia appaga, O Lingua' o Sensi' o Core, Beneditt'il Signiore.

Un altro, in medesimo Tono, ne' i versi poco immutato.

1. O peccatore' Ingrato, Emenda' il Tuo peccato, Ritorn' al Tuo Signiore.
   Che tutto per tuo' amore, Nel corpo sta piaghato, O peccator Ingrato.
2. Vedi che mente pura, Ch'alla colonna dura, Hebbi flagelli tali,
   Che tuoi commessi mali, A tal mod'ha pagato, O peccator Ingrato.
3. Risguarda quelle Spine, Ch'alle membra DIVINE, Dieder tanto dolore,
   Spargendo suo liquore, Dal cuore & ogni lato, O peccator Ingrato.
4. Mira lo su la croce, E senti la sua Voce, Ch'a penitenz'invita,
   La scelerata Vita, Va mutando' il tuo stato, O peccator Ingrato.
5. Contempla quel Martiro, Ch'i piedi e man' sentiro, E piangi amaramente,
   Quella ferita' ardente, Da lancia, del costato, O peccator Ingrato.
6. Deh non far piu di mora, Pio che Tu non sai l'hora, Che ti verra a morire.
   Ne giovera poi dire, Aime com'ho fallato, O peccator Ingrato.

Example 2. *Signior ti benedico* and *O peccatore ingrato*

in Prague, and while singing in the imperial chapel he also served as cantor in the Jesuit Marian sodality.[30] By 1594, he was enrolled at the Spanish-run Jesuit academy in Olomouc, the same school where Wallenstein would later matriculate in 1606 and convert to Catholicism. At the time of his promotion to Magister of liberal arts and philosophy in 1597, Sixt was also serving as cantor and rector of the choir at the Jesuit church.[31] One volume that speaks to the practice of *lauda* singing at Jesuit collegia is a copy of *Lodi, et canzoni spirituali* printed by Bartolomeo Merlo in Verona in 1618 now kept at the National Library of the Czech Republic (sign. 33 L 88). This book, assembled by the "compagnia della dottrina christiana di Verona," was first owned by Franciscus Godefridus Troilus à Lessoth, a Styrian nobleman who served in Prague as imperial advisor, before it was acquired by the Jesuits for use in their collegium in Český Krumlov. Among the anthology's 133 *lauda* texts is yet another version of *Lodiamo tutti Iddio* (paraphrased to suit its assignment to the Feast of the Holy Trinity, pp. 9–10). It is worth noting that *Chi vol seguir la guerra*, likewise, became a staple of the Jesuit repertory through repeated publication in massive *lauda* anthologies issued in the 1620s by the Florentine press of Alessandro Guiducci, some of which must have made their ways north through Jesuit networks.[32]

Jesuits were a constant presence among Tilly's regiments, whom they attended with spiritual and medical support, and they doubtlessly encouraged the singing of *laude* both old and brand new. Like the heavily reworked paraphrase of *Lodiamo tutti Dio*, the two remaining *laude* published by Sixt suggest that the culture of singing *laude* in Bohemia went well beyond passive absorption of Italian imports to include creative engagement with the genre that yielded new songs. Both *laude*—*O peccatore ingrato* and *Voi, capitani bravi*—survive as *unica* in this source, where they are presented as alternate texts to be sung, respectively, to the second two musical settings. If they represent local practices, it may well be in their very simplicity, for their regular poetic forms and syllabic, homophonic settings would have guided non-native speakers through the multiple stanzas of Italian text with recursive melodies and predictable rhymes. For instance, the six stanzas of *O peccatore ingrato* are each comprised of six short seven-syllable lines, whereby the final line serves as a refrain on the text "O peccator ingrato," a vestige of *lauda-ballata* form. The musical setting follows the AABBCC rhyme scheme with its organization into three couplets, and spondaic cadences preceded by quickened semiminim motion underscore the rhymes.

We might also see in this *lauda* the Jesuit practice of spiritual exercises Bohemian collegians learned in school and carried forward in life, a practice the Jesuit chaplains would have encouraged among the soldiers they attended.

Vn altro Sonetto, a4. Lingue Della Bataglia di Praga.
Per Cantare e Sonare. Sopra, Tutti Venite armati. di Castoldi'.
VIctoriosi Duces, concelebrate luces, Vestræ nunc Victoriæ,
VIctoriosi Duces, concelebrate luces, Vestræ nunc Victoriæ,
VIctoriosi Duces, concelebrate luces, Vestræ nunc Victoriæ,
VIctoriosi Duces, concelebrate luces, Vestræ nunc Victoriæ,
VIctoriosi Duces, concelebrate luces, Vestræ nunc Victoriæ,
Soldáti se hegbegte/ a Czechům Pokog degte/bydy bydy bydybom/
Frisch frölich jhr Soldaten/last sieden vnd auch braten/bidi bidi bidibom/
Voi che venist'armati, o forti miei Soldati, bidi bidi bidibom/
Si quis voluerit, poterit de Assumptione B. M. V. sic Cantare.
O Gaudium Cæleste, o Mundi Canticum, o Gloriosæ Virginis, Item.
Chtégili Czechowé, mohau této Pjsné, na Den Narozenj, aneb Wzkřjssenj Krysta Pána/ y w Kostele vžjwati.
Na Den Wzkřjssenj/ takto:
WZkřjsyteli swému/KRYSTV Pánu milému/ pleseg wssecko Stwořenj.
A na den Narozenj.
WYkupiteli swému/KRYSTV Pánu milému/plesseg wssecko Stwořenj.

Fig. 3. Jan Sixt of Lerchenfels, *Deo opt: max: trino et uni laus, honor, virtus, gloria, triumphus et victoria...*, fol. [45]r–v

From the outset, the three-fold repetition of "peccato-" establishes the theme of the inescapability of sin, and subsequent stanzas are launched by active commands that direct the eyes and mind of the "ungrateful sinner" to "see that pure mind," "gaze at those thorns," "observe him on the cross," and "contemplate that martyrdom." In its vivid engagement of body and imagination, this *lauda* harnesses the spiritual exercises to instill resolve in soldiers facing imminent battle, by drawing a parallel between physical pain and the example of Christ's martyrdom.

With its two-fold reference to Ferdinand II and exhortation to the Protestant Union, *Voi capitani bravi*, the second *unicum*, was clearly penned in response to Tilly's earlier victory at the Battle of White Mountain (1620), which led to the dissolution of the Protestant Union five months later. It is peppered with Italian military terms—*capitani, artelaria, salve, locotente, moschetiri, pezzi, bataglia, commando, gloria*, and *honore*—that were commonplace in the army and gradually slipping into the vocabularies of civilian speech communities. Through "wonderful songs," "suave voices," and volleys of musket fire, *Voi capitani bravi* calls for celebration of a battle quickly won, while admonishing the Union to end insurgency and unite with the Roman church. The soldiers, who know "neither month nor hour" as they journey through unfamiliar lands, joyfully command the vanquished to join them in singing a lexicon of Italian ecclesiastical and military terms. The eventual adaptation of these Italian terms by civilians was so pervasive that the practice would later be satirized by the Nuremberg poet Georg Philipp Harsdörffer, who complained in 1656, "[tiresome warfare] has imposed on us partly Italian and partly French words, so that even peasants keep such language masters at great expense and when faced with foreign things must call them by a foreign name."[33]

Multilingualism on the Bohemian battlefield

If the Italian *laude* dedicated to Tilly symbolically unite his regiments in the shared singing of Italian-texted songs, the final song in the book portrays battle itself as an inevitable linguistic potpourri. This composition, *Un altro sonetto a 4. lingue della bataglia di Praga*, again celebrates the Battle of White Mountain, where Tilly commanded the combined forces of the Catholic League and imperial armies, comprised of regiments from Naples, Florence, Milan, Spain, Wallonia, Germany, and Poland (see figure 3).[34] For the musical setting, Sixt simply adapted the music of Giacomo Gastoldi's *balletto*, *Amor vittorioso*, shortening the fa-la-la refrains that punctuate the verses in keeping with the import of the very real victory its new lyrics celebrate. By 1626, the musical style would have been somewhat antiquated, if not hackneyed: the first edition of Gastoldi's five-voice *balletti* had appeared twenty-five years earlier in 1591 and immediately became a European bestseller. Sixt capitalizes on the familiarity of this musical celebration of victory by underlaying a complex set of lyrics involving four stanzas in four different languages: Latin, Czech, German, and Italian. Through linguistic plurality, Sixt stages the combined imperial armies as a linguistically heterogeneous yet united formation of soldiers whose voices project the multiculturalism of the empire they defend.

The layout of the stanzas, stacked one on top of another, encourages readers to see them as translations of one another, but these stanzas mirror and respond to each another in meaningful ways. The stanza in Latin, the lingua franca of Central Europe, takes precedence: it is the only one laid under each of the five voices. Its opening salutation, "Victorious leaders," launches a series of imperatives to hail Ferdinand as the new King of Bohemia, support Maximilian I, Duke of Bavaria, and rout Frederick V of the Palatinate while Bohemia applauds and the Palatinate mourns. The three subsequent stanzas all begin with salutations to the soldiers, in—respectively—Czech ("Get moving, soldiers!"), German ("You good, cheerful soldiers"), and Italian ("You who came armed, oh my strong soldiers"), and hail the arrival of Ferdinand as king in Czech, emperor in German, and simply as "our Ferdinand" in Italian. In each stanza, Sixt replaces Gastoldi's "fa la la" refrain with the more military "bidi bidi bidibom." Although he differentiates the four languages through different typefaces—Roman for Latin and Italian, rotunda for Czech, and blackletter for German, helping orient the reader to the juxtaposition of these languages—the "bidibom" refrain is always printed in blackletter, perhaps an acknowledgment of the frequent use of the onomatopoeia in German battle songs. All five compositions included by Christoph Demantius in his 1600 print *Tympanum militare* harness the syllables to evoke the sound of battledrums, including one piece, *Praelium Ungaricum*, celebrating victory over the Ottomans which was sung, according to its title, in the presence of Rudolf II.[35] They also appear in a four-voice *battaglia* published in 1620 by Erasmus Widmann titled *Ein Schlacht oder Soldaten gsang* whose opening, "Wollauff, wollauff, Soldaten Blut / Sey frölich frisch und wolgemuth," is not unlike the beginning of the German stanza in Sixt's *battaglia*, "Frisch frölich ihr Soldaten."[36] These similarities, along with the epigrammatic character of the stanzas, demonstrate how Sixt drew on familiar stock phrases in putting the lyrics together. In contrast, a clear literary borrowing comes from Gastoldi's original Italian *balletto*, which begins with the text "Tutti venite armati, O forti miei soldati." Sixt added the pronoun "voi" and placed the first phrase in the past tense but kept the second phrase intact. These literary origins help explain why the Italian stanza, which unfolds as a complete sentence, is the least epigrammatic of all.

The technique of stringing together familiar stock phrases is one that would have helped his readers navigate the overload of multilinguistic information, and it is even more pronounced in the three alternative sacred texts Sixt provides beneath the *battaglia*. The first is a Latin song for the feast of the Assumption of the Blessed Virgin Mary comprised of such commonplaces as "gloriosae virginis," "fructus ventris," "dies est laetitiae," and "gaudeamus hodie," that recall a series of familiar sacred contexts that Sixt only partially organizes into a coherent rhyme scheme in favor of keeping them intact. Likewise, the repetition of phrases in the two sacred Czech stanzas for the birth and resurrection of Christ is made immediately apparent by their typographic placement on top of one another. This layout, which highlights the similarities in their construction, alerts singers to the way fragments of the texts can be extracted for use in any of a variety of celebrations. In providing these alternative texts, Sixt addresses a series of potential readerships, both military and civilian, that this music was designed to serve, even as he pitches it toward multiple occasions from the devotional to the bellicose. On the page immediately following the *battaglia*, Sixt prints his own coat-of-arms encircled by his personal motto, "Sustain, and Abstain" in four languages—Latin, German, Greek, and Czech. In this way, he presents himself as more than a Bohemian theologian or scholar, or the speaker of any one language, but as an imperial citizen, whose intersectional identities exceeded the proto-nationalist boundaries of a kingdom enflamed by war.

Plurilingualism during occupation and in exile

To understand the unconventional design of Sixt's book, and the ways it not only honored its dedicatees, but also responded to local readerships, it is important to bear in mind the social upheaval in the city of Litoměřice where Sixt's provostry and printshop stood, for the book's publication coincided with an alarming humanitarian crisis exacted under the authority of Ferdinand II against the city's predominantly non-Catholic population. Indeed, the ebullient celebration of Habsburg absolutism seems, at first glance, an affront to the very population Sixt was called to serve, since he must have borne daily witness to the cruel intimidations of his neighbors by imperial soldiers. Soon after the Battle of White Mountain, five companies from the regiment of Ferdinand of Bavaria, Elector of Cologne, claimed Litoměřice for the emperor, launching a succession of occupations by armies installed to administer and police the city: the Wallenstein regiments arrived after 1621, the Liechtenstein regiments in 1622–1623, and in 1624 the imperial regiment of Holstein, which stayed for more than a year.[37] These troops lived at the expense of city residents, whose resistance they slowly eroded in preparation for the arrival of the priests who were soon to follow. After the first order expelling non-Catholic preachers on March 13, 1621, foreigners were brought in from neighboring lands to fill the vacancies.[38] In 1625, the imperial field marshal Don Baltasar de Marradas y Vique was sent to Litoměřice with two Capuchins and his Spanish cavalrymen to enforce obligatory attendance at Mass and the spring Corpus Christi procession.[39] When Pavel Stránský, a municipal legal counsellor and Latin scholar, refused to attend the procession, a squadron of soldiers was sent to his house, which they proceeded to plunder while he was in hiding. When they found his wife Kateřina, they seized her keys, took possession of the home, cooked and ate any food they found, and emptied the wine cellar. Although they left that evening, it was typical for twelve to thirty soldiers to remain quartered in an individual house, where they did as they pleased until the host capitulated. These circumstances precipitated the first mass exodus in 1625, as seventy houses in the city were abandoned by Corpus Christi.[40] Stránský opposed the demand that citizens of Litoměřice convert to Catholicism in a two-day public disputation with the two Capuchins, during which he declared that he would sooner leave his home than his beliefs. In 1627 he finally departed for the city of Pirna in Saxony, never to return.[41]

In 1626, an additional military regiment was sent in, this time a battalion of infantry under the command of Philipp Friedrich Freiherr von Breuner, General of the Artillery (*Feldzeugmeister*) in the imperial army, and again, they were quartered in the homes of defiant inhabitants. An illuminating record of these torments can be found in the diary of the Litoměřice city clerk Václav Nosidlo, who writes on January 16, 1626,

> The soldiers were more learned than the Papist priests, for what the priests could not achieve in many years, neither through their lying and superstitious, rule-flattering doctrine nor through their cunning, these [soldiers] achieved through their vile and tyrannical behavior within a week. On account of their certain (that is, soldierly) instruction in religion, both the young as well as sixty-year-olds, who could barely learn their good faith from childhood to old age, now learned this Papist belief from the soldiers—some in a week, another in half an hour or even a quarter of an hour, in such a way that they did not want to leave this religion until their death.[42]

As Nosidlo recounts, most exiles were forced to abandon all their possessions, were banned from trade, separated from their immediate families, burdened with hefty fines, and finally resettled in Saxony with the permission of the Elector but "against the will and the hopes of the citizens in his cities, who did not want to receive us."[43] Being unwelcome in their new homes was for many, however, far better than the tortures they had just endured. By 1627, almost half the inhabitants of Litoměřice had left, with the Saxon town of Pirna as a favored destination.[44] Pirna was home to 2,123 Bohemian exiles by 1629,[45] and Stránský later estimated the number of emigrant families from Litoměřice alone at over 500, which he declared a testament to Litoměřice as the second most steadfast city in Bohemia after Prague in its resistance to re-Catholicization efforts.[46]

In the midst of this painful upheaval, Sixt's book of music more than affirms the doctrines of Catholic and imperial allegiance; it placed the language of those doctrines in the minds and mouths of its readers, so that they might figure out how to navigate the new world around them. Through acclamations, Biblical quotations, litanies, epigrams, and direct musical settings, readers learned the vocabulary that Sixt himself had acquired as *puer musicus* in the imperial chapel, where choirboys were taught the proper ways to address authorities, sing Catholic doctrine, honor soldiers, and position themselves as imperial citizens. One has the sense that Sixt, who seems never to have traveled far beyond the borders of Bohemia, learned Italian in much the same way. Typographical signposts on each page operate as aides-mémoires that guide the reader through the thickets of its diverse contents and help them recall melodies and phrases that were familiar from their own singing and that of others. The *laude* and the *battaglia* equip readers to welcome foreign regiments with Italian songs designed for widespread comprehensibility, while the *Te Deum* and Magnificat made the book useful on numerous occasions, both ceremonial and devotional, even for readers who maintained a different choice of faith. Meanwhile, the alternative Latin and Czech lyrics for the *battaglia* provided Bohemians with new, easy-to-learn songs that replaced the "sacrilegious" vernacular songs that had proliferated so wildly through Brethren songbooks.

Sixt prints in his book an historically grounded, plurilingual soundworld to remind readers of a distinctive Bohemian tradition to which the exiles in Saxony were losing access and for which they undoubtedly longed. Among them was Nicolaus Dionysius, a musician and former councilor of Prague's Old Town. After having his tongue nailed to the gallows for two hours and serving a two-year prison term in the aftermath of White Mountain, he fled Prague for Pirna in 1627, bringing with him a set of partbooks pinched from the Jesuit Marian confraternity.[47] When Dionysius later sang the passion at a church in Pirna loaned to Bohemian exiles, Nosidlo, transfixed in the audience, was stirred to recall "the customary Bohemian manner" of singing he once knew in his homeland.[48] For Nosidlo, this was a rare musical moment worthy of record and, for us, evidence of the tenacity of oral traditions, but also a reminder of the few opportunities taken to write them down. The stock phrases of oral traditions often evoke familiar tunes, an associative process of which Sixt and his contemporaries were acutely aware. By linking these phrases together into new forms, Sixt likewise designed his book to mobilize Bohemian memories through oral performance at a time when its documentation was in urgent peril.

The exceptional mobility at this time in Bohemia of so many people, forced to adapt to new surroundings, and the conflicting political and religious allegiances they were required to juggle call into question how Sixt's music book portrays a seventeenth-century understanding of selfhood. As Jacques Lezra has argued, early modern metalinguistic texts that included multiple languages and therefore multiple reading positions furnished "spectacularly deterritorialized, polyglot identities." The linguistic and textual heterogeneity of these texts formalized a fluid understanding of subjectivity, in conflict with nationalist forms of identification and even modern notions of individualism.[49] Historiographic treatment of this trauma in Bohemian history has cemented a thwarted nationalist narrative whose protagonists were driven out by an oblivious Catholic elite, predominantly foreign in origin. The pejorative meaning of the word "foreign" has proven difficult to shed, a situation made worse by the early modern division of nation according to language and the paucity of firsthand accounts from those forced to conform. Beneath the eye-catching monarchic bombast, Sixt also reminds us that Italian-speaking was as Bohemian as speaking Czech, German, or Latin, no matter the place of one's birth, and that linguistic identities overlapped in single individuals, who manipulated them according to necessity.

When Sixt's provostry and printshop inexplicably went up in flames on January 31, 1627, four months after his book was published, Nosidlo reports that Sixt was pulled out of bed as the fire raged, since he had drunken enormously with carnival guests the night before, a warning sent from God to repent, but things "only got worse." A little more than a week later, however, on February 8, 1627, when the deadline for the Nosidlo family to depart Litoměřice coincided with a heavy snowfall blocking passage northward, Nosidlo turned to Sixt, who intervened successfully with authorities to prolong their stay through the carnival season.[50] At this critical juncture, all sides were faced with conflicting allegiances. The mobile families of soldiers and civilians needed to figure out strategies for survival and living together, part of which involved figuring out how to exploit plurilingual identities in order to navigate speech communities typically pitted in opposition to one another. For all its "superstitious, rule-flattering doctrine," Sixt's music book deepens our understanding of the performance of deterritorialized subjectivities in an era of Habsburg absolutism, when the acquisition of multilingual lexica offered the possibility of security and mobility, whatever the status of one's "good faith."

Notes

1. This spectacle has been the object of several short studies, the most comprehensive of which is Dobalová and Muchka, "Ein unbekannter Text."

2. Slavata surmised that approximately 400 noble and 36,000 burgher families fled Bohemia and Moravia. Among them, it has been assumed that the vast majority of about 80,000 emigrated to Saxony. Despite skepticism toward these numbers in recent research, the considerable extent of this immigration remains undeniable. See Fialová, "K vývoji obyvatelstva přirozenou měnou"; idem, "Obyvatelstvo České Republiky"; Jančárek, "Populační vývoj českých zemí," 125–36; Lisa, *Die Chronik des Václav Nosidlo*, 12 n. 4; Maur, "Populační důsledky třicetileté války"; Metasch, *Exulanten in Dresden*, 20; Miller, *Urban Societies in East-Central Europe*, 12 and 23–26; and Nešpor, "Luteráni v českých zemích," 134–35.

3. This expansion was not consistent across the sixteenth and early seventeenth centuries. Some decades in some localities witnessed population decline or stasis due to disappearing economic sectors, environmental change (including the onset of a "small ice age" in the 1560s), crop failures in the 1580s, the outbreak of epidemics, and resulting shifts in mortality and birth rates, among other factors. See Fialová, "K vývoji obyvatelstva přirozenou měnou," and Fialová and Maur, "Příspěvek ke studiu přirozené měny."

4. A well-known case is the city of Joachimsthal. Following the discovery of silver around 1500, it grew to become the second-largest city in Bohemia with a population of around 18,000 in 1533. The depletion of its silver deposits reduced the population to only about 2,000 by 1600. See Jančárek, "Populační vývoj českých zemí," and Miller, *Urban Societies in East-Central Europe*, 24.

5. Miller, *Urban Societies in East-Central Europe*, 26.

6. The best study of the Italian diaspora in Prague remains Janáček, "Italové v předbělohorské Praze."

7. Earlier studies of this book are all rather cursory and tend to ignore much of its textual content. These include Haas, "Ein Leitmeritzer Musikdruck"; Niemöller, "Beziehungen kirchlicher Musikkultur"; and Žůrek, "Zapomenutí mistři starší české hudby."

8. This assessment is based on an examination of the three exemplars at the Österreichische Nationalbibliothek (A-Wn); the Knihovna Pražské konzervatoře (CZ-Kp); and the Bayerische Staatsbibliothek (D-Mbs). The CZ-Kp and D-Mbs exemplars retain original bindings prepared by the same bookbinder and have the same ordering of leaves. The A-Wn exemplar has a modern binding, and the collation of the book is different, with the six folios bearing the dedication to Eleonora Gonzaga repositioned as the first folios in that copy. It is clear, however, that its collation used to correspond to those of CZ-Kp and D-Mbs and that the leaves of A-Wn were later reshuffled prior to its modern binding. All folio numbers in this article correspond to those of the CZ-Kp and D-Mbs exemplars.

9. The copy in D-Mbs can be viewed here: https://stimmbuecher.digitale-sammlungen.de/view?id=bsb00082836, accessed April 1, 2019.

10. This date, September 27–28, 1626, is identified in all three exemplars as the occasion on which Christian IV of Denmark was defeated, although the battle of Lutter took place one month earlier on August 27. Printed in a fourth exemplar, however, at the Universitäts- und Stadtbibliothek in Cologne

(D-KNu) is the actual date of the battle. The reason for this discrepancy remains unknown. For facsimiles of eight pages from the D-KNu exemplar, see Niemöller, "Beziehungen kirchlicher Musikkultur," 238–41.

11. As reported to Maximilian I, Elector of Bavaria, in a letter from his agent in Vienna, Esaias Leuker, dated September 9, 1626. See Gindely, *Waldstein*, 114.

12. "Magnificat, quat. vel octo vocum. Cantus semper præcinit solus, cum tribus Violis &c. Respondent aliæ 4. Voces, cum Tubis & Organis," fols. [28]v–[29]r.

13. Jiří Žůrek writes that compositions similar to Sixt's Magnificat setting can be found in earlier Utraquist hymnbooks as well. See Žůrek, "Zapomenutí mistři starší české hudby," 28.

14. Khevenhüller, *Annales Ferdinandei*, 12:2405.

15. Sacchi, *La guerre de trente ans*, 1:368

16. Ibid., 1:387–88.

17. Winter, *Život cirkevní*, 2:841.

18. See Heilmann, *Kriegsgeschichte von Bayern*, 189; and Gindely, *Waldstein*, 76.

19. On the retinues accompanying armies in the Thirty Years War, see Asche, "Bellizität, Staat und Migration," 93–4; and Albrecht, *Maximilian I. von Bayern*, 527–28.

20. Jaroslav Miller calculates the population of Prague in 1650 to have fallen to between 26,450 and 30,300 inhabitants. See Miller, *Urban Societies in East-Central Europe*, 26.

21. Schiller, who also wrote a trilogy of plays about Wallenstein, parodies the "gesetzlose Soldateska" ("lawless Soldateska") in the third and fourth books of his *Geschichte des Dreißigjährigen Kriegs*, 248–52 and 402. On the replacement of the term *Landsknecht*, see Parrott, *The Business of War*, 160.

22. Wallenstein referred to his soldiers as "die ganze Soltadesca." See, for example, his letter to Moritz, Landgrave of Hesse-Kassel, of August 24, 1625, in Gindely, *Waldstein*, 63–64.

23. The borrowing of military terms of Latin, Italian, Spanish, and French origin became the subject of satirical songs in the 1640s and was lambasted by Johann Rist in his 1642 *Rettung der Edlen Teütschen Hauptsprache*. See Jones, *Images of Language*, 96–105.

24. He signs the dedication "Excell: Tuæ. Capellanus," fol. [40]v.

25. After *Il terzo libro delle laudi spirituali, stampate ad instantia delli reverendi padri della Congregatione dell'Oratorio* (Rome: Per li Heredi di Antonio Blado, stampatori camerali, 1577), both appeared in reprints issued by the oratory in 1583, 1585, and 1589, as well as the later *Lodi e canzonette spirituali* (Naples: Tarquinio Longo, 1608). See Rostirolla, Zardin, and Mischiati, *La lauda spirituale*, [88–89], [126], and [190].

26. In the fourth stanza, "O charitate immensa, che tal gratie dispensa" is altered to read "O charitate immensa, pur l'homo non la pensa."

27. On the genesis of this print and Animuccia's involvement with the oratorio, see Rostirolla, Zardin, and Mischiati, *La lauda spirituale*, [473–514].

28. This polyphonic anthology, *Lodi spirituali poste in musica da diversi eccellenti compositori, cantate nel duomo di Brescia per tramezo nella disputa generale della dottrina Christiana* (Brescia: Presso Vincenzo Sabbio, 1583), features the emblem of the society in its frontispiece. For a transcription of the dedication and musical incipits, see Rostirolla, Zardin, and Mischiati, *La lauda spirituale*, [376–81].

29. In *Lodate Dio*, the verses are "Sù, anime leggiadre. Vestitevi d'amore" from the first stanza and "Gustate i suoni e canti, che sono in paradiso. Orsù, gentili amanti" from the third stanza. In *Lodiamo tutti Dio*, these are modified respectively to read "Sù, anime leggiadre. Levate il puro cuore" and "Gustate i suoni e canti, che fanno in paradiso i spirti eletti e santi."

30. During his tenure as provost in Litoměřice, Sixt was also leading the Marian congregation at the Jesuit collegium in the Bohemian town of Chomutov. See Schlenz, *Johann Sixt von Lerchenfels*, 8 and 75.

31. Schlenz, *Johann Sixt von Lerchenfels*, 9.

32. Rostirolla, Zardin, and Mischiati, *La lauda spirituale*, [611–17].

33. Harsdörffer, *Der Teutsche Secretarius*, 142–43.

34. Polišenský, *The Thirty Years War*, 124–25; and Sacchi, *La guerre de trente ans*, 1:369.

35. This title, "Prælium Vngaricum, Divo Imperatori Rodolpho II, decantatum," appears in each of the print's partbooks as well as in the revised and expanded edition of *Tympanvm militare* published in 1615.

36. Widmann, *Ein Schöner Newer Ritterlicher Auffzug*, 82–87.

37. Lippert, *Geschichte der Stadt Leitmeritz*, 385–86.

38. Pescheck, *Geschichte der Gegenreformation*, 2:66, 103, and 466; and Schlenz, *Johann Sixt von Lerchenfels*, 62.

39. Pescheck, *Geschichte der Gegenreformation*, 2:205–7.

40. Lippert, *Geschichte der Stadt Leitmeritz*, 394.
41. Ibid., 396–400.
42. Lisa, *Die Chronik des Václav Nosidlo*, 70–71.
43. Ibid., 76–77.
44. On the censuses made in Pirna of Bohemian exiles in 1629, 1631, and 1636, see Bobková, *Exulanti z Prahy*. Following the destruction in 1639 of Pirna by Swedish troops, Dresden became the primary destination for exiles from northern Bohemia. See Lippert, *Geschichte der Stadt Leitmeritz*, 399, 407, and 468; and Lisa, *Die Chronik des Václav Nosidlo*, 23.
45. Bobková, *Exulanti z Prahy*, XXIII. Nosidlo writes in his chronicle in an entry dated February 23, 1629 that all exiles were summoned to the Pirna town hall to hear an electoral command fining anyone harboring an additional exile, since they did not want to allow in any more asylum-seekers. See Lisa, *Die Chronik des Václav Nosidlo*, 194–95.
46. As Lippert clarifies, Stránský's number of 500 immigrants refers only to the heads of urban and suburban families and does not account for wives, children, other family members, or servants. Moreover, this number is likely a considerable underestimate. According to the nineteenth-century historian Tomáš Bílek, the population was decimated, sinking from circa 6,000–7,000 to only about 600 people at the middle of the century, but it is impossible to distinguish the number of exiles from those who perished in the war. See Lippert, *Geschichte der Stadt Leitmeritz*, 399–400; and Lisa, *Die Chronik des Václav Nosidlo*, 26 n. 69.
47. This now fragmentary set of five partbooks is preserved at the Sächsische Landesbibliothek—Staats- und Universitätsbibliothek in Dresden (sign. Mus. Pi 2). For a list of the contents and more on Dionysius (Mikoláš Diviš z Doubravína), see Jan Baťa, "Between Prague and Pirna."
48. Lisa, *Die Chronik des Václav Nosidlo*, 206–9.
49. Lezra, "*Nationum origo*," 206.
50. Lisa, *Die Chronik des Václav Nosidlo*, 80–85.

Bibliography

Albrecht, Dieter. *Maximilian I. von Bayern 1573–1651*. Munich: R. Oldenbourg, 1998.

Asche, Matthias. "Bellizität, Staat und Migration im Alten Reich." In *Handbuch Staat und Migration in Deutschland seit dem 17. Jahrhundert*, ed. Jochen Oltmer. Pp. 87–116. Berlin and Boston: Walter de Gruyter, 2016.

Baťa, Jan. "Between Prague and Pirna: A Story from the Beginning of the Thirty Years' War." *De musica disserenda* 11 (2015): 41–50.

Bobková, Lenka. *Exulanti z Prahy a severozápadních Čech v Pirně v letech 1621–1639*. Prague: Scriptorium, 1999.

Demantius, Christoph. *Tympanvm militare, Vngerische Heerdrummel vnd Feldgeschrey / neben andern auch Vngerischen Schlachten vnd* Victorien *Liedern*. Nuremberg: Katharina Dieterichin, 1600. RISM A/I D 1531.

Demantius, Christoph. *Tympanvm militare, Allerley Streit vnd Triumph Lieder / Alß: Helden mut / Martialisches wesen / Heerdrum[m]el / Feldgeschrey / Schlachten / Venus Krieg / Friedseeligkeit / vnd Liebes verbündtniß*. Nuremberg: Balthasar Scherff, in Verlegung David Kauffmanns, 1615. RISM A/I D 1540.

Dobalová, Sylva, and Ivan P. Muchka. "Ein unbekannter Text zum Prager Fest *Phasma Dionysiacum Pragense* (1617)." *Acta Comeniana* 22–23 (2009): 207–47.

Fialová, Ludmila. "K vývoji obyvatelstva přirozenou měnou v českých zemí v 17. a 18. století." *Historická demografie* 18 (1994): 127–66.

Fialová, Ludmila. "Obyvatelstvo České Republiky v dlouhodobé perspektivě." *Geografické rozhledy: výuka a popularizace geografie, ekologická výchova* 17 (2007/2008): 26–27.

Fialová, Ludmila, and Eduard Maur. "Příspěvek ke studiu přirozené měny obyvatelstva Čech v 16. a první polovině 17. stolet." *Historická demografie* 41 (2017): 1–37.

Gindely, Anton. *Waldstein während seines ersten Generalats im Lichte der gleichzeitigen Quellen 1625–1630. Erster Band*. Prague: F. Tempsky; and Leipzig: G. Freytag, 1886.

Haas, Robert. "Ein Leitmeritzer Musikdruck von 1626." *Der Auftakt* 3 (1923): 106–7.

Harsdörffer, Georg Philipp. *Der Teutsche Secretarius. Das ist: Allen Cantzleyen, Studir- und Schreibstuben nützliches, fast nohtwendiges, und zum drittenmal vermehrtes Titular- und Formularbuch*. Nuremberg: In Verlegung Wolfgang Endters deß Aeltern, 1656.

Heilmann, Johann. *Kriegsgeschichte von Bayern, Franken, Pfalz und Schwaben. II. Band. Kriegsgeschichte und Kriegswesen von 1598–1651.* Munich: Literarisch-artistische Anstalt der J. G. Cotta'schen Buchhandlung, 1868.

Janáček, Josef. "Italové v předbělohorské Praze, 1526–1620." *Pražský sborník historický* 16 (1983): 77–118.

Jančárek, Petr. "Populační vývoj českých zemí v předbělohorském období a problematika jeho studia," *Historická demografie* 12 (1987): 125–36.

Jones, William Jervis. *Images of Language: Six Essays on German Attitudes to European Languages from 1500 to 1800.* Amsterdam: John Benjamins, 1999.

Khevenhüller, Franz Christoph. *Annales Ferdinandei Oder Wahrhaffte Beschreibung Kaysers Ferdinandi Des Andern, Mildesten Gedächtniß, Geburth, Aufferziehung und bißhero in Krieg und Friedens-Zeiten vollbrachten Thaten, geführten Kriegen, und vollzogenen hochwichtigen Geschäfften... Theil 12: Zwölfter und letzter Theil...* Leipzig: M. G. Weidmann, 1726.

Lezra, Jacques. "*Nationum Origo.*" In *Nation, Language, and the Ethics of Translation*, ed. Sandra Bermann and Michael Wood. Pp. 203–28. Princeton, NJ: Princeton University Press, 2005.

Lippert, Julius. *Geschichte der Stadt Leitmeritz.* Prague: Verlag des Vereines für Geschichte der Deutschen in Böhmen, 1871.

Lisa, Martina. *Die Chronik des Václav Nosidlo von Geblice: Aufzeichnungen aus der böhmischen Exulantengemeinde in Pirna zur Zeit des Dreißigjährigen Krieges. Edition und Übersetzung.* Stuttgart: Franz Steiner Verlag, 2014.

Maur, Eduard. "Populační důsledky třicetileté války." *Historická demografie* 12 (1987): 137–52.

Metasch, Frank. *Exulanten in Dresden. Die Einwanderung und Integration von Exulanten in Dresden während des 17. und 18. Jahrhunderts.* Schriften zur sächsischen Geschichte und Volkskunde 34. Leipzig: Leipziger Univ.-Verl., 2011.

Miller, Jaroslav. *Urban Societies in East-Central Europe, 1500–1700.* Aldershot and Burlington, VT: Ashgate, 2008.

Nešpor, Zdeněk R. "Luteráni v českých zemích v období protireformace a náboženské tolerance (1620–1861)." In *Luteráni v českých zemích v proměnách staletí*, ed. Jiří Just, Zdeněk R. Nešpor, Ondřej Matějka et al. Pp. 127–218. Prague: Lutherova společnost, 2009.

Niemöller, Klaus Wolfgang. "Beziehungen kirchlicher Musikkultur zwischen Böhmen/Mähren und dem Rheinland um 1600." In *Mitteleuropäische Aspekte des Orgelbaus und der geistlichen Musik in Prag und den böhmischen Ländern. Konferenzbericht Prag 17.–22. September 2000*, ed. Jaromír Černý and Klaus-Peter Koch. Pp. 233–44. Sinzig: Studio Verlag, 2002.

Parrott, David. *The Business of War: Military Enterprise and Military Revolution in Early Modern Europe.* Cambridge: Cambridge University Press, 2012.

Pescheck, Christian Adolph. *Geschichte der Gegenreformation in Böhmen: Nach Urkunden und anderen gleichzeitigen Quellen bearbeitet. Zweiter Band. Hauptgeschichte seit 1621 und Nachgeschichte. Zweite Ausgabe.* Leipzig: Arnoldische Buchhandlung, 1850.

Polišenský, Josef V. *The Thirty Years War*, trans. Robert Evans. London: B. T. Batsford, 1971.

Rostirolla, Giancarlo, Danilo Zardin, and Oscar Mischiati. *La lauda spirituale tra cinque e seicento: Poesie e canti devozionali nell'Italia della controriforma.* Rome: IBIMUS, 2001.

Sacchi, Henri. *La guerre de trente ans, Tome I: L'ombre de Charles-Quint.* Paris: L'Harmattan, 2003.

Schiller, Friedrich. *Geschichte des Dreißigjährigen Kriegs.* Frankfurt and Leipzig: n.p., 1792.

Schlenz, Johann. *Johann Sixt von Lerchenfels, Propst von Leitmeritz.* Prague: Im Selbstverlage des Vereines für Geschichte der Deutschen in Böhmen, 1911.

Sixt of Lerchenfels, Jan. *Deo opt: max: trino et uni laus, honor, virtus, gloria, triumphus et victoria, qui, justitia & pietate, unionem, non unam: et confoederationem hæreticorum pestiferam... auspitiis, serenissimi ac potentissimi principis ac domini, divi Ferdinandi Austriaci... virtute excellentiss: ac illustriss: domini, domini Joannis, Sterclaes, comitis de Tilli, &c. totius catholicæ ligæ ducis supremi... dissolvit...* Litoměřice: Typis Domesticis, D. Præpositi, Collegiatæ Ecclesiæ S. Stephani, & c., September 8, 1626. RISM A/I L 2036 and S 3563.

Widmann, Erasmus. *Ein Schöner Newer Ritterlicher Auffzug vom Kampff vnd Streyt zwischen* Concordia *vnd* Discordia. Rothenburg ob der Tauber: Hieronymus Körnlein, 1620. RISM A/I W 1039.

Winter, Zikmund. *Život cirkevní v Čechách. Kulturně-historický obraz z XV. a XVI. století. Svazek druhý.* Prague: Nákladem České akademie císaře Františka Josefa pro vědy, slovesnost a umění, 1896.

Žůrek, Jiří. "Zapomenutí mistři starší české hudby: Jan Sixt z Lerchenfelsu aneb Nově příležitostném skladateli z doby počátků baroka." *Harmonie* 8 (2009): 26–28.

PART III

The Spanish and French Empires

Music and Social Ordering in Colonial Latin America: Stasis and Mobility, Sameness and Difference

Geoffrey Baker

The colonial period in Latin America began with movement: voyages, expeditions, campaigns, missions. Yet one of the first things the *conquistadores* did on reaching a new territory was to found a town—to fix a node on a blurry map. Nevertheless, a town was surprisingly mobile: it could exist as a legal construct even before its site was actually determined, and in some cases its physical location was subsequently changed, for reasons relating to environment, climate, sanitation, or insecurity. Trujillo, in modern-day Venezuela, is known as "the portable city" for the number of times it changed location. In the case of the Guatemalan capital Santiago de los Caballeros, the formal act of foundation was carried out in 1524 before a site had even been chosen, epitomizing the notion of the city as performance.[1] A subsequent development was the forced resettlement of the native population into new towns called *reducciones* or *congregaciones*. Yet in the Viceroyalty of Peru, Indigenous labor was often required elsewhere, and large movements of people were necessary in order to provide workers in mines, on haciendas, and in textile mills. In such cases, the *reducciones* might be considered as forced movement in pursuit of a stability that permitted further forced movement.

At the heart of the pacification of the Indies lay *policía*, a complex term that encompassed order, good government, Christianity, and civilization.[2] *Policía* was a central goal of Spanish colonialism, and since it was considered to be fostered by urbanism, it underpinned the foundation of towns across the Spanish domain. The program of mass resettlement into *reducciones* or *congregaciones*, too, was driven by the Spaniards' pursuit of *policía* and concomitant concern over excessive mobility in the native population. To quote from a sixteenth-century Mexican church document: "if Indians are truly to become Christians and civilized like rational men, it is necessary to congregate and organize them in towns and prohibit them from living scattered about and dispersed in the mountains and hills."[3]

In this broad-brush sketch of the early colonial period, a back-and-forth or counterpoint can be discerned between mobility and stasis, fluidity and fixity. What does music have to do with any of this?

Musicians were found among some of the early voyages and expeditions. Music also played a part in the ceremony for the foundation of a new town. As described by Bernardo de Vargas Machuca in his *Milicia y descripción de las Indias* (1599), city foundation was to be accompanied by a mass "with all the soldiers present and with full devotion and solemnity in order to impress the native population and move their hearts; and with many salvos from the guns, celebrating the event with trumpets and drums."[4] More broadly, imperial expansion and domination was carried out in the name of salvation (conversion to Christianity, a civilizing mission), and music was one of the prime evangelical tools. The royal *Ordinances for the Discovery, New Settlement and Pacification of the Indies* proposed a kind of religious ambush on Indigenous groups that were more resistant to the Christian message. Priests were instructed that "should they wish to generate greater admiration and attention among the infidels—and if available—they might use music, by way of singers and high and bass wind instruments, in order to entice the Indians to join them."[5]

Policía entailed forced urbanization and curtailment of mobility, and as such it had an ugly face. Richard Kagan, describing a woodcut of the Bolivian city of Potosí in Pedro Cieza de León's *Primera parte de la crónica de la conquista de Perú* (1553), writes: "The human head stuck onto a pike and prominently displayed at the town gate served as a sign that the Spaniards had introduced *policía* into this part of the world."[6] Yet *policía* had another side, of which music was a prime example. Evangelical activities were at the heart of the *reducciones*, and music was an important means of attracting the Indigenous population to participate in them.[7] It was also understood as a means of instilling *policía* within the local populace.

In Renaissance Spain, music was attributed with considerable powers over both individual and collective human behavior. In her study of the music theorist Juan Bermudo, Paloma Otaola González writes that music's capacity to instill order not only affects the individual human body and psyche but also "extends to society, since music has not just ethical but also *political* value, contributing to the common good."[8] An eyewitness account of the ceremonies held in Seville for the Beatification of Saint Ignatius Loyola describes the different kinds of music performed along the route of the procession, "so that everything together created a heavenly consonance and harmony, inciting fervent devotion in the listeners who crowded along the route."[9] Music was widely accredited with the power to reproduce the harmony of the spheres within and among men;[10] it was therefore ideally suited to the propagation of *policía* within colonial Latin American society. Ceremonies in public spaces, invariably rich in music and sound, were one means of impressing messages on the colonial populace: "the plaza served both as a school and a theatre where the rudiments of *policía* were taught."[11]

Policía was pursued through music education as well as performance. The notion of music education as a means of social ordering, too, had deep roots in Europe.[12] The emblematic institution of European music education, the conservatoire, has its origins in the orphanages (or *conservatorios*) of Renaissance Italy. In Venice, for example, young female orphans were trained in music at the *ospedali grandi*, the primary purpose of which was to regulate the city's social environment. Along with the musical opportunities provided to impoverished girls went strict control over their day-to-day lives.[13] The young musicians had to submit to an inflexible monastic routine: silence, lots of work, and little leisure time. When the English music historian Charles Burney visited in the eighteenth century, he described one *ospedale* orchestra as "under the most exact discipline," with its musicians "under that kind of subordination which is requisite in a servant to a superior."[14] In some ways, then, musical training was an extension of the orphanages' imposition of social control.

The connection between musical training and a will to order migrated along with Europeans and their culture to the New World, and if anything, it was amplified in the new environment. Here, it was not orphans who were targeted but rather the Indigenous population—in particular, the native elite. Felipe Guaman Poma de Ayala's chapter on the *maestro de coro* (choirmaster) in Peru in his *El primer nueva corónica y buen gobierno* (c.1615) concludes with the words: "if possible, there should be a school and Christianity and *policía* in every village, large or small, throughout the realm."[15] In other words, the choirmaster was considered to play a central role in spreading *policía*.

Music was thus implicated in the forced mass migration, pacification, and indoctrination of Indigenous people; it was considered an instrument of social ordering and control. Transatlantic circulation brought an intensification and a broadening of the idea of music education not just as training musicians but also as ordering society, one that could now be employed over vast territories and extended populations. Joanne Rappaport and Tom Cummins write of the New World as "a projection of desires or plans—architectural, political, and social—not realized in Spain."[16] It might be productive to consider music in a similar light. Ideas of music, harmony, and social ordering had a long history in Europe, going back to Plato and Aristotle, but the colonization of the New

World provided a vast new canvas on which to develop them. With the mass movements of imperial expansion, music grew into its role as a tool of conquest and civilization.

However, music also provided a route to social mobility or consolidation of power for some Indigenous members of colonial society.[17] Indigenous musicians were granted social and economic advantages, such as salaries, sporadic payments, and/or exemption from taxes and tribute, which made the profession distinctly appealing in many locations.[18] As a consequence, by the middle of the sixteenth century colonial officials had begun to complain about the large number of native musicians; a 1561 royal decree expressed the Crown's concern over the "great excess and superfluity of music in the churches."[19] During the post-Conquest upheaval of social structures, service as a church musician allowed some Indigenous men to maintain their elevated position and others to break away from their subservient status and engage in "social climbing."[20] It was not just the Spanish, then, who employed music as an instrument of social (re)ordering.

In colonial Peru, a number of more senior musicians came from elite families with a long history in their parishes.[21] Some belonged to the social rank of *principal*, a position of leadership among Indigenous communities one rank below the *cacique* (local chief). A *principal* might be the son of a cacique other than the firstborn (who would normally take over his father's role), or a legitimate nephew. After the Spanish conquest, hereditary leaders sought to consolidate their status and maintain their privileges in the new social order by obtaining positions of responsibility within the colonial power structure. The Church was unwilling to sanction the establishment of a native priesthood in many areas, so the music profession became a substitute ecclesiastical career, a power base for native elites within the colonial Church. In the case of the priest's absence, which was a regular or even semi-permanent occurrence in some parishes, the *maestro de coro* was de facto head of the church, and as such, an important intermediary between the most widely established arm of the Spanish state and the native population. He and the singers were expected to officiate in church rituals when the priest was away. He not only wielded power over the church musicians and congregation but he also came to occupy the position of *maestro de escuela*, or schoolmaster.

Guaman Poma de Ayala recognized the power and authority that musicians exercised within their communities in early seventeenth-century Peru, though he did not regard the influence of the *cantores* and other church servants as entirely benign: he accused them of behaving as though they were Inkas (or native leaders), and on several occasions he denounced them for corrupting the village women, especially when their husbands were away on community duties. If the chronicler is to be believed, musicians and other minor church officials acted in some parishes like a local gang that knew how to exploit its central position in local life.[22]

However it is viewed, the post of parish *maestro de coro* was one of the highest to which an Indigenous man could aspire in colonial Peru. The privileges and powers that accompanied it were allied to a salary or other rewards, giving the position economic as well as social weight. The *maestro de coro* in an Indigenous parish was far more than a choirmaster: he was the key Indigenous figure in education and religion, a community leader, and an important point of contact between the Spanish and Andean republics.

Furthermore, in the face of the forced migration of the native population, the music profession provided a way for some individuals to resist movement and to stay put. *Reducciones* facilitated access to Indigenous labor as well as evangelization. In the Andes, the Spanish exacted a notorious form of tribute from the Indigenous population called the *mita*, which involved forced migration to and labor in mines, textile mills, and plantations. Musicians, however, were generally exempt from the *mita*. In other words, music in the *reducciones* might be considered as a kind of "social glue" that created and maintained a degree of stasis, within the larger policy of *policía*—also associated with immobility—of which it formed a part.

Both musicians and priests had something to gain from a static arrangement. Priests had good reason to support music ensembles within their communities, as church servants formed part of the stable core of the male town population on which priests depended. The commitment to musical provision by the Church might be seen as a way to resist the pressure on Andean males to migrate away, whether to fulfil the obligation to perform tribute labor or to avoid that duty, and thus to combat the decimation of this population—potentially to the benefit of the priest and the local church. Meanwhile, Andean males, through these positions of responsibility, were afforded a degree of influence over local life. Crucially, musicians' ties to their community and local context underpinned their accumulation of power. If the music profession provided positions of privilege as intermediaries between the Indigenous and Spanish worlds, and opportunities to exploit the social and economic possibilities that went with them, these possibilities were bound up with local resources, both human and material. As a result, it seems that few Indigenous musicians were inclined to move. The contrast between the stasis of these officeholders and the (often enforced) mobility of many other Andeans is striking.

It is also the case that the limited financial means of many parish churches had a dampening effect on the mobility of musicians. Churches generally preferred to train local boys, who could later—as members of the community—be rewarded for their musical services in a variety of non-monetary forms. Outsiders, on the other hand, usually had to be hired for cash, so they were generally contracted only as a last resort. Parishes seemed to rely on the fact that local musicians felt some degree of social or religious obligation to their churches and would therefore settle for lower wages, payments in kind, or no payment at all. As a result, the circulation of musicians between churches seems to have been limited and kept to a necessary minimum. With parish authorities showing a reluctance to allow musicians to leave after subsidizing their musical education, there seem to have been more incentives and pressures to remain in situ than to move.

Furthermore, in Peru there was a "glass ceiling" that limited the professional advancement of Indigenous musicians. Whereas in Spain, an ambitious parish *maestro de capilla* might aim for the equivalent post in a cathedral or another prestigious institution, the racial discrimination practiced by Peruvian cathedrals meant that this was effectively out of the question. Mobility at the top end of the Indigenous musical profession thus seems to have been curtailed by structural constraints as well as the benefits of stasis.

Stability, rather than mobility, was also a feature of Hispanic musical life in the Peruvian city of Cuzco for much of the colonial period.[23] There was a brief period in the late sixteenth and early seventeenth centuries when a few famous Spanish musicians such as Pedro Bermúdez were hired by Cuzco Cathedral, but they did not stay long, lured by higher salaries offered in other cathedrals.[24] After this time, the *maestros de capilla* were generally individuals born in Cuzco, trained locally, and who spent their whole career there. The advantages of remaining in a city where they occupied a place near the heart of the colonial power structure apparently outweighed the attractions of more prestigious or better-paid posts elsewhere. What we see is not "horizontal" mobility—moving to a similar post in a different city—but rather "vertical," in the sense that several Cuzco *maestros de capilla*, having reached the pinnacle of musical achievement in the city, were promoted (or sought promotion) to higher ecclesiastical positions in the same cathedral—ones that were not music-related.[25] It appears that neither their economic position nor their social status depended on their musical career. They seemed more interested in mobility *away* from music than migrating *with* their music.

The fact that a number of Cuzco's musicians sought promotion within church ranks, a pattern also observed by Bernardo Illari in Tucumán (Argentina), would seem to suggest that Javier Suárez-Pajares's claim that social climbing was more of a driving force than artistic vocation within the Hispanic music profession holds particularly true for Cuzco.[26] For many of its incumbents, the post of *maestro de capilla* seems to have been simply one of a range of ecclesiastical posts that ambitious students of the local seminary might seek to fill, more of a stepping-stone on the ecclesiastical career path than a vocation or end in itself.

In order to understand this geographical stasis we must also consider the issue of land ownership. Successful musicians in Cuzco, both Indigenous and Hispanic, usually owned land and one or more houses. Property ownership was not only an investment but it also served to generate cash flow, since houses or land could be rented out to provide an annual income and could also serve as security for loans. Investment in property was a gateway to full involvement in the urban economy and to diversification of income, and it was characteristic of both Andean and Spanish elites in the seventeenth century.[27] The first known examples of Andean musicians in Cuzco purchasing land date from the 1620s and involved the buying and selling of arable plots by the cathedral cornettist Pedro Juan Tinco and the shawm player Nicolás Guaman. In the following decade, parish singers and organists too can be found engaging in such transactions. It is not hard to see why migration might have held relatively little appeal in such a context.

In considering the importance of mobility, it is therefore important not to neglect its other. Stasis was generally more beneficial than movement for both Indigenous and Spanish musicians in and around Cuzco in the mid-colonial period. Physical stasis fostered other kinds of mobility, particularly social and economic. Musicologists have good reason to be interested in the movements of musicians between Spain and the Americas and their circulation between the cathedrals and other prominent institutions of the New World, but we should also pay due attention to those who moved "vertically" rather than "horizontally," who climbed socially rather than traveled physically.

Certainly, high mobility might be a sign of success in the case of a Spanish *maestro de capilla* around 1600. But if we look at Cuzco two centuries later, we find the following reference to the singers of the parish of San Pedro in 1796: "as they have no land which might provide them with food, they support themselves with their voices, doing the rounds of the churches."[28] Cuzco experienced a profound economic decline during the eighteenth century, and one consequence was greatly increased mobility of musicians in search of sustenance. More than half the members of Cuzco's guild of barbers and musicians were listed as absent in 1786, implying that many musicians had left the city in search of work. In the 1780s, there are repeated references to *violinistas forasteros* (nonlocal violinists) in the accounts of the parishes of the Urubamba Valley, near Cuzco, further suggesting that musicians were increasingly leaving their place of origin around this time. Cuzco's records show a concentration of payments to nonlocal musicians to perform at one-off events in the late eighteenth century.

There is some evidence that musicians' exemption from tribute payments—the foundation on which the Indigenous music profession had been built—was eroded in the late eighteenth century. The year 1779 saw the reform of the tribute system as royal officials sought ways to increase state revenue. As a result, *indios reservados*—those who had for so long benefited from various exemptions through filling community posts—were increasingly obliged to pay tax. In 1785 the sub-delegate of Aymaraes claimed that church servants and community officeholders in his district were now all paying tribute.[29] This suggests that the basic system of compensating musicians may have been undermined, and it would explain why music became markedly more professionalized in rural areas around this time. Musicians were obliged to become less dependent on a single church to support them and more like modern freelance musicians, traveling in order to earn fees. If tribute exemptions were eroded, the profession must have lost much of its stability.

The case of the singers of San Pedro in 1796 is another reminder of the importance of land ownership. Here, circulation is associated with those too poor to own land. In the late eighteenth century, then, increased movement was an indication of straitened economic circumstances, and the rather forlorn picture of parish musicians "doing the rounds of the churches" points to a darker side to mobility, which was associated with a breakdown in the longstanding structures of the music profession.

Difference and sameness

In the contemporary world, musical change and differentiation tend to be associated more with mobility and the urban than with stasis and the rural. However, an opposing dynamic was also quite prevalent in colonial Latin America, and so it is in fact unsurprising that Philippe Canguilhem's discovery of possible traces of a "mestizo musical culture" stems from musical manuscripts originating from rural Guatemala. Adriaan van Oss describes a pervasive religious syncretism in the remote parishes of the Western Guatemalan Highlands, which "remained a bastion of Indigenous language, race, and culture."[30] Claims of a mestizo culture are thus plausible in the case of Guatemalan villages because of the nature of colonial society in such places. In the context of colonial Latin America, margins and backwaters offered advantages when it came to cultural mixing; centers were more firmly under the colonial eye, and more closely connected to—or even in competition with—the metropolis.

In the diocese of Cuzco, evidence of musical hybridization comes largely from the rural parishes.[31] The performance of *chanzonetas* was recorded in documentation from rural confraternities in the late seventeenth and early eighteenth centuries. According to the early seventeenth-century *Tesoro de la lengua castellana o española* of Sebastián de Covarrubias, "Chanzonetas are villancicos that are sung on Christmas Eve in churches in the vernacular, with a particular kind of lively and joyful music."[32] References to such hybrid musical practices are particularly concentrated in the late eighteenth century, when rural parish records include references to *comedias* and to ensembles of violin, harp, and harpsichord performing both church music and popular secular music.

In 1790 a Spanish geographer named Pablo José Oricaín visited the village of Andahuaylillas, near Cuzco. There he composed a "Brief Compendium of Various Discourses on Different Matters," which included his impressions of music-making in the rural parish churches of the region, which was notable for its musical mixing:

> I cannot gloss over the fact that on Christmas Eve in general, and especially in the villages, those who play the instruments in the choir disturb the faithful at the moment of the Mass, as they are not well versed in musical compositions suitable for divine worship, but rather adapt them, with four or six [musicians] who do not even perform them half-decently; and to vary, they introduce profane contradanzas, minuets, *yaravís*, and lascivious songs.[33]

Nevertheless, it is striking just how hard it is to find written traces of a mestizo musical culture in Latin America. Even in the highly propitious context of the remote Guatemalan parishes, Canguilhem has to search around the edges of what is largely an orthodox repertoire. In Cuzco, formerly the capital of the Inka Empire, José Quezada Macchiavello's exhaustive study of the many surviving sources revealed no evidence of a hybrid culture in either the written music or anywhere else—not that this stopped him from labeling it a "mestizo musical culture" anyway.[34] Why is this musical mixture so hard to find? And why might a musicologist like Quezada Macchiavello be so keen to find it that he was not dissuaded by the lack of evidence?

In her book on architecture in early colonial Peru, Valerie Fraser poses her central question as: "where are the Indians?"[35] Canguilhem provides one answer in his chapter in this volume: in the margins. Fraser, meanwhile, located them not in the physical forms of provincial Andean churches but in the notarial records, the contracts, the artisans and laborers who had created the buildings. The answer, then, was: they are everywhere, if we know where to look for them. The same is true for music. Just as with the construction of the early colonial churches, the Indigenous presence is to be found in the sheer quantity of production, in the proliferation of musical culture, in the parish and notarial records. A significant difference, though, is music's performative nature, and in certain colonial contexts, as Leonardo Waisman argues, we may plausibly imagine local influences in performance (for example, in features such as timbre or tuning) that did not leave a trace in notation.[36] As Inga Clendinnen wrote about Mexico in the sixteenth century: "The Indians persisted in making a song and dance of their religion."[37] She describes the Indigenous population's enthusiasm and exuberance as constantly pushing at the limits of what the Spanish churchmen considered acceptable. We may never know for sure whether or how Indigenous musicians "made a song and dance" of European(-style) music, but it seems highly likely that they did in some form, in some locations, and at some times.

Nonetheless, an important issue to consider is that church music may often have been a domain for the performance of sameness rather than difference. Notarial documents are again relevant here. Rappaport and Cummins underline that influential Indigenous figures often made headway in colonial society by emphasizing their success at conforming to Spanish dictates and norms. Referring to notarial records concerning such figures, they note: "these documents do not broadcast alterity. Instead, they champion conformity within a Spanish system."[38] The absence of signs of cultural difference in legal documentation is perfectly comprehensible, since this was a sphere in which resemblance to Europeans was advantageous and viewed positively. Different forms of colonial culture may thus display different degrees of transculturation, and if written music is a realm where signs are very limited, then it is important to consider possible reasons beyond simply the limitations of musical notation.

The valorization of race mixture now informs the cultural politics of many postcolonial Latin American nations. In the contemporary world more broadly, as Timothy Taylor suggests, hybridity is the new authenticity.[39] But we need to be a little cautious or at least reflexive in searching for an El Dorado of mestizo musical culture in the colonial past. Today, many would find such a culture fascinating, but we need to remember that for the *criollo* (Spanish-descended) population of colonial Latin America, "mestizo" was not generally a positive word, concept, or cultural trait, nor a desirable goal. The absence of signs of a mestizo musical culture in Cuzco's cathedral and seminary archives is therefore less a consequence of the limitations of musical notation or a loss of sources than of the fact that the repertoire belonged to elite *criollo* institutions dedicated to the reproduction of European cultural values.

If today there is a tendency to appreciate stylistic difference, in the colonial period it was sameness that was prized by elite social groups: the highest praise that could be bestowed on a group of Latin American musicians was that they were indistinguishable from a European cathedral choir. *Criollo* competition with the old continent was often expressed through attempts to outshine Europeans, but on European terms. Ricardo Miranda, writing on music in the cathedrals of New Spain, describes a distinctively *criollo* combination of orthodoxy and exaggeration that is far from cultural *mestizaje*.[40] The margins may have been a different story: I have no doubt that the taverns on the periphery of major cities like Lima and Mexico City were, like remote mountain villages, hotbeds of hybridity. But there is good reason to believe that in urban centers, many professional musicians were less interested in creating fusions of European and Indigenous music than in sounding like Spaniards, even in the occasional piece in which they parodied Africans.

This was true of Indigenous as well as Hispanic musicians: for example, the Andean *maestro (compositor) de música* Don Matías de Livisaca owned copies of Domenico Pietro Cerrone's *El melopeo y maestro* (1613) and Andrés Llorente's *El porqué de la música* (1672), and he sold his musical services and compositions to elite Hispanic institutions such as convents and monasteries and their confraternities.[41] He was clearly fluent in European idioms, and he had little to gain professionally from musical *mestizaje* and much to lose. We should be wary, therefore, of assuming that music produced at the interface of Spanish and Indigenous cultures is necessarily hybrid. It was sameness, rather than difference, that had most value in the music profession and in the process of social ordering.

In sum, colonial expansion undoubtedly led to a great flowering of music in the New World, but it was one that left only limited traces in the realms of notation or composition. Whether the Guatemalan repertoire gives clues about a mestizo musical culture or not, there is considerable value in reflecting on why we find this music in such a context, who performed it and how, and what it might have meant to them. Certainly, the circulation of music and musicians to such remote locations is a fascinating topic, but it is also worth focusing on the movements of musical practices and ideologies, particularly educational ones. I conclude with the suggestion that the migration of lettered music from the Old World to the New produced innovation mainly in areas beyond the written page, with a prime example being the widespread implementation of the idea of musical performance and education as social ordering. With music now conceptualized as an instrument of *policía*, the conquest and colonization of the Americas in the sixteenth century saw the mobilization and materialization of age-old ideas about the power of music to shape the world—ideas that continue to resonate across Latin America to this day.[42]

Notes

This essay was written for presentation at the I Tatti conference in 2017, and it appears here largely in its original form, with most of its idiosyncrasies intact. It was intended to serve as a conversational opening gambit and to provoke discussion on the themes of the conference, bringing in some elements of my earlier research on music in colonial Cuzco and responding to Philippe Canguilhem's paper on Guatemala. While there are a few wider points of comparison drawn in, there is no attempt at comprehensive coverage of its topics or the relevant literature, and there is plenty here to be nuanced, fleshed out, and contradicted by scholars of colonial Latin American music. For a more systematic musicological treatment of the Spanish colonial project and Indigenous responses to it, see Waisman, "La América española."

1. Kagan, *Urban Images of the Hispanic World, 1493–1780*, 30.

2. Ibid.

3. Cited in ibid., 37. Translations in English-language sources are by their authors; translations from Spanish-language sources are mine.

4. Cited in Guarda, "Tres reflexiones en torno a la fundación de la ciudad indiana," 92–93. Similarly, the first step in occupying a new territory was the performance of a ritual in which the singing of litanies and hymns played their part; these acts of (dis)possession illustrate clearly the link between music and the imposition of colonial order.

5. Garr, *Hispanic Urban Planning in North America*, 30–31.

6. Kagan, *Urban Images of the Hispanic World, 1493–1780*, 103.

7. Stevenson, *Music in Aztec and Inca Territory*; Turrent, *La conquista musical de México*; Clendinnen, "Ways to the Sacred: Reconstructing 'Religion' in Sixteenth-Century Mexico"; van Oss, *Catholic Colonialism: A Parish History of Guatemala, 1524–1821*.

8. Otaola González, *Tradición y modernidad en los escritos musicales de Juan Bermudo*, 76.

9. Quoted in Knighton, "'Through A Glass Darkly': Music and Mysticism in Golden Age Spain," 424.

10. See e.g. León Tello, *Estudios de historia de la teoría musical*.

11. Kagan, *Urban Images of the Hispanic World, 1493–1780*, 34.

12. Gouk, "Music as a means of social control: some examples of practice and theory in early modern Europe."

13. Tonelli, "Women and music in the Venetian ospedali."

14. Cited in ibid., 38, 65.

15. Guaman Poma de Ayala, *El primer nueva corónica y buen gobierno*, 635.

16. Rappaport and Cummins, *Beyond the Lettered City: Indigenous Literacies in the Andes*, 30.

17. Farriss, *Maya Society under Colonial Rule: The Collective Enterprise of Survival*; Baker, *Imposing Harmony: Music and Society in Colonial Cuzco*.

18. Baker, *Imposing Harmony: Music and Society in Colonial Cuzco*, 155.

19. Cited in Turrent, *La conquista musical de México*, 131.

20. Spalding, "Social Climbers: Changing Patterns of Mobility among the Indians of Colonial Peru."
21. Baker, *Imposing Harmony: Music and Society in Colonial Cuzco.*
22. Guaman Poma de Ayala, *El primer nueva corónica y buen gobierno*, 816, 824, 857, 864.
23. Cuzco is the main focus of my research on music in colonial Latin America: see Baker, *Imposing Harmony: Music and Society in Colonial Cuzco.*
24. Stevenson, "Cuzco Cathedral: 1546–1750."
25. For example, Alonso Fernández de Velasco, who was *maestro de capilla* between 1626 and 1647, was promoted to *racionero* in 1647 and canon in 1657. Alonso de Zúñiga y Anaya, *maestro de capilla* from 1647 until the start of the eighteenth century, repeatedly sought such a promotion, although he was unsuccessful. Basilio Pancorbo was *maestro de capilla* for just three years starting in 1724, and he went on to pursue a non-musical ecclesiastical career in Cuzco for another four decades, although he served for a while as the cathedral's organist.
26. Illari, "La música que, sin embargo, fue: La capilla musical del obispado del Tucumán (siglo XVII)," 44; Suárez-Pajares, *La música en la catedral de Sigüenza, 1600–1750*, 145.
27. Garrett, *Shadows of Empire: The Indian Nobility of Cusco, 1750–1825*, 134.
28. Cited in Baker, *Imposing Harmony: Music and Society in Colonial Cuzco*, 187.
29. Cahill, "*Curas* and Social Conflict in the *Doctrinas* of Cuzco, 1780–1814," 251–52.
30. van Oss, *Catholic Colonialism: A Parish History of Guatemala, 1524–1821*, 71.
31. Baker, *Imposing Harmony: Music and Society in Colonial Cuzco*, 224–26.
32. Covarrubias, *Tesoro de la lengua castellana o española*, 432.
33. Maurtua, *Obispados y audiencia del Cuzco*, 338–39.
34. Quezada Macchiavello, *El legado musical del Cusco barroco: Estudio y catálogo de los manuscritos de música del seminario San Antonio Abad del Cusco.*
35. Fraser, *The Architecture of Conquest: Building in the Viceroyalty of Peru, 1535–1635*, 156.
36. Waisman, "La América española."
37. Clendinnen, "Ways to the Sacred: Reconstructing 'Religion' in Sixteenth-Century Mexico," 115.
38. Rappaport and Cummins, *Beyond the Lettered City: Indigenous Literacies in the Andes*, 122.
39. Taylor, *Beyond Exoticism: Western Music and the World*, 141.
40. Miranda, "Éxtasis de luz y fe: la policoralidad en la Nueva España a través de la obra de Juan Gutiérrez de Padilla."
41. Baker, *Imposing Harmony: Music and Society in Colonial Cuzco*, 182–84.
42. Baker, *El Sistema: Orchestrating Venezuela's Youth.*

Bibliography

Baker, Geoffrey. *Imposing Harmony: Music and Society in Colonial Cuzco*. Durham: Duke University Press, 2008.

Baker, Geoffrey. *El Sistema: Orchestrating Venezuela's Youth*. New York: Oxford University Press, 2014.

Cahill, David. "*Curas* and Social Conflict in the *Doctrinas* of Cuzco, 1780–1814." *Journal of Latin American Studies* 16 (1984): 241–76.

Clendinnen, Inga. "Ways to the Sacred: Reconstructing 'Religion' in Sixteenth-Century Mexico." *History and Anthropology* 5 (1990): 105–41.

Covarrubias, Sebastián de. *Tesoro de la lengua castellana o española* [1611], ed. Felipe C. R. Maldonado, rev. Manuel Camarero. 2nd ed. Madrid: Editorial Castalia, 1995.

Farriss, Nancy M. *Maya Society under Colonial Rule: The Collective Enterprise of Survival*. Princeton: Princeton University Press, 1984.

Fraser, Valerie. *The Architecture of Conquest: Building in the Viceroyalty of Peru, 1535–1635*. Cambridge: Cambridge University Press, 1990.

Garr, Daniel (ed.). *Hispanic Urban Planning in North America*. New York: Garland Publishing, 1991.

Garrett, David T. *Shadows of Empire: The Indian Nobility of Cusco, 1750–1825*. Cambridge: Cambridge University Press, 2005.

Gouk, Penelope. "Music as a means of social control: some examples of practice and theory in early modern Europe." In *The Emotional Power of Music: Multidisciplinary perspectives on musical arousal, expression, and social control*, ed. Tom Cochrane, Bernardino Fantini, and Klaus R. Scherer. Pp. 307–13. Oxford: Oxford University Press, 2013.

Guaman Poma de Ayala, Felipe. *El primer nueva corónica y buen gobierno* [c.1615], ed. John V. Murra and Rolena Adorno. 3 vols. Mexico City: Siglo Veintiuno, 1980.

Guarda, Gabriel. "Tres reflexiones en torno a la fundación de la ciudad indiana." In *Estudios sobre la ciudad iberoamericana*, ed. Francisco de Solano. Pp. 89–106. Madrid: Consejo Superior de Investigaciones Científicas, 1983.

Illari, Bernardo. "La música que, sin embargo, fue: La capilla musical del obispado del Tucumán (siglo XVII)." *Revista argentina de musicología* 1 (1996): 17–54.

Kagan, Richard. *Urban Images of the Hispanic World, 1493–1780*. New Haven: Yale University Press, 2000.

Knighton, Tess. "'Through A Glass Darkly': Music and Mysticism in Golden Age Spain." In *A New Companion to Hispanic Mysticism*, ed. Hilaire Kallendorf. Pp. 411–36. Leiden: Brill, 2010.

León Tello, Francisco José. *Estudios de historia de la teoría musical*. Madrid: Consejo Superior de Investigaciones Científicas, Instituto Español de Musicología, 1962.

Miranda, Ricardo. "Éxtasis de luz y fe: la policoralidad en la Nueva España a través de la obra de Juan Gutiérrez de Padilla." In *Polychoralities: Music, Identity and Power in Italy, Spain and the New World*, ed. Juan José Carreras and Iain Fenlon. Pp. 263–86. Kassel: Reichenberger, 2013.

Maurtua, Victor. *Obispados y audiencia del Cuzco*. Vol. 11 of *Juicio de límites entre el Perú y Bolivia*. Barcelona: Henrich y Companía, 1906.

Otaola González, Paloma. *Tradición y modernidad en los escritos musicales de Juan Bermudo*. Kassel: Reichenberger, 2000.

Quezada Macchiavello, José. *El legado musical del Cusco barroco: Estudio y catálogo de los manuscritos de música del seminario San Antonio Abad del Cusco*. Lima: Fondo Editorial del Congreso del Perú, 2004.

Rappaport, Joanne, and Tom Cummins. *Beyond the Lettered City: Indigenous Literacies in the Andes*. Durham: Duke University Press, 2011.

Spalding, Karen. "Social Climbers: Changing Patterns of Mobility among the Indians of Colonial Peru." *Hispanic American Historical Review* 50 (1970): 645–64.

Stevenson, Robert. *Music in Aztec and Inca Territory*. Berkeley and Los Angeles: University of California Press, 1968.

Stevenson, Robert. "Cuzco Cathedral: 1546–1750." *Inter-American Music Review* 2 (1980): 1–25.

Suárez-Pajares, Javier. *La música en la catedral de Sigüenza, 1600–1750*. Madrid: Instituto Complutense de Ciencias Musicales, 1998.

Taylor, Timothy. *Beyond Exoticism: Western Music and the World*. Durham: Duke University Press, 2007.

Tonelli, Vanessa M. "Women and music in the Venetian ospedali." Master's thesis, Michigan State University, 2013.

Turrent, Lourdes. *La conquista musical de México*. Mexico City: Fondo de Cultura Económica, 1993.

van Oss, Adriaan. *Catholic Colonialism: A Parish History of Guatemala, 1524–1821*. Cambridge: Cambridge University Press, 1986.

Waisman, Leonardo J. "La América española: proyecto y resistencia." In *Políticas y prácticas musicales en el mundo de Felipe II*, ed. John Griffiths and Javier Suárez-Pajares. Pp. 503–50. Madrid: Ediciones del ICCMU, 2004.

Encounters in the Margins: Considering the Local in the Lilly Library Music Manuscripts from Sixteenth-Century Guatemala*

Philippe Canguilhem

On Holy Saturday in April 1541, the Florentine engineer and man of letters Luca Martini wrote from Bologna to his friend Giovanbattista della Fonte in Florence, giving him an account of the musical life he had discovered in the Emilian city. Alongside his description of the beautiful singer Susanna Ferrarese and his disappointment at finding no new madrigals to send to his friend, his letter also contains a general appraisal of Bolognese musical habits that is worth quoting in full: "I have never been anywhere on earth where I have heard singing more frequently; but they sing such poor things and in such a strange way, a thing I impute to the fact that I haven't stuffed my body with ravioli, even though you know that there are exceptions to every rule."[1]

While the last part of Martini's sentence may be interpreted as ironic, it nevertheless documents how dramatically musical (and culinary) habits could vary even at a short distance like the eighty kilometers separating Florence from Bologna. But how would Martini have reacted when confronted with more radical differences like those being experienced by the Spaniards arriving for the first time in the New World in those same years? To be sure, music played only a small part in the cultural shock that followed from the encounters between Indigenous peoples and the first Europeans to land in Central America during the early decades of the Spanish conquest, but from various reports, we know that dance and music as practiced by the native inhabitants did not have much in common with what the Iberians were used to.[2]

Even though pre-contact musical practice is only known through the reports of Spanish witnesses (and thus, cannot really be called "pre-contact"), a number of iconographical documents have been preserved, including some created by native peoples, such as those in the Codex Durán in Madrid and the even more famous Codice Fiorentino compiled by Bernardino de Sahagún, now in the Laurenziana library; moreover, a corpus of texts in Náhuatl that were sung during Aztec ceremonies has also been preserved, sacred songs known today as *Cantares mexicanos*.[3]

Whereas no melodies for these *cantares* have survived, we do nevertheless possess numerous musical sources produced in Central and South America in the sixteenth and seventeenth centuries, mostly manuscripts, which document how rapidly and faithfully the Spaniards imported their own musical tradition and repertoire to the Americas. As a matter of fact, the choirbooks copied in Mexico and across the whole of New Spain beginning in the sixteenth century were conceived as musical tools that were essential for Christian worship, which ruled throughout the continent. As a result, the music copied into these manuscripts reflects the taste of the Iberian Peninsula. These documents are well known to musicologists and were thoroughly studied in the second half of the twentieth century, since they preserve pieces by important composers such as Cristóbal de Morales, Francisco Guerrero, and Tomás Luis de Victoria.[4]

The present study is dedicated to a group of sources copied in Central America and containing Spanish polyphonic music for the church. They are unique in a number of ways. First and foremost is that they were copied far from the urban and political center of Mexico City and its surrounding network of cities, and—even more significantly—far from any urban center whatsoever. Considering a complex of musical sources produced in small villages of the Western highlands of Guatemala at the end of the sixteenth century may be interesting in its own right, since, as Geoffrey Baker recognizes, "little sustained attention has been paid to rural music making in colonial Latin America." In his opinion, this lack of interest is explained by the fact that "the urban focus of colonial ideology has been largely maintained by musicologists' privileging of elite city institutions."[5]

To be sure, the manuscripts of the Lilly Library have not languished in obscurity: in the first part of the 1980s, two master's theses and a PhD dissertation were dedicated to them, all focusing on the musical works they convey, namely a mixture of European masses and motets, mostly Spanish, as well as local compositions, especially sacred villancicos.[6] In a nutshell, these valuable and very helpful studies approached these sources in a manner typical of Renaissance source studies at the time, treating them as if they had been written in Europe. In the introduction of his doctoral dissertation, Paul Borg stated that his main goal was to "assay the musical style of the polyphonic works" present in the manuscripts.[7] While I have always considered this type of work to be extremely useful and necessary, I would like to shift perspective by looking at everything in these sources that was written down by their scribes *except* the repertoire, in order to grasp the elements that might record a musical encounter between local Indigenous culture and the European one. In trying to find some traces of what Serge Gruzinski has called a "*mestizo* mind" in his seminal book, I wish to explore "how the performative nature of music documented instances of ethnic encounter, creolization, and cultural métissage that are otherwise difficult to trace," as Kate van Orden has put it.[8]

Of the fifteen Guatemalan music manuscripts that came into the possession of the Lilly Library between 1967 and 1969, four contain plainchant, two are fragmentary, and nine contain polyphony in choirbook layout. To this well-known corpus must be added another manuscript, preserved today at Princeton University Library, and a tract of music theory written in Náhuatl that was transcribed and translated into Spanish in 1980 and 1997.[9] All these sources, copied between 1582 and the first decades of the seventeenth century, come from three villages (Santa Eulalia, San Juan Ixcoi, San Mateo Ixtatán) in the Huehuetenango region in the western highlands of Guatemala. Among the various names that appear in the manuscripts, two—Francisco de León and Tomás Pascual—are believed to have been the scribes and composers of a part of the repertory, and scholars have therefore referred to them as "maestros de capilla," the former at Santa Eulalia, the latter at San Juan Ixcoi.[10] So far, no other documentation has surfaced that could provide further information about them. The first step to a fuller understanding of these musicians is deeper consideration of the places they lived and worked.

The area known as Los Altos Cuchumatanes, or the Sierra de los Cuchumatanes, stands out for its remoteness. As ethnologist Oliver La Farge described it in 1932, "The Heights of Cuchumatán form an isolated region of high ridges and precipitous valleys, hard to approach, hard to cross in any direction, and, in the main, high, cool, fertile, and beautiful beyond the possibility of expression."[11] Nearly four hundred years earlier, the opinion registered by the Spaniard Diego de Garcés was concordant only in part, as he considered the region to be "a poor and unfruitful land, good only for raising corn and chickens, which are to be found in great number." Regardless of its beauty and fertility (or infertility), the Cuchumatán region was above all an isolated and forgotten land, a "periphery within a periphery," as historian George Lovell has described it.[12] And so, even in 1932, La Farge could write about the village of Santa Eulalia: "At the time that this study was made, none of the area could be reached by wheeled vehicle."[13] As a result, the villages were barely controlled by the authorities. In 1556, Pedro Ramírez de Quiñones reported about them to the Consejo de Indias: "There is great disorder among the Indians in matters that relate to their government and administration. Things are chaotic, lacking proper direction. [...] In most *pueblos de indios,* people live as they wish to, or can, and since the court cannot arrange for visitations to be made, we, its officers, cannot vouch for one-tenth of the district we govern."[14] This situation would remain unchanged for a long time: during a visit to the region in 1689, the Bishop of Guatemala declared that the Cuchumatanes highlands, because of their rugged terrain and severe cold, had not been visited by one of his predecessors since the time of conquest.[15]

The region had been colonized, though. Between 1525 and 1530, the Spaniards organized various military expeditions in the Cuchumatán highlands in order to take control of the area, but it took them two more decades before they could establish an effective colonial government. This means that only from 1550 onwards did the Indigenous population begin to be systematically evangelized. This process was implemented through a specific administrative organization, known as *congregaciones,* or forced native resettlements. Because the population was dispersed in the mountains, it was felt that resettlement in newly created villages would allow the friars to convert the local population more easily. In 1551, an article of the *Leyes de Indias* (Laws of the Indies) stipulated that, in order to allow them to "forget their ancient erroneous rites and ceremonies and to live in concert and order," the Indians "should be reduced to villages and not be allowed to live divided and separated in the mountains and wilderness, where they are deprived of all spiritual and temporal comforts, the aid of our ministers, and those other things that human necessities oblige men to give one to another."[16] The three villages where our manuscripts were copied, then, had been artificially formed and forcibly populated only a few decades before. Their inhabitants, who originally lived in various areas scattered throughout the Cuchumatanes, spoke different languages more or less related to Mayan, in particular the Mam, Chuj, and Kanjobal languages. In the *congregación* of Santa Eulalia, Kanjobal was spoken by a majority of inhabitants, but Ixil was also spoken, after the populations from the hamlet of Ilom were moved to the village.[17]

It comes as no surprise, then, to find these languages set to music in some of the Lilly manuscripts. According to Robert Stevenson, who was the first musicologist to study these documents, they contain texts written in Chuj, Kanjobal, Jacaltec, and Náhuatl. We know that this last one, the language of the Mexican Aztecs, was used by Indigenous peoples as a *lingua franca,* but as we shall see, other factors might also explain its presence in the manuscripts.[18]

The *congregaciones* of San Mateo Ixtatán, Santa Eulalia, and San Juan Ixcoi were founded between 1549 and 1560, first under the supervision of Dominican missionaries and subsequently by members of the Mercedarian Order (Orden de Nuestra Señora de la Merced), who built the church of Santa Eulalia in 1586.[19] It is important to stress that these friars were the only non-native people to live there, since a 1563 article of the *Leyes de Indias* states very clearly that the *congregaciones* should only be populated by Indigenous peoples, and that they were strictly forbidden to sub-Saharan Africans, mestizos, and Spaniards, who could not settle there.[20] It appears that in the Cuchumatanes, this law was rather faithfully respected. Therefore, we have to imagine these villages as closed communities exclusively populated by native peoples and a few Spanish missionaries, completely cut off from the world.[21]

Most probably, then, both Tomás Pascual and Francisco de León were not, as they are called in the current literature, "maestros de capilla," at least not in the sense that term was intended in the Spanish cathedrals of the Siglo de Oro. Our two scribes and composers were arguably Dominican or Mercedarian friars skilled in plainchant and mensural music. The Dominican Antonio de Remesal, who settled in Guatemala in 1614 and wrote his *Historia* between 1615 and 1617, which was eventually published in Spain in 1619 and 1620, singles out a number of his Dominican brothers who were particularly gifted in music and taught it in Guatemala. He also states that some of the missionaries who were not musicians took pains to learn music thoroughly so that they could teach mensural music and musical instruments to the Indians.[22]

If we look further, though, another passage of Antonio de Remesal's *Historia* points to a more intriguing possibility. Remesal's book not only recounts the conquest of Guatemala and Chiapas, it also chronicles the work of Bartolomé de las Casas, whom Remesal very much admired. Remesal relates how Bartolomé de las Casas came to realize that music was instrumental in the process of Christianization, as the Indians were fascinated by the sound of instruments and the singing of the Spaniards. Seeking to pursue his missionary work in the Tezulutlan province of Guatemala, las Casas convinced the Spanish authorities to help him in his task by issuing a decree directed to the Minister General of the Franciscan order in the New World. The decree, dated 1540 and signed by the cardinal Garcia de Loaysa y Mendoza, regent of the Indies, stipulates that las Casas and his companions

> have told us that they are in need of some Indians who play shawns, sackbuts and recorders, and also some singers, who are to be found in the convents of your Order in your Province. And this because thanks to music, they could better convert the Indians of your Province to our Christian faith. [...] And thus I ask you to give to the aforementioned friar Bartolomé de las Casas, friar Rodrigo de Adrada, and friar Pedro de Angulo Indian singers and instrumentalists who

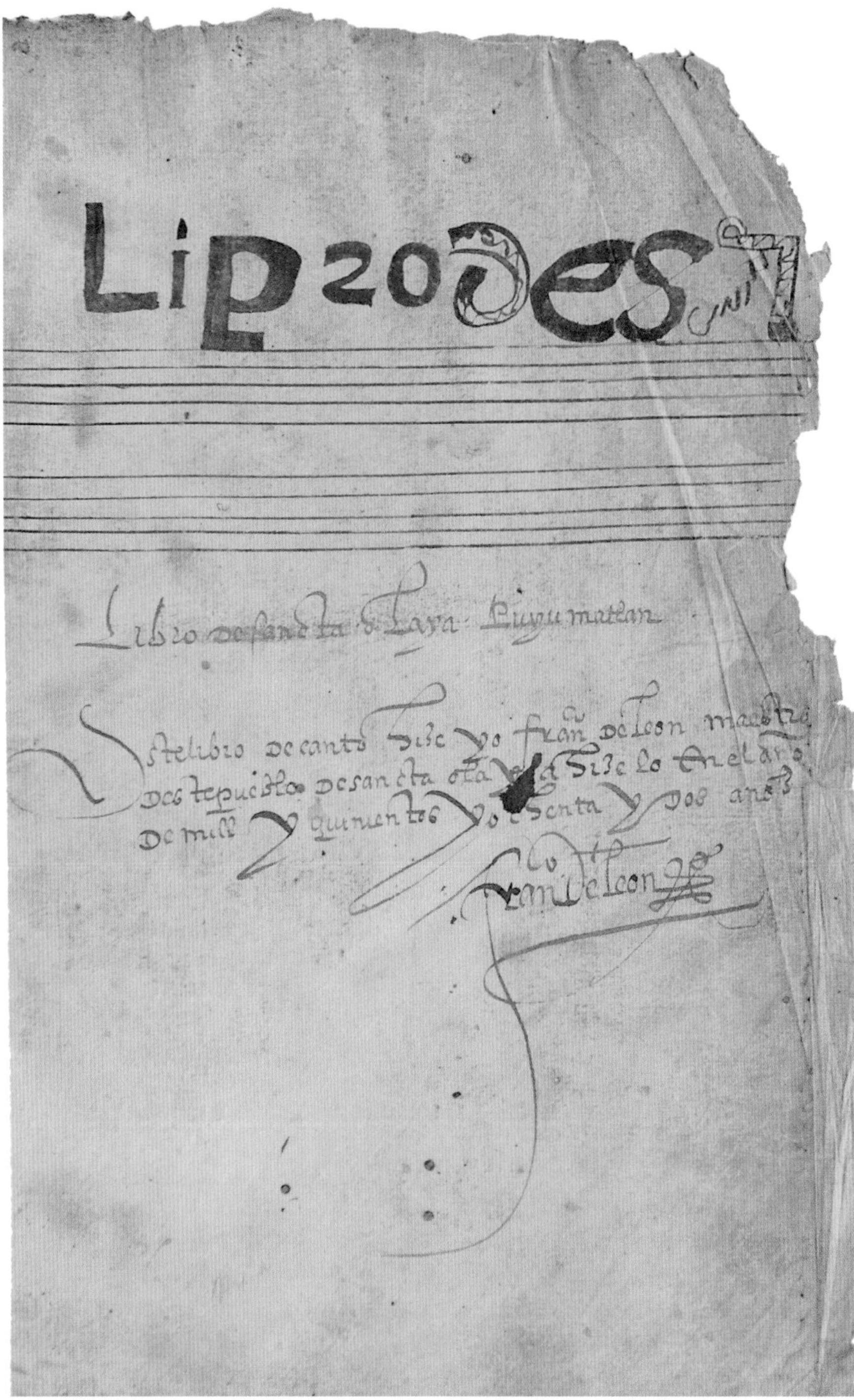

Fig. 1. Bloomington, Indiana University, Lilly Library, Music Ms. 1, fol. 1

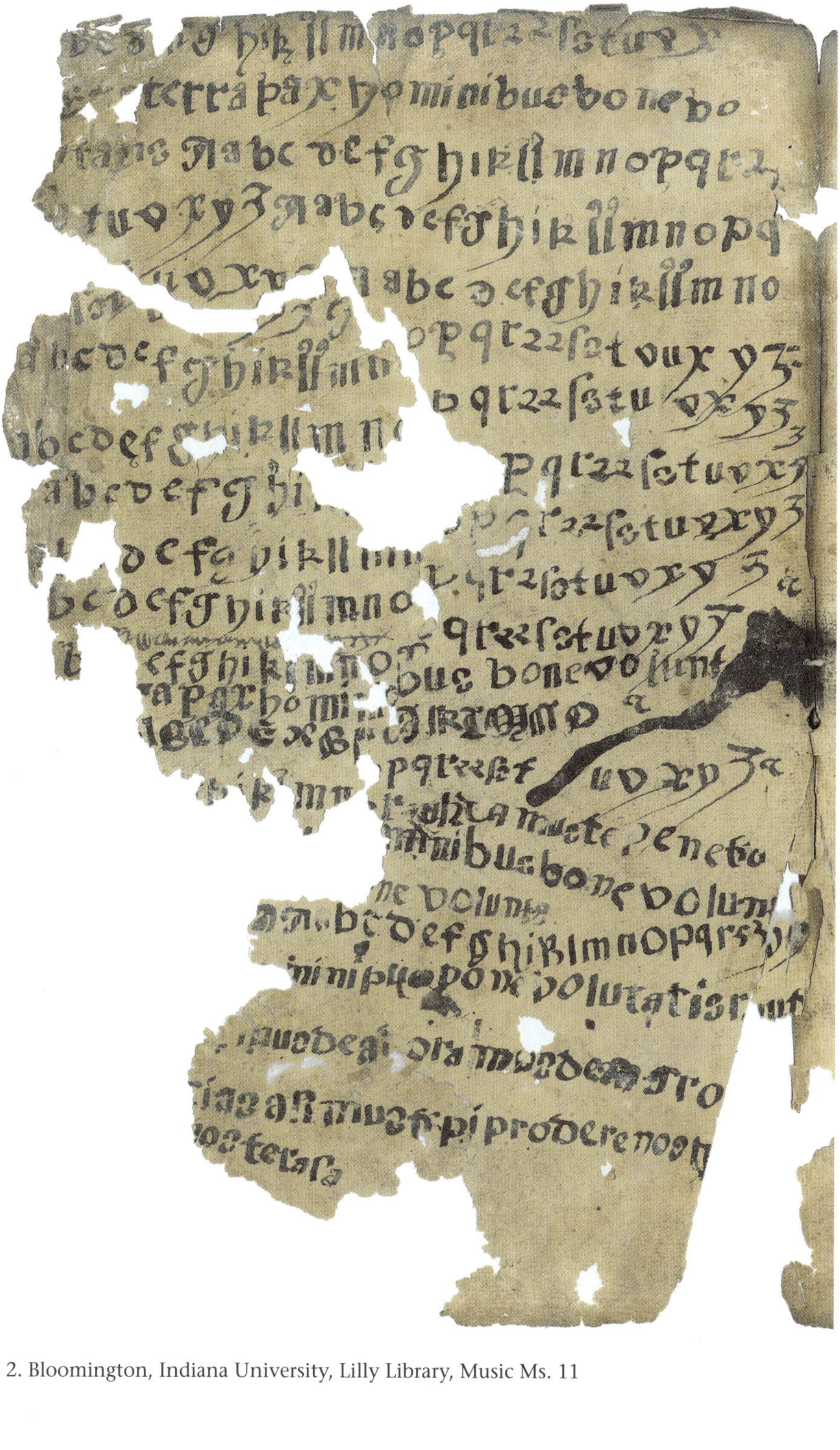

Fig. 2. Bloomington, Indiana University, Lilly Library, Music Ms. 11

Fig. 3. Bloomington, Indiana University, Lilly Library, Music Ms. 10, fol. 39v

> are staying in the convents of your Order in your Province, especially those you consider the most gifted, so that they could go with them and work at the aforesaid conversion, and in doing this you will serve me.[23]

Could Tomás Pascual and Francisco de León be Mexican Indians, brought up in Dominican convents in Mexico and for this reason bearing Christian names? This possibility should not be ruled out, since in addition to items in the local Mayan dialect, Náhuatl language also surfaces in the manuscripts in prayers without music, marginal notes, and a few musical works. Moreover, the manuscripts are marked by a diversity of scripts, which appear to be those of students and teachers: to quote Paul Borg, who has conducted the most thorough study of these sources to date, "the many individual works and fragments of works that appear in yet different hands often seem to be the result of some student or apprentice practicing his copying skills."[24] Indeed, contributions to the manuscripts show an only approximate mastery of Western script, as seen on the first page of Ms. 1 where a title has been added by a non-professional scribe above the inscription written by Francisco de León, who describes himself as "maestro deste pueblo de santa olaya" (see figure 1). The alphabet exercises that fill the flyleaves of another manuscript reveal the true function of this "Maestro Francisco" and his colleagues, who taught not only music, but gave also basic instruction to their pupils (see figure 2). Leafing through the manuscripts, modern readers will also be struck by their decoration, with capital letters in a style not found in any extant European choirbook (see figure 3).

The manuscripts are full of such traces of local visual culture, which affect the design of numerous pages and tie the manuscripts firmly to their immediate context, where Mexican missionaries fluent in Spanish musical practices were proselytizing in the Western Guatemalan Highlands. We can thus infer from this overview of the sources and the geographic, social, and cultural conditions in which they were produced, that they merit attention not only for the repertoire they contain, but as complex objects that may convey some evidence of a local culture and the intricacies of the broader Iberian diaspora of which they were a part. But to what extent could one argue that this blending of cultures goes beyond the decorative aspects of the manuscripts and affects the music itself? At the very least, it is clear that many marginal additions are musical and aim to script performances beyond those indicated by the polyphony copied in mensural notation, something exemplified by the diminution formulas written down in various places and probably intended for instruments.[25] Considering these leads, then, it is tempting to look further for instances where the scribes

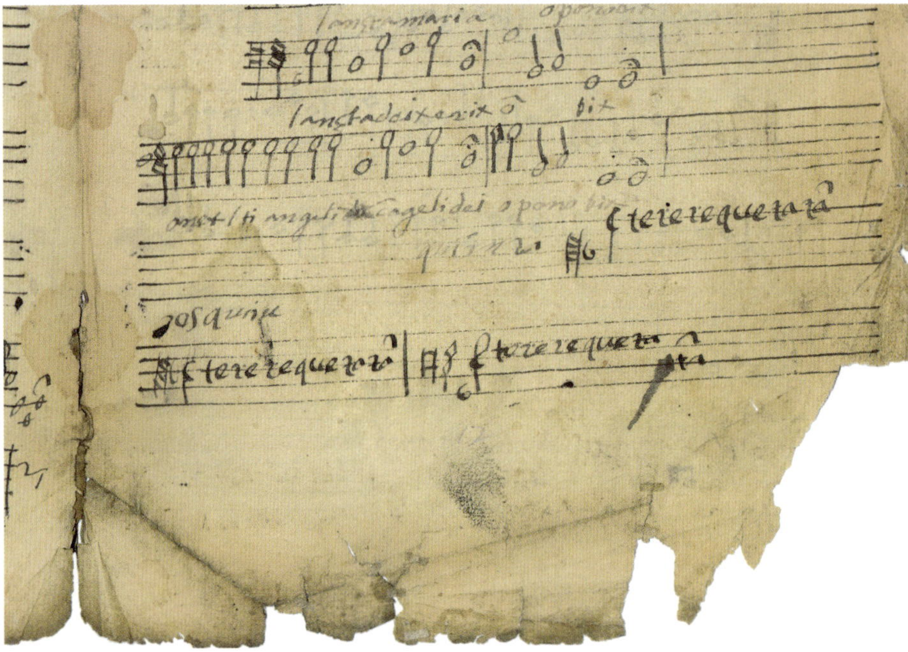

Fig. 4. Bloomington, Indiana University, Lilly Library, Music Ms. 6, fol. 9

might have left traces of some native musical practice. But this issue, as we shall see, is a delicate one.

As a case study in how we might approach such questions of music and cultural encounter, I will concentrate here on a unique example: an enigmatic musical phrase that appears in Ms. 6 at the bottom of folio 9, on the recto side (see figure 4). This piece has been neither transcribed nor listed in the inventory of the manuscript made by Paul Borg in his otherwise very thorough dissertation, perhaps due to its marginal status, but probably also because of its unusual musical notation. As written, each of the three parts of the piece has been notated by placing the syllables of the sung text directly on the five-line staff, each on the line or space where it has to be sung. I know of very few other examples of such a practice, but it is striking to note that it first appears in the *Musica enchiriadis,* a musical treatise dated to the ninth century. There, the description of organum technique is illustrated with an example that represents the very first notated polyphony in the West. Despite the chronological and geographic separation of these two sources, the anonymous author of *Musica enchiriadis* places the syllables of the text *Sicut gloria Domini in secula* on the staff in the same manner as the scribe of Ms. 6, except for the fact that the parts are superimposed in the organum example whereas in the Guatemalan manuscript they are separated.[26]

Fig. 5. Adam Gumpelzhaimer, *Compendium musicae* (Augsburg, 1611), fol. 3v (detail)

The three other examples known to me come from the Renaissance: the Glogauer Liederbuch, copied around 1470–80, contains a neo-Latin polyphonic song, *Alga iacet humilis,* for the celebration of Easter and Spring, that employs a similar style of notation. A century later, a music treatise known as "Scottish Anonymous" copied circa 1580 has the plainchant melody of a Magnificat inscribed this way, while a few years later, in 1591, Adam Gumpelzhaimer's cruciform riddle canon, *Ecce lignum crucis,* includes an analogous piece of notation above the cross, indicating in this way that two voices should sing the formula *Iesus Nazarenus Rex Iudæorum* on the note E an octave apart (see figure 5).[27]

Clearly this notational procedure was not unknown to European musicians, although it must be considered rare. A second puzzling feature of the Guatemalan piece is the text itself, the six syllables that are put on the three staves: terere quezaza.[28] These appear to be onomatopoeic nonsense, not only in Spanish, but also in Náhuatl and the other local languages, if we assume that the syllables were supposed to be sung. How can we understand this kind of musical expression in light of what we know of native musical practice? Some evidence can be gleaned from the repertoire of Aztec sacred songs, now called *Cantares mexicanos,* which were written down in the second half of the sixteenth century by Spanish witnesses who understood Náhuatl. In fact, some are preceded by headings including nonsense syllables, as in song no. 44: "Here begin log-drum songs Tico tico toco toto. And when the song ends: tiquiti titito titi."[29] These syllables seem to take the form of percussion cadences, as Gary Tomlinson explains: "We do not know much about the origins of this syllabic notation. [...] by the middle of the seventeenth century, a whole genre of colonial Mexican song, the *tocotin,* could be named after it. It may well reflect pre-Hispanic oral mnemonic practices for teaching, disseminating, and preserving percussion cadences."[30]

Fig. 6. Girolamo Fantini, "Sparata di buttasella," *Modo per imparare a sonare di tromba* (Frankfurt, 1638), 12

Given that Aztec songs typically included series of nonsense syllables, some of them related to percussion rhythms, it is tempting to consider this "terere quezaza" as in some way reminiscent of the "pre-Hispanic oral mnemonic practices" present in the *Cantares mexicanos*. But here, too, this example might just as easily refer to European practices. The trumpet treatise published by Girolamo Fantini in 1638 employs similar syllables as mnemonic devices for students learning trumpet fanfares (see figure 6). When reading a phrase such as "teghe teghe da ta na no" out of context, who would guess that these syllables made perfect sense to an Italian trumpet player of the seventeenth century? And even more striking is a passage in the French dance treatise published by Thoinot Arbeau in 1589 under the title *Orchésographie,* where the author inserts what he calls a "tablature" for the drummer with the rhythmic formulas used to accompany the dancers. These formulas are notated with three sets of syllables, "tan," "fre," and "tere," that are combined in all possible ways.[31] Note, as well, the coincidence that "tere" was being used around the same time by the Frenchman Arbeau and the Latin American scribe of the Guatemalan manuscript.

A third unusual feature of this piece concerns the harmonic result of the three parts, assuming that they were meant to be heard simultaneously (see example 1). The flat in the signature, the three different clefs, the cut-C time signature, and the fermata at the end of the line provide multiple indications that the three parts were intended to be played—or sung—together. Nonetheless, the resulting counterpoint is far from correct, both because of the fourths between the lowest and middle part on the first five syllables, and because the "cadential resolution" on the last syllable produces a chord made up of two fourths in internal inversion. Whereas we can be fairly sure that such sonorities

Example 1. Indiana University, Lilly Library, Music Ms. 6, fol. 9

are not be related to European models, it would be dangerous, given our complete ignorance of Indigenous music, to claim that they reflect a local tradition. Conversely, it would be equally rash to discount "terere quezaza" as a senseless musical example resulting from scribal error simply because it does not fit expectations shaped by the musical conventions of Renaissance Europe. To sum up, then, this musical enigma employs a number of European notational features, namely a peculiar form of music notation that uses syllables on the staff instead of notes, and vocables reminiscent of some trumpet and percussion techniques current in the Old World. But it also bears some elements that elude decipherment. The fact that it was copied in the local circumstances I posit above raises a number of questions that remain unresolvable, especially about the presence of Indigenous elements that might have been incorporated here and elsewhere in the manuscripts.

As with "terere quezaza," numerous artistic creations and artifacts produced during the first decades of the colonial period resist analysis because it remains so difficult to identify and parse Indigenous elements from European ones. This difficulty has been theorized by Serge Gruzinski as a distinctive quality of what he has called a "*mestizo* mind." Analyzing a number of artistic productions of sixteenth-century Mexico, Gruzinski explains that they are not simply the result of adding or juxtaposing traits from two different cultures, but, on the contrary, represent original blended creations in which the dialogue between the two cultures is multidimensional: "The Indigenous Renaissance that occurred in Spanish Mexico is teeming with inexplicable forms, aborted experiments, startling articulations. The absence of an overall trend in forms and combinations, amazing stylistic dispersion, and an apparently endless capacity for inventiveness all paint a complex picture full of ruptures, transformations, and bifurcations."[32] Other recent authors also emphasize that the concept of acculturation, first coined by Redfield in 1935, should be abandoned for the term "transculturation," which more accurately describes the process of exchange and transformation that pertains when different cultures come into contact.[33] In this regard, the Lilly manuscripts should be evaluated more as products of transculturation than as Guatemalan counterparts to European polyphonic manuscripts. Only with this perspectival shift will be begin to see them as carriers of the unique cultural relationships indigenous to what would become Latin America.

Notes

* This article relies on a direct examination of the original sources during a two-week Summer Repository Research Fellowship at Indiana University's Institute for Advanced Study in July 2018. I would like to thank the staff of the Lilly Library, who were so helpful in making my research possible, and Giovanni Zanovello for his welcome at Bloomington and the fruitful discussions about the sources. These preliminary thoughts are intended to show how deeper study of this material could produce significant results.

1. "Io non sono stato in terra mai che io sentissi più cantare che in questa e peggior cose con più strano modo, il che ne do la colpa al non aver io nutrito il corpo di raviuoli, ma ogni regola sapete che patisce eccetione." Canguilhem, "The madrigal en route to Florence," 66.

2. See the classical study by Stevenson, *Music in Aztec and Inca Territory,* chap. 2.

3. See Madrid, Biblioteca Nacional de España, Ms. Vitr/26/11 fols. 158v and 305 [Diego Durán, *Historia de las Indias de Nueva España e islas de la tierra firme,* available online at the *Biblioteca Digital Hispánica*], and Florence, Biblioteca Medicea Laurenziana, Med.Palat. 218, fol. 262 [Bernardino de Sahagún, *Historia universal de las cosas de Nueva España,* available online at the *World Digital Library*]. On the *Cantares mexicanos,* see the studies cited by García Gómez, "Música en la conquista espiritual de Tenochtitlan," 170.

4. An overview of these sources is offered by Stevenson, *Renaissance and Baroque Musical Sources in the Americas.* For a recent update focused on the cathedral of Mexico City, see Marín López, *Los libros de polifonía de la catedral de Mexico,* and idem, "The musical inventory of Mexico cathedral, 1589."

5. Baker, *Imposing Harmony,* 194. More recently, a number of studies address rural music issues in early modern Latin America, in particular those by Dutcher Mann, *The Power of Song,* Tello, *Huellas musicales,* and Navarrete Pellicer, *Ritual sonoro.*

6. Garven, "San Juan Ixcoi Mass"; Baird, "*Santa Eulalia M.Md. 7*"; Borg, "Polyphonic Music." The first mention of the manuscripts appears in Stevenson, "European Music in 16th-Century Guatemala." More recently, the manuscripts have been discussed by Waisman, "La América española," 531–33, and Marín López, "Musical Cultures," 355–63.

7. Borg, "Polyphonic Music," 1. More recently, Paul Borg considered the Indigenous aspects of the manuscripts in "Music Notation as Visual Culture: Examples from 17th-century Guatemala," paper read at the Visual Culture Colloquium, School of Art, Illinois State University, August 8, 2007. My warmest thanks to him for providing me with a copy of his paper and drawing my attention to the existence of the Princeton manuscript (see below).

8. See, respectively, Gruzinski, *The Mestizo Mind,* and van Orden, opening remarks at the international conference "Music in the Mediterranean Diaspora," I Tatti, Florence, May 18–19, 2017.

9. Princeton University Library, Garrett-Gates Mesoamerican Ms. 258, belongs to the same corpus of manuscripts as those at the Lilly Library. It was copied by Tomás Pascual between 1622 and 1635 at San Juan Ixcoi. This manuscript has been studied by Timothy Watkins in two unpublished papers, "A New Source for Colonial Guatemalan Music: Princeton Garret-Gates MS. 258," read at the Annual Meeting of the Society for Seventeenth-Century Music, Minneapolis, April 2011, and "Cultural and Musical Identities in Princeton Garret-Gates MS. 258," read at the 19th Congress of the International Musicological Society, Rome, July 2012. A manuscript of music theory written in Náhuatl known as the "Santa Eulalia Music Theory manuscript" shares the same provenance, although its present location is unknown. It has been transcribed and translated by Lemmon and Horcasitas, "El tratado de Santa Eulalia." The Latin American Library at Tulane University still owns a microfilm of the manuscript under the shelfmark Rare MT 88/.Se. I would like to thank Dr Hortensia Calvo, director of the Latin American Library, for this information. Finally, another manuscript related to this series is described by Borg, "The Jacaltenango Miscellany." It is still preserved at the parish of Santa Eulalia, according to Marín López, "Musical Cultures," 355. As Kirstin Haag discovered, these surviving 18 manuscripts represent only a small part of an original number of 50 that were originally preserved in the Cuchumatanes and brought to the U.S. by Maryknoll missionaries in the 1960s. I would like to thank Kirstin Haag, who is finishing her PhD dissertation at Stanford, for sharing this information with me.

10. Apart from the Princeton manuscript mentioned above, Tomás Pascual copied Ms. 7 between 1595 and 1600 and Ms. 13 in 1635, while Francisco de León is responsible for copying Mss. 1 and 2 in 1582. See Borg, "Polyphonic Music," 10–13.

11. La Farge, *Santa Eulalia,* 1.

12. Lovell, *Conquest and Survival in Colonial Guatemala,* 174. The quotation of Diego de Garcés, who wrote around 1560, appears on page 84, and the original Spanish ("tierra pobre y estéril, salvo de maíz y gallinas que hay en abundancia") in the Spanish edition of the same book, 87.

13. La Farge, *Santa Eulalia,* 1.

14. Lovell, *Conquest and Survival,* 191. Spanish original: "En los pueblos de los naturales hay gran desorden en lo que toca a la policia. Hay muy poco orden entre ellos, ni instrucción. [...] En lo mas los pueblos de indios viven cada uno como quiere o como puede y como la audiencia no puede enviar visitadores, no pueden cumplir de visitar la decima parte del distrito" (Lovell, *Conquista y cambio cultural,* 99).

15. Ibid., 84.

16. Ibid., 76. Spanish original: "olvidando los errores de sus antigos ritos y ceremonias vivan en concierto y policía, y para que esto se executasse con mejor acierto se juntaron diversas vezes los de nuestro Consejo de Indias y [...] resolvieron que los indios fuessen reducidos a pueblos y no viviessen divididos y separados por las sierras y montes, privándose de todo beneficio espiritual y temporal, sin socorro de nuestros ministros, y del que obligan las necesidades humanas que deben dar unos hombres a otros" (Lovell, *Conquista y cambio cultural,* 78). The original text was published in *Recopilación de las leyes,* 3:198.

17. Lovell, *Conquest and Survival,* 22 and 82. See also La Farge, *Santa Eulalia,* vi-viii.

18. Stevenson, "European Music in 16th-Century Guatemala," 347–49. The use of Náhuatl as a *lingua franca* is confirmed by Antonio de Remesal, who explains that Pedro de Angulo, Juan de Torres, and other Dominicans arriving in Guatemala "con infinito trabajo juntaron los pueblos de caserías o familias de indios tan apartadas unas de otras que cada una tenía lengua diferente, como se echa de ver en la particular que cada uno habla, usando de la mexicana como general y común." Remesal, *Historia de la provincia de San Vincente de Chyapa y Guatemala,* 149. English translation, Lovell, *Conquest and Survival,* 79.

19. Hinz, *Existence and Identity,* 36. Remesal, *Historia,* 508–12, explains why and how the *pueblos de indios* were established in the region. Toward the end of the seventeenth century, thirty villages were under the control of the Mercedarians and six under the Dominicans. On the process of *congregación* in sixteenth-century Guatemala, see Lovell et al., *"Strange Lands and Different Peoples,"* chapter 5.

20. Lovell et al., *"Strange Lands and Different Peoples,"* 103. Original text, *Recopilación de las leyes,* 2:200.

21. According to Fuentes y Guzmán, *Recordacion florida,* 3:88, who provides an accurate description of these villages at the end of the seventeenth century, 800 inhabitants lived in Santa Eulalia, "gente pobre y miserable," and 560 in San Juan Ixcoi, "gente cerril y miserable." On Guatemalan parish churches in general, see the useful study of van Oss, *Catholic Colonialism.*

22. Remesal, *Historia,* 733. Earlier in the book, Remesal speaks of the Dominican Alonso de Cervantes, "destrissimo en musica, assi de canto como de tecla" (565). Remesal's *Historia* reappeared a year later in

Madrid with a new title, *Historia general de las Indias occidentales*. But except for the title-page, the book is the same as that printed in 1619.

23. Remesal, *Historia*, 155–56: "Acordavase muy bien el padre fray Bartolomé de las Casas del modo con que conociendo el natural de los indios, avia entrado el conocimiento de los misterios de nuestra sagrada Religion en los primeros fieles de tierra de Guerra, que fue por musica y por el canto de los mercaderes. Y aviendo de proseguir con su conversión adelante, no era bien dexar el medio que le dio tan buen principio, que era el mismo canto y musica. Y como los naturales de aquellas partes yvan creciendo y perficionandose en las cosas de nuestra sagrada religion, quiso el Padre fray Bartolomé que se perficionassen tambien en el gusto de oyrla con vozes concertadas e instrumentos musicos, que los deleytassen y hiciessen apetecer por el gusto del oydo las cosas de Dios y de su divino culto. Y para esto sacò la cedula siguiente: *EL REY venerable Provincial de la orden de san Francisco en la Nueva España, o a vuestro Vicario General.* Sabed, que fray Bartolomé de las Casas y fray Rodrigo de Adrada y fray Pedro de Angulo y Otros Religiosos de su Orden con zelo de servir a nuestro Señor, quieren procurar con predicacion y persuasion, de traer de paz y a nuestro servicio y obediencia, y en conocimiento de nuestra santa Fè Catolica los Indios de las Provincias de Tezulutlan, que son en la Provincia de Guatemala, y de otras a ellas comarcanas. Los quales nos han hecho relacion, que por poder mejor efetuar lo susodicho, avrian menestér algunos Indios que supiesen tañer ministriles altos è chirímías, è sacabuches, e flautas, e algunos cantores de los que ay en los Monasterios de vuestra Orden de essa Provincia; porque con la musica podrian mas brevemente atraer a los Indios de las dichas Provincias al conocimiento de nuestra santa Fè. Y me suplicaron vos mandasse escrivir, para que se los diessedes, ò como la mi merced fuese. E porque como veys, si lo susodicho se efetuasse, Dios nuestro Señor e Nos seriamos dello muy servido. Por ende yo vos encargo y mando que de los Indios cantores y que supieren tañer ministriles è chirimias y sacabuches y flautas que oviere en los Monasterios de vuestra Orden de essa Provincia, deys a los dichos fray Bartolomé de las Casas y fray Rodrigo de Adrada è Fr. Pedro de Angulo ò qualquiera dellos, lo que os pareciere que pueden aprovechar, para que vayan con ellos a entender en la dicha pacificacion, que en ello me servireys. Fecha en la villa de Madrid, a diez y siete dias del mes de Octubre de mil y quinientos y quarenta años. Frater Garsias cardinal Hispalensis."

24. Borg, "Polyphonic Music," 50. According to Stevenson, "European Music in 16th-Century Guatemala," 347–49, Mayan languages do not discriminate between "d" and "t," and this could explain some odd wordings in the manuscripts, like "dible," "denor," or "condaraldo," all of this suggesting Indigenous scribes.

25. See the transcriptions in Borg, "Polyphonic Music," 518 and 625.

26. This page of *Musica enchiriadis* can be seen on fol. 16v of Paris, Bibliothèque nationale de France, Ms. Latin 7211, available online at *Gallica*.

27. Glogauer Liederbuch: Kraków, Biblioteka Jagiellonska, Berlin Ms. Mus 40098, n° 140. Scottish Anonymous: London, British Library, Ms. Add. 4911, fol. 37.

28. Two puzzling inscriptions also appear next to the "score," apparently written by the same hand: "qui ínza" and "josquin" [?]

29. Tomlinson, "Ideologies of Aztec Songs," 368. Other "meaningless song syllables or vocables" like "ayao ayao o ayya yyao ay" also appear in the body of the songs. Tomlinson discusses and rejects the "meaningless" nature of these syllables on pages 368–70. His arguments are more fully developed in *The Singing of the New World*, chapter 3.

30. Tomlinson, "Ideologies of Aztec Songs," 373. On percussion cadences, see his *The Singing of the New World*, 42–45 and 87–90. On the *tocotin*, see Stevenson, *Music in Aztec and Inca territory*, 46–50 and 165. Another example of percussion syllables used in Mexican native songs from the Zapotec region is studied by Tavárez, "Cristo en la Sierra Norte," 209–14.

31. Arbeau, *Orchésographie*, fols. 9v-15r, available online at *Gallica*.

32. Gruzinski, *The Mestizo Mind*, 147.

33. On this point, see Levin Rojo and Navarrete, *Indios, mestizos y españoles*. This idea is also expressed in analogous terms by Geoffrey Baker, *Imposing Harmony*, 207, where he suggests that colonial musical culture in rural churches should be considered "less an instrument of domination or a cultural invasion by the Catholic Church than the result of negotiations between colonial religious authorities and Indigenous leaders."

Bibliography

Manuscript Sources

D-B, Berlin, Staatsbibliotek, Ms. Mus 40098

E-Mn, Madrid, Biblioteca Nacional de España, Ms. Vitr/26/11

F-Pn, Paris, Bibliothèque nationale de France, Ms. Latin 7211

GB-Lbl, London, British Library, Ms. Add. 4911

I-Fl, Florence, Biblioteca Medicea Laurenziana, Med.Palat. 218

PL-Kj, Kraków, Biblioteka Jagiellonska, Glogauer Liederbuch

US-BLl, Indiana University, Lilly Library, Music Mss. 1, 6, 10, 11

US-PRu, Princeton University Library, Garrett-Gates Mesoamerican Ms. 258

Printed Sources

Arbeau, Thoinot. *Orchésographie et traicté en forme de dialogue, par lequel toutes personnes peuvent facilement apprendre et practiquer l'honneste exercice des dances*. Langres: Jehan des Preys, 1589.

Baird, Sheila Raney. "*Santa Eulalia M.Md. 7*: A Critical Study and Edition of Sacred Part-Music from Colonial Guatemala." Master's thesis, North Texas State University, 1981.

Baker, Geoffrey. *Imposing Harmony: Music and Society in Colonial Cuzco*. Durham: Duke University Press, 2008.

Borg, Paul. "The Jacaltenango Miscellany: A Revised Catalogue." *Inter-American Music Review* 3 (1980): 55–64.

Borg, Paul. "The Polyphonic Music in the Guatemalan Music Manuscripts of the Lilly Library." PhD diss., Indiana University, 1985.

Borg, Paul. "Music Notation as Visual Culture: Examples from 17th-century Guatemala." Paper read at the Visual Culture Colloquium, School of Art, Illinois State University, August 8, 2007.

Canguilhem, Philippe. "The madrigal en route to Florence (1540–1545)." *Recercare* 21 (2009): 35–73.

Dutcher Mann, Kristin. *The Power of Song: Music and Dance in the Mission Communities of Northern New Spain, 1590–1810*. Stanford: Stanford University Press, 2010.

Fantini, Girolamo. *Modo per imparare a sonare di tromba*. Frankfurt: Daniel Vuastch, 1638.

de Fuentes y Guzmán, Francisco Antonio. *Recordacion florida*. Guatemala City: Tipografía nacional, 1933.

Garven, Richard O. "San Juan Ixcoi Mass: A Study of Liturgical Music in Northwestern Guatemala." Master's thesis, North Texas State University, 1979.

García Gómez, Arturo. "Música en la conquista espiritual de Tenochtitlan." *Acta musicologica* 85 (2013): 169–85.

Gruzinski, Serge. *The Mestizo Mind. The Intellectual Dynamics of Colonization and Globalization*, trans. Deke Desinberre. New York: Routledge, 2002.

Gumpelzhaimer, Adam. *Compendium musicae*. Augsburg: Schoenigius, 1611.

Hinz, Eike. *Existence and Identity: Reconciliation and Self-organization through Q'anjob'al Maya Divination*. Hamburg: the author, 2010.

La Farge, Oliver. *Santa Eulalia. The Religion of a Cuchumatán Indian Town*. Chicago: University of Chicago Press, 1947.

Lemmon, Alfred E., and Fernando Horcasitas. "El tratado de Santa Eulalia: un manuscrito musical náhuatl." *Tlalocan* 12 (1997): 71–116 [first ed. *Revista Musical Chilena* 34/152 (1980): 37–79].

Levin Rojo, Danna, and Federico Navarrete. *Indios, mestizos y españoles. Interculturalidad e historiografía en la Nueva España*. Mexico City: Universidad Autónoma Metropolitana, 2007.

Lovell, W. George. *Conquest and Survival in Colonial Guatemala. A Historical Geography of the Cuchumatán Highlands, 1500–1821*. Montreal and Ithaca: McGill-Queen's University Press, 2015. [Spanish translation: *Conquista y cambio cultural: La sierra de los Cuchumatanes de Guatemala 1500–1821*, trans. Eddy Gaytán. La Antigua: Centro de Investigaciones Regionales de Mesoamérica, 1990.]

Lovell, W.George, Christopher H. Lutz, Wendy Kramer, and William R. Swezey. *"Strange Lands and Different Peoples": Spaniards and Indians in Colonial Guatemala*. Norman: University of Oklahoma Press, 2013.

Marín López, Javier. "The musical inventory of Mexico cathedral, 1589: a lost document rediscovered." *Early Music* 36 (2008): 575–96.

Marín López, Javier. *Los libros de polifonía de la catedral de Mexico*. Jaén: Universidad de Jaén, 2012.

Marín López, Javier. "Musical Cultures in the Reinos de Indias at the Time of Isabel and Ferdinand." In *Companion to Music in the Age of the Catholic Monarchs,* ed. Tess Knighton. Pp. 324–63. Leiden and Boston: Brill, 2017.

Navarrete Pellicer, Sergio, ed. *Ritual sonoro en catedral y parroquias.* Mexico City: Ciesas, 2013.

Recopilación de las leyes de los reynos de las Indias. 3 vols. Madrid: Ediciones Cultura Hispanica, 1973.

Remesal, Antonio de. *Historia de la provincia de San Vincente de Chyapa y Guatemala de la orden de nuestro Glorioso Padre Sancto Domingo.* Madrid: Francisco de Angulo, 1619.

Stevenson, Robert. "European Music in 16th-Century Guatemala." *The Musical Quarterly* 50 (1964): 341–52.

Stevenson, Robert. *Music in Aztec and Inca Territory.* Berkeley and Los Angeles: University of California Press, 1968.

Stevenson, Robert. *Renaissance and Baroque Musical Sources in the Americas.* Washington D.C.: General Secretariat, Organization of American States, 1970.

Tavárez, David. "Cristo en la Sierra Norte: La reinterpretación del cristianismo en un género ritual y musical zapoteco." In Navarrete Pellicer, *Ritual sonoro en catedral y parroquias.* Pp. 203–29. Mexico City: Ciesas, 2013.

Tello, Aurelio. *Huellas musicales de San Diego Metepec, Tlaxcala. Una colección de manuscritos del siglo XVIII.* Tlaxcala: Instituto Tlaxcalteco de Cultura, 2013.

Tomlinson, Gary. "Ideologies of Aztec Songs." *Journal of the American Musicological Society* 48 (1995): 343–79.

Tomlinson, Gary. *The Singing of the New World. Indigenous Voice in the Era of European Contact.* Cambridge: Cambridge University Press, 2007.

van Oss, Adriaan C. *Catholic Colonialism: A Parish History of Guatemala: 1524–1821.* Cambridge: Cambridge University Press, 1986.

Waisman, Leonardo J. "La América española: proyecto y resistencia." In *Políticas y prácticas musicales en el mundo de Felipe II,* ed. John Griffiths and Javier Suárez-Pajares. Pp. 503–50. Madrid: IICMU, 2004.

Watkins, Timothy. "A New Source for Colonial Guatemalan Music: Princeton Garret-Gates MS. 258." Paper read at the Annual Meeting of the Society for Seventeenth-Century Music, Minneapolis, April 2011.

Watkins, Timothy. "Cultural and Musical Identities in Princeton Garret-Gates MS. 258." Paper read at the 19th Congress of the International Musicological Society, Rome, July 2012.

Gendered Geographies in Lully's *Proserpine* (1680)

Olivia Bloechl

Mobility and displacement were integral to early European opera. This is true of its production and casting, as composers, designers, instrumentalists, and singers often relocated to distant courts and theaters in support of opera productions.[1] Indeed, a growing body of research is revealing the transregional and even global range of these travels, as European opera artists and materials made their way to world cities via the great land and sea routes of the early modern period.[2] We are just beginning to integrate these extra-European opera centers into our sense of opera's geography before 1800, but Julia Prest's extensive database of performances in Saint-Domingue (Haiti), for example, suggests the need for similar documentation elsewhere.[3]

Geographic mobility also characterized opera's *storytelling* from the outset, as characters routinely moved between fictional settings in ways that mattered dramatically and, often, politically. It is this fictional mobility that I will explore here, focusing especially on the repertory of serious French operas (*tragédies en musique*) produced in the 1670s and 1680s by the royal opera company, the Académie Royale de Musique. At the helm of the king's academy (or Opéra, as it is often called) was the composer and impresario, Jean-Baptiste Lully, who, together with a team of other artists, produced roughly one new *tragédie* per year, which they programmed alongside revivals of older operas. Performances began with an extended prologue and proceeded through five fully sung, orchestrally accompanied acts, each with its own embedded choral and dance *fête* (the *divertissement*). Singers, choruses, and dancers were exquisitely costumed, and they worked their magic with sets and machines crafted by some of the finest designers in Europe.

Audiences engaged with operas' dramatic settings most immediately through these sets and machinery, as well as through scenic descriptions in printed librettos sold at the Palais Royal.[4] Normally the location of the plot action changed multiple times within a performance, and corresponding set changes were carried out in full view of the audience.[5] Librettists often called for the action to move locally within the fictional setting—say, from a garden to a public square—in ways that adhered loosely to the neo-Aristotelian principle of unity of place, which governed spoken tragedy.[6] However, Lully's librettists, especially his primary collaborator, Philippe Quinault, drew their subject matter mainly from mythology and (later) chivalric epic, and the protagonists of *these* stories tend to wander farther afield than the "rules" of tragedy prescribed. Taking advantage of Italian advances in scenic design and engineering, the creators of *tragédie* embraced this theatrical mobility, which reveled in characters' movement between familiar settings and marvelous ones and asked audiences to experience extraordinary places as possible worlds.[7]

The underworld was one of these marvelous settings. By the late 1660s, French productions of mythological *pastorales* and court ballets included spectacular *enfers* (as the French called underworld sets and scenes), something audiences also experienced in the Italian opera productions that Cardinal Mazarin had brought to Paris before and after the Fronde.[8] With the institution of annual French opera productions in the early 1670s (Lully received the license in 1672), the Opéra's machinists regularly repurposed the underworld set type, and sometimes actual sets, for *tragédies en musique* at court and at the Palais Royal in Paris. While infernal or magical settings appeared in many of Lully's operas and ballets, full-fledged descents to the underworld were included in only three of his *tragédies*: *Alceste* (1674), *Psyché* (1678), and *Proserpine* (1680). I will focus here on the last of these, *Proserpine*, a mythological opera whose set designs and action offer especially rich insight into the genre's spatial imaginary and its political stakes in Louis XIV's France.

Underworld settings were generally well-suited for Baroque opera because of the opportunities they offered for spectacle and technical marvels.[9] However, during the golden age of the *tragédie en musique* (from the 1670s through the 1730s) librettists sometimes turned to these hellish scenes as backdrops for stories and themes that were not at home to the genre's more realist locales, for aesthetic and political reasons. Elsewhere I have considered the underworld as a setting for this repertory's strain of biopolitical theater, which centers on heroic encounters with numinous figures possessing an outsized power over others' bodies and lives.[10] Dramatic encounters of this sort were often staged in the underworld because of its strong association with death and violence, a "dark side of politics" that debased the forms of power librettists could reasonably imagine there. Crossing the threshold of *les enfers* exposed characters like Orpheus, Psyche, Theseus, or Alcestis to the "left-sacred" side of the genre's clement princes, and their journeys plunged them into drastic experiences of sovereign violence, emergency rule, banishment, and sacrifice.

Interestingly, all three of Lully's operas with *enfers* center on female characters who travel to underworld realms. In Lully and Quinault's last essay on this trope, *Proserpine*, the creative team dramatized the rape of Proserpina, and they used this well-known myth to explore a specifically feminine experience of sovereign biopower. Quinault based the libretto of *Proserpine* mainly on Ovid's version of this myth in book 5 of the *Metamorphoses*, which had been edited, dramatized, and translated into French many times during the seventeenth century.[11] Although Quinault adhered closely to Ovid, he, Lully, and the royal designer Jean Bérain also adapted the tale to current tastes and social concerns, including concerns over the erotic and reproductive lives of noblewomen in the orbit of the king. Among the artists' creative adaptations was their choice to locate the opera's mythological action in pastoral and palatial settings that were relatively familiar to elite audience members, from previous theatrical productions and from life at court. They also organized the characters' movements within and between these settings in ways that created a gender-inflected hierarchy among them, by differentiating between each character's ability to transcend natural limits on space, time, and action.

Neoclassical opera, especially its courtly forms, tended to spatialize and spectacularize power, and this tendency is apparent in *Proserpine*'s organization of space. The *enfer* sets in acts 4–5 of *Proserpine* (see table 1) were key components of what Edward Said would have called its "imaginative geography." Said coined this term to describe "a way of making geographical distinctions that *can be* entirely arbitrary" but that nevertheless perform the important cultural work of designating "a familiar space which is 'ours' and an unfamiliar space beyond ours which is 'theirs'."[12] This "cultural work" of dividing the known world is sometimes discernible in the *tragédie*'s Orientalist treatment of far-flung realist settings in the Eastern Mediterranean (like Thrace or Damascus) and beyond (like Ethiopia, "Tauris," or Colchis). Most often, artists highlighted religious, legal, and political differences in representing French opera's real-world "elsewheres," but climatic and other period forms of racialism also inflected its geographical imaginary.

Said's framework is especially helpful for understanding the political significance of marvelous settings in mythological operas like *Proserpine*. As I have argued, we might think of these non-realist settings as establishing an imaginative political cosmography, or a make-believe order comprised of the genre's celestial, terrestrial, and infernal realms.[13] In *Proserpine*, the most important

Act, scene	Set description
1, 1	*Le Theatre represente le Palais de Ceres.*
1, 1	*Sur la fin de cette Feste on entend un tremblement de terre qui fait tomber une partie du Palais de Ceres.*
1, 1	*Le Tonnerre tombe sur le Mont* Ætna, *qui paroist dans l'esloignement; et ce coup acheve d'accabler le Chef des Geants, qui s'efforçoit de se relever.*
2, 1	*Le Theatre change, et represente les Jardins de Ceres.*
3, 1	*Le Theatre change, et represente le Mont* Ætna *vomissant des flâmes, et les lieux d'alentour.*
4, 1	*Le Theatre change, et represente les Champs Elysées*
5, 1	*Le Theatre change, et represente le Palais de Pluton*
5, 2	*Le Theatre change, et represente une Solitude.*
5, 5	*Le Ciel s'ouvre, et Jupiter paroist accompagné des Divinitez celetes.*

Table 1. Set descriptions in a *livret* for the court debut, Quinault/Lully, *Proserpine* (Paris: Christophe Ballard, 1680)

distinction is between the opera's infernal and celestial settings. The opera's negative characterization of Pluto's underworld created a strong moral and political contrast with its other realms, especially the idealized celestial realm presided over by the king of the gods, Jupiter.[14]

Baroque opera audiences generally loved spatial variety, which pressured librettists to arrange characters' mobility in ways that were entertaining but still adhered to rational precepts. Mobility between settings was a crucial element of the *tragédie*'s imaginative geographies, because it let artists and audiences assign differential meaning to the settings themselves and to the figures who move between them. Unlike in most *tragédies en musique*, the characters in *Proserpine* are exclusively supernatural, so they all enjoy the special license afforded to the actions and expression of gods by French poetics. However, even these exceptional characters related to one another in a nuanced hierarchy of rank and power, as was customary in courtly opera across Europe. Freedom of movement across realms was an important index of power in this opera's roving cosmic drama, yet only male gods could move between realms at will. By far the most visibly mobile characters are the messenger Mercury (acting on Jupiter's behalf) and Pluto, who readily moves between worlds together with his confident Ascalaphe (see table 2). In contrast, even the powerful earth goddess Ceres travels only within her own realm until Proserpina's apotheosis in the final scenes, and the other female characters move between realms involuntarily (Proserpina) or by permission of a male god (Arethuse).

Act, scene	Character(s)	Description of stage action
1, 2	Mercure	*Mercure descend du Ciel*
1, 2	Mercure	*Mercure...s'envole pour aller au Ciel retrouver Jupiter.*
1, 3	Cérès	*Ceres va voir Proserpine avant que de partir pour aller en Phyrgie.*
1, 7	Cérès	*Ceres sur son Char tiré par des Dragons aislez.*
1, 7	Cérès	*Ceres fait partir son Char volant.*
2, 9	Divinités infernales	*Une troupe de Divinitez infernales sort de la Terre, et le Char de Pluton paroist en mesme temps.*
2, 9	Pluton, Ascalaphe, Proserpine, Divinités infernales	*Pluton, Ascalaphe, et les Divinitez infernales, descendans aux Enfers avec Proserpine.*
3, 3	Nymphes et dieux de bois, Alphée, Arethuse, Cérès	*Les Nymphes et les Dieux de Bois se cachent, Alphée et Arethuse descendent aux Enfers, le Char volant de Ceres s'arreste, et la Déesse en descend.*
4, 3	Ascalaphe	*Ascalaphe se transforme en Hibou, et s'envole.*
5, 4	Alphée, Arethuse	*Alphée et Arethuse sortent des Enfers.*
5, 5	Mercure	*Mercure descend du Ciel.*
5, 5	Jupiter, Divinités celestes, Pluton, Proserpine, Cérès, Divinités infernales, Divinités de la Terre	*Le Ciel s'ouvre, et Jupiter paroist accompagné des Divinitez celestes. Pluton et Proserpine sortent des Enfers assis sur un Trône, ou Ceres va prendre place prés de sa Fille. Une Troupe de Divinitez Infernales richement parées, accompagnent Pluton. Et une Troupe de Divinitez de la Terre viennent prendre part à la joye de Ceres, et à la gloire de Proserpine.*

Table 2. Movement of characters and troupes between settings, according to descriptions of stage action in a *livret* for the court debut, Quinault/Lully, *Proserpine* (Paris: Christophe Ballard, 1680)

Spatial confinement and surveillance are also recurring themes in *Proserpine*, and they are similarly gendered, as I discuss below. For now, we might consider why the opera's creators assigned gendered meanings to mobility and constraint, and how this aspect of its imaginative geography related to the world audiences knew. Contemporary witnesses found a range of allegories in *Proserpine*, as several scholars have noted, mostly relating to royal and aristocratic marriages, as well as the king's treatment of his former mistresses and their children.[15] This emphasis on royal love and marriage makes sense, as the opera's court premiere was intended to celebrate the dauphin's wedding to Marie-Anne de Bavière. Although the opera was eventually performed before the new dauphine's arrival, dynastic marriage—especially in the patrilocal form practiced by Europe's royal families—would have been on everyone's minds as they watched *Proserpine*.[16]

The opera's themes of marriage, mobility, and power were thus legible partly through its allegorical references to current events. They also were easily rationalized by analogy with the patriarchal nature of French sovereignty, which in Louis XIV's time was justified through appeals to the "natural" male right of succession.[17] Sovereignty on the French model was masculine and reproductive, excluding women from any formal political role (except as regents) while nevertheless relying on them as diplomatic pawns and dynastic mothers.[18] Moreover, Louis' government increasingly sought to control his subjects' family lives, especially their marriage and sexuality, through a series of royal laws beginning with the pronatalist edict of 1666.[19] Although this history takes us well beyond my topic here, it does suggest how *Proserpine*'s fictions might also have resonated with day-to-day life beyond the elite circles where opera mattered most.

Despite the real-world resonances of its storytelling, French opera tended to engage the political most effectively not through reference to everyday life but through fantasy and feeling, as a kind of dream of the world of experience.[20] We modern opera lovers and scholars can also approach *Proserpine*'s imaginary from this phenomenological perspective, which potentially grants insight into non-rational aspects of its imaginary. In particular, thinking from the theatrical organization of space and spatial relations in *Proserpine* highlights its artistic engagement with several experiences of absolutist power: as forced mobility and constraint, as surveillance, as a disregard of boundaries, and as a potentially cataclysmic force.

Each of these forms of power is, moreover, patriarchal. Female characters are at the heart of *Proserpine*'s storytelling, and the power they confront is explicitly masculine and gender-based. We can see, hear, and—perhaps most importantly—feel this patriarchalism in how the opera's singers and troupes experience dramatic space, in modern productions as in early modern ones. In Lully and Quinault's time, the opera's performers enacted its source myth as a story of the displacement and confinement of noblewomen in patrilocal marriage, as a story of being monitored as a sexed body, and as a story of vulnerability to dispossession or violence in patriarchal spaces. I will focus on these themes in turn, before concluding with thoughts about the difference that gender makes in the opera's imaginative cosmology.

Dynastic marriage and its discontents

The royal wedding of the dauphin and dauphine was the event of the season in the spring of 1680, but other dynastic pairings also invited comparison with the match in *Proserpine*. As many have noted, the opera celebrates the

Fig. 1. *L'Alliance renouvellée entre la France et l'Espagne, par l'auguste mariage de Charles, IIe, Roy d'Espagne avec Marie Louise d'Orléans, fille aisnee de Monsieur* (Paris: la Veuve P. Bertrand, [1680])

treaties of Nijmegen, which brought an end to the Dutch Wars, and the peace provisions included an arranged marriage between Louis XIV's niece, Marie-Louise d'Orléans, and the Hapsburg king of Spain, Charles II.[21] The young

Marie-Louise begged Louis XIV, her uncle, not to send her far from home in marriage to a man known to have significant impairments, and Madame de Sévigné described the dramatic scenes that played out at court as the princess sought support:

> The queen of Spain [Marie-Louise d'Orléans] cries endlessly for mercy, and throws herself at everyone's feet; I don't know how Spanish pride puts up with all this despair. She held up the King the other day past the time for mass; he said to her: "Madame, it would be a fine thing if the Catholic Queen prevented the Most Christian King from going to mass."[22]

Royal almanacs commemorating Marie-Louise's marriage in August and September, 1679, depicted its key events, including her tearful farewells, wedding procession, proxy marriage at Fontainebleau, and reception in Burgos.[23] One almanac for 1680, *L'Alliance renouvellée entre la France et l'Espagne*, stressed the diplomatic advantages of the match for France, and the engraver underlined this theme with an allegorical grouping featuring Ceres as "l'Abondance" offering her gifts to "la France" and "l'Espagne," shown as two royal women clasped in an embrace (figure 1).[24]

Buford Norman points out that Quinault would certainly have known of Marie-Louise's forced marriage as he worked on the libretto the fall and winter of 1679–1680, and he speculates that "it is quite possible that this marriage played a role in the choice of the subject of the new opera."[25] The almanac's allegorical use of Ceres is certainly consistent with Quinault's treatment of this character: after dramatizing Ceres's resistance to her daughter's fate, the poet includes her in the final apotheosis, seated in glory alongside the married pair, Pluto and Proserpina.[26]

Anne Duggan likewise finds in Quinault's libretto an allegorical treatment of patrilocal diplomatic marriages, like that of Louis XIV's niece. "Marie-Louise's displacement south of the border," she writes, "is allegorized in Proserpine forcibly having to reside in Hades." However, she also finds strikingly different treatments of diplomatic marriage in the period's literary fairy tales (or *contes de fées*), a female-authored salon genre that was influenced by the Opéra's productions.[27] Among the best-known contemporary fairy tales were those by Madame d'Aulnoy, a noblewoman who had herself been given in an arranged marriage at the age of fifteen. D'Aulnoy's story "Babiole" (1697) centers on a magically disguised princess who refuses to enter a diplomatic arranged marriage with the ape king, Magot; and Duggan argues that, with tales like this, "d'Aulnoy seems to rewrite stories like that of Marie-Louise [d'Orléans], the princess sacrificed to a monster to end a war."[28]

D'Aulnoy and other female authors of fairy tales of the 1690s and early 1700s inherited a skepticism toward dynastic marriage from the salon writers of the Fronde generation, including Madeleine de Scudéry and the exiled princess known at court as "La Grande Mademoiselle," Anne-Marie-Louise-Henriette d'Orléans, Duchesse de Montpensier.[29] Like Scudéry before her, Montpensier viewed aristocratic marriage as, in the words of her friend, Madame de Motteville, "an honorable slavery that the Church dignifies by calling it a sacrament."[30] Among the princess's writings were pastoral utopias whose woman-centered communities prioritized friendship and placed strict limits on marriage: imagined communities that closely resembled the exilic "counter-court" that she created with her friends at her estate of Saint-Fargeau.[31] Juliette Cherbuliez argues that these pastoral elsewheres offered an alternative to the "social aesthetics of constrained space and people" that Louis XIV had created by regulating noble presence and absence at court, whether through royals summons, domestic exile, or arranged marriage.[32]

Quinault was himself a former *salonnier* and as such was steeped in this sort of pastoral fantasy during his formative years as a poet. A protegé of Tristan l'Hermite, Quinault was supported by the Parisian salons in the 1650s and was influenced throughout his career by the sentimental novels and other genres that they favored.[33] Patricia Ranum points out that the salon theme of freedom from marriage and romantic attachments to men recurred in Quinault's librettos, as in *Isis* (1677) and *Proserpine*.[34] Choruses in praise of "la liberté" (freedom) are prominent in both operas, voicing an indifference to opposite-sex love that salon writers had championed for several decades.[35]

However, *Proserpine* debuted in 1680, not 1660, and in the intervening years the *salonnières'* vision of a gentle society of friends was the target of both social and literary backlashes.[36] By the last quarter of the century Quinault himself was also playing for bigger stakes than the approval of the salons. He had been named a member of the exclusively male Académie Française in 1670 and, in 1674, was invited to join Colbert's Académie des Inscriptions et Médailles (the *petite Académie*), a working group established to review public representations of the reign. When he served as the main librettist for Lully's opera productions, then, Quinault took on the challenging task of pleasing the public, including *mondain* circles in Paris and at court, while serving the king.

These competing pressures help to explain Quinault's handling of pastoral spaces and their relationship to the opera's courtly settings. The most important pastoral setting is Ceres's gardens ("Les Jardins de Cérès"), where Proserpina and her nymphs amuse themselves with a *fête* while her mother is away. Ceres's gardens are a feminized dramatic space, and, as was often true of Lullian opera settings, their layout and social meanings echoed those of real-life spaces familiar to members of the court: in this case, the king's own gardens.

Les Jardins de Cérès

Act 2 of *Proserpine* is set in Ceres's garden, a bucolic space that Quinault took directly from Ovid.[37] In the sixth scene, the nymph Arethusa describes the garden as a place set apart from the previous act's palatial setting ("Le Palais de Cérès"/ Ceres's palace), where Proserpina finds respite from the court and the other gods:

> Dans l'innocent repos de cette solitude
> Elle évite les dieux
> De la terre et les cieux:[38]
>
> [In the innocent repose of this solitary retreat / She avoids the gods / Of the earth and the heavens:]

Other characters describe the goddess's garden as a "beau séjour" (Crinise, 2.1) and a "lieu charmant" (Pluton, 2.6), and Lully reinforced these descriptions with his music for the nymphs' *fête* (2.8). Drawing on his five-part orchestra and a *concertante* trio of oboes, Lully gave the nymphs a pair of instrumental dances interspersed with vocal numbers for Proserpina and a *petit chœur* of high-voiced singers (G2, C1, C3).[39] His use of parallel thirds/sixths, oboes, and gavotte dance rhythms was appropriate for this pastoral *fête*, and the choice of a high tessitura for the choral and oboe passages underlined the feminine character of the garden setting and its community.[40]

The nymphs' verses celebrate freedom from love and voice their determination to escape its sorrows:

> Pour nous défendre
> D'un amour tendre
> Avec fierté,
> Nous avons pris les armes;
> Nos biens n'ont point coûté
> De tristes larmes,

La liberté
N'a jamais que des charmes.[41]

[In order to defend ourselves / against tender love /with dignity, / we took up arms; / our pleasures cost us / no sad tears, / freedom / has only charms.]

Proserpina herself has similar sentiments in the scene's solo-choral exchanges. As was often true of Quinault's festive verse, Proserpina's lines are a series of maxims that she exchanges with the nymphs in their vocal gavotte. (Her first couplet gives a sense of the verse: "Belles fleurs, charmant ombrage, / Il ne faut aimer que vous" [Lovely flowers, charming glade, / One must love nothing but you].) With this scene, Quinault transposed the salon posture of *l'indifférence* into an ethos governing the *fête*.

Like other pastoral spaces in mythological *tragédies en musique*, Ceres's garden is "a peaceful, verdant setting" symbolically opposed to "the dangers and marvels of mythological places and characters put into motion by machines."[42] In reality these other "places and characters" were never very far removed from spectators' experience. The machines that transported magical characters regularly entered its pastoral sets, most often carrying a singer impersonating a god. *Proserpine*'s pastoral act also culminates in a god's entrance, but not one of the celestial Olympians (e.g., Jupiter, Diana, or Venus) who usually descend in splendor. In this case, the god Pluto enters Ceres's garden surreptitiously, and his hidden presence at the edge of the garden and its *fête* is felt as a menace to the nymphs' freedom.

Midway through act 3, Pluto enters Ceres's garden and manages to catch a glimpse of Proserpina. Quinault's stage description has Pluto and his confidante Ascalaphe hiding behind onstage bushes, in order to watch the goddess and her companions dancing and singing in the *fête*.[43] This prolonged surveillance does not appear in the *Metamorphoses*—there, Pluto gives Proserpina a swift, desiring look ("paene simil visa est dilectaque raptaque Diti:")—which suggests that Quinault inserted it to maintain dramatic tension during the *divertissement*.[44] One effect of this decision was to introduce spectators onstage, always a metatheatrical gesture and one that, in the Palais Royal, would have echoed the practice of seating real spectators on either side of the stage. In this case, the gods' onstage surveillance introduced a specifically masculine model of spectatorship that allowed audience members identifying with the male characters to vicariously experience the desiring gaze and listening of the gods, and identify with their assertion of control over the

Fig. 2. Atelier of Jean Bérain, pen and ink drawing with watercolor, engraved as one of two frontispieces for Philippe Quinault, *Proserpine* (Paris: Christophe Ballard, 1680). Paris, Bibliothèque nationale de France

garden and its users. (Earlier in the act, Pluto described just such an experience of watching and hearing Proserpina in a dialogue with Ascalaphe.) In contrast, for female-identified spectators the scene set by Quinault held no viable spectator position, but only the objective one of being watched and overheard by a menacing presence.

The introduction of predatory surveillance into Ceres's garden is in keeping with the Ovidian landscape tradition, in which the peace and sensual fullness of pastoral idylls presage violent disruption.[45] As Stephen Hind puts it, Ovid wove his plots of predation into "the ideal landscape's potential to turn frightening and uncontrollable when... its groves thicken into pathless forests, its shade into darkness, its inherent numinousness into menace."[46] Yet the staged experience of being surveilled in *Proserpine*'s act 2 also belonged to the seventeenth-century present, whether as the quotidian gendered experience of sexual predation, courtiers' experience of being monitored at every turn, or the experience of royal governmental control common to many social groups in Louis XIV's France.[47]

One such experience, of royal control over natural landscapes and their users, would have been familiar to anyone who had visited the formal gardens of the king's chateaus.[48] In fact, the Opéra's designers sometimes referred to the king's gardens in their sets and backdrops, and the pastoral setting of Ceres's garden was linked in this way to the landscaping works underway at Versailles.[49] One of Bérain's frontispieces for *Proserpine*'s 1680 librettos showed the opera's key event, Pluto's kidnapping of Proserpina (act 2), unfolding in a formal garden that resembles Versailles' fountains dedicated to the seasons, especially the *bassin de Cérès* (1672, allegorizing summer) (see figure 2).[50] Like the chateau's other waterworks, the fountains of the seasons were controlled through a precise whistle system, so that the king would be able to enjoy their beauty whenever he passed by, despite the water shortages that plagued his engineers.[51] Through the artificial magic of pumps, windmills, and whistles, Versailles' workers imposed order on the chateau's landscape so the king could enjoy privileged access to its beauties, unhampered by natural constraints. Bérain's frontispiece reminded readers of the king's real-life mastery over pastoral settings like those in *Proserpine*, while warning of the violence and disorder lurking at its boundaries.

Mastering space and sound

Like the king in his castle, only the most powerful or magical characters in *tragédies en musique* have full mastery over the genre's dramatic settings. Some cross between its cosmic realms with ease, while others do so with the help of magical aids or more powerful characters who can carry them from place to place. Regardless, crossing the threshold between operatic worlds was always an extraordinary action, because it involved moving characters between immanent and transcendent stage realities. Gary Tomlinson notes a "circumscribing of theatrical space" in the scenic design of seventeenth-century Italian opera that, he argues, "reflects...the emergence of early modern [European] subjectivity and its novel relation to metaphysical regions." Among other changes, he finds a clearer demarcation of boundaries between "physical and metaphysical" spaces in Giacomo Torelli's pastoral sets for Venice, where stage machinery enabled transitions between what were now distinct, if still contiguous realms.[52]

Torelli's scenography influenced French opera directly through his mid-century designs for Paris, and *tragédies en musique* also used machines as well as transitional music (*entr'actes*) to dramatize movement to and from magical realms.[53] Claude-François Ménestrier explained this use of machines in his 1681 treatise on musical theater, *Des Représentations en musique anciennes et modernes*. "Machines," he wrote, "are a great aid to this [type of] marvel, because all at once they let [it] pass from the earth to Heaven, from the Sea to the Underworld, from Heaven to Earth, from a Garden, and from a Forest into a Wilderness, from a Palace, to an Arsenal, etc."[54] Transport machines abound in *Proserpine*, as when Ceres comes and goes in her dragon cart. But the most spectacular one by far is Pluto's chariot in act 2, which according to the libretto erupted into Ceres's garden from below stage before descending again into Hades carrying Pluto, Proserpina, and the "Divinités infernales."[55]

The entrance of Pluto with his retinues asserts a jurisdiction over Ceres's garden just as surely as he asserts control over Proserpina by removing her to *les enfers*. It is hard to overstate how shocking this abduction would have been in the context of a genre that normally avoided onstage violence, even though audience members would have known the story. Sylvie Bouissou labels this type of action a "catastrophe lyrique," and one of the places where such exceptional irruptions of violence could occur was at the boundaries between opera's realms.[56] As Martha Feldman has argued in the context of opera seria, liminal spaces let singers and other artists suspend "normal time and action" in order to play out myths of origins:

> In its widest interpretation, myth here suggests how things in the present first came into existence and showed themselves: codes of behavior, forms of power, the social order, and the institutions that sustain it. The stories of opera seria

Example 1. Jean-Baptiste Lully, *Proserpine* (Paris: Christophe Ballard, 1680), act 2, scene 9

> present models of what those who know the tale in the present can hope to "master" and "manipulate" as a result of that knowledge. And yet...the tales of opera seria, like other myths, were not learned primarily as content but as feeling, feeling internalized through the expressive power of a ceremonial recitation, itself justified by the myth.[57]

In *Proserpine*, the boundary between Ceres's garden and *les enfers*—at the Palais Royal, the trap door leading to the area below stage—let the artists play out a violent tale about the origins of patriarchal sovereign government, presented in its barest form as the capture of women's bodily life as means to an end.

Despite the spectacular display of violence in *Proserpine*, it has the form of an open secret: known to witnesses (both onstage and in the audience) but kept from public acknowledgment because of the scandalous nature of violence by a ruler figure, particularly against innocent characters. However, Quinault did allow onstage figures and groups to express a range of feeling in response to Pluto's actions, including the negative effects of fear, horror, and despair. In act 3, for instance, Ceres and the chorus have an extended lament sequence, and Quinault even incorporated a voice of protest in the act 2 kidnapping scene itself. There Cyane, a Sicilian nymph and Ceres's confidant, responds to the violence with horrified outrage, which later makes her a target of retribution:

> CYANÉ, *retenant Proserpine*
> Quelle barbare violence!
>
> PLUTON
> Nymphe, crains ma vengeance:
> Sur peine de perdre la voix
> Garde-toi de parler de tout ce que tu vois.[58]
>
> [CYANE, *restraining Proserpina*: What barbarous violence! / PLUTO: Nymph, fear my vengeance: / on pain of losing your voice, / say nothing about what you see.]

Lully set Cyane's brief protest as a triadic fusillade of a melody whose harmonic support tries unsuccessfully to move away from C, a key that Pluto had appropriated from the preceding *fête* (see example 1). Nevertheless, her outrage, as well as that expressed by Ceres (in act 3) and by Proserpina herself (in act 4), contrasts with the response modeled in several solo and group numbers extolling the erotic surrender of women to male suitors, especially powerful ones. The most succinct (and catchy) response is a maxim sung over and over by "Ombres Heureuses" (Happy Ghosts) in the underworld:

> Aimez qui vous aime,
> Rien n'est si charment.[59]
>
> [Love the one who loves you, / Nothing is as charming.]

Although Proserpina is unimpressed by the advice of the Ghosts, the theatrical power of numbers like these lay in their pleasurable, repetitive delivery in easily remembered group song, which invited feelings of communality and commonsense among spectators. Telling the truth about Pluto's violence is generally suppressed in the opera (in Cyane's case, dramatically so), despite a shared knowledge of what has happened. Instead, personas and groups struggle over how to feel and comport themselves in response to the violence revealed at the edges of their world.

Conclusion

After Proserpina's kidnapping in act 2, her voice is never again heard on earth. The last word she sings in her mother's garden is "innocence," in her plea for protection ("O Ciel! protegez l'innocence") [O Heaven! protect innocence].[60] Although her vocal role continues through act 4, its action takes place in the underworld. Moreover, near the end of act 4 and throughout act 5 Proserpina is gradually silenced as she becomes an object of celebration in the last two *divertissements*.

Cyane too loses her voice, in keeping with Ovid's tale. Her backstory is, if anything, more violent than Proserpina's, and Quinault retained a vestige of this patriarchal brutality in the dissolution scene in act 3. When Cyane tries to tell Ceres who kidnapped Proserpina (in act 3, scene 6), her recitative breaks off mid-line, and it is left to the chorus to narrate her fate: "Cyané perd la voix et n'est plus qu'un Ruisseau" (Cyane has lost her voice and is no more than a brook).[61] This episode of Proserpina's tale was reproduced many times over in visual art of the seventeenth century, suggesting its cultural importance.

Her pastoral companions also find that their voices are not powerful enough to overcome Pluto's actions. At the opening of act 3, they sing an echo chorus while they search for Proserpina, but it ends in despair, as they hear nothing except the sound of their own echoed voices: "Proserpine? ah faut-il qu'en vain (en vain) on vous appelle?" [Proserpina? Ah, must we call you in vain (in vain)?].[62] Lully altered certain of the chorus's repeated words to imply an answer to its questioning, so that the chorus itself repeats the words "en vain," softly and without orchestral support. Like Orpheus's exchange with Echo in Claudio Monteverdi's *Orfeo,* the chorus's vocal appeal to the pastoral world as a source of presence and repair fails audibly and in real time.[63] Instead, it demonstrates the limited powers of its own song, even despite the mechanical "supplement" of Lully's formidable orchestra, which abandons the singers.[64]

With all this silencing and failure, the role of Ceres comes as a relief. Her character has plenty to say about her former lover (Jupiter) and his brother (Pluto), some of it scathing and much of it very moving. (Laura Naudeix is right when she argues that her character is the central one of the opera.)[65] Yet Ceres is also limited in ways that are relevant to the opera's spatial imaginary. She never crosses into the underworld to go after her daughter, but instead remains mainly on earth, as was fitting for an earth deity. It is true that she travels in a dragon-drawn chariot, probably the same one that the character of Medea had used in Quinault and Lully's *Thésée* five years earlier. Ceres's flying chariot also anticipated those used by magical characters in *tragédies* of the 1680s and 1690s, especially Armida and Medea.[66] Unlike the divine Ceres, though, these are heroines drawn from romance and placed in more realistic (though still magical) settings than the mythological realms of *Proserpine*. Their powers are also more occult and threatening. After all, they congress freely with underworld powers, travel at will between fantastic and natural settings, and, as Susan McClary has noted, avoid the consequences of their actions by escaping in their flying machines.[67] In the process, they wreak havoc on the martial, diplomatic, and dynastic projects of the men around them.

Proserpine was a different kind of opera, created for a different moment of the reign. It was practically a hymn to diplomatic marriage, despite the upheaval of its first three acts. In its final scene, the gods of the three realms ("l'enfer, la terre, et les cieux") assemble to witness the marriage of Proserpina and Pluto, and Bérain's set placed them in a cosmic hierarchy, with the divine couple enthroned at its center. Lully represented this cosmography musically with a triple chorus ("Que l'on enchaîne pour jamais") comprised of "celestial deities who sing in the [upper] machines" and two "troupes of singing terrestrial and infernal deities" on the stage, joined by a group of instrumentalists costumed as celestial gods. On the chorus's third line, "Dans les enfers, dans les cieux, sur la terre" (In Hades, in the heavens, on earth), Lully subdivided the singers into antiphonal groups with contrasting tessituras, audibly reinforcing the spatial order onstage.

This lieto fine, with its tableau of a carefully ordered cosmos, enshrines dynastic marriage as the ideal outcome of conflict, rape, and "homosocial rivalry" among male rulers.[68] Like most political theologies, though, *Proserpine*'s glorification of marriage rests on a sacrifice, in this case one that its creators played out literally in Proserpina's descent to the underworld. Her character's journey dramatized, in the hyperbolic, affective mode of fantasy, the experience of aristocratic women, whose bodily lives were so routinely taken up by the patriarchal family and state, as value and a means to an end.

I have argued that librettists in the French tradition used the underworld descent and its set types to dramatize violent and otherwise indecorous aspects of political life without offending verisimilitude.[69] In this way, Quinault and his successors were able to displace the monstrous, death-dealing capacity of absolutist sovereignty from the terrestrial and celestial settings of most scenes to, in Said's words, "an unfamiliar space beyond ours which is 'theirs'," namely the underworld of the dead.[70] For *Proserpine*'s female protagonists, the cosmos is also divided into "a familiar space which is 'ours' and an unfamiliar space beyond ours which is 'theirs'," as Said has it, except that for much of the opera the distinction of "us" from "them" rests on gender.

If Proserpina's descent, then, stressed a different kind of sacrifice than that depicted in the underworld tales of a Hercules, Orpheus, or Theseus, its creators nonetheless preserved the basic dramatic structure of a confrontation with the most menacing aspect of sovereign power, as the French knew it. The difference is that Proserpina's descent addressed the most menacing aspect of sovereignty *for women*. When the singer creating Proserpina sang to Pluto, in act 4, that even his cleaned-up underworld is a "hell" for her, she communicated an experience that many women in attendance would have understood too well. Unlike in the opera, I will give her poignant arioso the final word:

> Mon triste cœur ne peut connaître
> La douceur des appas qu'on voit ici paraître,
> Hélas! ces lieux si beaux où je frémis d'effroi
> Sont toujours les Enfers pour moi.[71]
>
> [My sad heart cannot know / The sweetness of the charms revealed to the sight here, / Alas! these places, so beautiful, where I tremble with fright / Are still a hell for me.]

Notes

1. Marvin and Thomas, eds. *Operatic Migrations*; and Stein, "How Opera Traveled," 843–61.

2. Brito, "Portugal and Brazil," 233–43; Stein and Leza, "Opera, Genre, and Context"; and Prest, "*Iphigénie en Haïti.*"

3. Prest, "Theatre in Saint-Domingue." Most colonial opera houses were not founded until the nineteenth century, before which European-style opera and musical theater was often performed by itinerant troupes. See Yamomo, "Global Currents, Musical Streams."

4. As Calhoun argues, "Like the spectator facing the pastoral setting, the libretto reader is being asked, as soon as the *didascalie*, to be a complicit participant in a fictional world that is man-made...but nevertheless coherent and possible." Calhoun, "Architecture of Arcadia," 119. On scenography in this tradition see also Naudeix, *Dramaturgie de la tragédie en musique.*

5. Coeyman, "Opera and Ballet"; and Ferrero, "Stage and Set."

6. Lyons, *Kingdom of Disorder*; Thomas, *Aesthetics of Opera*; Kintzler, *Poétique de l'opéra française.*

7. Kintzler, *Poétique de l'opéra française*, 295, 520–23.

8. Powell, *Music and Theatre*, 21–28, 230–42. The underworld featured prominently in one of the first operas staged in the kingdom, Luigi Rossi's *Orfeo* (1647), though the Parisian public was already familiar with underworld settings from mythological machine plays of the 1630s. Cardinal Mazarin's last opera commission, Francesco Cavalli's *Ercole amante* (1661), also included an *enfer* that Louis XIV ordered reused a decade later for the *tragédie-ballet Psyché* (1671).

9. As Ménestrier wrote in 1681, subjects drawn from "fables" were better suited to the operatic stage "parce qu'il y entre plus de machines extraordinaires, & de decorations, des Cieux ouverts, des Enfers, des Mers, des Naufrages, des nuées...." Ménestrier, *Représentations*, 239.

10. Bloechl, *Opera and the Political Imaginary*, 156–203.

11. Gros, *Philippe Quinault*, 544–52; Apostolidès, *Roi-machine*, 79; Néraudau, *L'Olympe du roi soleil*, 16–18; Norman, *Touched by the Graces*, 214–36.

12. Said, *Orientalism*, 54.

13. Bloechl, *Opera and the Political Imaginary*, 157–59. Naudeix discusses the *tragédie*'s cosmos in *Dramaturgie de la tragédie en musique*; and Naudeix, "Proserpine au croisement des mondes."

14. See also the discussion of Pluto in Cowart, *Triumph of Pleasure*, 39–40, 146–47.

15. Research on allegories in *Proserpine* includes Norman, *Touched by the Graces*, 222–27; Duggan, "Women and Absolutism," 309; and Norman, "Rôle de la femme."

16. The court premiere was on February 3, and the dauphine did not arrive until March. Norman, *Touched by the Graces*, 214–15.

17. See Hanley, "Salic Law, " 15; and Hanley, "Family, the State, and the Law."

18. Hanley, "Engendering the State"; Merrick, "Fathers and Kings"; and Hanley, "Monarchic State."

19. Tuttle, *Conceiving the Old Regime.*

20. Bloechl, *Opera and the Political Imaginary*, x-xiii.

21. Norman, *Touched by the Graces*, 50–51.

22. Marie de Rabutin-Chantal, marquise de Sévigné, to Françoise-Marguerite de Sévigné, comtesse de Grignan, Sept. 18, 1679, in Sévigné, *Correspondance*, 2:680. My translation. Cited in Norman, *Touched by the Graces*, 229.

23. Her emotional departure is commemorated in a vignette, "Les Adieux de la Reine d'Espagne," included with Jean Lepautre's engraved almanac, *La Célèbre et auguste cérémonie du mariage du Roi d'Espagne avec Mademoiselle....*

24. Larmessin, *L'Alliance renouvellée entre la France et l'Espagne.*

25. Norman, *Touched by the Graces*, 229.

26. "Pluton et Proserpine sortent des Enfers assis sur un Trône, ou Ceres va prendre place prés de sa Fille." Quinault, *Proserpine*, 65.

27. Duggan, *Salonnières, Furies, and Fairies*, 223–30.

28. Ibid., 231–32.

29. See DeJean, *Tender Geographies*; Duggan, *Salonnières, Furies, and Fairies*; Goldsmith, "*Galant* Culture," 98–100.

30. Montpensier, *Against Marriage*, 63.

31. Ibid., 18. See also Cherbuliez, *Place of Exile*, 42–107; and Arenberg, "Idyllic Spaces."

32. Cherbuliez, *Place of Exile*, 43.

33. Gros, *Philippe Quinault*, 18; Howard, "Influence of the *Précieuses*"; Howard, "Quinault, Lully, and the *Précieuses*"; and Brooks, *Philippe Quinault*, 157–61.

34. Howard, "Influence of the *Précieuses*," 60.

35. Ray also reads Proserpina as a tragic version of *L'Indifférente* (the "Indifferent Woman") whom, she finds, had also appeared in older court ballets and comedies and reappeared in the opéra-ballets and cantatas of the early eighteenth century. Ray, "Savage Love."

36. This is documented in a number of studies, but Ray summarizes these reactions in the context of music and musical theater, in "Savage Love," 583–84.

37. Gros stresses the extent to which Quinault took his cues for *Proserpine*'s settings from Ovid, in *Philippe Quinault*, 551–52.

38. Quinault, *Proserpine*, 26.

39. The libretto for the court premiere lists eight male dancers in the troupe of "Nymphes dançantes," and it lists fourteen singing nymphs in the *petit chœur*, of whom only five were female singers. The remaining nine male singers presumably took the lower two vocal parts. Ibid., 28, 33.

40. This feminine character is not undermined by the mixed-gender chorus. The high tessitura of their music associated it with women's voices, as the French did not use castratos in opera. Also, every early image of this scene shows the nymphs in feminine costumes, suggesting that the chorus was either costumed as such or accepted as feminine despite its mixed-gender makeup.

41. Quinault, *Proserpine*, 32.

42. Calhoun, "Architecture of Arcadia," 117.

43. "Pluton et Ascalaphe se retirent et se cachent, et Proserpine et ses nymphes s'avancent en dançant et en chantant." Quinault, *Proserpine*, 29.

44. Ovid, *Metamorphoses*, V: 395.

45. Segal, *Landscape in Ovid's Metamorphoses*; and Johnson, *Ovid Before Exile*, 67–68.

46. Hinds, "Landscape with Figures," 132.

47. For example, see Foucault's analysis of royal efforts to curb plague outbreaks as a nascent panopticism, in Foucault, *Discipline and Punish*, 195–228.

48. See Mukerji, *Territorial Ambitions*.

49. La Gorce, *Carlo Vigarani*, 131.

50. The *bassin* was flanked by grand verdant arches with perspectival vistas, like the garden shown in Bérain's frontispiece. See the engraving of the *bassin de Cérès* created by the Pérelle family in the late seventeenth century, reproduced in Garrigues, *Jardins et jardiniers de Versailles*, 271.

51. "Ordre à observer pour les fontaines de Versailles," F-Pan, O1 1854, 1, published in Mousset, *Les Francine*, 86–88.

52. Tomlinson, *Metaphysical Song*, 68–72. See also Glixon and Glixon, *Inventing the Business of Opera*, 227–76; and Ferrero, "Stage and Set."

53. Bjurström, *Giacomo Torelli*.

54. "Les Machines sont d'un grand secours pour ce merveilleux, parce que tout d'un coup elles font passer de la terre au Ciel, de la Mer aux Enfers, du Ciel en Terre, d'un Jardin, & d'une Forest dans un Désert, d'un Palais dans un Arsenal, &c." Ménestrier, *Représentations*, 263–64.

55. Quinault, *Proserpine*, 33–34.

56. Bouissou, *Crimes, cataclysmes, et maléfices*.

57. Feldman, *Opera and Sovereignty*, 32–33.

58. Quinault, *Proserpine*, 33.

59. Ibid., 48.

60. Ibid., 34.

61. Ibid., 41.

62. Ibid., 35.

63. On the echo scene in *L'Orfeo*, see Chua, "Untimely Reflections"; and Gordon, "Orfeo's Machines."

64. Gordon, "Orfeo's Machines," 216.

65. Naudeix, "*Proserpine*," 42.

66. These characters appeared in Quinault and Lully, *Armide* (1686), and in Corneille and Charpentier, *Medée* (1693).

67. McClary, *Desire and Pleasure*, 258–74.
68. Stanton, *Dynamics of Gender*, 74.
69. Bloechl, *Opera and the Political Imaginary*, 171–73.
70. Said, *Orientalism*, 54.
71. Quinault, *Proserpine*, 52.

Bibliography

Apostolidès, Jean-Marie. *Le Roi-machine: Spectacle et politique au temps de Louis XIV*. Paris: Editions de Minuit, 1981.

Arenberg, Nancy. "Idyllic Spaces: Marriage and Politics in the Montpensier-Motteville Correspondence." *Papers on Seventeenth-Century French Literature* 40 (2013): 65–79.

Bjurström, Per. *Giacomo Torelli and Baroque Stage Design*. Stockholm: Almquist & Wiksell, 1961.

Bloechl, Olivia. *Opera and the Political Imaginary in Old Regime France*. Chicago: University of Chicago Press, 2018.

Bouissou, Sylvie. *Crimes, cataclysmes, et maléfices dans l'opéra baroque en France*. Paris: Minerve, 2011.

Brito, Manuel Carlos de. "Portugal and Brazil." In *The Cambridge Companion to Eighteenth-Century Opera*, ed. Anthony R. DelDonna and Pierpaolo Polzonetti. Pp. 233–43. Cambridge: Cambridge University Press, 2009.

Brooks, William. *Philippe Quinault, Dramatist*. Oxford: Peter Lang, 2009.

Calhoun, Alison. "The Architecture of Arcadia: Quinault, Lully, and the Complicit Spectator of the *Tragédie en Musique*." *Seventeenth-Century French Studies* 33 (2011): 114–26.

Cherbuliez, Juliette. *The Place of Exile: Leisure Literature and the Limits of Absolutism*. Lewisburg, PA: Bucknell University Press/Rosemont, 2005.

Chua, Daniel K. L. "Untimely Reflections on Operatic Echoes: How Sound Travels in Monteverdi's *L'Orfeo* and Beethoven's *Fidelio* with a Short Instrumental Interlude." *The Opera Quarterly* 21 (2005): 573–96.

Coeyman, Barbara. "Opera and Ballet in Seventeenth-Century French Theaters: Case Studies of the Salle des Machines and the Palais Royal Theater." In *Opera in Context: Essays on Historical Staging from the Late Renaissance to the Time of Puccini*, ed. Mark A. Radice. Pp. 37–72. Portland, OR: Amadeus, 1998.

Cowart, Georgia. *The Triumph of Pleasure: Louis XIV and the Politics of Spectacle*. Chicago: University of Chicago, 2008.

DeJean, Joan. *Tender Geographies: Women and the Origins of the Novel in France*. New York: Columbia University Press, 1991.

Duggan, Anne E. "Women and Absolutism in French Opera and Fairy Tale." *The French Review* 78 (2004): 302–15.

Duggan, Anne E. *Salonnières, Furies, and Fairies: The Politics of Gender and Cultural Change in Absolutist France*. Newark, NJ: University of Delaware Press/Rosemont, 2005.

Feldman, Martha. *Opera and Sovereignty*. Chicago: Chicago University Press, 2007.

Ferrero, Mercedes Viale. "Stage and Set." In *Opera on Stage*, ed. Lorenzo Bianconi and Giorgio Pestelli, tr. Kate Singleton. Pp. 1–69. Chicago: University of Chicago Press, 2002.

Foucault, Michel. *Discipline and Punish: The Birth of the Prison*, tr. Alan Sheridan. 2d. ed. New York: Vintage Books, 1995.

Garrigues, Dominique. *Jardins et jardiniers de Versailles au grand siècle*. Seyssel: Champ Vallon, 2001.

Glixon, Beth, and Jonathan Glixon. *Inventing the Business of Opera*. Oxford: Oxford University Press, 2006.

Goldsmith, Elizabeth C. "*Galant* Culture." In *The Cambridge Companion to French Literature*, ed. John D. Lyons. Pp. 85–101. Cambridge: Cambridge University Press, 2016.

Gordon, Bonnie. "Orfeo's Machines." *The Opera Quarterly* 24 (2008): 200–22.

Gros, Etienne. *Philippe Quinault. Sa vie et son œuvre*. Geneva: Slatkine Reprints, 1970.

Hanley, Sarah. "Engendering the State: Family Formation and State Building in Early Modern France." *French Historical Studies* 16 (1989): 4–27.

Hanley, Sarah. "The Monarchic State in Early Modern France: Marital Regime Government and Male Right." In *Politics, Ideology, and the Law in Early Modern Europe*, ed. Adrianna E. Bakos. Pp. 107–26. Rochester, NY: University of Rochester Press, 1994.

Hanley, Sarah. "The Salic Law." In *Political and Historical Encyclopedia of Women*, ed. Christine Fauré, translated by Richard Dubois. Pp. 2–17. New York: Routledge, 2003.

Hanley, Sarah. "The Family, the State, and the Law in Seventeenth- and Eighteenth-Century France: The Political Ideology of Male Right versus an Early Theory of Natural Law." *The Journal of Modern History* 78 (2006): 289–332.

Hinds, Stephen. "Landscape with Figures: Aesthetics of Place in the *Metamorphoses* and its Tradition." In *The Cambridge Companion to Ovid*, ed. Philip Hardie. Pp. 122–49. Cambridge: Cambridge University Press, 2002.

Howard, Patricia. "The Influence of the *Précieuses* on Content and Structure in Quinault's and Lully's *Tragédies Lyriques*." *Acta Musicologica* 63 (1991): 57–72

Howard, Patricia. "Quinault, Lully, and the *Précieuses*: Images of Women in Seventeenth-Century France." In *Cecilia Reclaimed: Feminist Perspectives on Gender and Music*, ed. Susan C. Cook and Judy S. Tsou. Pp. 70–89. Champaign: University of Illinois Press, 1994.

Johnson, Patricia J. *Ovid Before Exile: Art and Punishment in the Metamorphoses*. Madison: University of Wisconsin Press, 2008.

Kintzler, Catherine. *La Poétique de l'opéra française*. 2d ed. Paris: Minerve, 2006.

La Gorce, Jérôme de. *Carlo Vigarani: Intendant de plaisirs de Louis XIV*. Paris: Perrin, 2005.

Larmessin, Nicolas de. *L'Alliance renouvellée entre la France et l'Espagne, par l'auguste mariage de Charles, IIe, Roi d'Espagne avec Marie Louise d'Orléans, fille aînée de Monsieur*. Paris: la Veuve P. Bertrand, [1680].

Lepautre, Jean. *La Célèbre et auguste cérémonie du mariage du Roi d'Espagne avec Mademoiselle épousée par M.[r] le Prince de Conty à Fontainebleau le 31 Aout 1679*. Paris: Gerard Jollain, [1680].

Lyons, John D. *Kingdom of Disorder: The Theory of Tragedy in Classical France*. West Lafayette, IN: Purdue University Press, 1999.

Marvin, Roberta Montemorra, and Downing A. Thomas, eds. *Operatic Migrations: Transforming Works and Crossing Boundaries*. London and New York: Routledge, 2006.

McClary, Susan. *Desire and Pleasure in Seventeenth-Century Music*. Berkeley: University of California Press, 2012.

Ménestrier, Claude-François. *Des Représentations en musique anciennes et modernes*. Paris: René Guignard, 1681.

Merrick, Jeffrey. "Fathers and Kings: Patriarchalism and Absolutism in Eighteenth-Century French Politics." *Studies on Voltaire and the Eighteenth Century* 308 (1993): 281–303.

Montpensier, Anne-Marie-Louise-Henriette d'Orléans, duchesse de. *Against Marriage: The Correspondence of La Grande Mademoiselle*, ed. and tr. Joan DeJean. Chicago: University of Chicago Press, 2002.

Mousset, Albert. *Les Francine, créateurs des eaux de Versailles*. Paris: A. Picard, 1930.

Mukerji, Chandra. *Territorial Ambitions and the Gardens of Versailles*. Cambridge: Cambridge University Press, 1997.

Naudeix, Laura. *Dramaturgie de la tragédie en musique (1673–1764)*. Paris: Éditions Champion, 2004.

Naudeix, Laura. "*Proserpine* au croisement des mondes." In Proserpine, *tragédie lyrique de Jean-Baptiste Lully, Saint-Germain-en-Laye, 1680. Un collectif autour de l'opéra* « Proserpine », ed. Benoît Dratwicki. Pp. 38–49. San Lorenzo de El Escorial: Glossa Music, 2008.

Néraudau, Jean-Pierre. *L'Olympe du roi soleil: Mythologie et ideologie royale au Grand Siècle*. Paris: Les Belles Lettres, 1986.

Norman, Buford. *Touched by the Graces: The Libretti of Philippe Quinault in the Context of French Classicism*. Birmingham, AL: Summa, 2001.

Norman, Buford. "Le Rôle de la femme dans *Proserpine*," in Proserpine, *tragédie lyrique de Jean-Baptiste Lully, Saint-Germain-en-Laye, 1680. Un collectif autour de l'opéra* « Proserpine », ed. Benoît Dratwicki. Pp. 51–62. San Lorenzo de El Escorial: Glossa Music, 2008.

Ovid. *Metamorphoses, with an English Translation by Frank Justus Miller*. 2 vols. Cambridge, MA, and London: Harvard University Press, 1976.

Powell, John S. *Music and Theatre in France, 1600–1680*. Oxford: Oxford University Press, 2004.

Prest, Julia. "*Iphigénie en Haïti*: Performing Gluck's Paris Operas in the French Colonial Caribbean." *Eighteenth-Century Music* 14 (2017): 13–29.

Prest, Julia. "Theatre in Saint-Domingue, 1764–1791, Plays, Ballets, and Operas." https://www.theatreinsaintdomingue.org/, accessed September 1, 2019.

Quinault, Philippe. *Proserpine, tragédie en musique; ornée d'entrées de ballet, de machines, et de changements de théâtre. Representée devant Sa Majesté à Saint Germain en Laye, le 15. de Février 1680*. Paris: Christophe Ballard, 1680.

Ray, Marcie. "Savage Love: The Indifferent Woman, Violent Seduction, and 18th-Century French Cantatas." *Early Music* 44 (2016): 579–91.

Said, Edward. *Orientalism*. New York: Vintage Books, 1979.

Segal, Charles. *Landscape in Ovid's Metamorphoses: A Study in the Transformations of a Literary Symbol*. Wiesbaden: F. Steiner Verlag, 1969.

Sévigné, Marie de Rabutin-Chantal, marquise de. *Correspondance*, ed. Roger Duchêne. 3 vols. Paris: Gallimard, 1972–1978.

Stanton, Domna C. *The Dynamics of Gender in Early Modern France: Women Writ, Women Writing*. Farnham, UK, and Burlington, VT: Ashgate, 2014.

Stein, Louise K. "How Opera Traveled." In *The Oxford Handbook of Opera*, ed. Helen M. Greenwald. Pp. 843–61. Oxford: Oxford University Press, 2014.

Stein, Louise K., and José Máximo Leza. "Opera, Genre, and Context in Spain and its American Colonies." In *The Cambridge Companion to Eighteenth-Century Opera*, ed. Anthony R. DelDonna and Pierpaolo Polzonetti. Pp. 244–69. Cambridge: Cambridge University Press, 2009.

Thomas, Downing A. *Aesthetics of Opera in the Ancien Régime, 1647–1785*. Cambridge: Cambridge University Press, 2002.

Tomlinson, Gary. *Metaphysical Song: An Essay on Opera*. Princeton: Princeton University Press, 1999.

Tuttle, Leslie. *Conceiving the Old Regime: Pronatalism and the Politics of Reproduction in Early Modern France*. New York: Oxford University Press, 2010.

Yamomo, Melê. "Global Currents, Musical Streams: European Opera in Colonial Southeast Asia." *Nineteenth-Century Theatre and Film* 44 (2017): 54–74.

L'amant statue: Staging Slavery in Pre-Revolutionary Haiti*

Pedro Memelsdorff

Some years ago during a conference on late-medieval music in Cyprus and the Eastern Mediterranean, Lorenzo Calvelli introduced his presentation with an overview of historical geography.[1] He illustrated the complex relations between Cyprus's ruling Lusignan family and certain European hegemonic powers—such as Pisa, Genoa, and above all France and Venice—as well as some Eastern Mediterranean realms including the eastern Roman Empire, Egypt, Tripoli, Cilicia, and Antioch.[2] That extraordinary crossroad of multiplex traditions seemed like a microcosm: a limited geographic area marked by special political circumstances enabling, or perhaps forcing, a large number of extremely different cultures—and musical cultures—to coexist almost by symbiosis.

True, any historical moment can be seen as a microcosm—or a dynamic encapsulation of countless influences—as shown, for example, by fifty-odd years of worldwide micro-historical research;[3] and yet, as does Gérard Genette in a different field, one could argue that some of these moments and locales are more exposed to complex cultural interaction than others.[4]

In response to these ideas, in 2016 I proposed a methodological reflection on two extremely different music-historical phenomena, pairing them by the concept of microcosm: late-medieval Cyprus in the Eastern Mediterranean and the early modern French colonies in the Caribbean.[5] An important feature common to each area was its strategic function within its respective macro-economic and political backgrounds; a shared musical feature was the impact of European (and specifically French) hegemonic cultures upon a complex stratification of local and imported ones: Eastern Mediterranean, Orthodox, and French-Italian in Cyprus; (almost vestigial) Indigenous-American, sub-Saharan, and French in the French Caribbean.[6]

In the present essay I will focus on one of France's colonies in the late eighteenth century, Saint-Domingue (present-day Haiti), and especially on the reception there of French stage music following the construction of the first public theaters on the island, in the early 1760s.[7] After a quick summary of current historiography on the topic, I will reflect on some specific connotations that conventional theatrical and musical *topoi* may have acquired in the colonial context. In order to do so, I will comment on the career of the first known French opera singer of color to be cast in a title role, named Minette, active in Saint-Domingue in the 1780s, and provide a close reading of one particular piece she performed in 1786, Desfontaines's *L'amant statue*, set to music by Nicolas Dalayrac.[8] This bravura piece in itself projects a kaleidoscope of semiotic and social implications and merits sustained consideration. Finally, I will briefly return to the concept of microcosm through a short anecdote.

Methodologically, I will survey historiography both immediately and not immediately related to the subject, and reconsider sources that are printed or accessible online. Theoretically, I will agree with some recent reflections on the potential ties between historical musicology, theories of postcolonialism and decoloniality,[9] and (as framed by Olivia Bloechl) "scholarly, pedagogical, or artistic projects."[10]

The context

Limitations of space force me to skip many historiographical details, but it is nonetheless crucial to begin by remarking that the terms of recent scholarship on pre-revolutionary Haitian theater and music have been set by major local historians such as Adolphe Cabon and especially Jean Fouchard.[11] Their stunning archival findings and historiographic framings have been adopted by two generations of Caribbean and Anglo-Saxon scholars, in the latter case sometimes without acknowledgment.[12] Strikingly, almost no "hexagonal" French literature exists on this topic.

Basing his work on eyewitness historians (such as Moreau de Saint-Méry), travel literature, and the contemporary local press, Fouchard reconstructed the life of the eight opera theaters active in the colony in the late eighteenth century (see figure 1).[13] By 1789 they could seat approximately 3,800 viewers (one out of every fifteen potential white or free-colored spectators), thus proportionally three times more than Parisian theaters of the same period.[14] Between 1764 and 1791 over 8,000 European-style concert evenings were staged in Saint-Domingue, including some 1,200 performances of operas that arrived from France and, if necessary, were newly arranged on the island.[15] Saint-Domingue was therefore one of the major opera centers of the ("Western") world, certainly the largest in the Americas. Its influence on Caribbean, American, and perhaps even European theater and opera can hardly be exaggerated.

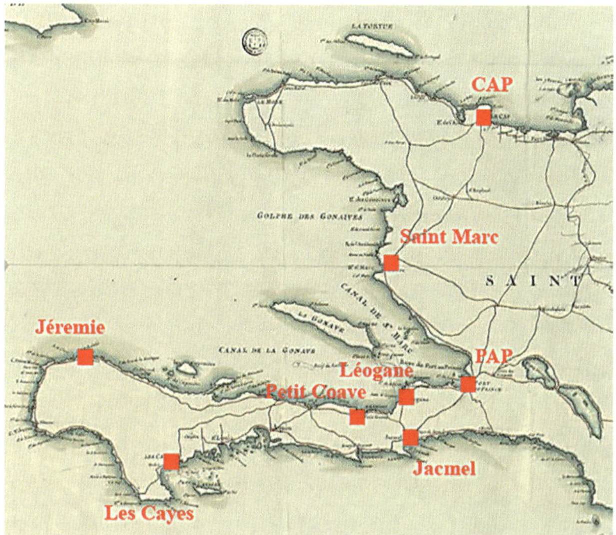

Fig. 1. Saint-Domingue, location of theaters in 1780. Rubrics added to the *[Carte routière de l'île de] Saint-Domingue*. Paris, Bibliothèque nationale de France, Collections, GESH18PF146DIV1P27/1. CAP stands for Cap Français, and PAP for Port-au-Prince

Regarding the opera singer of color, Minette, she was one of the brightest stars to play in one of these theaters. Biographies of her have been published by Jean Fouchard, Bernard Camier, and David M. Powers, and a novel based on her life appeared in 1957.[16] Fouchard's biography romanticizes her career at several points (on which more below) and makes some incorrect assumptions—such as Minette's birthdate, deduced from the date of her performance of Pierre Laujon and Johann Paul Aegidius Martini's comedy *L'amoureux de quinze ans* on October 2, 1781.[17] Camier's several publications on Minette partially differ on her parentage, for he first supposed François Saint-Martin, then Joseph Sartre, and finally Marin Ferrand to have been Minette's father.[18] Ferrand's paternity is supported by consistent evidence, however (see below, figure 2), though some facts concerning his whereabouts in the 1780s remain obscure, as do some perhaps minor documentary matters—such as the order of Minette's names (Elisabeth Alexandrine Louise, or Louise Elisabeth Alexandrine) and her age at death.[19] These discrepancies prompted Powers (and with her, cautiously, Julia Prest) to doubt Camier's genealogy and account of Minette's final years.[20]

None of these scholarly works examines in full detail the public *artistic persona* fashioned by her presenters and conditioned by her social context; but they offer a stunning amount of information, which may be summarized as follows.[21] Elisabeth Alexandrine Louise, who from 1784 on went by the stage name Minette, was born in Port-au-Prince in July 1767 as the mixed-race daughter of the white treasurer Marin Ferrand—who was stationed at the harbor of Port-au-Prince in the 1760s—and the mixed-race Elisabeth "Fillette" "Mahaultière" Daguin, herself the daughter or granddaughter of a freed person of color.[22]

Notarial documents witness Elisabeth Daguin's ownership of a house with a *case à nègre* in the center of Port-au-Prince, suggesting relative wealth and the possession of enslaved persons.[23] Minette herself, moreover, inherited two enslaved persons from the geographer and engineer Louis Alexandre Longuet de Montplaisir.[24] Thus both Minette and her mother apparently belonged to the upper middle-class society of free people of color.

Their political connections with the *grands blancs* and the administration of Port-au-Prince seems to have been quite impressive.[25] The godparents of Minette's younger daughter Louise Françoise Théodore were Théodore Roberjot and Anne-Françoise Duvivier de la Mahaultière: they were, respectively, the son of Minette's father's successor in the harbor of Port-au-Prince and the daughter of Marthe-Jerôme Duvivier de la Mahaultière, member of the *Conseil supérieur* of Port-au-Prince. Moreover, Mme Duvivier was married to Joseph Sartre, business partner of Alexandre Saint-Martin, who was himself the godfather of Minette and perhaps relative of François Saint-Martin, director of the theater of Port-au-Prince, and so Minette's sponsor and superior.[26]

In short, Minette's position seems to have been fairly privileged. And yet, according to Moreau de Saint-Méry—and further documented by Fouchard and Camier—pervasive racial discrimination seems to have hindered her opera debut in February 1781.[27] This debut merits much more attention than can be given it here.[28] Suffice it to say that it featured the *scène-lyrique Pygmalion* of Jean-Jacques Rousseau and Horace Coignet, a piece that Minette performed in September of the same year, and which probably conditioned some of her later performances (on which more below).[29]

In the following eight years she pursued an unparalleled performing career in Port-au-Prince, acting and singing in some forty operas and comedies, as well as concerts of several types.[30] Almost the entire list of these performances is reconstructible by cross-referencing the data published by Fouchard, Camier, and Powers, which can occasionally be further nuanced by directly consulting the local newspapers of the time.[31] It shows a stunning sequence of increasingly demanding title roles, performed by a first-rank coloratura soprano who was at the same time a comic and occasionally tragic actress.[32]

Scholars have repeatedly noted a particular feature of Minette's career: her refusal to perform creole or "popular" pieces, favoring—unlike her sister Lise—classical European repertoires instead.[33] This has led to various conclusions: Fouchard supposed that Minette was a kind of assimilated "aristocrat," while Camier suggested that she refused the idealized—and therefore indirectly denigrating—tone of creole comedies.[34] Powers, finally, stressed her condition of

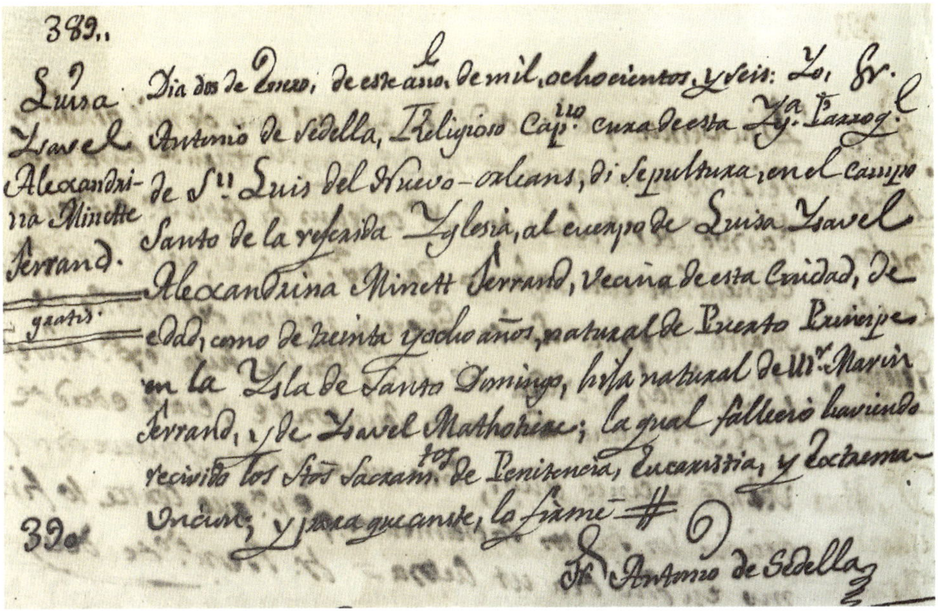
389.
Luisa Isavel Alexandrina Minette Ferrand.
gratis
Dia dos de Enero, de este año de mil ochocientos y seis: Yo, Fr. Antonio de Sedella, Religioso Capuchino cura de esta Yglesia Parroquial de Sn. Luis del Nuevo-orleans, di Sepultura en el Campo Santo de la referida Yglesia, al cuerpo de Luisa Ysavel Alexandrina Minett Ferrand, vecina de esta Ciudad, de edad como de treinta y ocho años, natural de Puerto Principe en la Ysla de Santo Domingo, hija natural de Mr. Mario Ferrand, y de Ysavel Mathorine; la qual fallecio haviendo recivido los Stos. Sacramentos de Penitencia, Eucaristia, y Extrema-Uncion, y para que conste, lo firme #
Fr. Antonio de Sedella
390

Fig. 2. Archdiocese of New Orleans, St. Louis Cathedral, *Funeral Records 1803–1807*, II, 112, act #389: Funeral of Luisa Isavel Alexandrina Minette Ferrand, 1807 (note that the date 1806 is a *lapsus*, as corroborated by the entries before and after the document)

semi-enslavement and limited freedom to choose her repertoire, for Minette—at least in the first three years of her career—was *not* paid for her performances.[35]

At any rate, some time after her last performance in 1789, Minette left Saint-Domingue. According to Camier, she was registered as an exile in Santiago de Cuba in 1802, and in 1806 her—perhaps last—performance was announced in the theater of New Orleans (eventually postponed for health reasons).[36] Her funeral record, first cited by René Le Gardeur, reconsidered by Camier, and doubted by Powers, is dated January 2, 1807, here published for the first time (see figure 2).[37]

Minette and *L'amant statue*

Skipping a number of crucial aspects of Minette's career—such as the possible agenda behind her nine known benefit concerts, her rivalry with the white star singer Jeanne-Marie Marsan, and her denigration by some racist reviews in the press—I will instead focus my discussion on one of Minette's hits, which aptly exemplifies her complex bond with the mixed-race audiences of Port-au-Prince.[38] As is well known, (some) free people of color normally had their special seats in the so-called *Paradise* or upper sections of theaters, while white people used all other balconies and the parterre, sharing them with an as-yet unquantifiable number of enslaved domestics in their service.[39]

Of her many successes, Minette was perhaps best known for three performances: *L'amant statue*, *Nina*, and *La belle Arsène*, the first two set to music by Nicolas Dalayrac, the third by Pierre Alexandre Monsigny.[40] *La belle Arsène* and especially *Nina* prompted something of a scandal in their critical reception—which again for reasons of space I will have to skip;[41] and *L'amant statue* was the most frequently and successfully repeated piece in Minette's career.[42]

First staged in Paris in 1785, the *comédie mêlée d'ariettes L'amant statue*, by monsieur Desfontaines and Nicolas Dalayrac was premiered in Port-au-Prince on October 10, 1786.[43] In it, Dorval loves the young widow Célimène (Minette), who likes his letters but refuses to meet him because she has sworn never to love men again. After trying several tricks, Dorval convinces Célimène's maid Rosette to let him slip into Célimène's garden, which lacks a statue. He then pretends to be a mechanical statue of a shepherd who plays a flute, which enchants Célimène (more on Dorval's performance below). She declares that she will love the statue forever, at which point Dorval reveals himself, and the lovers get engaged.

Dorval's idea was, of course, not new. Magic transformations of or into statues were a common conceit in eighteenth-century theater, from Alain-René Lesage's *La statue merveilleuse* (staged in 1719–1720) and George Frideric Handel's *Admeto* (1727), to Carlo Gozzi's *Il re cervo* (1762), Gaetano Martinelli and Niccolò Jommelli's *Le avventure di Cleomede* (1772), and of course a number of *Pygmalions* (on which more below).[44] In the last quarter of the century, moreover, magic statues were almost endlessly present on stage, both in *tragédie lyrique* and in *opéra comique,* quite often with a derisive or social-critical undertone: pieces issued by everyone from Vincenzo Righini and Nunziato Porta, Joseph Schuster and Caterino Mazzolà, Joseph Haydn and Joseph Kurz, to Lorenzo da Ponte and Wolfgang Amadeus Mozart.[45]

On the other hand, the *topos* of the *flute-playing* statue opened at least two further semantic fields. The first is the stereotypical instrumentation of magic scenes with recorders or flutes in the eighteenth century: its prevalence has been thoroughly cataloged by David Buch.[46] Flutes were already used in scenes of enchantment, magic transformation, sleep, or dreams in Jean-Baptiste Lully's *Atys* and *Thésée*, in André Campra's *Tancrède* and *Alcina*, and in Louis Lacoste's *Philomèle*.[47] They continue to appear in later works by François Rebel and François Francœur, Jean-Philippe Rameau, Gluck, and Niccolò Piccinni,[48] and so the association of flutes with magic (or fake magic) probably would not

Fig. 3. Antoine Coysevox, *Le Berger flûteur*, 1709. Paris, Musée du Louvre, Département des Sculptures

have escaped the notice of Dorval's listeners in Saint-Domingue.

The second semantic field is that of flute-playing automata—objects that were very much admired in eighteenth-century France, Europe, and the Americas—which now merit some attention. The most celebrated prototype of these automata was probably Jacques de Vaucanson's "Joueur de Flûte" of 1738: a wooden android that could play up to twelve different pieces on a real flute, itself a (mobile) copy of a marble statue by the sculptor Antoine Coysevox that could be seen on the terrace of the Tuileries (see figure 3). Coysevox (1640–1729), let us remember, was celebrated for sculpting the tombs of Jean-Baptiste Colbert and of Cardinal Mazarin—as well as the votive sculpture featuring Louis XIV on the high altar of Notre-Dame. As for Jacques de Vaucanson (1709–1782), Voltaire called him "the new Prometheus," and the *Mercure de France* called his "Joueur de Flûte" "un phénomene de méchanique."[49] Vaucanson described it in a treatise in two parts, the first of which consisted of a digression on the instrument itself (with an acoustic description and consideration of a number of technical problems, including the regulation of the breath for dynamics, the embouchure technique for correction of intonation, and the articulation of the tongue); part two provided a detailed explanation of the automaton's mechanism.[50] A second edition of the same treatise appeared in 1741, but with the date of the first publication. It featured the important addition of a letter by Vaucanson presenting two further automata—the "Joueur de tambourin" and the famous "Canard digérateur"—as well as an illustration of the three automata by the engraver Gravelot, which inspired later versions (see figures 4 and 5).[51]

More important than these bibliographic details is the philosophical dimension of Vaucanson's discourse, which engaged anew with Kircherian issues concerning the origin, intentionality, and comprehensibility of semiotic

LE
MÉCANISME
DU FLUTEUR
AUTOMATE,
Preſenté a Meſſieurs de l'Académie Royale des Sciences.
Par M. VAUCANSON, *Auteur de cette Machine.*
Avec
La deſcription d'un Canard Artificiel, mangeant, beuvant, digerant & ſe vuidant, épluchant ſes ailes & ſes plumes, imitant en diverſes manieres un *Canard* vivant. Inventé par le meſme.
Et auſſi
Celle d'une autre figure, également merveilleuſe, jouant du Tambourin & de la Flute, ſuivant la relation, qu'il en a donnée depuis ſon Mémoire écrit.
A PARIS,
Chez JACQUES GUERIN, Imprimeur-Libraire, Quai des Auguſtins.
ET SE VEND
Dans la Sale de dite figures Automates.
M. DCC. XXXVIII.
AVEC PERMISSION DU ROI.

Fig. 4. Vaucanson—Gravelot, *Le mécanisme du fluteur automate*, 2nd edition, 1738 (but 1741). Paris, Bibliothèque nationale de France, département Arsenal, 4-S-4798

phenomena. The android was not simply a music box inside a mobile statue but a mechanical object blowing into a *real* flute. On the one hand this added verisimilitude to the flutist, even as it highlighted the complexity of the mechanism. Moreover, by mimicking human lips, lungs, fingers, and even tongue so as to create sounds and phrasing "dans le goût le plus parfait" the android challenged the very concept of musical intelligence.[52]

Vaucanson's invention was imitated by numerous followers: in 1746 a certain M. Defrance presented at the Tuileries a new model of the mechanical flutist, and in the 1760s the Abbé Mical presented two mechanical flutists he called Annette and Lubin.[53] The tradition, as will be seen, was soon exported to the Americas and would survive colonial times (to be explored below). Regarding its reception in the music scene, finally, Vaucanson's android would still be remembered in the nineteenth century, as witnessed by the comedy of Adolphe de Leuven and Luigi Bordèse, *L'automate de Vaucanson: opéra-comique en un acte*, published in 1840.[54]

In the context of Minette's performance of *L'amant statue*, the polysemy may have been even more complex, however. In the first place, the audience could not but compare the fake automaton with Minette's own performance of Galathée, the animated statue in Rousseau's-Coignet's *Pygmalion*, and of Myris, the

Fig. 5. Anon., *Vaucanson's automata*, after 1746. Paris, Bibliothèque nationale de France, département Estampes et photographie, RESERVE QB-201 (100)-FOL

parody of Galathée in Favart's-Monsigny's *La belle Arsène*—two roles she had played in 1781. Moreover, Desfontaines-Dalayrac made fully explicit the link between music and animation (the act of conferring or receiving, or the state of possessing a soul), which neither Rousseau nor Favart had done.

As for the association with *Pygmalion* or Pygmalionesque roles, an obvious referent for European and perhaps colonial contemporaries must have been the fact that as early as 1766 Jean-Auguste Jullien dit Desboulmiers had published his parody *Le nouveau Pygmalion: Histoire véritable*,[55] and that in 1774 Christoph Rheineck had premiered in Lyon his *L'amante statue, ou le nouveau Pigmalion* (libretto by monsieur de B. Desgagniers), a comedy inspired by, and actually reversing, Rousseau's plot.[56] Both titles—*L'amant* (or *L'amante*) *statue* and *Pygmalion*—were therefore associable even before the version of Dalayrac and Desfontaines. Their version, too, reversed Rousseau's, but in new ways: first, Célimène (the female protagonist) was no longer the statue but its observer, and second, what animated the statue was no longer Pygmalion's misogynous talent, but the revelation of Dorval's fake magic. In short, it is almost as if Célimène's overcome misandry was meant to prove the impossibility of loving inanimate objects, or, reversing the perspective, the impossibility that a non-human musician could possibly stir emotion in the audience.[57]

As for the relationship between animation and music, in *L'amant statue* it was no longer the beauty of the statue, but the beauty of the statue's music that ultimately implied its animation, which suggests that Dalayrac was also responding to—and inviting audiences to recall—prior *musical* settings of the scene. These must have included the extremely popular *Pigmalion* of Jean-Philippe Rameau from 1748 and its Rousseauian critique.[58] Perhaps not coincidentally, Rameau's version—as Dalayrac's—was scored with flutes accompanying the coming to life of the statue, whose first words, parodied by Dalayrac (on which more below), seem to quote John Locke, David Hume, or André-François Boureau-Deslandes with the sensualist questions "Que vois-je? Où suis-je? Et qu'est-ce que je pense?"[59] Summarizing, then: the fake android in *L'amant statue* ingeniously mocked the complex philosophical and musical implications of its serious and comic models from Rameau to Rousseau, Desboulmiers, and Rheineck.

Perhaps only a selection of colonial viewers was fully aware of the complexities of these models.[60] One specifically colonial association, conversely, would hardly have passed unnoticed by anyone in Port-au-Prince: the link between the playing statue and the actual flutist who accompanied the scene from the orchestra.

Fouchard and Camier have compiled a list of some eighty names of enslaved instrumentalists—mostly violin players—that staffed Saint-Domingue's orchestras in the decades of Minette's career.[61] Considering the dimensions of the orchestras on the island and the usual dimension of the orchestra in Port-au-Prince, with eleven players, it seems plausible that a good number of them, if not the majority, were indeed enslaved.[62] Some may have been enslaved *wind players*, but specific information about them is rather scanty, even if not totally missing.

The first flutist originating in Saint-Domingue that we know of by (nick?)name was called Atys, and he is mentioned briefly by Jean-Benjamin Laborde, Alexandre Choron, and François Fayolle.[63] Born on the island in 1715, he lived in Paris in the 1750s and 1760s. He also spent some time in Vienna, where a wound to his jaw suffered in a duel harmed his playing. Returning to Paris, he devoted the remainder of his career to teaching and composing. In Laborde's words:

> Atis, né à Saint-Domingue vers 1715, avait beaucoup de talent pour jouer de la flûte. Une affaire qu'il eut en Autriche, l'obligea de se battre, & une balle qu'il reçut dans le menton, lui fit perdre une grande partie de sa facilité, sur-tout pour l'embouchure. Il revint en France, où il s'est fixé depuis, & s'y est occupé à faire des écoliers, & à composer un grand nombre de sonates, duo, trio, symphonies, &c. où l'on trouve des morceaux agréables.[64]

To this scant data, François-Joseph Fétis added some bibliography and precise dates taken from Moriz Bermann's *Oesterreichisches Biographisches Lexikon*:[65]

> Atys, ou Atis [...] créole, né à Saint-Domingue, vers 1715. [...] De retour à Paris [de Vienne], il s'y livra à l'enseignement, et composa beaucoup de sonates, duos, trios et quatuors pour la flûte. On trouve de lui, en manuscrit, à la Bibliothèque impériale de Paris, un œuvre de six sonates pour deux flûtes, en forme de conversation. Suivant M. Bermann (*Oesterreich. Biograph. Lexikon*, t. 1, p. 287), la date précise de la naissance d'Atis serait le 18 avril 1715; il aurait été à Vienne en 1760; et il serait mort le 8 août 1784. M. Bermann *sait les dates d'une manière effrayante*.[66]

The origin of Atys's (nick?)name may or not be the present village Atis near Titanyen in Saint-Domingue, but the frequent spelling with a 'y' may also allude to his having participated in Lully's celebrated tragedy or—perhaps more plausibly—in one of its numerous late parodies.[67] Theatrical names were quite frequent in Saint-Domingue, however, and were typically given to enslaved or *affranchis*.[68] In fact, the lack of a family name in all of his biographies, published compositions, and flute treatises suggests that Atys may well have been an *affranchi* before arriving in France.[69] According to Bermann and Fétis, Atys died in 1784, two years before Minette's *L'amant statue*. His fame as an extraordinary flute teacher and composer in Paris may have reached Saint-Domingue's flutists and flute teachers of the time—such as Héricourt or Barbier.[70]

Another flutist, the European M. Macarty, is reported as playing in the opera orchestra of Port-au-Prince from late 1780.[71] Traces of him disappear in 1783, and it is not known who succeeded him immediately thereafter.[72] From July 1782, however, a certain Louis is recorded as a clarinetist performing at the theater of Port-au-Prince.[73] Fouchard believes he belonged to the theater's orchestra, where flute and clarinet were normally played by the same person.[74] Documents omit his family name, suggesting—once again—that he may have been an enslaved person or an *affranchi*, that is, an enslaved flautist in the years of Minette's stage career.

Returning to *L'amant statue* in Port-au-Prince, then, it is perfectly possible that the comedy's fake android alluded to the enslaved condition of the very flutist who was playing from the orchestra in his place, drawing the attention to his own mental and expressive faculties—or, more precisely, to his animation. Because in fact, despite the proclaimed acceptance of the centuries-old Aristotelian concept of enslaved persons as "animated property," and article 2 of the *Code noir*, which mandated the baptism of enslaved persons, their animation remained a problematic issue throughout the French colonial era.[75] One need only recall the ambiguities inherent in Charles-Louis de Montesquieu's *De l'esclavage des nègres* of 1748: "One cannot possibly imagine how God in his wisdom could have put a soul, especially a good soul, in such a Black body."[76] As Catherine Reinhardt argues in *Claims to Memory*, not all of the critics understood Montesquieu's remarks as ironic.[77]

In this light, it seems worthwhile to examine the plot of Desfontaines's *L'amant statue* in greater detail.[78] In scene 10, the maid Rosette sings in Célimène's garden while Dorval's servant Frontin arrives disguised as a sculptor and holding a spring and a crank. After setting them down next to the empty pedestal he explains the plan: while Dorval will feign being the mechanical statue, he will feign being a deaf sculptor—so as to hide his plebeian accent.[79] In scene 11 the three of them sing the trio *Céladon pour fléchir sa belle* (which praises untruth) and finally, in scene 12, Dorval poses on the pedestal and Célimène arrives.[80]

The climax can be summarized as follows: first Célimène admires the statue; then Rosette provokes her curiosity by teasing her:

> R: You would like it even more if you knew that...
> C: Knew what? You won't tell me? Speak!
> R: ...that people say it has a soul.
> C: A soul![81]

At this point Rosette explains the mechanism, Frontin turns the crank, and the statue starts to play. First it performs a clumsily-ended prelude, and then an *air* said to imitate the *sérinette. Sérinettes*, let us remember, were small mechanical organs with which birds were taught songs; and so Dorval's performance turns into something like a *mise en abîme*, or a metaphor, to say the least: for he not only pretends to be an inanimate being (the statue), but a (mechanical) intelligence teaching others.[82]

Finally as a sort of litmus test the statue "improvises" a flute accompaniment while Frontin sings "a famous air." This turns out to be Monsigny's *O ma tendre musette* to new words (by Desfontaines) that allude to Dorval's plot with the Pygmalionesque final sentence "Si le Marbre s'enflame / dans ce bois enchanté / c'est que tout prend un âme / pour plaire à la beauté."[83] After these words, Frontin falls silent and the statue concludes with a long and magnificent solo flute cadenza. The ensemble moves Célimène to surrender—leading Dorval to unveil his lie and Célimène to escape in embarrassment. In her stupor, she then utters the words: "Ciel, que vois je ... ah que je suis émue ... quel moment ...

Fig. 6. Alexandre-Nicolas Théroude, *Automate mécanique, Jouer de Flûte*, 1878. Marseille, Mucem (Musée des civilisations de l'Europe et de la Méditerranée), inv. 2015.15.1

Fig. 7. Gustave Vichy, *Flutist*, ca. 1878. Private collection

Fig. 8. Jean Roullet Decamps, *Flutist*, n.d. Private collection

quel torment," mimicking Rameau's and Rousseau's statue while exploiting the burlesque potential of the reversal of roles.[84]

Considering the colonial context, the burlesque elements of this scene may have taken yet another turn. For Célimène's (Minette's) exclamation "une âme!"—a soul—(referring to the animated statue accompanied by the enslaved flutist) must have set off a chain of associations in which her own status was also called to attention. As a "freed" *chose mobiliaire* (chattel), perpetually marked by the *tache de l'esclavage* (stain of slavery), she would unavoidably have been likened to the figure of the disguised Dorval and his enslaved, wordless voice.[85] Moreover, Frontin's last words "tout prend une âme / pour plaire à la beauté"—followed by Dalayrac's flute cadenza played by Louis—would have strengthened the controversial link between animation and slavery. In other words (to put it more bluntly): if what proved the statue's animation was the intelligence of the enslaved player in the orchestra, then the heuristic and political potential of the exclamation "une âme!" in 1786 Saint-Domingue becomes dramatically clear.

This brings us back to Vaucanson's automaton, which also inspired a long tradition of *colored*-flutist music boxes in France and the Americas well into the nineteenth century. They featured sub-Saharan flutists richly dressed in European attire—thus probably meant to be seen as enslaved domestics—playing on European Classical or Romantic flutes (see figures 6–8).[86] They bear witness to the proliferation of enslaved flutists in colonial societies.

In conclusion: if in Paris *L'amant statue* was a comedy with an only slightly ironic plot, when played in Saint-Domingue it could not but bring to the mind of spectators a number of controversial issues. As in Minette's debut piece *Isabelle et Gertrude* in 1781 and in many of her benefit evenings during her career, it was once again not the piece alone—or not the piece at all—that amplified gendered and racial conflicts, but the superimposition of piece, casting, and viewer.[87]

Minette's biography, at any rate, seems to end on an ambiguous trope: while Fouchard suspected she died in the fires of the revolt in 1791, Camier—as mentioned before—at first doubted and then confirmed her identification with the singer deceased in New Orleans in 1807. Ironically, her last recorded performance in Saint-Domingue was a newly composed piece called *La Répétition interrompue*.[88]

Epilogue

The perception of certain "microcosmic" geographic areas—such as the modern Caribbean and late-medieval Cyprus—as multicultural crossroads seems to have been, at least sometimes, an emic one.

By way of a final conclusion, we might consider the work of Voltaire, whose tragedy *Zaïre* (1732) takes place in a fictional medieval Jerusalem, putting on stage the Muslim slave owner Orosmane, who wants to free his slave Zaïre in order to marry her. She discovers she is the daughter of a Christian crusader named Lusignan (the medieval rulers of Jerusalem and Cyprus), and agrees with her family to be baptized in secret before marrying. Orosmane discovers the plot, kills her, and commits suicide.

Voltaire's rendering of the story for his contemporaries stressed issues such as the complexities of multicultural environments, clan loyalty, and religious intolerance.[89]

Strikingly, similar issues are raised by a document from Saint-Domingue, written in Saint-Marc (some one hundred kilometers north of Port-au-Prince) and dated 1793.[90] In it—as brilliantly discussed by Camier and Dubois—the Black slave owner Laurent Jolicœur petitions the government to recognize his freeing of an enslaved woman (called Zaïre after Voltaire's play) by openly comparing her to Voltaire's heroine in the cross-cultural medieval Eastern Mediterranean. Jolicœur's extraordinary parallel, in an apparently legal document, stands as a reminder of the far-reaching social significance of French theater in Saint-Domingue, which not only dramatized imported repertoires for mixed-race audiences, but did so—at least occasionally—with mixed-race casts as well.[91] Not least, it also stands for a late eighteenth-century, Caribbean fictionalized perception of the French-medieval enclaves in the Eastern Mediterranean: the same ventured parallel with which this study started.

Postscript

After this article was submitted in August 2018, some important discoveries emerged concerning the lives of Minette and Lise that are essential to report here. Bernard Camier has provided substantial additions to their biographies in two new contributions.[92] Julia Prest has published an important article on Minette and Mme Marsan, which integrates some of the data briefly mentioned in my essay.[93] Finally, I have found a number of new documents on Minette's life, whereabouts, presumed "stage name," family, properties, and social background, including information about her main partner and autographs of her mother and siblings. One of these documents has meanwhile been published.[94] All the others will be presented or discussed in my aforementioned volume on music and race in the eighteenth-century French Caribbean.

A summary of new information that most closely relates to this article is reported in the following paragraphs.

1. According to new archival records recently published by Camier, Minette had four further children besides those already known: Jean, born in Port-au-Prince in 1793; Charles, in Baltimore in 1794; Charlotte, in Philadelphia in 1796; and Benjamin, on the high seas in 1798.[95] However, new evidence concerning further children has recently emerged.

2. These documents imply that Minette was exiled not once but at least twice; and that the first exile began sometime after September 6 (or maybe after October 7), 1793, taking her first to Maryland and then to Pennsylvania.[96]

3. Moreover, the birth certificate of her (perhaps) last child—Benjamin—provides further information: Minette was traveling on the "brik parlementaire" (that is, a neutral ship) *L'aimable Adèle*, which on that day navigated at the coordinates 25° North and 60°51´ West (approximately at the latitude of Miami and about seven hundred kilometers north-west of the Virgin Islands).[97] Building on this data, I would like to advance that Minette was traveling to, or returning from Europe; and so, that she most likely was in France shortly before

or after August 21, 1798. Nothing is known about that journey; but the name Benjamin seems to suggest that for unknown reasons Minette envisaged no further children. In addition, given that Minette's first signature containing her family name Ferrand dates to 1799, it seems possible that the European stop was linked to her recovery of an acknowledgment of paternity.

4. At any rate, this first exile ended sometime before March 8, 1799, when she was back in Port-au-Prince to declare the three children born outside Saint-Domingue.[98]

5. Regarding Minette's second and, as it seems, definitive exile, Camier had dated it to 1802 based on a document presumably drafted in Santiago de Cuba in that year.[99] My own research at the ANOM in Aix-en-Provence has produced new results, however: the document cited by Camier is actually dated January 16, 1805 (26 Nevôse An XIII); and a further document suggests that the person referred to in both documents may not be the same as the singer of Port-au-Prince. Details of these findings can be found in my article "Minette à Cuba?"

Notes

* This essay is a revised version of a paper read in Florence in May 2017 and Pittsburgh in March 2018, and it constitutes part of a forthcoming volume on music and race in the eighteenth-century French Caribbean. My warmest thanks to I Tatti, The Harvard University Center for Italian Renaissance Studies, and its Director, Alina Payne, as well as to Kate van Orden, for their great support; and to Attilio Bottegal, librarian at the Morrill Music Library, I Tatti, for his kind and efficient assistance.

1. Lorenzo Calvelli, "When East meets West: Royal Courts and Monastic Orders in Frankish Cyprus," paper read at the conference *Cyprus: Plainchant and Ars subtilior in the Latin East*, Venice, Fondazione Giorgio Cini, May 22, 2011.

2. That is: the Byzantine Empire, the Mamluk Sultanate in Egypt, the County of Tripoli, the Armenian Kingdom of Cilicia, and the principality of Antioch. The conference discussed forms of religious and musical hybridization, for instance cases of simple polyphony in the Venetian style sung with Orthodox words and melodies, or sections of the Greek Easter ritual adjusted to Latin polyphony shortly after the fall of the Eastern Empire in the 1450s and copied in northern Italy. On the latter phenomenon see Memelsdorff, "Cantus grecus."

3. Surveyed by Carlo Ginzburg in his "Microstoria." I thank Carlo Ginzburg for having read and commented this paper, and for his always generous advice and most illuminating conversations.

4. Genette, *Palimpsests*, 9.

5. Pedro Memelsdorff, "Microcosmos: Historicizing Musical Multiculturality," paper read at the Third Singapore Heritage Science Conference: *The Treasure of Human Experiences*, Singapore, Nanyang Technological University, January 25–26, 2016.

6. Seminal thoughts on Caribbean history and musical culture—conceived as a microcosm—are summarized in Kuss, "Prologue," xvii: "A history that assigns the same value to all traditions and is defined by a heterogeneity 'of which there need be no synthesis' and by an infinite number of intersections of time, place, and peoples" (single quotation marks refer to González Echevarría, *Alejo Carpentier*, 266). See also eadem, "The Caribbean." My warmest thanks to Malena Kuss for her continual encouragement and inspiring support.

7. Fleurant, "Haiti"; and, in the same volume, Ramos Venereo, "Haitian Traditions in Cuba," 266–80.

8. François-Georges Fouques Deshayes, aka Desfontaines (1733–1825, librettist), and Nicolas Dalayrac (1753–1809, composer) [henceforth: Desfontaines and Dalayrac], *L'amant statue mise en musique*.

9. Quijano, "Coloniality and Modernity/Rationality"; Mignolo, "Delinking"; Bhambra, "Postcolonialism and Decoloniality"; Reinhardt, *Claims to Memory*.

10. Bloechl, "Race, Empire, and Early Music," 104.

11. Cabon, *Histoire d'Haïti*; Fouchard, *Le théâtre à Saint-Domingue*; idem, *Plaisirs de Saint-Domingue*; idem, *Artistes et répertoire*.

12. Undoubtedly the most eminent scholar of St. Dominguan music history is Bernard Camier, who has produced an impressive number of excellent works. The following list of authors—fully detailed in the appended bibliography—is of course not exhaustive: Cale, "French Secular Music"; Stevenson, "Caribbean Music History"; Mintz and Price, *Focus: Caribbean*; Largey, "Musical Ethnography in Haiti"; McClellan, *Colonialism and Science*; all works by Camier, alone and in collaboration; Fleurant, "Haiti"; Ramos Venereo, "Haitian Traditions in Cuba"; Hazaël-Massieux, *Textes anciens en créole français*; Dubois, "Gendered Freedom"; Curtis, "Utopian (Post)Colonies"; Gay, "The Performance of Colonialism"; Clay, *Stagestruck*; Lemmon, ed., *French Baroque Music of New Orleans*; Powers, *From Plantation to Paradise*; Prest, "*Iphigénie en Haïti*." See also the recent website: https://www.theatreinsaintdomingue.org (last accessed on July 7, 2018), produced by Julia Prest, which features "a bilingual (French-English) database of public performances of plays, ballets and operas as documented in the local newspapers between 1764 and 1791." I thank Julia Prest for her careful remarks on this essay.

13. Fouchard, *Le théâtre à Saint-Domingue*, 1–119; Moreau de Saint-Méry, *Description topographique*, *passim* (see the entry "Comédie" in the index, 3:1435–36). Travel literature includes Du Tertre, *Histoire generale des Antilles*, 4 vols.; Labat, *Nouveau voyage aux isles de l'Amérique*; Thibault de Chanvalon, *Voyage à la Martinique*; [Girod-Chantrans], *Voyage d'un Suisse*; Isert, *Voyages en Guinée*; Malouet, *Mémoire sur l'esclavage*; Wimpffen, *Voyage à Saint Domingue*; Descourtilz, *Flore pittoresque*; Sansay, *Secret History*. See also: Camier, "Musique coloniale," 29. The local press basically (but not exclusively) consists of the *Affiches Américaines* (published weekly from January 1, 1776 to November 4, 1786, then twice a week until December 30, 1790), and *Supplément aux Affiches Américaines* (published weekly from July 10, 1769 to March 21, 1789, then twice a week until December 29, 1790).

14. Camier and Dubois, "Voltaire et Zaïre," 44, according to whom in 1789 the theater of Saint-Domingue seated 3,800 of some 59,000 potential viewers and Paris some 13,000 of 600,000. For a similar calculation see Clay, *Stagestruck*, 208. In a lecture published on http://www.lameca.org/dossiers/musiquecoloniale/p3.htm and announced in https://guadeloupeattitude.wordpress.com/category/opera/, Camier differed from some of his previously published statistics by stating: "à Saint Domingue à la même période on compte à peu près 3.000 places pour environ 20.000 spectateurs libres potentiels des villes (une place pour 6 ou 7 habitants libres, en incluant les militaires de passage) [...]; nous arrivons à un total d'environ 1.200 soirées et 1.900 représentations d'œuvres diverses." I thank Prof. Camier for having clarified that he believes these second statistics to be correct (private communication July 15, 2018). Cf. also his "Musique et société coloniale," 16–17 (I thank Camilla Cavicchi for having provided me with a copy of this and other texts).

15. Camier, "Les concerts dans les capitales," 76.

16. Fouchard, *Le théâtre à Saint-Domingue*, 303–44; Camier, "Minette artiste"; idem, "Minette, chanteuse"; idem, "Musique coloniale," 269–74; idem, "Minette, situation"; Powers, *From Plantation to Paradise*, 90–104 (who does not quote Camier's PhD dissertation, however). Finally, Minette's career inspired Marie Vieux-Chauvet's novel *La Danse sur le volcan*, entirely based on Fouchard.

17. Fouchard, *Le théâtre à Saint-Domingue*, 316.

18. See respectively Camier, "Minette, artiste," 7; idem, "Minette, chanteuse," 4023; idem, "Musique coloniale," 272; and idem, "Minette, situation," 4639. These publications are now summarized and supplemented with extensive archival transcriptions in Camier's most recent article "Minette: une étude biographique," which I will only quote where it contains data or views that are new or differ from his previous publications. I thank Prof. Camier for having sent me the manuscript of this article prior to publication, and for his very helpful comments. On two further articles published by Camier after the submission of this study, see my "Postscript."

19. Camier, "Minette, artiste," 6; idem, "Minette, situation," 4639–40, and idem, "Minette: une étude biographique." As it appears, the consultation of the original funeral certificate could have solved much earlier the issue of Minette's paternity.

20. Powers, *From Plantation to Paradise*, 121; Prest, *"Iphigénie en Haïti,"* 19 n. 25 and 22 n. 41. See also figure 2 on p. 281 of this study.

21. The present genealogy basically follows Camier's "Minette, situation," and "Minette: une étude biographique." But see also my "Postscript" at the end of this essay.

22. On Minette's stage name see Camier, "Minette, artiste," 9 (but see also my "Postscript"). On her mother's surname and nickname variants or errors such as Mahotière and Daquin—*recte* Mahaultière and Daguin—see the clarifications by Bernadette and Philippe Rossignol, who appended substantial genealogical information on Minette's ancestors to Camier's article "Minette, situation," in *Généalogie et Histoire de la Caraïbe* 185 (2005), in a separate section entitled "Compléments," on pp. 4640–42 of the same issue of the journal. Both nicknames—Mahaultière and Daguin—are used in a notarial document naming Minette's mother, dated to 1782 in Port-au-Prince (Camier, "Minette, situation," 4638 and 4640 n. 4; idem, "Musique coloniale," 272 n. 92, which cites Dominique Rogers, "Les libres de couleur dans les capitales de Saint-Domingue," 111).

23. Camier, "Minette, situation," 4638.

24. Ibid., and idem, "Minette: une étude biographique," where more information on Longuet is provided.

25. Camier, "Musique coloniale," 272.

26. Idem, "Minette: une étude biographique." The baptismal certificate of Minette's youngest daughter confirms Minette's full name and contains her autograph signature (I thank Prof. Camier for having sent me a photograph of this document). Minette's mother's nickname Mahaultière suggested to Bernadette and Philippe Rossignol that Minette's grandmother Elisabeth Dougé had been raised by the family Duvivier de la Mahaultière, related to Minette's great-grandfather Alexandre Dougé (whose brother Matthieu married Marie Anne Françoise, a sister of the aforementioned council member Marthe-Jerôme Duvivier de la Mahaultière). Cf. Fouchard, *Le théâtre à Saint-Domingue*, 304; B. and Ph. Rossignol, "Compléments," 4641–42; Camier, "Minette, situation," 4638–39 and idem, "Minette: une étude biographique"; Powers, *From Plantation to Paradise*, 39.

27. Moreau de Saint-Méry, *Description topographique*, 2:989; Fouchard, *Le théâtre à Saint-Domingue*, 309; Camier, "Minette, situation," 4638, but cf. his conclusions in "Minette: une étude biographique." Two months before her opera debut Minette had sung her first public concert—though the precise repertoire remains unknown—on which cf. Fouchard, *Le théâtre à Saint-Domingue*, 305–06; Camier, "Musique coloniale," 355; Powers, *From Plantation to Paradise*, 91.

28. Fouchard, *Le théâtre à Saint-Domingue*, 305–12—paraphrased by Powers, *From Plantation to Paradise*, 91–95.

29. Camier, "Musique coloniale," 811; Powers, *From Plantation to Paradise*, 95 and 218. On the *scène-lyrique* of Rousseau and Coignet, see Jean-Jacques Rousseau and Horace Coignet, *Pygmalion*; and Simeone Antonio Sografi and Giovanni Battista Cimador, *Pimmalione*, which includes a facsimile of Coignet's score reproducing Ms. 6 R 13, vol. VII:313–42, of the Archives de la Comédie Française in Paris. On the Lyon edition of 1770—and for its collation with further extant sources—see Rousseau and Coignet, *Pygmalion*. I wish to thank Brenno Boccadoro for his precious advice concerning the latter work.

30. Camier's list in his "Musique coloniale," 811–13, includes Minette's Easter concert on 15 April 1781, not her debut in December 1780—because of its unknown repertoire. See also his "Minette, artiste," 3–4.

31. The information provided in the *Affiches Américaines* about operas in Saint-Domingue can presently be consulted at https://www.theatreinsaintdomingue.org (last accessed on July 20, 2018).

32. Only two serious operas were in Minette's repertoire: Gluck's *Orphée* (March 19, 1782; January 5, 1787, role: L'amour) and *Iphigénie en Aulide* (possibly only the duo "Ne doutez jamais de ma flamme," sung during a concert on January 18, 1785; role: Iphigénie); cf. Prest, *"Iphigénie en Haïti,"* 24 n. 49. On Minette's characterization as coloratura singer see the announcement on *Affiches Américaines* quoted below in n. 40; and on her skills as an actress, see pp. 14–15 of Julia Prest's new article cited in my "Postscript" at the end of this essay.

33. This is, alas, not the place to discuss the—stunning—career of Minette's sister, Lise, whose life seems even more evanescent than Minette's, perhaps due to her talent—and preference?—for more "local," creolized types of plays (as mentioned, a repertoire disdained by Minette, see *Supplément aux Affiches Américaines* of October 10, 1783, 594). Lise would certainly deserve a monograph devoted to her alone. On her, see Fouchard's possibly idealized reconstruction in *Le théâtre à Saint-Domingue*, 310; and Powers,

From Plantation to Paradise, 90–122. On a new article on Lise published by Camier, see my "Postscript" at the end of this essay.

34. See Fouchard, *Le théâtre à Saint-Domingue*, 321–22 (and Prest, *"Iphigénie en Haïti,"* 20, who does not refer to Fouchard, however); Camier, "Musique coloniale," 226–27; Camier and Dubois, "Voltaire et Zaïre," 55.

35. Powers, *From Plantation to Paradise*, 100.

36. Camier, "Musique coloniale," 273–74. On Camier's evidence and on Minette's exile in general, however, see my "Postscript" at the end of this essay.

37. Le Gardeur, *The First New Orleans Theatre*, 13–14; Camier, "Minette, chanteuse," 4023; Powers, *From Plantation to Paradise*, 120.

38. On Jeanne-Marie Marsan and Minette's critics see Fouchard, *Artistes et répertoire*, 56–59; idem, *Le théâtre à Saint-Domingue*, 337; Camier, "Musique coloniale," 270; Powers, *From Plantation to Paradise*, 103–4. But see also the "Postscript" at the end of this essay.

39. Camier and Dubois, "Voltaire et Zaïre," 47–48; Clay, *Stagestruck*, 216–19. On the seating policy of Saint-Domingue's theaters see also Fouchard, *Le théâtre à Saint-Domingue*, 179–83; and Powers, *From Plantation to Paradise*, chapter 3 (Port-au-Prince's theater discussed on pp. 73–77).

40. On Minette's performance of the title role in *L'amant statue*, see the announcement in *Affiches Américaines* October 7, 1786, 477–78, where she is equated with "Demoiselle *Renaud*" (Rose Renaud, aka Mlle Renaud l'aînée; sometimes spelled as Renault), who sang the coloratura soprano lead role of Célimène in the Parisian premiere of *L'amant statue* in 1785 (on the piece more below; on Rose Renaud described as "première chanteuse à roulades" [coloratura singer] in the Comédie Italienne, see for instance Fétis, *Biographie universelle*, 229). *Nina, ou la folle par amour*, based on a libretto by B. J. Marsollier des Vivetières, was premiered in Paris on May 15, 1786 and in Port-au-Prince on March 4, 1787 (*Affiches Américaines* March 1, 1787, 97–98). *La belle Arsène*, based on a libretto by Charles-Simon Favart, was premiered in Fontainebleau on November 2, 1773, in Paris on August 14, 1775, and in Port-au-Prince on October 25, 1778. Minette performed its title role during her benefit on 5 May 1787 (*Affiches Américaines* May 3, 1787, 230).

41. But see, for instance, the exceedingly long review in *Affiches Américaines* March 10, 1787, 123–24.

42. The piece was repeated in Port-au-Prince only two months after its premiere. Three of its six further repetitions in the same theater were benefits for one of the four soloists of the first cast (two for Sieur Saint-Léger and one for Sieur Durosier, the latter having been the beneficiary of the premiere as well), and so it seems likely that Minette was included in those three: March 16, 1787, March 23, 1787, and January 19, 1788. If so, *L'amant statue* would be her most frequently repeated performance altogether, perhaps matched by *La fée Urgele*. According to Fouchard and Powers it was still being presented as late as 1789 (cf. Fouchard, *Le théâtre à Saint-Domingue*, 330 and 340; Powers, *From Plantation to Paradise*, 102 and 166), while the website https://www.theatreinsaintdomingue.org gives February 23, 1788 as the last date of performance in the colony. Other pieces frequently repeated in Port-au-Prince during Minette's career (1781–1789) include *La fée Urgele, ou ce qui plaît aux dames* by Egidio Romoaldo Duni and Charles-Simon Favart; *L'épreuve villageoise* by André-Ernest-Modeste Grétry and Pierre-Jean-Baptiste Desforges; *Blaise et Babet, ou la suite des trois fermiers* by Nicolas Dezède and Jacques-Marie Boutet de Monvel; *L'infante de Zamora* by Giovanni Paisiello and Nicolas-Étienne Framery; and *La belle Arsène*.

43. Desfontaines had already published his libretto in 1781 (Paris, chez Vente), with arias to be sung on various known melodies. Another, like-named libretto, written by Jean-François Guichard and set to music by Charles de Lusse, had been published in 1759—but the plot was totally different. The presentation of Dalayrac-Desfontaines's piece in Port-au-Prince was preceded by the aforementioned announcement in the *Affiches Américaines* October 7, 1786, 477–78, probably ordered by the beneficiary, M. Durosier. It ended by saying: "[c'est] une pièce qu'on regarde avec raison comme l'écueil des meilleures chanteuses."

44. Carr, "Pygmalion and the *Philosophes*"; but see also below, nn. 55–60. On the pieces by Alain-René Lesage, George Frideric Handel, Carlo Gozzi, Gaetano Martinelli, and Niccolò Jommelli see Buch, *Magic Flutes*, 113, 163, 215, and 220 respectively.

45. Buch, *Magic Flutes*, 227–50. In the present context the young Haydn's pantomime *Arlequin, der neue Abgott Ram in America* is particularly interesting for the way it touches on issues of racial mixture. Composed on a libretto by Joseph Felix Kurz, it was performed in Vienna in 1759; see Kurz, *Der neue Krumme Teufel*.

46. Reviewers of Buch's book include Nicholas Till, Leonardo J. Waisman, Laurel E. Zeiss, Alice Bellini, and Amber Youell; most of them agree that the book is repetitive and the examples redundant, though they acknowledge the author's archival zeal.

47. Buch, *Magic Flutes*, 37, 50–51.

48. Respectively *Le Prince de Noisy* (1749), *Les Boreades* (1763), *Armide* (1777), and *Roland* (1778); see Buch, *Magic Flutes*, 70–87.

49. *Œuvres complètes de Voltaire*, 15:363; see also *Mercure de France* (April 1738, pp. 738–39), where the flûteur is—wrongly—said to perform 14 pieces. On Vaucanson's fame and production, see Gaillard, Goffi, Roukhomovsky, and Roux, eds., *L'Automate*. See also Metzner, *Crescendo of the Virtuoso*, 165, 241, 338.

50. Vaucanson, *Le mécanisme du fluteur automate* (1738). In January 1739 (p. 87) the *Mercure* announced the publication of Vaucanson's treatise—clearly quoting the title-page of its first edition.

51. The reason for the misdating of the second edition remains unknown, but the real date can be deduced from D'Alembert's entry "Automate," from Vaucanson's "Lettre [...] à M. l'Abbé D.F.," and from the "Lettre d'un Persan, Au sujet des nouveaux Automates de M. Vaucanson," an anonymous letter probably written by Charles-Étienne Pesselier dated October 8, 1741 (my thanks to Dr. Alfredo Damanti for having clarified this issue for me).

On Hubert-François Bourguignon d'Anville, aka Gravelot (1699–1773), famous for his illustrations of Boccaccio, Tasso, Ovid, and Shakespeare, see Sullivan, "Gravelot."

The engraving that appears in fig. 5 was used to illustrate the announcement of an exhibition of the three automata once Vaucanson had become a member of the Académie Royale des Sciences, thus datable after January 28, 1746; see http://www.academie-sciences.fr/fr/Liste-des-membres-depuis-la-creation-de-l-Academie-des-sciences/les-membres-du-passe-dont-le-nom-commence-par-v.html.

52. *Mercure de France*, April 1738, 739.

53. Metzner, *Crescendo of the Virtuoso*, 173. The names of these automata are reminiscent of the popular morality tale by Jean-François Marmontel of 1762, or one of its early theatrical arrangements, for instance Favart's and Blaise's *Annette et Lubin*.

54. Leuven and Bordèse, *L'automate de Vaucanson*.

55. Jullien, *Le nouveau Pygmalion*. A second edition was published in Amsterdam and Bordeaux in 1776. See Coulet, *Pygmalions des Lumières*, 13–15, and 79–98 (where Jullien's text is reproduced), who compares a series of earlier and later parodies, and also Carr, "Pygmalion and the *Philosophes*," 252. For an enlightening account of the genesis and diachronic reception of the Pygmalion myth and its complex interaction with the arts see Stoichita, *L'effet Pygmalion*.

56. Rheineck and Debresme-Desgagniers, *L'amante statue*. Rheineck had seen Rousseau's melodrama in 1770; his parody was premiered at the Hôtel de Ville of Lyon on August 9, 1774. The libretto was printed in Lyon the same year, but the music is lost.

57. And, of course, the end of *L'amant statue* must have recalled Rousseau's disapproval of the supernatural effects employed in contemporary tragedies.

58. Rameau, *Pigmalion*. Based on the literary version of Houdar de La Motte, it premiered in Paris on August 27, 1748 with a libretto by Ballot de Sauvot. On the relationship between Rameau's *Pigmalion* and Rousseau's *Pygmalion* see Gullstam, "Pygmalion's Power Struggles." On the medieval origin (and post-medieval survival) of the function of music in the animation of Pygmalion's statue see Stoichita, *L'effet Pygmalion*, especially 76–88, 160–62, and 189.

59. Rameau, *Pigmalion*, 14–15; a description of the scene can be found in Gullstam, "Pygmalion's Power Struggles," 127, and Buch, *Magic Flutes*, 64–65. Also see Boureau-Deslandes, *Pigmalion, ou la Statue Animée*, a short work that uses the myth of Pygmalion to introduce a libertine treatise on gnosiology, aesthetics, and morality. On this text see Mastrogiacomo, *Libertinismo e lumi*, 56–70; and on its stunning illustrations by Emmanuel De Ghendt (after Charles Eisen) see Stoichita, *L'effet Pygmalion*, 178–82.

60. Only Rameau's chaconne from *Les Indes galantes* is known to have been performed in Saint-Domingue (cf. Camier, "Musique coloniale," 110).

61. Fouchard, *Le théâtre à Saint-Domingue*, 345–48; Camier, "Musique coloniale," 259–61.

62. On the orchestra of Port-au-Prince see Moreau de Saint-Méry, *Description*, 2:987. Its precise instrumentation remains unknown, but that of Saint-Marc of 1779 survives: two flutes or clarinets, one horn, four violins, one viola, one bass (see Camier, "Les concerts," 84 and 86). Occasional performers would nevertheless not be represented by these figures. On enslaved musicians Camier writes: "La formation connue la plus importante est celle de Port-au-Prince mais on sait seulement qu'elle comportait onze instrumentistes. Cette absence d'informations peut avoir deux explications, le désintérêt encore très vivace dans la fin du XVIIIème pour tout ce qui touche à la musique instrumentale, et peut-être aussi la présence de musiciens esclaves, donc 'transparents' pour les commentateurs, dans ces orchestres. Les deux arguments peuvent d'ailleurs très bien s'adosser l'un à l'autre, la fonction subalterne des instrumentistes justifiant l'emploi d'esclaves musiciens" ("Musique coloniale," 104).

63. Laborde, *Essai sur la musique*, 3:493; Choron and Fayolle, *Dictionnaire historique*, 1:31, col. II.

64. Laborde, *Essai sur la musique*, 3:493

65. Fétis, *Biographie universelle*, 1:162, who quotes Bermann, *Oesterreichisches Biographisches Lexikon*, in whose *Drittes Heft* the entry on "Atis" is found on pages 287–88 (I thank most warmly Dr. Scott Edwards, who provided me with a photographic reproduction of this entry). Ljungar-Chapelon, ed., *Atys*, 9, incorrectly posits the identity of Fétis's "M. Bermann" as Jeremias Bermann (1770–1855), "who was an art and music dealer in Vienna."

66. Last italics added. Fétis's skepticism suggests that Bermann's dates may be somewhat tentative.

67. Lully's *Atys* featured one of the earliest recorder/flute solos in a magic-sleep scene (cf. Buch, *Magic Flutes*, 37). On its parodies see Rubellin, "Stratégies parodiques"; and eadem, ed., *Atys burlesque*.

68. On the website *Le marronnage dans le monde atlantique: sources et trajectoires de vie* (https://www.marronnage.info/fr/accueil.php) the name Atis (thus spelled) occurs in eight announcements of runaways in Saint-Domingue between 1767 and 1787. Five of them include names of other theatrical characters such as Hippolite, Castor, or Lindor. I thank the anonymous reader of this essay for having directed me to this website.

69. However, Atys cannot be identified with any of the other like-named persons listed in Noël, ed., *Dictionnaire des gens de couleur*, 1:21 (no. 89) and 232 (no. 1123), and 2:141 (no. 1052), 581 (no. 5058), 805 (no. 7386), 821 (no. 7544), and 839 (no. 7670); I could not consult vol. III, however.

70. Among his Parisian students was Antoine Hugot (1761–1803), who taught at the Conservatoire in Paris along with François Devienne (1759–1803) and Johann Georg Wunderlich (1755–1819); see Ljungar-Chapelon, ed., *Atys*, 9, who describes in detail Atys's pioneering interest in the notation of dynamics and rhetorical punctuation. On flutists in Saint-Domingue see Camier, "Musique coloniale," 215. Not all of Atys's many works are detailed in the *Grove Music Online* article by Cotte, "Atys [Atis; first name unknown]." [*sic*] A comprehensive works list will be included in my forthcoming study of music and race in the eighteenth-century French Caribbean.

71. A composer, oboist, flutist, and bassoonist, he shared with Minette the concerts for Christmas 1780 and Easter 1781 (see respectively *Supplément aux Affiches Américaines* December 19, 1780, 411, and April 10, 1781, 138), and the performance on December 4, 1781 (*Supplements aux Affiches Américaines* November 20, 1781, 459). See also Fouchard, *Artistes et répertoire*, 56.

72. After a benefit concert for him on April 11, 1783 (*Supplements aux Affiches Américaines* April 5, 1783, 176), his next recorded performance is dated January 31, 1789, when Macarty performs a *Symphonie concertante* by Stamitz and Minette sings twice: an air from l'*Olympiade* and the *Grand Chœur* of *Phèdre* (*Affiches Américaines* January 29, 1789, 50).

73. Qualified as "Louis, musicien du Régiment d'Agenois" in *Supplément aux Affiches Américaines* of Port-au-Prince, July 27, and August 10, 1782 (respectively on pages 283 and 301), and, previously, as "Sieur Luis" in *Affiches Américaines* of Le Cap, March 30, 1779 (on page 105, misprinted as 30/33/79 in Camier, "Musique coloniale," 354). However, Louis is paired with another clarinetist called "Henri"—supposed by Fouchard to have been a musician active in the theater of Le Cap (see *Artistes et répertoire*, 45).

74. Fouchard, *Artistes et répertoire*, 55. On the doubling of wind players cf. Camier, "Les concerts," 84 and 86; idem, http://www.lameca.org/dossiers/musique_coloniale/p3.htm. A similar practice is reported in Havana in 1802 by Escudero, "Noticias sobre música," 48.

75. For a discussion of Aristotle's ambiguous statements concerning the souls of enslaved persons see, for example, Thalmann, *The Swineherd and the Bow*, 29–37. On the nuanced application—and radicalization—of the *Code noir* in the eighteenth-century Caribbean see Reinhardt, *Claims to Memory*, 33–35, and 109.

76. "By an irony in the second degree, Montesquieu's ironical defence of slavery shared the common fate and was misunderstood; it was taken for the very thing it was designed to expose": Fletcher, "Montesquieu's Influence," 415.

77. Reinhardt, *Claims to Memory*, 29. See also Lafontant, *Montesquieu et le problème de l'esclavage.*

78. The following summary is based on the Parisian print of 1785, since no traces are known of a different arrangement in Saint-Domingue.

79. See the brilliant analysis of a similar case in an earlier repertoire in Wilbourne, "*Lo Schiavetto*," 11.

80. *Céladon*'s refrain reads: "J'ai lu que plus une Bergere parait sévere; / et plus on doit prendre l'essor. / Oui, bien souvent, pour mieux nous plaire, / il faut avoir tout-à-fait tort" (Dalayrac and Desfontaines, *L'amant statue mise en musique*, 72–73; punctuation added from the libretto: [Desfontaines], *L'amant statue, comédie*, 24–25).

81. R: "Il vous plairait bien davantage, si vous saviez..." C: "Eh bien? quoi? parleras-tu?" R: "C'est qu'on dit qu'il a une âme." C: "Une âme!" Desfontaines and Dalayrac, *L'amant statue mise en musique*, 75.

82. See Diderot (?), "Sérinette," in *Encyclopedie*, 15: 96–7.

83. The original words of the "famous air" were by La Harpe. Desfontaine's full replacement text reads: "Sous sa forme nouvelle / si Daphné soupira, / c'est qu'elle était fidelle / au Dieu qu'elle adora: / Si le Marbre s'enflame / dans ce bois enchanté, / c'est que tout prend une âme / pour plaire à la beauté." (Dalayrac and Desfontaines, *L'amant statue mise en musique*, 77–78). While the first quatrain establishes a classical *exemplum e contrario* (Daphne's stiffening), the second obviously alludes to Dorval's animation in Célimène's garden. Variations of Pierre-Alexandre Monsigny's melody crowd the repertoire of the time. Examples include Beauvarlet-Charpentier, *Airs choisis variés*; Krumpholtz, *Cinquième concerto*; or Wunderlich, *O ma tendre musette, varié*.

84. Dalayrac and Desfontaines, *L'amant statue mise en musique*, 80–83. The model alluded to is Rameau's *Pigmalion*, 14–15. A further mocking of Rameau's statue seems implicit in Célimène's phrase "il a l'air de me fixer" at 176—perhaps reminiscent of Rameau's "Ciel quel objet? mon âme en est ravie," which the statue utters on p. 15.

85. "Chose mobiliaire," a definition of enslaved persons used in paragraphs 45 and 46 of both issues of the *Code noir* (1685 and 1724); respectively: "[...] ainsi qu'il se pratique pour les sommes de deniers et autres *choses mobiliaires*"; "[...] que la condition des esclaves soit réglée en toutes affaires comme celle des autres *choses mobiliaires* [...]" (italics added). On the "tache de l'esclavage" see Hilliard d'Auberteuil, *Considérations sur l'état présent*, 2:73: "[...] mais à Saint-Domingue, l'intérêt et la sureté veulent que nous accablions la race des Noirs d'un si grand mépris, que quiconque on descend jusqu'à la sixième génération, soit couvert d'une tache inéfaçable."

86. Flute-playing automata include ones fabricated by Gustave Vichy (ca. 1870); Jean Roullet (1870); and Alexandre Nicolas Théroude (1855, 1862, 1878). See, for example, Nocks, *The Life Story*.

87. Mindful of Genette's "minimal parodies," cf. *Palimpsests*, 12 and 431.

88. Mozard, *La Répétition interrompue*, premiered in Port-au-Prince on October 4, 1789, and is described in *Affiches Américaines* (*Nouvelles Diverses*) October 7, 1789, 542. Also see Fouchard, *Artistes et répertoire*, 252; idem, *Le Théâtre à Saint-Domingue*, 340; Powers, *From Plantation to Paradise*, 119 (who misidentifies the work, however).

89. Voltaire, *La Zayre, tragédie*. The piece was performed at least eight times in Saint-Domingue between 1768 and 1786. On Voltaire's tragedy, see Madelyn Gutwirth, "The Intolerable Other," 178–80.

90. Camier and Dubois, "Voltaire et Zaïre," 55.

91. Laujon, *Souvenirs de trente années*, 1:166–67; Clay, *Stagestruck*, 223.

92. Bernard Camier, "Minette Ferrand. Actualisation des résultats de recherche"; idem, "Jeanne, Louise, Anne Beauvernet dite Lise (Port-au-Prince 1773 - Paris circa 1840?)."

93. Julia Prest, "Parisian Palimpsests and Creole Creations."

94. Pedro Memelsdorff, "Minette à Cuba?"

95. Camier, "Minette Ferrand. Actualisation des résultats de recherche," 4–5.

96. Ibid.

97. Ibid.

98. Ibid.

99. Camier, "Musique coloniale," 273

Bibliography

Affiches Américaines. Saint-Domingue newspaper (1766–1791), digitized by the University of Florida (www.ufdc.ufl.edu).

Beauvarlet-Charpentier, Jean-Jacques. *Airs choisis variés pour le clavecin ou forte-piano [...] Œuvre V*. Paris: Cousineau, n.d.

Bermann, Moriz. *Oesterreichisches Biographisches Lexikon: Genaue Lebensbeschreibungen berühmter und denkwürdiger Personen jedes Standes in der österreichischen Monarchie; von der frühesten Zeit bis auf unsere Tage*. 3 vols. Vienna: Bei Sigmund Bermann's Witwe und Sohn, 1851.

Bhambra, Gurminder. "Postcolonialism and Decoloniality, A Dialogue." *Postcolonial Studies* 17 (2014): 115–21.

Bloechl, Olivia. "Race, Empire, and Early Music." In *Rethinking Difference in Music Scholarship*, ed. Olivia Bloechl, Melanie Lowe, and Jeffrey Kallberg. Pp. 77–107. Cambridge: Cambridge University Press, 2015.

Boureau-Deslandes, André-François. *Pigmalion, ou la Statue Animée*. London: Samuel Harding, 1741.

Buch, David. *Magic Flutes & Enchanted Forests: The Supernatural in Eighteenth-Century Musical Theater*. Chicago: University of Chicago Press, 2008.

Burnard, Trevor and Garrigus, John. *The Plantation Machine: Atlantic Capitalism in French Saint-Domingue and British Jamaica*. Philadelphia: University of Pennsylvania Press, 2016.

Cabon, Père Adolphe. *Histoire d'Haïti*. 4 vols. Port-au-Prince: Éd. de la Petite revue, [1930–1938].

Cale, John G. "French Secular Music in Saint-Domingue (1750–1795) Viewed as a Factor in America's Musical Growth." PhD diss., Louisiana State University and Agricultural & Mechanical College, 1971.

Camier, Bernard. "Minette (1767–1807), artiste de couleur à Saint-Domingue." *Revue de la Société haïtienne d'Histoire et de Géographie* 205 (2000): 1–11.

Camier, Bernard. "Minette, chanteuse de couleur à Saint-Domingue." *Généalogie et histoire de la Caraïbe* 165 (2003): 4023.

Camier, Bernard. "Musique coloniale et société à Saint-Domingue dans la seconde moitié du XVIIIème siècle." PhD diss., Université des Antilles-Guyane, 2004.

Camier, Bernard. "Minette, situation sociale d'une artiste de couleur à Saint-Domingue." *Généalogie et histoire de la Caraïbe* 185 (2005): 4638–40.

Camier, Bernard. "Moreau de Saint-Méry et la musique coloniale." In *Moreau de Saint-Méry ou les ambiguïtés d'un créole des Lumières, Actes du colloque Moreau de Saint-Méry (Fort-de-France, 9–11 septembre 2004)*. Pp. 173–87. Fort-de-France: Société des Amis des archives et de la recherche sur le patrimoine culturel des Antilles, 2006.

Camier, Bernard. "Les concerts dans les capitales de Saint-Domingue à la fin du XVIIIe siècle." *Revue de musicologie* 93 (2007): 75–98.

Camier, Bernard. "Musique et société coloniale: Saint-Domingue à l'époque de Chabanon." In *Michel Paul Guy de Chabanon et ses contemporains*, Éd. Laurine Quetin. Pp. 13–34. Tours: Université François Rabelais, 2008.

Camier, Bernard. "Minette (Elisabeth, Alexandrine, Louise Ferrand dite): artiste libre de couleur à Port-au-Prince à la fin du XVIIIème siècle: une étude biographique." *Revue haïtienne d'histoire, de géographie et de géologie* 259–62 (2018): 214–37.

Camier, Bernard. "Jeanne, Louise, Anne Beauvernet dite Lise (Port-au-Prince 1773—Paris circa 1840?) demi-sœur de Minette et chanteuse de couleur à Saint-Domingue à la fin du XVIIIème siècle," *Généalogie et Histoire de la Caraïbe*. www.ghcaraibe.org/, accessed July 21, 2019.

Camier, Bernard. "Minette Ferrand. Actualisation des résultats de recherche." *Généalogie et Histoire de la Caraïbe*, www.ghcaraibe.org/, accessed July 29, 2019.

Camier, Bernard, and Laurent Dubois. "Voltaire et Zaïre, ou le théâtre des Lumières dans l'aire atlantique française." *Revue d'histoire moderne et contemporaine* 54 (2007): 39–69.

Camier, Bernard, and Marie-Christine Hazaël-Massieux. "*Jeannot et Thérèse* de Clément: Un opéra-comique en créole à Saint-Domingue au milieu du XVIIIème siècle." *Revue de la Société Haïtienne d'Histoire et de Géographie* 215 (2003): 135–66.

Carr, J. L. "Pygmalion and the *Philosophes*: The Animated Statue in Eighteenth-Century France." *Journal of the Warburg and Courtauld Institutes* 23 (1960): 239–55.

Choron, Alexandre, and François Fayolle. *Dictionnaire historique des musiciens artistes et amateurs, morts ou vivans [...]*. 2 vols. Paris: Chez Valade, Imprimeur; chez Lenormant, 1810–1811.

Clay, Lauren R. *Stagestruck: The Business of Theater in Eighteenth-Century France and Its Colonies*. Ithaca, NY: Cornell University Press, 2013.

Cotte, Roger J. V. "Atys [Atis; first name unknown]." In Grove Music Online. www.oxfordmusiconline.com, accessed January 16, 2019.

Coulet, Henri. *Pygmalions des Lumières*. Paris: Éditions Desjonquères, 1998.

Curtis, Lesley Shannon. "Utopian (Post)Colonies: Rewriting Race and Gender after the Haitian Revolution." PhD diss., Duke University, 2011.

D'Alembert, Jean le Rond. "Automate." In *Encyclopédie, ou dictionnaire raisonné des sciences, des arts et des métiers*, ed. Denis Diderot and Jean Le Rond d'Alembert. 28 vols. Vol. 1 (1751): 896–97. Geneva, Paris, Neuchatel: Chez Briasson [and others], 1754–1772.

Descourtilz, Michel Étienne. *Flore pittoresque et médicale des Antilles, ou Traité des plantes usuelles des colonies françaises, anglaises, espagnoles, portugaises*. 8 vols. Paris: Chez Pichard; Chez Gauthier, 1821–1829.

Desfontaines (François-Georges Fouques Deshayes). *L'amant statue. Comédie en un acte et en prose, mêlée d'ariettes [...]*. Paris: Chez Brunet, 1785.

Desfontaines (François-Georges Fouques Deshayes) and Nicolas Dalayrac. *L'amant statue. Comédie en un acte et en prose [...] dédiée à Monsieur le Bailli de Crussol [...]. Mise en musique par M. Dal...* [*sic*]. Paris: Chez Le Duc, [1785].

Diderot, Denis (?). "Sérinette." In *Encyclopédie, ou dictionnaire raisonné des sciences, des arts et des métiers*, ed. Denis Diderot and Jean Le Rond d'Alembert. 28 vols. Vol. 15 (1765): 96–97. Geneva, Paris, Neuchatel: Chez Briasson [and others], 1754–1772.

Du Tertre, Jean-Baptiste. *Histoire generale des Antilles habitées par les François*. 4 vols. Paris: Chez Thomas Iolly, 1667–1671.

Dubois, Laurent. "Gendered Freedom: Citoyennes and War in the Revolutionary French Caribbean." In *Gender, War and Politics: Transatlantic Perspectives, 1775–1830*, ed. Karen Hagemann, Gisela Mettele, and Jane Rendall. Pp. 58–70. Basingstoke, Palgrave Macmillan, 2010.

Escudero, Miriam. "Noticias sobre música en el *Papel Periódico de la Havana* (1790–1805)." In *Música de salón en publicaciones periódicas, La Habana, 1829–1867*, ed. eadem, Zoila Lapique, Claudia Fallarero, and Indira Marrero. Pp. 21–48. Havana: Ediciones Cidmuc, 2017.

Favart, Justine, and Adolphe-Benoît Blaise. *Annette et Lubin, comédie en 1 acte et en vers, mêlée d'ariettes et de vaudevilles, par Mme Favart et M**** [*sic*]. Paris: N.n, 1762.

Fétis, François-Joseph. *Biographie universelle des musiciens et bibliographie générale de la musique*. 2nd ed. 8 vols. Paris: Firmin-Didot, 1860–1865.

Fletcher, F. T. H. "Montesquieu's Influence on Anti-Slavery Opinion in England." *The Journal of Negro History* 18 (1933): 414–25.

Fleurant, Gerdès. "Haiti." In *Performing the Caribbean Experience*, ed. Malena Kuss. Vol. 2 of *Music in Latin America and the Caribbean: An Encyclopedic History*. Pp. 252–63. Austin, TX: University of Texas Press, 2007.

Fouchard, Jean. *Artistes et répertoire des scènes de Saint-Domingue*. Port-au-Prince: Imprimerie de l'État, 1955.

Fouchard, Jean. *Le théâtre à Saint-Domingue*. Port-au-Prince: Imprimerie de l'État, 1955.

Fouchard, Jean. *Plaisirs de Saint-Domingue, notes sur la vie sociale, littéraire et artistique*. Port-au-Prince: Imprimerie de l'État, 1955.

Gaillard, Aurélia, Jean-Yves Goffi, Bernard Roukhomovsky, and Sophie Roux, eds. *L'Automate: Modèle, Métaphore, Machine, Merveille*. Pessac: Presses Universitaires de Bordeaux, 2013.

Gay, Pamela. "The Performance of Colonialism: The Theater of the Haitian Revolution." In *Essays: Exploring the Global Caribbean*, ed. Susan Roberson. Pp. 87–104. Newcastle upon Tyne: Cambridge Scholars Publishing, 2013.

Genette, Gérard. *Palimpsests: Literature in the Second Degree*, trans. Channa Newman and Claude Doubinsky. Lincoln, NE: University of Nebraska Press, 1997.

Ginzburg, Carlo. "Microstoria: Due o tre cose che so di lei." In idem, *Il filo e le tracce: Vero, falso, finto*. Pp. 240–69. Milan: Feltrinelli, 2006.

[Girod-Chantrans, Justin]. *Voyage d'un Suisse dans différentes colonies d'Amérique pendant la dernière guerre [...]*. Neuchâtel: Imprimerie de la Société Typographique, 1785.

González Echevarría, Roberto. *Alejo Carpentier: The Pilgrim at Home*. Austin, TX: University of Texas Press, 1990.

Gullstam Maria. "Pygmalion's Power Struggles: Rousseau, Rameau and Galathée." In *Rousseau on Stage: Playwright, Musician, Spectator*, ed. Maria Gullstam and Michael O'Dea. Pp. 119–37. Oxford: Voltaire Foundation, 2017.

Gutwirth, Madelyn. "The Intolerable Other." In *Discourses of Tolerance and Intolerance in the European Enlightenment*, ed. Hans Erich Bödeker, Clorinda Donato, and Peter Reill. Pp. 170–91. Toronto: University of Toronto Press, 2008.

Hazaël-Massieux, Marie-Christine. *Textes anciens en créole français de la Caraïbe: Histoire et analyse*. Paris: Éd. Publibook, 2008.

Hilliard d'Auberteuil, Michel-René. *Considérations sur l'état présent de la colonie française de Saint-Domingue. Ouvrage politique et législatif*. 2 vols. Paris: Chez Grangé, 1776–1777.

Isert, Paul Erdmann. *Voyages en Guinée et dans les îles Caraïbes en Amérique [...] Traduits de l'Allemand*. Paris: Chez Maradan, 1793.

Jullien, Jean-Auguste, dit Desboulmiers. *Le nouveau Pygmalion*. In *Pygmalions des Lumières*, ed. Henri Coulet. Pp. 79–98. Paris: Éditions Desjonquères. 1998.

Krumpholtz, Jean-Baptiste. *Cinquième concerto pour la harpe [...] dans lequel est renfermé l'air de O ma tendre musette [...]*. Paris: Chez l'Auteur, Chez M. Naderman, Chez Mad.[me] Oger, [1779].

Kurz, Joseph. *Der neue Krumme Teufel: Eine Opera-Comique von zwey Aufzügen; Nebst einer Kinder-Pantomime, Betitult: Arlequin Der neue Abgott Ram in America*. N.p., [ca. 1759].

Kuss, Malena. "Prologue." In *Performing Beliefs: Indigenous Peoples of South America, Central America, and Mexico*, ed. Malena Kuss. Vol. 1 of *Music in Latin America and the Caribbean: An Encyclopedic History*. Pp. ix-xxvi. Austin, TX: University of Texas Press, 2004.

Kuss, Malena. "The Caribbean: A Reflective Overview." In *Performing the Caribbean Experience*, ed. Malena Kuss. Vol. 2 of *Music in Latin America and the Caribbean: An Encyclopedic History*. Pp. 9–15. Austin, TX: University of Texas Press, 2007.

Labat, Jean-Baptiste. *Nouveau voyage aux isles de l'Amérique, contenant l'histoire naturelle de ces Pays, l'Origine, les Mœurs, la Religion et le Gouvernement des Habitans anciens et modernes. Les Guerres et les Evenemens singuliers [...]*. 6 vols. Paris: Chez Guillaume Cavelier, 1722.

Laborde, Jean-Benjamin de. *Essai sur la musique ancienne et moderne*. 4 vols. Paris: Ph.-D. Pierres, 1780.

Lafontant Julien. *Montesquieu et le problème de l'esclavage dans* L'esprit des lois. Sherbrooke: Éd. Naaman, 1979.

Largey, Michael D. "Musical Ethnography in Haiti: A Study of Elite Hegemony and Musical Composition." PhD diss., Indiana University, 1991.

Laujon, Alexandre Paul Marie de. *Souvenirs de trente années de voyages à Saint-Domingue, dans plusieurs colonies étrangères et au continent d'Amérique*. 2 vols. Paris: Schwartz et Gagnot, 1835.

Le Gardeur, René. *The First New Orleans Theatre, 1792–1803*. New Orleans: Leeward Books, 1963.

Le marronnage dans le monde atlantique: sources et trajectoires de vie. https://www.marronnage.info/fr/accueil.php, accessed August 15, 2020.

Lemmon, Alfred E., ed. *French Baroque Music of New Orleans: Spiritual Songs from the Ursuline Convent (1736)*. New Orleans: The Historic New Orleans Collection, 2014.

Leuven, Adolphe de, and Luigi Bordèse. *L'automate de Vaucanson: Opéra-comique en un acte*. Paris: Henriot et Cie, 1840.

Ljungar-Chapelon, Anders, ed. *Atys: Six sonates en duo œuvre IV, 1760; Clef facile et méthodique œuvre V, 1763*. Flöjtisten vademecum (The flautists vademecum). Malmö: Lund University, Malmö Academy of Music, 2015.

Malouet, Victor. *Mémoire sur l'esclavage des nègres dans les possessions françaises*. Neuchâtel: n.p., 1788.

Mastrogiacomo, Elisabetta. *Libertinismo e lumi: André-François Boureau-Deslandes (1689–1757)*. Naples: Liguori Editore, 2010.

McClellan, James E. *Colonialism and Science: Saint Domingue in the Old Regime*. With a New Foreword by Vertus Saint-Louis. Chicago and London: The University of Chicago Press, 2010 (first ed. 1992).

Memelsdorff, Pedro. "Cantus grecus: Greek Liturgy *more Latinorum* in the Codex Faenza 117." In *Mondo latino e civiltà bizantina: Musica, arte e cultura nei codici del '400*, ed. Antonio Lovato and Dilva Princivalli. Pp. 203–23. Padua: CLEUP Editrice, 2014.

Memelsdorff, Pedro. "Minette à Cuba? Notes sur un document retrouvé," *Bulletin de la Société d'Histoire de la Guadeloupe* 186 (2020): 89–100.

Mercure de France. French journal (1672–1789).

Metzner, Paul. *Crescendo of the Virtuoso: Spectacle, Skill, and Self-Promotion in Paris during the Age of Revolution*. Berkeley and Los Angeles: University of California Press, 1998.

Mignolo, Walter. "Delinking: The Rhetoric of Modernity, the Logic of Coloniality and the Grammar of De-Coloniality." *Cultural Studies* 21 (2007): 449–514.

Mintz, Sidney W., and Sally Price, eds. *Focus: Caribbean*. Washington, DC: Latin American Program, Woodrow Wilson International Center for Scholars, 1984.

Moreau de Saint-Méry, Médéric-Louis-Elie. *Description topographique, physique, civile, politique et historique de la partie française de l'isle Saint-Domingue*. 3 vols. Paris: Publications de la Société française d'histoire d'outre-mer, 2004.

Mozard, Charles Théodore. *La Répétition interrompue: Divertissement national*. Port-au-Prince: De l'Imprimerie de l'Auteur, 1789.

Noël, Érick, ed. *Dictionnaire des gens de couleur dans la France moderne*. 3 vols. Bibliothèque des Lumières 77, 82, 91. Geneva: Droz, 2011–2017.

Nocks, Lisa. *The Life Story of a Technology*. Westport, CT: Greenwood Press, 2007.

[Pesselier, Charles-Étienne]. "Lettre d'un Persan, Au sujet des nouveaux Automates de M. Vaucanson." *Amusements du Cœur et de l'Esprit* 13 (1742): 452–62.

Prest, Julia. "*Iphigénie en Haïti*: Performing Gluck's Paris operas in the French colonial Caribbean." *Eighteenth-Century Music* 14 (2017): 13–29.

Prest, Julia. "Parisian Palimpsests and Creole Creations: Mme Marsan and Dlle Minette play *Nina* on the Caribbean Stage." *Early Modern French Studies* 41 (2019): 1–19.

Powers, David. M. *From Plantation to Paradise? Cultural Politics and Musical Theatre in French Slave Colonies, 1764–1789*. East Lansing, MI: Michigan State University Press, 2014.

Quijano, Aníbal. "Coloniality and Modernity/Rationality." *Cultural Studies* 21 (2007): 168–78.

Rameau, Jean-Philippe, and Sylvain Ballot de Sauvot. *Pigmalion, acte de ballet*. Paris: Chez l'Auteur; Chez la Veuve Boivin; Chez M. Leclair, 1748.

Ramos Venereo, Zobeyda. "Haitian Traditions in Cuba." In *Performing the Caribbean Experience*, ed. Malena Kuss. Vol. 2 of *Music in Latin America and the Caribbean: An Encyclopedic History*. Pp. 266–80. Austin, TX: University of Texas Press, 2007.

Reinhardt, Catherine A. *Claims to Memory: Beyond Slavery and Emancipation in the French Caribbean*. New York and Oxford: Berghahn Books, 2006.

Rheineck, Christophe, and Deb[resme]-Desgagniers. *L'amante statue, ou le nouveau Pigmalion, comédie en 1 acte et en prose, mêlée d'ariettes, par M. de B... Desgagniers*. Lyon: Chez Castaud, 1774.

Rogers, Dominique. "Les libres de couleur dans les capitales de Saint-Domingue." PhD diss., University of Bordeaux III, 1999.

Rossignol, Bernadette, and Philippe Rossignol "Compléments." *Généalogie et Histoire de la Caraïbe* 185 (2005): 4640–42.

Rousseau, Jean-Jacques, and Horace Coignet. *Pygmalion: scène lyrique*, ed. Jacqueline Waeber. Geneva: Droz, 1997.

Rubellin, Françoise. "Stratégies parodiques: Les dénouements d'Atys." In *Le Théâtre en musique et son double (1600–1762)*, ed. Delia Gambelli and Letizia Norci Cagiano. Pp. 141–91. Paris: Éditions Champion, 2005.

Rubellin, Françoise, ed. *Atys burlesque: Parodies de l'opéra de Quinault et Lully à la Foire et à la Comédie-Italienne, 1726–1738*. Montpellier: Éditions Espaces 34, 2011.

Sacramental records of the Roman Catholic Church of the Archdiocese of New Orleans, ed. Earl C. Woods and Charles E. Nolan. 19 vols. New Orleans: Archdiocese of New Orleans, 1987–2004.

Sansay, Leonora (Hassal, Mary). *Secret History, or, The Horrors of St. Domingo*. Philadelphia: Bradford and Inskeep. R. Carr, printer, 1808.

Sografi, Simeone Antonio, and Giovanni Battista Cimador. *Pimmalione*, ed. Emilio Sala. Milan: Casa Ricordi, 1996.

Suppléments aux Affiches Américaines. Saint-Domingue newspaper (1766–1791), digitized by the University of Florida (www.ufdc.ufl.edu).

Stevenson, Robert. *Caribbean Music History: A Selective Bibliography with Musical Supplement*. Special issue of *Inter-American Music Review* 4 (1981).

Stoichita, Victor. *L'effet Pygmalion. Pour une anthropologie historique des simulacres*. Geneva: Droz, 2008.
Sullivan, M. G. "Gravelot [formerly Bourguignon], Hubert-François." In *Dictionary of National Biography*. www.oxforddnb.com/view/article/11307, accessed 13 January 2018.
Thalmann, William G. *The Swineherd and the Bow: Representations of Class in the Odyssey*. Ithaca, NY: Cornell University Press, 1998.
"Theatre in Saint-Domingue, 1764–1791, Plays, Ballets, and Operas." https://www.theatreinsaint-domingue.org, accessed July 20, 2018.
Thibault de Chanvalon, Jean-Baptiste. *Voyage à la Martinique, contenant diverses observations sur la physique, l'histoire naturelle, l'agriculture, les mœurs et les usages de cette isle, faites en 1751 & dans les années suivantes [...]*. Paris: Chez Cl. J. B. Bauche, 1763.
Vaucanson, Jacques. *Le mécanisme du fluteur automate présenté à messieurs de l'Académie royale des sciences*. Paris: Chez Jacques Guerin, 1738.
Vaucanson, Jacques. *Le mécanisme du fluteur automate présenté à messieurs de l'Académie royale des sciences [...] avec la description d'un Canard Artificiel [...] et aussi celle d'une autre figure [...] jouant du Tambourine & de la Flute [...]*. Paris: Chez Jacques Guerin, 1738 [actually 1741].
Vaucanson, Jacques. "Lettre [...] à M. l'Abbé D.F." In Pierre-François Guyot Desfontaines, and François Granet, *Observations sur les écrits modernes*. 33 vols. Vol. 23 (1740, recte 1741):346–53. Paris: Chez Chaubert, 1733–1746.
Vieux-Chauvet, Marie. *La Danse sur le volcan*. Paris: Plon, 1957.
Voltaire (Arouet, François-Marie). *Œuvres complètes de Voltaire*. 75 vols. Paris: Baudouin, 1825–1828.
Voltaire (Arouet, François-Marie). *La Zayre ... représentée à Paris aux mois d'aoust, novembre et décembre 1732*. Paris: Chez J. B. Bauche, 1733.
Wilbourne, Emily. "*Lo Schiavetto* (1612): Travestied Sound, Ethnic Performance, and the Eloquence of the Body." *Journal of the American Musicological Society* 63 (2010): 1–43.
Wimpffen, Alexandre-Stanislas de. *Voyage à Saint Domingue, pendant les années 1788, 1789 et 1790*. Paris: Chez Cocheris, 1797.
Wunderlich, Johann Georg. *O ma tendre musette, varié pour la flûte avec acc. de violon*. Paris, n.d.

CONTRIBUTORS

Geoffrey Baker is a professor of Music at Royal Holloway, University of London. He has written extensively on music in Latin America. His books include *Imposing Harmony: Music and Society in Colonial Cuzco* (Duke, 2008); *Music and Urban Society in Colonial Latin America* (Cambridge, 2010, with Tess Knighton); and *El Sistema: Orchestrating Venezuela's Youth* (Oxford, 2014). His most recent book is *Rethinking Social Action Through Music: The Search for Coexistence and Citizenship in Medellín's Music Schools* (Open Book Publishers, 2021).

Olivia Bloechl is a professor of Music at the University of Pittsburgh, with research interests in the early modern Atlantic world, French Baroque opera, postcolonialism, feminist ethics, and global music history. She is the author of *Native American Song at the Frontiers of Early Modern Music* (2008) and *Opera and the Political Imaginary in Old Regime France* (2017), and co-editor of *Rethinking Difference in Music Scholarship* (with M. Lowe and J. Kallberg, 2015).

Philippe Canguilhem is a professor of Musicology at the University of Tours (France), and a senior member of the Institut Universitaire de France. His work focuses on Italian music in the sixteenth century, with special emphasis on Florentine musical life. On this topic, he has published two books: on Vincenzo Galilei (2001) and Andrea and Giovanni Gabrieli (2003). He is also interested in improvised counterpoint in the Renaissance, with two publications: an edition and translation of Vicente Lusitano's counterpoint treatises (Brepols, 2013), and a book on polyphonic improvisation in the Renaissance published in 2015 (Classiques Garnier).

Scott Lee Edwards is presently working on an edition of the collected works of Ludwig Senfl (New Senfl Edition), a project funded by the Austrian Academy of Sciences and hosted at the University of Music and the Performing Arts Vienna. His research interests and publications seek to understand musical performance through the contexts of book culture, censorship, and diaspora, in addition to multilinguistic musical practices and auditory histories in a variety of literary forms within and beyond Central Europe in the sixteenth and seventeenth centuries.

Dinko Fabris is an associate professor of Musicology at the University of Basilicata in Matera; external supervisor at the University of Leiden; and member of the Academia Europaea, the Pontifical Council for Culture, and the Agency for the Evaluation of Research in Italian Universities (ANVUR). He is a member of the Commission Mixte of RILM and RISM, was first Italian elected president of the International Musicological Society (2012–2017), and is currently past president and chair of the IMS Study Group "Mediterranean Music Studies." His 170 publications include *Music in Seventeenth-Century Naples* (Ashgate 2007; repr. Routledge 2016). Since 2020 he has been chair of the Department of Research and Communication at San Carlo Theater in Naples.

Cory M. Gavito is a scholar of the early guitar in Italy (1580–1700), with special emphasis on its engagement with improvisation, music pedagogy, and the transmission of song repertories. His publications include a critical edition of Giovanni Stefani's three guitar songbooks, and articles in the *Journal of Musicology*, *Recercare*, and *Early Music*. He has held research fellowships at the University of Texas at Austin, the Newberry Library, Harvard University, and in 2016–2017 served as the Melville J. Kahn Fellow at I Tatti, The Harvard Center for Italian Renaissance Studies.

Musician/musicologist **Pedro Memelsdorff** has long performed with Jordi Savall's Hespèrion XXI, and in 1987 founded the medieval ensemble Mala Punica. He has been a fellow at I Tatti; Ernest Bloch Lecturer at Berkeley; Blodgett Distinguished Artist; and Christoph Wolff Distinguished Scholar at Harvard. He is also an affiliate researcher at the University of Tours and a member of the college of the Swiss Confederal Graduate School in Italian Civilization. He directs the Early Music Seminars at the Fondazione Cini in Venice and belongs to the scientific board of the Galleria dell'Accademia in Florence. He also served as the director of the Schola Cantorum in Basel.

Théodora Psychoyou is *maître de conferences* (associate professor) at the Sorbonne University in Paris, and member of the *Institut de recherche en musicologie*. She has been a fellow at Villa Medici–French Academy in Rome (2005-2007), member of the RISM group (early music manuscripts) at the Bibliothèque nationale de France (1997-2005), and an associate researcher at the Centre de musique baroque de Versailles (1997-2007). Her research focuses on history of music theory and sacred music in the seventeenth century. Her current projects concern the quarrel between Ancients and Moderns in music, Catholic music practices in the Greek isles, and the relationship between music and science in the early modern era.

For more than fifty years, **Jordi Savall**, one of the most versatile musical personalities of his generation, has rescued musical gems from obscurity. A tireless researcher into early music, he interprets and performs the repertory both as a gambist and conductor. Together with Montserrat Figueras, he founded the ensembles Hespèrion XXI (1974), La Capella Reial de Catalunya (1987), and Le Concert des Nations (1989), with whom he has released more than 230 discs of Medieval, Renaissance, Baroque, and Classical music, with a special focus on Hispanic and Mediterranean musics. They have received numerous awards, including multiple Grammy Awards. In 2008, Savall was named a UNESCO "Artist for Peace."

Francesco Spagnolo (PhD Hebrew University, 2007) is the curator of The Magnes Collection of Jewish Art and Life at the University of California, Berkeley, where he is also an associate adjunct professor in the Department of Music. He is also a host for Italian National Radio, and the Scholar-in-Residence for the "Jews & Music" initiative of the Philharmonia Baroque Orchestra. Among his publications are *Italian Jewish Musical Traditions* (Accademia Nazionale di Santa Cecilia–Hebrew University, 2001) and *The Jewish World* (Rizzoli-Skira, 2014).

Kate van Orden is a cultural historian and the Dwight P. Robinson Jr. Professor of Music at Harvard University. Her prize-winning publications include *Materialities: Books, Readers, and the Chanson in 16th-c. Europe* (Oxford, 2015), *Music, Discipline, and Arms in Early Modern France* (Chicago, 2005), and articles in *Renaissance Quarterly* and *Early Music History*. In 2016, she received a French Medaille d'Honneur. She will serve as president of the International Musicological Society beginning in 2022. She is also a professional performer on the baroque and classical bassoon and can be heard on over sixty recordings on Sony, Virgin Classics, and other labels.

Emily Wilbourne is an associate professor of Musicology at Queens College, in the City University of New York, and at the CUNY Graduate Center. Her first book, *Seventeenth-Century*

Opera and the Sound of the Commedia dell'Arte, was published in 2016 by the University of Chicago Press; a collection of essays, co-edited with Suzanne G. Cusick, entitled *Acoustemologies in Contact: Sounding Subjects and Modes of Listening in Early Modernity,* was published in early 2021 and is available via open access. Dr. Wilbourne is currently working on a second book, tentatively titled, *Race, Voice, and Slavery in Seventeenth-Century Florence.*

PHOTO CREDITS

Bloomington, Indiana University, Lilly Library: p. 240 fig.1, p. 241 fig. 2, p. 242 fig. 3, p. 244 fig. 4

Bologna, Museo internazionale e biblioteca della Musica: p. 158 figs. 3-4

Bruxelles, Bibliothèque royale de Belgique: pp. 38-39 fig. 1

Marseille, Mucem - Musée de les civilisations et de la Méditerranée: p. 289 fig. 6

München, Bayerische Staatsbibliothek, daten digitale sammlungen: p. 194 fig. 1, pp. 206-207 fig. 3

Naples, Biblioteca Nazionale Vittorio Emanuele III (I-Nn), Ms. Mus. XVII.300: p. 152 fig. 1

New Orleans, Archdiocese, Courtesy of the Office of Archives and Records: p. 281 fig. 1

Paris, Bibliothèque nationale de France: p. 40 fig. 2, p. 152 fig. 2, p. 259 fig. 1, p. 264 fig. 2, p. 279 fig. 1; Département Arsenal, 4-S-4798: p. 284 fig. 4; Département Estampes et photographie: p. 285 fig. 5; © Gallica: p. 71 fig. 2, p. 72 fig. 3, p. 78 fig. 4

Paris, Musée du Louvre, © 2011 Musée du Louvre (Photo Philippe Fuzeau): p. 283 fig. 3

Psychoyou, Théodora: p. 70 fig. 1, p. 82 fig. 5, p. 84 fig. 6, p. 91 fig. 11, p. 92 fig. 12

Tinos, Archive of the Catholic bishopric of Tinos: p. 86 fig. 8, p. 86 fig. 9, p. 87 fig. 10, p. 94 fig. 13

Washington, D.C, Library of Congress, Prints and Photographs Division: p. 200 fig. 2

Wikimedia Creative Commons, files licensed under the Creative Commons Attribution-Share Alike 4.0 International license: p. 15 fig. 1, p. 16 fig. 2, p. 245 fig. 5, p. 246 fig. 6

INDEX

Numbers in italics refer to figures or music examples.

I Tatti Research Series

The I Tatti Research Series is dedicated to ongoing projects at the Harvard University Center for Italian Renaissance Studies. Its volumes expand on themes explored during conferences and seminars and cover a wide spectrum of disciplines including art history, architecture, history, philosophy, literature, music, and the history of science.

The series examines all aspects of the Italian Renaissance — broadly understood to include the period from the fourteenth to the seventeenth centuries. At the same time, it investigates dialogues between Renaissance Italy and other regions around the world, in addition to the period's roots in classical antiquity and its enduring impact on modernity.

PUBLISHED AND FORTHCOMING VOLUMES

Vol. 1 ***The Renaissance in the 19th Century: Revision, Revival, and Return,*** **edited by Lina Bolzoni and Alina Payne**

Vol. 2 ***Seachanges: Music in the Mediterranean and Atlantic Worlds, 1550–1800,*** **edited by Kate van Orden**

Vol. 3 *Sacrifice and Conversion in the Early Modern Atlantic World,* edited by Maria Berbara

Vol. 4 *Ariosto and the Arabs: Contexts for the Orlando Furioso,* edited by Mario Casari, Monica Preti, and Michael Wyatt

Printed in the month of December 2021 on the presses of Esperia, Lavis (Trento).

Ex Officina Libraria Jellinek et Gallerani

FSC www.fsc.org MISTO Carta da fonti gestite in maniera responsabile FSC® C021437